Germain Doucet (Sieur de La Verdure)
My Paternal Ancestry

Michele Doucette, M.Ed.

Germain Doucet (Sieur de LaVerdure): My Paternal Ancestry

Copyright © 2012, 2019 by Michele Doucette, St. Clair Publications

All rights reserved. No part of this publication may be reproduced or transmitted in any form or by any means, electronic or mechanical, including photocopying, recording, or by any information storage and retrieval system, without written permission from the author.

ISBN 978-1-935786-35-1

Printed in the United States of America by

St. Clair Publications

PO Box 726

McMinnville, TN   37111-0726

http://stclairpublications.com

Inside cover image of Port Royal, Nova Scotia © Paul Clarke Photography

http://www.pcphotography.ca

Table of Contents

Dedication 1

Acknowledgments 2

Author's Note 7

Updated Author's Note 9

Setting the Doucet Stage 10

Germain Doucet 23

Generation 1 25

Doucet Surname Family Tree DNA Project 28

The Lejeune Sisters 35

Generation 2 45

Michele's Direct Lineage 81

July 2013 Addendum to Doucet DNA 175

May 2016 Addendum to Doucet DNA 183

June 2018 Addendum to Doucet DNA 186

April 2019 Addendum to Doucet DNA 192

Alström Syndrome 193

Michele's Letter to F. René Perron 195

Letter from F. René Perron 198

Translation of Letter from F. René Perron 203

Origin Maps 208

Blank Consanguinity Chart 210

Charts: Jean-Avite Doucet 213

Charts: Beatrice Muise 223

Aboriginal Ancestry 232

Acadian Family Names	264
Amirault 1A	266
Amirault 1B	268
Bajolet 1	270
Bajolet 2	271
Bernard	272
Bornstra	273
Boudrot 1A	274
Boudrot 1B	276
Boudrot 1C	278
Bourg 1A	281
Bourg 1B	283
Bourgeois	285
Boutier	287
Brassaud	290
Brun	291
Chebrat	292
Clémenson	294
Comeau	295
Corporon	298
Deveau	300
Doucet 1A	307
Doucet 1B	318
Doucet 1C	319
DuFosset	320
Dugas	321
Dulain	323
Duon	329

de Forest	331
Frontain	338
Gaudet 1A	339
Gaudet 1B	341
Gaudet 2	342
Hébert 1	344
Hébert 2A	345
Hébert 2B	348
Hébert 2C	349
Housseau	353
Lafleur	354
de La Grange	356
Landry 1	357
Landry 2	358
LeBlanc	360
Lefebvre	364
Lejeune	366
Maillard	367
Martin 1	368
Martin 2	371
Meunier	373
Mius	375
Mius d'Entremont 1A	380
Mius d'Entremont 1B	411
Mius d'Entremont 1C	421
Mius d'Entremont 1D	426
Mius d'Entremont 2	429
A Little Controversy	431

O'Bird 1A	432
O'Bird 1B	435
Pellerin	438
Pesseley	439
Pinet	441
Pitre	443
Poirier	447
Pothier	448
Préjean	449
Roach	450
Robichaud 1A	456
Robichaud 1B	458
Savoie 1A	461
Savoie 1B	462
Savoie 1C	463
A Little More Controversy	464
Surette 1A	466
Surette 1B	468
Thériot	470
Thibodeau	471
Trahan	473
Viger	475
Vigneau	476
Kinship List	477
Marriage List	501
Genealogy Forms	513
Associations	519
Bibliography 1	524

Bibliography 2 527

About the Author 539

Dedication

As an individual, I have always been driven by a love of history. I have been as equally passionate about my Acadian ancestry. This project, as you will see, quickly became a merger of these two strong influences in my life.

My father, Albert Doucette (May 3, 1936 - July 24, 2000) was eager to learn more about his family. Despite my father's passing, I have continued to strive towards answers in his name. I will always cherish our trips to Yarmouth. This one is for you Dad, because life and love are eternal.

Acknowledgments

In the organizing of this genealogical data, there are many individuals who need to be thanked for their time, their patience and their most valuable assistance in enabling this project to become a reality. E-mail is truly a wondrous thing to behold.

Barbara Atwood, first cousin to my father, who was instrumental in helping me establish connections, back in the very beginning (1989).

Roger Aubé, cousin, personal translator and 1998 New Brunswick tour guide.

Jackie Auclair, Doucet cousin and LDDM member.

Jane Doucette Barber, a detective cousin willing to sleuth for me in Reading, Massachusetts.

Florian Bernard, Québec cousin and author of *Heritage Acadian: Revue d'Histoire de Genealogie*, for amply intriguing me with his knowledge of Acadian heritage.

Marielle Bourgeois, a cousin who always attempts to answer my questions.

Paul Pierre Bourgeois, author of <u>À la recherche des Bourgeois d'Acadia (1641 à 1800)</u>, now deceased, but instrumental in my forging ahead with the Doucet and Bourgeois mystery.

Kenneth Breau, maternal cousin and Archivist at the Université de Moncton.

Linda Campbell, first cousin once removed to my father, former Heritage Coordinator for the Municipality and Town of Yarmouth, who was inspirational in uncovering records, and obtaining documents, in Yarmouth, Nova Scotia and area.

Peter Crowell, chief historian at the Argyle Courthouse Archives in Tusket, Nova Scotia.

Carol Doucet, Louisiana cousin and LDDM member.

Père Clarence d'Entremont, author of <u>Histoire de Quinan, Nouvelle-Écosse</u>, now deceased, who thought, in our exchanged letters, that I was actually a male (named Michel).

Pauline d'Entremont, a dear cousin, in Pubnico, dedicated to genealogical pursuits and preserving the work of Père Clarence d'Entremont.

Colonel John B. Devoe, author of <u>Devoe-deVaux Family History 1691 to 1991</u>, who passed away on January 27, 2012, after a long illness.

Betty Doucet, paternal aunt, who was instrumental in helping me put the puzzle pieces together, despite the conflicting family stories.

Robert (Bob) Doucet, who willingly shared the research conducted by his uncle, Wilfred Doucette, now deceased.

Léo Doucet, cousin, personal translator and Family Tree Maker teacher.

Edwina Doucette, a Yarmouth cousin and MSVU chum since 1980, who never thought we could be related and then was delighted to find out that we were.

Vincent Giles, friend and researcher in Digby County who keeps me abreast of his findings, both DNA related as well as genealogical, while doing his best to answer my questions.

Pat Doucette Hayes, cousin, personal translator, from time to time, and LDDM member.

Tim Hébert, fellow historian, researcher and webmaster, now deceased, of Acadian-Cajun Genealogy, History and Culture website located at http://www.acadian-cajun.com/index.htm

Janet Jehn, author of *Acadian Genealogy Exchange (AGE)*, for publishing countless queries, way back when.

William (Bill) Johnson, for sending me copies of photos taken on his trip to LaVerdure, France, in 1999.

Lucie LeBlanc Consentino, fellow historian, researcher and webmistress of the Acadian and French Canadian Ancestral Home website located at http://www.acadian-home.org

Pauline Moulaison Kimball, another detective cousin willing to sleuth for me in Wakefield, Massachusetts.

Kindale Library Staff in Stephenville, NL, for their continued efforts in securing copious material through inter-library loan.

Sheila Hubbard Macauley, author of The Hubbard Family of Nova Scotia, for her incredibly valuable research.

Florence Doucet MacKenzie, an elderly patient of my sister Lynette, albeit deceased, who first introduced me to *The Argus* (as published by the Argyle Municipality Historical and Genealogical Society).

David A. MacLeod, aka Davel, who has been, and continues to be, a devoted email companion.

Jan D. Marshall, geneticist at the Jackson Laboratory in Maine (researching Alström Syndrome specific to Yarmouth County).

Lorraine Newman, researcher at the Argyle Courthouse Archives in Tusket, Nova Scotia, for her valuable assistance.

Seán Ó Conaill (Sean O'Connell), my Gaelic speaking French cousin from northern New Brunswick, for updating me on the resrach of F. René Perron of Sèvres, France.

François Roux, researcher in France, who answered many emails, way back when.

Stephen A. White, Acadian genealogist/researcher/historian at the Université de Moncton. An incredibly brilliant mind, he is the author of <u>Dictionnaire Généalogique des Famille Acadiennes</u> that spans the time frame from 1636 to marriages of 1714. I am anxiously awaiting the upcoming installment of the next portion of the Dictionnaire.

Of course, I must not forget to make mention of those with whom I have corresponded over the years; namely,

Rich Bergeron, Susan Cann (mother of Lesley Anne Doucet, a dear Acadian cousin, from Yarmouth, who, while continuing to remain brave in her battle with Neimann-Pick Disease, transitioned on January 15, 2003, at the tender age of eighteen years), Edouard Comeau, Jacques Comeau, Joe Crochet, Lloyd d'Entremont, Gaetan Doucet, Dean Doucet, Genesta Doucette, Dr. Francis (Bob) Doucette, George Doucette (thanks for the shared trip to Yarmouth to meet Lesley Anne), John E. Doucette, Jeff Deveaux, James Frotten, Marc Graziadei (a fellow Beatles enthusiast), Karen Hesson, Peter Landry, David A. Mallet, Sally Mallet, Marcel Muise, Darlene Nielson, Marie Doucet O'Brien, Matt O'Keefe, Tina Prokopsky (a Yarmouth cousin), Shirley Muise Belliveau, Karen Muise Rediker, Owen Robb (a *Doucet wannabe*, to use his words), Susan Surette, Lark Szick, Ellie Doucette Turnage, Fred Chandler Union III, Rod Violette, Leona Doucette Walsh (a Yarmouth cousin) and Karen White.

In addition, a special thank you is herein extended to Gillian Barfoot of St. John, New Brunswick, whose Port Royal photograph graces the front cover of this book. As soon as I saw it, I said to myself ... *I think this is the one.*

Gillian is a reliable and enthusiastic writer, editor and photographer experienced in both print and electronic communications. Feel free to visit her Flickr home at http://www.flickr.com/photos/eye_gillian/ for many other eye catching visuals. Likewise, one can visit her online home at www.gillianbarfoot.com to learn more.

As always, a distinctive thank you must be extended to Kent Hesselbein [1] of Manchester, Tennessee, owner of Kent Grey-Hesselbein Design Studio, who weaves his special brand of magic when creating my book cover designs. He certainly came through, yet again, on this majestic, and historic, looking beauty.

---

[1] kghdesignstudio.com/index.html

Author's Note

What follows on the pages herein is not a history of the Acadian people. There are countless books available that enable one to revisit the history of Acadie. Instead, you will find the history of my family. It is my sincere hope that this work shall inspire others to do the same.

Here are some of the abbreviations that have been used throughout the text.

BIM = Belle-Île-en-Mer, Bretagne, France

Bbn = Beaubassin, Acadie (present day Amherst, Nova Scotia)

Cbd = Cobequid, Acadie (present day Truro, Nova Scotia)

CS = Cap-de Sable, Acadie (present day Cape Sable, Nova Scotia)

GP = Grand Pré, Acadie (present day Grand Pré, Nova Scotia)

ISJ = Îsle-St-Jean (Prince Edward Island)

Lbg = Louisbourg, Acadie (Louisbourg, Nova Scotia)

LM = Les Mines, Acadie (present day Horton, Nova Scotia; Minas Basin area)

MA (exile) = Massachusetts (while in exile)

PLJ = Port Lajoie, Îsle St-Jean, Acadie (present day Charlottetown, Prince Edward Island)

PR = Port Royal, Acadie (present day Annapolis Royal, Nova Scotia)

SAR = Sainte-Anne-du-Ruisseau, Eel Brook, Yarmouth County, Nova Scotia c = circa (about)

s/o = son of

d/o = daughter of

Updated Author's Note

This genealogical reference was initially published on June 27, 2012.

Whilst I can no longer lay claim to Germain Doucet (Sieur de LaVerdure) as a paternal ancestor (due to DNA evidence that proves Germain Doucet, born about 1641, carries the C3b Y-DNA signature, which is Native American, now referenced as C-P39), I am able to lay claim to him as a maternal ancestor (denoted in <u>Men and Women of Renown: My Maternal Ancestry</u>); hence, the information shared within this text shall continue to remain as is, so that other family historians will be able to make note of the route that has been taken.

Please also refer to the *July 2013 Addendum to Doucet DNA* chapter. If anyone still finds themselves confused, they can reach me at michele.doucette@nf.sympatico.ca

Michele Doucette

December 13, 2015

Setting the Doucet Stage

Cardinal Richelieu, born of an ancient family of the lesser nobility of Poitou, in 1585, the third son of François du Plessis, Seigneur de Richelieu, dominated the history of France from 1624 until his death in 1642. [2] [3]

In 1627, after having been convinced by Samuel de Champlain of both the riches available in France as well as of the necessity to expand colonization in New France, Richelieu created the Company of One Hundred Associates; it was through this very company that supplies and new colonists would be sent to Québec, in New France, to join Champlain's growing settlement. [4]

Isaac de Razilly, born July 5, 1587 at the Château d'Oiseaumelle in Chinon, [5] situated 15 kilometers north of Loudun, was from a noble family. [6] His father, François de Razilly, a Knight in the Order Du Roi (Chevalier de l'Ordre du roi), was Governor of Loudun. [7]

In his youth, Isaac joined a strict military/religious order that forbade him to marry, but it was his bravery in battle that caught the attention of many; he would soon become a high ranking French naval officer. [8] As a result, Isaac was chosen by his cousin, Cardinal Richelieu, to reclaim Acadie from the English following the St. Germain-en-Laye Treaty, signed March 29, 1632.

---

[2] https://en.wikipedia.org/wiki/Cardinal_Richelieu
[3] https://www.historylearningsite.co.uk/france-in-the-seventeenth-century/cardinal-richelieu/
[4] www3.sympatico.ca/goweezer/canada/z16champ6.htm
[5] White, Stephen A. (1999) Dictionnaire Généalogique des Familles Acadiennes, Volume H to Z, page 1369.
[6] www.oocities.com/weallcamefromsomewhere/devils_loudun.html
[7] Ibid.
[8] Ibid.

In 1632, at the time of his expedition to Acadie, Charles de Menou d'Aulnay de Charnizay, known as D'Aulnay, was an officer in the Navy with a Royal Commission; having grown up in luxury, he personally financed the initial 40 families who accompanied him and his cousin, Isaac de Razilly, to Acadie. [9]

According to author Andrew Hill Clark, de Razilly "sailed from France on July 4, 1632 in L'Espérance à Dieu [captained by D'Aulnay], shepherding two transports, and disembarked some three hundred people (mostly men) and a variety of livestock, seeds, tools, implements, arms, munitions, and other supplies at La Have (LaHève, at the mouth of La Have River in present day Lunenburg County) on September 8." [10]

According to authors Sally Ross and J. Alphonse Deveau, it was in September that "Isaac de Razilly arrived in Acadia with three sailing vessels, 300 hand-picked men, three Capuchin Fathers and a few women and children." [11]

Amongst these hand-picked men was Germain Doucet, Sieur de LaVerdure, my ancestor.

For three years, D'Aulnay acted as a Lieutenant and Second in Command, to Isaac de Razilly at Acadie; it was only after de Razilly's death at La Hève on July 2, 1636 [12] that he would assume the leadership placed upon him by Isaac's brother, Claude, becoming embroiled in numerous battles with his nemesis, Charles de Saint-Étienne de La Tour, all in an effort to secure control of Acadie. [13]

---

[9] www.oocities.com/weallcamefromsomewhere/devils_loudun.html
[10] Clark, Andrew Hill. (1968) <u>Acadia: The Geography of Early Nova Scotia to 1760</u> (page 91). Madison: University of Wisconsin Press.
[11] Ross, Sally and Deveau, J. Alphonse. (1992) <u>The Acadians of Nova Scotia: Past and Present</u> (page 16). Halifax, Nova Scotia: Nimbus Publishing.
[12] White, Stephen A. (1999) <u>Dictionnaire Généalogique des Familles Acadiennes</u>, Volume H to Z, page 1369.
[13] www.oocities.com/weallcamefromsomewhere/devils_loudun.html

On a document signed July 14, 1640, Germain Doucet was Captain of the Army at Fort Pentagoët (present day Castine, Maine), the capital of their new colony. This was a most important trading post, situated at the mouth of the Penobscot River.

Both a loyal and trusted friend, he was also the right-hand man of Charles de Menou d'Aulnay de Charnizay, the Governor of Acadie. At the time of the sudden death of the Governor, by drowning, on May 24, 1650, Germain was the Commander at the fort of Port Royal as well as Deputy Guardian of the Governor's children.

Let us now fast forward to August 16, 1654, when 500 Bostonian soldiers, under the command of Robert Sedgewick, attacked the fort at Port Royal. Germain was wise enough to give up without a struggle, mainly because he had only 100 men to oppose them. As a result, so, too, was he able to obtain both honourable terms for his soldiers, as well as transportation for them back to France.

Germain left his brother-in-law, Jacques Bourgeois, surgeon, as both Lieutenant of Port Royal as well as a witness to see that the conditions of the treaty were carried out. The inhabitants were given a choice; they could remain, with liberty of conscience, and enjoy their property, or they could sell it and return to France. The missionary priests were allowed to remain, providing they lived some distance from the fort itself.

In the words of my cousin, Léo Doucet ... *While Sedgwick's men were, more or less, military types, all able and bent on invading, ravaging and conquering, the men under Germain Doucet were mainly artisans along with some Indians; in other words, all of the types, including the Indians, that for reasons of age and medical fitness (or unfitness) were left at Port Royal, it not being thought that Port Royal would be attacked at that time. A strong defense would have put the general civilian population in danger, making it subject to far more severe forms of reprisals from the attackers. It is not a wonder, then, that Germain Doucet sought (and obtained) an honourable cessation of hostilities.*

An artist's rendition of what Germain Doucet may have looked like.

According to the research of Wilfred Doucette (one of the Directors of the Acadian Heritage and Culture Foundation Incorporated in Erath, Louisiana), Germain Doucet wrote a letter from Villy, France, dated October 13, 1660 to Demoiselle de Charnisay [14] thereby putting his date of death sometime after 1660; unfortunately, this information has never been validated.

The beginnings of my own research, in 1989, led me to explore the works of Adrien Bergeron, author of Le Grand Arrangement Des Acadiens au Québec, and Bona Arsenault, author of Histoire et Généalogie des Acadians. During the time of their publication, each set of books proved to be an outstanding source of information. Up until these books came to print, we had never been exposed to such detailed Acadian research.

David MacLeod, a Maine cousin whose mother was a Doucet, received a letter from Stephen A. White (Généalogiste, Centre d'études acadiennes, Université de Moncton), dated May 8, 1992.

It was here that evidence first came to light upon the fact that Germain Doucet (born about 1641 in Port Royal) was not the son of Pierre Doucet (born about 1621 in France), eldest son of Germain Doucet, Sieur de LaVerdure, as previously surmised by many, including Adrien Bergeron and Bona Arsenault.

This, of course, sparked my immediate interest. In March of 1999, I sent an e-mail letter to Stephen White, in care of my cousin Kenneth Breau, an Archivist at the Université. At that time, however, I was unsure if he would be able to pass the letter onto Stephen for me.

---

[14] Murdoch, Beamish. (1865) *A History of Nova Scotia or Acadie: Volume 1* (page 136). Halifax, NS: James Barnes, Printer and Publisher. Online digitized copy accessed on July 29, 2011 at https://archive.org/stream/historyofnovasco01murdiala#page/136

The information that I received certainly solidified what David had shared.

Dispensations in the 3rd degree had been granted by the Catholic Church (St. Jean-Baptiste in Port Royal, Acadie) on November 26, 1726, so that Germain Doucet (grandson of Germain) could marry Françoise Comeau (granddaughter of Pierre).

Herein was the undisputed evidence that Pierre Doucet (born about 1621 in France) was the brother, or half brother, of Germain Doucet (born about 1641 in Port Royal).

Pierre married Henriette Pelletret about 1660. Children born of this union were: Marie-Anne (born about 1661), Toussaint dit François (born about 1663), Jean (born about 1665), Pierre (born about 1667), Madeleine (born about 1671), Louis (born about 1674), Louise dite Jeanne (born about 1675), René (born about 1678), Marguerite (born about 1680) and Mathieu (born about 1685). It was Marguerite who married Alexandre Comeau (s/o Étienne Comeau and Marie-Anne Lefebvre). Marguerite and Alexandre had a daughter Françoise.

Germain married Marie Landry about 1664. Children born of this union were: Charles (born about 1665), Bernard dit LaVerdure (born about 1667), Laurent (born about 1669), Jacques dit Maillard (born about 1671), Claude dit Maître Jean (born about 1674), Marie (born about 1678), Jeanne (born about 1680), Alexis (born about 1682) and Pierre (born about 1685). It was Charles who married Huguette Guérin (d/o François Guérin and Anne Blanchard). Charles and Huguette had a son Germain.

"Dispensation in the 3rd degree was granted Nov 26, 1726, at Port-Royal to Germain Doucet (grandson of Germain) to marry Françoise Comeau (granddaughter of Pierre)." [15]

---

[15] https://novascotia.ca/archives/acadian/archives.asp?ID=1137

Germain Doucet Sieur de LaVerdure	Pierre Doucet born about 1621	Marguerite Doucet born about 1680	Françoise Comeau born 1703
Germain Doucet born about 1641	Brother Sister	Aunt Uncle Nephew Niece	Great Aunt Great Uncle Great Nephew Great Niece
Charles Doucet born about 1665	Aunt Uncle Nephew Niece	FIRST Cousin	FIRST Cousin Once Removed
Germain Doucet born about 1697	Great Aunt Great Uncle Great Nephew Great Niece	FIRST Cousin Once Removed	**SECOND Cousin**

ADDENDUM

In April 2010, the Family Tree DNA Doucet Surname Project was launched; test results show that Pierre Doucet (1621) is an R1b Doucet while Germain Doucet (1641) is a C3b (now referenced as C-P39) Doucet. Please refer to the chapter entitled *July 2013 Addendum to Doucet DNA*. As you can see, DNA testing is serving to rewrite history.

While there were many males with the nickname dit LaVerdure, some in Acadie (as in Pierre Melanson dit LaVerdure) and some in the Antilles (as in Anthoine Galois dit LaVerdure), Germain Doucet, Commander of the Army at Port Royal, a military man, was Sieur *de* LaVerdure; this is a most important distinction. [16]

In reviewing what the documents tell us, researcher genealogist F. René Perron of Sèvres, France, instructs us to begin with the January 20, 1649 will of Charles de Menou d'Aulnay de Charnizay.

---

[16] Perron, F. René. *De La Verdure aux Ant-Isles et Vice-Versa* article.

When he makes note of Germain Doucet being from *the parish of Couperans-en-Brie*, he hardly gives any supplementary indication. [17] The will also references the wife of Germain Doucet, without ever mentioning her family name. In keeping, her given name is also unaccounted for.

Perron shares that Charles de Menou d'Aulnay de Charnizay was extremely generous, in spite of the enormous debts that he had incurred, his will stating that Germain Doucet would be given "only 200 pounds, but the assistance which I render to his *nephews and nieces and to all who concern him*, amounts to 100 pounds. One does not choose so precisely; he well deserves 100 crowns per year for his salary and his food and that of *his wife*." [18]

Perron Inference number 1 → Germain Doucet's wife, as attested to by the will of Charles de Menou d'Aulnay de Charnizay, is still alive in 1649. Was she alive in 1654?

Perron Inference number 2 → Did this Doucet couple really have children? On this matter, he agrees with Maurice Caillebeau, a cousin from Poitiers, who thought that Germain Doucet and his wife were raising, as their own children ... their *nephews and nieces*.

Historians tell us that Germain Doucet, Sieur de LaVerdure, returned to France. Of course, this brings additional questions: did he return alone or did he return with his wife? Unfortunately, we do not have an answer to either question.

The only thing we can be sure of is that "his children" remained in Acadie, an act that Perron sees as outside the boundaries of what would constitute normal behavior with regards to family. This act, according to Perron, certainly <u>makes plausible</u> the idea that the Doucet individuals, remaining behind, namely, Pierre and Marguerite, were, in fact, his nephew and niece.

---

[17] Perron, F. René. *De La Verdure aux Ant-Isles et Vice-Versa* article.
[18] Ibid.

In keeping with the updated research of Stephen A. White, this is what he has to say ……

There is no documentation showing that Germain Doucet, Sieur de La Verdure, had any children, but it is known that he had a wife, so he might have had some.

D'Aulnay's will mentions Germain and "his wife" as well as "his nephews and nieces." There is nothing that identifies the latter. Marguerite Doucet might have been his niece, but she also might have been his daughter.

There are two dispensations that indicate that Marguerite Doucet was closely related to the younger Germain Doucet. These do not agree on the exact relationship, one pointing to them being siblings, and the other to them being mother and son. Before the DNA showed that the younger Germain was not a "French" Doucet, I presumed that the former was the correct interpretation, partly because at the time a 3-4 relationship could have been dispensed as fourth degree (which would give the siblings result), but a fourth degree relationship would not have correctly received a 3-4 dispensation (which would give the mother-son result).

Marguerite was born about 1625. Current DNA results show that her mother was European, meaning that we now have persuasive evidence that Marguerite was born in Europe, and thus to European parents, so she *could not have had* the same father as Germain Doucet the younger; this, then, eliminates the sibling possibility, so it would appear that this Germain must have been her illegitimate son. If that is so, the fact that she named him Germain suggests that there must have been a very close relationship between her and the older Germain Doucet, but this still does not prove that she was the older Germain's daughter.

Regarding the older Germain's wife (or wives), we do know that the capitulation of Port Royal in 1654 describes Jacques Bourgeois as Germain's brother-in-law. We have ample proof that Jacques Bourgeois was married to Jeanne Trahan, so Germain must have been married to either Jacques's sister, or to Jeanne's sister.

Of course, a half-sister would be also possible in either case, although we really have no reason to suspect that Jeanne Trahan had a half-sister.

If the older Germain Doucet was in fact brother-in-law to Jacques Bourgeois, because he had married the second of the two children of Jacques's father-in-law Guillaume Trahan who accompanied their father to Acadia in 1636, and if the older Germain was Marguerite Doucet's father, then the older Germain must have been married more than once, because Guillaume Trahan was only married in 1627, and Marguerite Doucet was born about 1625.

If the older Germain Doucet had no children, it is likely that both Marguerite Doucet and Pierre Doucet were among those described in d'Aulnay's will as his nephews and nieces. And it remains likely (although not certain) that Marguerite Doucet had a sister who married Pierre Lejeune.

That is all we can say about the Doucets at this point.

In accordance with the online <u>Dictionnaire Généalogique des Familles Acadiennes</u> [19] additions and corrections, the information states that instead of Germain Doucet having been from Couperans-en-Brie (or Conflans in Brye), as initially denoted on page 526 of Volume 1, it should now be amended to read Couperoue in Brye (or Coupru in Brie); a small village in the south of the department of Aisne. As well, Jean-Marie Germe, through Les Amitiés Généalogiques Canadiennes-Françaises, [20] published an article entitled *Origine de Germain Doucet* in 1999 (Volume 9) that also references Couperoue. Unfortunately, the records of this parish (which might have confirmed this as a possible place of birth) are preserved only from 1674 onwards (over 40 years after his departure).

---

[19] http://www.umoncton.ca/umcm-ceaac/files/umcm-ceaac/wf/wf/pdf/corrections.pdf (page 55)

[20] poitou-acadie-quebec.pagesperso-orange.fr/

As the actual birthplace of Germain Doucet has not yet been definitively established, Perron tells us that La Verdure lies east of St. Cyr-Sur-Morin, near departmental highway 407 (which goes from La Ferté-sous-Jouarre to Montmirail) and about 12 kilometers north of La Ferté-Gaucher, situated near Coutran in the Bassevelle Parish. [21]

Perron has also told us that La Verdure, the fiefdom of Germain Doucet, was located near Bassevelle (north of the present day Seine and Marne Rivers) in the Île de France region.

While there "exists no trace of Doucet in the oldest register of the church of Saint-Romain in La Ferté-Gaucher, the surname Doucet is known in the area, including in Montmirail, the ancient fiefdom of persons who were important in the 17th century French court." [22]

There is nothing to prove that Germain Doucet was born in the Bassevelle/LaVerdure area. As is the case with many other individuals, "he may have purchased property there, and, in this way, became *Sieur de LaVerdure*. This act was very common among members of the Court, particularly east of Paris, as we have come to realize through notarized documents." [23]

La Verdure was part of Bassevelle. Unfortunately, the Baptismal certificates between 1599 and 1635 do not exist, thereby eliminating "any possibility of finding records of Germain Doucet's children." [24]

---

[21] Perron, F. René. (1991). "*De Germain Doucet à Jacob Bourgeois*" as as published by La Société Historique Acadienne, Les Cahiers, Octobre – Décembre 1991 (Volume 22, Number 4), page 90.
[22] Perron, F. René. *Mystère de la famille Doucet* article.
[23] Ibid.
[24] Perron, F. René. (1992). "*Bourgeois & Doucet: À Bassevelle, Des Suites Surprenantes*" as published by La Société Historique Acadienne, Les Cahiers, Janvier – Mars 1992 (Volume 23, Number 1), page 32.

The church at Bassevelle (Barry Cuttell)

https://www.ww1cemeteries.com/bassevelle-communal-cemetery.html

It was certainly "in this church that Germain Doucet came to pray before his departure for Acadie in 1632; unfortunately, documents are missing in the registry." [25]

---

[25] Perron, F. René. (1992). *"Bourgeois & Doucet: À Bassevelle, Des Suites Surprenantes"* as published by La Société Historique Acadienne, Les Cahiers, Janvier – Mars 1992 (Volume 23, Number 1), page 32.

According to Perron, "there is no possible doubt: La Ferté-Gaucher, Coutran, La Verdure, Les Groseilliers and Bassevelle formed a unit; placed under the protection of the local Bailiff, linked to the Knights of Malta, in which was formed a location for the recruitment of settlers for New France with Jean de Biencourt." [26]

For Perron, this return to France meant that Germain Doucet, Sieur de LaVerdure, was "probably tempted to return to the place from whence he had initially departed, namely the Headquarters of the Order of Malta of La Ferté-Gaucher, Coutran. As a Soldier of the Order, in one way or another, he was obliged, once again, to put himself at the disposition of the Knights." [27]

In accordance with a Catholic News Agency [28] article, the Order of Malta is a chivalric order which was founded in 1099, originally to provide protection and medical care to Holy Land pilgrims.

The Sovereign Military Hospitaller Order of Saint John of Jerusalem of Rhodes and of Malta (Supremus Ordo Militaris Hospitalis Sancti Ioannis Hierosolymitani Rhodius et Melitensis) is not the same as the Poor Fellow Soldiers of Christ and of the Temple of Solomon (Pauperes commilitones Christi Templique Solomonici) which was eventually shortened to Knights Templar.

---

[26] Perron, F. René. (1992). "*Bourgeois & Doucet: À Bassevelle, Des Suites Surprenantes*" as published by La Société Historique Acadienne, <u>Les Cahiers</u>, Janvier – Mars 1992 (Volume 23, Number 1), page 37.
[27] Perron, F. René. *De La Verdure aux Ant-Isles et Vice-Versa* article.
[28] https://www.catholicnewsagency.com/news/knights-of-malta-grand-master-to-resign-at-request-of-pope-francis-42917

Germain Doucet

Germain Doucet was also known as Sieur de La Verdure. He was Captain of the Army at Pentagoët as well as the right-hand man of the Governor of Acadia (Charles de Menou d'Aulnay de Charnizay).

In accordance with the January 20, 1649 will of Charles de Menou d'Aulnay de Charnizay, Germain Doucet is noted as being from *the parish of Couperans-en-Brie*. In keeping with corrections to the Dictionnaire Généalogique des Familles Acadiennes, [29] instead of Couperans en Brie (ou Conflans en Brye), it should read Couperoue en Brye (Coupru en Brie). It needs to be remembered, that whilst Germain Doucet may have come from this area, we still know naught where he was born. At the time of the death of the Governor in 1650, Germain was both Commander at the Fort of Port Royal, as well as Deputy Guardian of the Governor's children.

According to an article entitled *Mystère de la famille Doucet* written by F. René Perron of Sèvres, France, there is reference to a letter sent by Germain Doucet, in France, to Marie de Menou, Demoiselle de Charnisay, in 1660, concerning land-owners in Acadia; as stated earlier, this would place his death sometime after 1660.

Given the August 16, 1654 capitulation of Port Royal, we know that Germain Doucet left his brother-in-law, Jacques Bourgeois, surgeon, as both Lieutenant of Port Royal as well as a witness to see that the conditions of the treaty were carried out. It is quite possible that Germain Doucet married a second time, before 1654. Even though the wife has never been

---

[29] http://www.umoncton.ca/umcm-ceaac/files/umcm-ceaac/wf/wf/pdf/corrections.pdf (page 55)

identified, Stephen A. White states that she may have been either the daughter of Guillaume Trahan or the sister of Jacques Bourgeois; no children have been traced to this marriage.

It is important to make mention of further notations per Stephen A. White as noted in the <u>Dictionnaire Généalogique des Familles Acadiennes</u>, Volume A to G, page 527.

[i]. It is not possible that the mother of the children of Germain Doucet is a sister of Jacques Bourgeois' wife, as certain authors have proposed, given that the in-laws of Jacques Bourgeois did not get married until 1627. There exists the possibility that Germain Doucet nevertheless married, in second nuptials, to a daughter of Guillaume Trahan who gave him no surviving children; but it is as possible that such a second wife is the sister of Jacques Bourgeois and not the sister of his wife. (Refer to *La Société Généalogique Canadienne Française*, Volume VI, 1955, page 372)

[ii]. The dispensation of third to the fourth degree of consanguinity granted at the time of the marriage of Pierre Doucet, grandson of Germain Doucet and of Marie Landry, with Anne Marie Dugas, great grand-daughter of Abraham Dugas and of Marguerite Doucet (PR Parish Register dated January 27, 1749), gives us the certainty that Germain and Marguerite were brother and sister.

[iii]. The dispensation of fourth degree of consanguinity granted at the time of the marriage of Claude Trahan with Anne LeBlanc (GP Parish Register dated April 18, 1746) suggests that the wife of Pierre LeJeune dit Briard, great grandfather of Claude, was the sister of Marguerite Doucet, great grandmother of Anne.

[iv]. The dispensation of third degree of consanguinity granted at the time of the marriage of Germain Doucet, grandson of Germain Doucet and of Marie Landry, with Françoise Comeau, granddaughter of Pierre Doucet and Henriette Pelletret (PR Parish Register dated November 26, 1726), assures us that the spouse of Marie Landry was the brother of Pierre Doucet.

Generation 1

Family 1 [30]

Pierre Doucet (born c. 1621 in France), son of Germain Doucet and unknown, married Henriette Pelletret (d/o Simon Pelletret and Perrine Bourg) c. 1660. He died in PR on June 1, 1713 and was buried on June 2, 1713.

1. Marie Anne (born c. 1661) (1.1)

2. Toussaint dit François (born c. 1663) (1.2)

3. Jean (born c. 1665) (1.3)

4. Pierre (born c. 1667) (1.4)

5. Madeleine (born c. August 1671) (1.5)

6. Louis (born c. 1674) (1.6)

7. Louise dite Jeanne (born c. 1675) (1.7)

8. René (born c. 1678) (1.8)

9. Marguerite (born c. 1680) (1.9)

10. Mathieu (born c. 1685) (1.10)

---

[30] White, Stephen A. (1999) <u>Dictionnaire Généalogique des Familles Acadiennes</u>, Volume A to G, pages 526, 528 and 529.

Family 2 [31]

Marguerite Doucet (born c. 1625 in France), daughter of Germain Doucet and unknown, married Abraham Dugas c. 1674. She died in PR on December 19, 1707 and was buried on December 20, 1707 in the cemetery at the head of the St-Laurent chapel river.

1. Marie (born c. 1648) (2.1)

2. Claude (born c. 1649) (2.2)

3. Anne (born c. 1654) (2.3)

4. Martin (born c. 1656) (2.4)

5. Marguerite (born c. 1657) (2.5)

6. Abraham (born c. 1661) (2.6)

7. Madeleine (born c. 1664) (2.7)

8. Marie (born c. 1667) (2.8)

Family 3 [32] [33]

An unnamed daughter (according to Stephen A. White) married Pierre Lejeune dit Briard c. 1650. This information was based on the declaration made at BIM.

1. Pierre dit Briard (born c. 1656) (3.1)

2. Martin dit Briard (born c. 1661) (3.2)

---

[31] White, Stephen A. (1999) <u>Dictionnaire Généalogique des Familles Acadiennes</u>, Volume A to G, pages 526 and 562.
[32] Ibid, page 526.
[33] White, Stephen A. (1999) <u>Dictionnaire Généalogique des Familles Acadiennes</u>, Volume H to Z, pages 1048 and 1049.

Family 4 [34]

Germain Doucet (born c. 1641), son of Germain Doucet and unknown, married Marie Landry (d/o René Landry and Perrine Bourg) at PR c. 1664. He died before the PR census of 1698.

1. Charles (born c. 1665) (4.1)

2. Bernard dit Laverdure (born c. 1667) (4.2)

3. Laurent (born c. 1669) (4.3)

4. Jacques dit Maillard (born c. 1671) (4.4)

5. Claude dit Maître Jean (born c. 1674) (4.5)

6. Marie (born c. 1678) (4.6)

7. Jeanne (born c. 1680) (4.7)

8. Alexis (born c. 1682) (4.8)

9. Pierre (born c. 1685) (4.9)

---

[34] White, Stephen A. (1999) Dictionnaire Généalogique des Familles Acadiennes, Volume A to G, pages 526, 530 and 531.

Doucet Surname Family Tree DNA Project

In genetic genealogy, we are now working with three types of DNA.

[1] Y-DNA, which MEN have on the Y chromosome

[2] mtDNA which MEN and WOMEN both get from their mothers, and

[3] atDNA which makes up the other 21 chromosomes

Autosomal DNA (atDNA), found in both MEN and WOMEN, is an inherited collection from all of your ancestors.

As per above, Y-DNA is passed from father to son, in a line of unbroken descent, unless there has been an adoption (or an illegitimate birth) somewhere in the family. As a result, Y-DNA is significantly valuable in following a specific surname.

While Mitochondrial DNA (mtDNA) is passed from a mother to all of her children, including the sons, it is only passed successively through the females (from mother to daughter). The only difficulty with mtDNA is that the surname changes every generation, making it more challenging, but not impossible, to track.

By comparison, atDNA, in any individual, is a random collection of some of the DNA of all your ancestors, inherited 50% from each parent. Autosomes contain such things as hair color, eye color, facial features, height, body structure, health issues, etc.

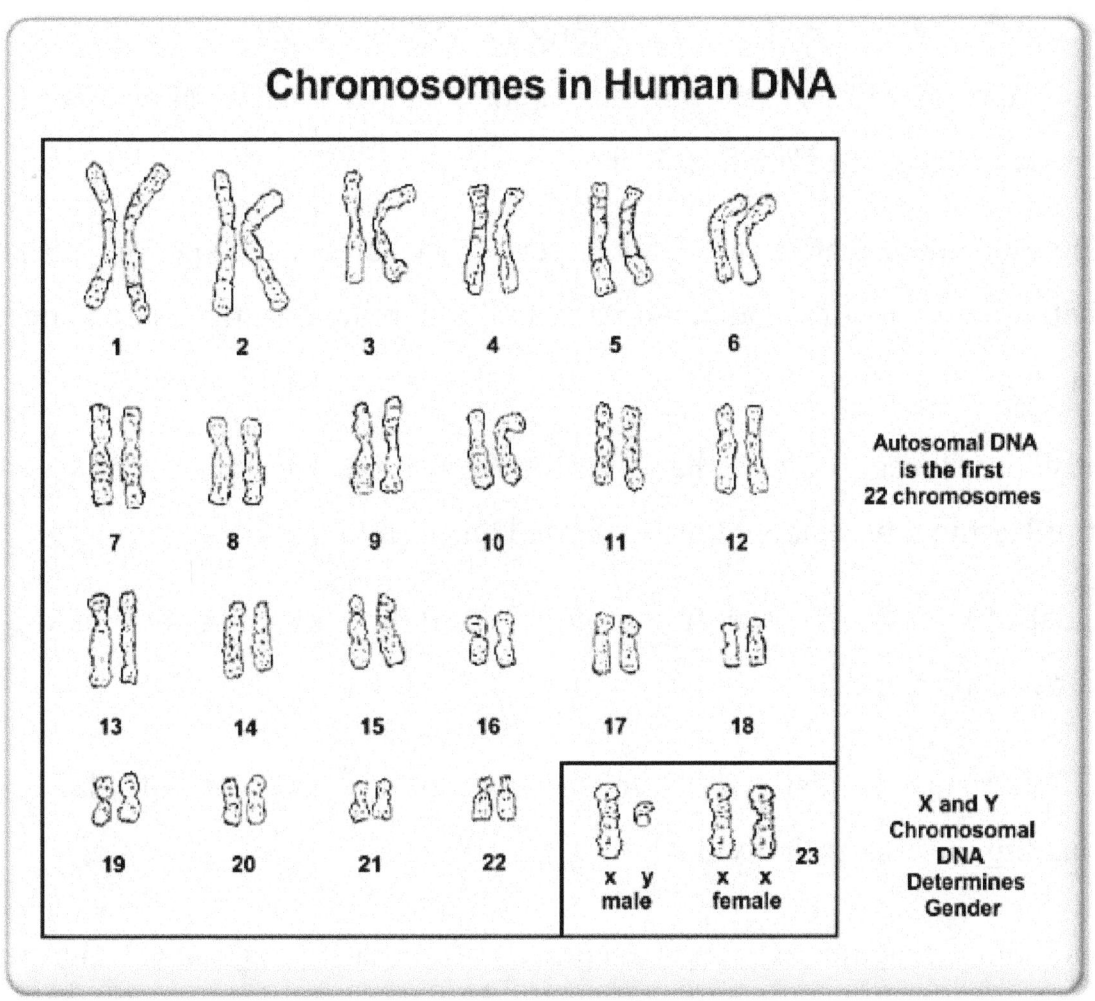

In humans, autosomes are the set of chromosomes pairs labelled 1 to 22. Chromosome 23 is the sex chromosome. Since autosomal DNA (atDNA) is made up of random combinations of genetic blocks of information, its uses in genealogy have been limited, thus far. [35]

In truth, it is becoming clearer that genetic testing, for genealogical purposes, is currently the most powerful tool for genealogists.

---

[35] *atDNA in Depth* article, courtesy of the The Phillips DNA Project, accessed on July 23, 2011 at
https://phillipsdnaproject.com/faq-sections/27-dna-questions-faqs/316-atdna-in-depth

Doucet is a relatively common French family name that exists among the Acadians and Cajuns, among the other French in Louisiana, among the Mi'kmaq in Nova Scotia, as well as among the early colonists of Canada (Québec).

It is also known that there are many Doucet persons (whatever the spelling variation), even in Nova Scotia, the home of Acadie, who are totally unrelated to the shared ancestry of the Acadian branch.

Consequently, the Doucet Surname Family Tree DNA project was launched (April 2010) in the interest of learning more about these various Doucet families.

The chief goal of this Y-DNA surname project is to discover more about the origins of the people who bear this name.

An equally important secondary objective is to explore the possibility of relationships, near or remote, among these same individuals.

According to the Dictionnaire Généalogique des Familles Acadiennes, Germain Doucet (Sieur de LaVerdure) had four children, as already highlighted in the Generation 1 chapter, namely;

[1] Pierre, born in France about 1621,

[2] Marguerite, born in France about 1625,

[3] a daughter, name unknown, who married Pierre Lejeune dit Briard, according to the records at Belle-Île-en-Mer, Bretagne, France, and

[4] Germain, born at Port Royal about 1641.

In keeping with the Y-DNA, we can only follow **direct male descendents** of both Pierre and Germain.

At the present time, there are C-P39 Doucets and R1b Doucets.

As more men join the project, it is to be expected that there will be some who are neither C-P39 nor R1b.

The preponderance of the evidence will eventually cause the emergence of patterns from which conclusions about the first ancestors, of the various clusters of results, may be drawn.

Matches are determined based on both haplogroup designations (and in this case, thus far, we have but two) as well as definitive marker comparisons (which is why a Y-DNA 67 marker test, later combined with deepclade SNP testing, is the best choice to date).

R1b1a2 is the most frequent haplogroup in Western Europe. They were most successful breeders, which is why deepclade SNP testing and getting out to 67 markers is so important.

A deep clade test is a test for single nucleotide polymorphisms (SNPs) that determines a male's precise placement (branch) on his ancestral tree. Deep clade testing offers in-depth information about the ancient ancestry and historic migrations of the direct paternal line.

Haplogroup C-P39 is the Native American branch of Y-DNA paternal haplogroup C. Most Native American males fall into haplogroup Q, making the participants of this C-P39 haplogroup quite unusual and unique.

All of the C-P39 Doucet participants trace their lineages back to Germain Doucet (born about 1641). Of Native American, paternal-line ancestry, his father, therefore, would have been a Native American, meaning that there is *no genetic relationship* between himself and Germain Doucet (Sieur dit Laverdure), the commander of Port Royal.

By comparison, the original descendants of Germain Doucet (Sieur de Laverdure) carry haplogroups of R1b1a2, clearly European, just as one would expect.

The Acadian people settled in the eastern-most region of Canada; they mixed freely with the Native people and intermarried.

Beginning in 1710 and continuing until 1755, when they were forcibly deported, they were in conflict with the English government, refusing to sign an oath of loyalty to England.

The families were highly endogamous, marrying within their own ethnic group. As a result, if you discover you descend from an Acadian family, you will discover that you descend from many Acadian families.

Based on the <u>significant</u> haplogroup differences that exist, some of them may well be the result of either errors in genealogical documentation (clerical errors) or non-paternal events (NPEs), meaning adoption, silent assimilation, infidelity and/or the like, all of which would discontinue Y-DNA from a father to a son.

The *only* conclusion that can be reached, at this time, is the <u>need for more testing</u>, <u>more markers and deep subclade determination of all cases</u>, as well as the gathering of <u>more members</u> (along with the obtaining of rigorous, first-hand, documentation of the ancestry of each member).

Simply put, we need <u>more direct line</u> Doucet(te) males (meaning an unbroken line of descent from father to son to son to son to son) who are willing to add to these current results.

If you have not already been DNA tested, and are willing to join the project, go the Group Join Request Login page [36] and click PURCHASE A TEST TO JOIN THIS PROJECT. You can then proceed by ordering a Y-DNA 37 (marker) test, unless, of course, you select a Y-DNA 67 (marker) test.

Given that Family Tree DNA seek to ensure that their customers obtain the highest resolution Y-DNA test in the world, several groups of families have still not been able to completely determine the relatedness of group members with their flagship 37 marker test; as a result, the Y-DNA67 kit can further refine their estimate of how closely related two individuals are. By using additional markers, groups of related participants have a better chance of finding mutations which identify sub-branches in the family.

A Y-DNA 37 marker match gives you a 95% probability of having a common ancestor within the last 300 years.

A Y-DNA 67 marker match gives you a 95% probability of having a common ancestor within the last 150 to 200 years.

If you are a Doucet(te) male that has already been tested through Family Tree DNA, just go to your personal page at the Family Tree DNA site [37] and look for the JOIN PROJECTS link in the upper, left margin.

After clicking that link, you will be taken to a JOIN A PROJECT page. This is where you will need to enter DOUCET in the search window.

This will take you to a list of projects, including ours; clicking on the DOUCET project link will take you to the JOIN THE DOUCET PROJECT page. Thereafter, simply click on the orange JOIN button.

---

[36] https://www.familytreedna.com/group-join-request.aspx?group=Doucet&vGroup=Doucet
[37] https://www.familytreedna.com/

You can also read more about the Doucet Surname Family Tree DNA Project [38] at our denoted website.

If you are not interested in being tested, but wish to make a donation [39] to help fund our DNA project, you may certainly do so.

In many cases, as was the case for me, whereby one does not have a brother, one could then contribute monies towards having a brother, an uncle or a first cousin tested.

Special thanks are to be extended to Jacques Beaugrand (cousin and co-admin of the French Heritage DNA Project), [40] Lucie LeBlanc Consentino, David Dugas, Al Aburto (admin of the J-L24 Family Tree DNA Project), [41] Steve St. Clair (admin of the Sinclair/St. Clair DNA Study) [42] and Stephen White (Université de Moncton) for their input and assistance into these specific DNA matters.

If it were not for a first male Doucet cousin agreeing to be DNA tested, I would not have known that my father was of the R1b haplogroup, the most frequent haplogroup in Western Europe, meaning that I now have my own DNA Mystery to solve.

---

[38] https://www.familytreedna.com/public/Doucet/
[39] https://www.familytreedna.com/group-general-fund-contribution.aspx?g=Doucet
[40] www.frenchdna.org/
[41] https://www.familytreedna.com/public/J-L24-Y-DNA/default.aspx
[42] www.stclairresearch.com/

The Lejeune Sisters

In having secured my own mtDNA results in 2006, I came to discover that my most distant maternal mtDNA ancestress was Edmée Lejeune. As I continued to further my paternal ancestry, I quickly came to realize that my father's most distant maternal mtDNA ancestress was none other than Catherine Lejeune, biological sister to Edmée. Of course, this means that both my parents had the same mtDNA.

PATERNAL	MATERNAL
Catherine Lejeune and François Savoie	**Edmée Lejeune** and François Gautrot
Françoise Savoie and Jean Corporon	**Marie Gautrot** and Claude Thériot
Jeanne Corporon and Antoine Hébert	**Marguerite Thériot** and Claude Landry
Agnès Hébert and Jean Baptiste Duon dit Lyonnais	**Jeanne Landry** and François dit Manne Boudreau
Jeanne Duon and François Mius	**Marie Josèphte Boudrot** and Jacques Haché dit Gallant
Marie Suzanne Mius and Michel Doucet	**Marie Haché dit Gallant** and Pierre Doucet
Marie Anne Doucet and Jean O'Bird (Hubbard) JR	**Pélagie Doucet** and Raphaël Blanchard
Marie Madeleine O'Bird (Hubbard) and Jean Séraphin Deveau	**Marie Blanchard** and Jean Lanteigne
Marie Elizabeth Deveau and William Henry Roach	**François Lanteigne** and Agapit Doiron
Martha Roach and Peter Muise	**Romaine Doiron** and Jacques (Jim) Mallet
Beatrice Muise and Jean Avite (Harvey) Doucet	**Marie Philomène Mallet** and André Breau
Albert Doucette (my father)	**Marie Catherine (Kay) Breau** and James Henry (Harry) Feeley
	Anne Elizabeth Feeley (my mother)
	Michele Anne Doucette

My father had several sisters who lived to marry and have children. They, too, belong to the U6a haplogroup. In having had daughters, so, too, was this mtDNA passed along to them; likewise for any female grandchildren and great grandchildren.

I am not sure what the end result will be in keeping with all of the agencies and organizations that had previously issued Band cards, Métis cards and the like, based on the controversy surrounding the LeJeune sisters, Edmée and Catherine.

It had been erroneously inferred, and for many years, that they were Native American, but there had never been any documented proof to this allegation.

There had also been much speculation surrounding a possible connection between these sisters and Pierre Lejeune dit Briard, spouse of ---------- Doucet (d/o Germain Doucet, Sieur de LaVerdure, and unknown).

When I first began researching my French Acadian lines, well over 20 years ago, I learned the importance of sourcing as well as validating. Some sources, it was later proven, were more reliable than others.

Not wanting to continue to perpetuate false information, I decided to concentrate solely on what was coming out of the CEA at the Université de Moncton, courtesy of Stephen White.

Matrilineality is a system in which one belongs to one's mother's lineage.

A <u>matriline</u> is a line of descent from a female ancestor to a descendant in which the individuals in all intervening generations are female. Such can be traced both maternally as well as paternally.

However, it is the uterine ancestry of an individual that is a person's pure female ancestry, meaning a matriline leading from a female ancestor to that individual (from mother to daughter to daughter to daughter to daughter).

The fact that mitochondrial DNA (mtDNA) is maternally inherited enables matrilineal lines of individuals to be traced through genetic analysis.

On November 30, 2006, my Family Tree mtDNA results were released, directly affiliating me with the U6a haplogroup.

Information supplied regarding this U6a result states that "the mitochondrial super-haplogroup U encompasses haplogroups U1 to U7 and haplogroup K. Haplogroup U6 is *among the oldest of the U haplogroups* with an origin approximately 50,000 years ago. It is *a rare, but ancient haplogroup*, and individuals bearing this lineage out of the Near East may have encountered Neanderthals as they moved around what is now the southern Mediterranean basin. In modern populations, it is found at highest frequency in Berber-speaking populations of North Africa and the Canary Islands. Its presence in Portugal and Spain is the result of recent admixture most likely related to the Moorish occupation of Iberia." [43]

Additional research led me directly to the work of Bryan Sykes, author of The Seven Daughters of Eve, Professor of Human Genetics at Oxford University, one of the world's leading geneticists who has been involved in high-profile cases dealing with ancient DNA.

Professor Sykes has "identified 36 women, who lived thousands of years ago, from whom almost everyone on Earth is directly descended through the maternal line. He has named these women and been able to determine upon which continent they lived. The so-called

---

[43] Information received courtesy of the Family Tree DNA project at https://www.familytreedna.com/ (upon accessing personal mtDNA test results).

Seven Daughters of Eve subgroup represents the seven-clan mothers from whom almost all native Europeans are descended."[44]

In addition, Africa is able to "lay claim to 13 of the maternal clans. Although these are easily the most ancient clans in the world, a reflection of Africa's status as the cradle of humankind, it is still possible to construct the genetic relationship between them. By doing this, it is possible to show there is one maternal ancestor for all of Africa, and therefore for the rest of the world. She is referred to as *Mitochondrial Eve*."[45]

This particular Eve has no connection to the biblical Eve; apparently, she was coined in such a way by popular media. Also known as African Eve, she lived approximately 200,000 years ago.

Professor Sykes tells us that, while not the only woman alive at the time, it is <u>only her maternal lineage</u> that has been able to survive, unbroken, to the present day. One cannot help but be absolutely astounded by such a revelation.

According to Professor Sykes, "she lived about 45,000 years ago in what is now northern Greece. She was among the first arrivals of a new, modern human to set foot in Europe. She was slender and graceful, in marked contrast to the thickset Neanderthals with whom she and her clan shared the land for another 20,000 years. Her kind brought with them a new and more sophisticated type of stone tool with which to hunt and butcher the abundant game animals that soon appeared on the walls of limestone caves as the first expression of human art. They spread right across Europe, west across France and north as far as the British Isles. As the climate deteriorated 25,000 years ago, the clan began its long migration south; eventually reaching Spain and founding what became a refuge for all humans during

---

[44] http://www.tsakanikas.net/matclans.html
[45] Ibid.

the coldest millennia of the last Ice Age. As the climate warmed, the scattered clan led the march back to the North to reclaim the once frozen lands." [46]

In accordance with the company started by Bryan Sykes, called Oxford Ancestors, [47] one that is based in England, "broadly speaking the following clans and clades are similar although not exactly the same: U1 - Una, U2 - Uta, U3 - Uma, U4 - Ulrike, U5 - Ursula, U6 - Ulla and U7 - Ulaana. Groups U1 to U7, along with K (Katrine) all share a common maternal ancestor." [48]

It appears, therefore, that I belong to the Ulla clan, being of the U6a haplogroup.

Eileen Krause (Anthrogenealogy Response Center with the Family Tree DNA) has stated the following description of Haplogroup U6a:

This is a very interesting lineage for several reasons. First, I'm positive this lineage is not Native American in origin. The haplogroup U6a is not found in Native American populations, and generally haplogroup U6 is understood to be an African haplogroup. Out of curiosity, I checked our database, which is largely European so understand it is biased to show more European samples than African, for individuals who are in haplogroup U6. Of the people who reported a country of origin, it turns out the country of origin with the greatest number of individuals in our database is France.

When someone belongs to a haplogroup that is found in both Native American and non-Native American populations, we often look at the matches to determine which lineage this person is matching. In your case, your group members [meaning the French Heritage DNA Project] are an exact match for four out of five of the U6a samples from France.

---

[46] www.oxfordancestors.com/
[47] Ibid.
[48] www.brian-hamman.com/IntroductionClanUrsulaHaplogroupU5.htm

In addition, several of the participants in our database who are U6a, who are an exact match in the HVR1 region, and who did not report a country of origin, have distinctly French surnames.

While the surname isn't necessarily descriptive of the origin of the direct maternal line, when I combine this with the fact that France was the country with the most U6a individuals in our database, it is very interesting.

From this information, I would conclude that the direct maternal line of your participants is not a Native American line; perhaps there is a European ancestor along that line further than the paper trail is able to trace, or perhaps the Native American ancestor is a male or a different female on that side of the family.

At this point, we still have the interesting question of how did U6a, which research indicates is primarily an African lineage, make it to Europe? Despite U6a's African origins, <u>I'm certain these lineages came to Canada from France based on the matches</u>.

How, then, did they get to France from Africa, where this haplogroup branch is most commonly found?

There are a number of possibilities.

U6 may have originated in Europe and this lineage simply did not migrate to Africa. On the other hand, if it originated in Africa, a family could have simply migrated into Europe, but there are also some historical events that would have brought some African lineages into the area.

For example, the Moors who invaded Spain left some lineages behind, which could have easily migrated into France.

Romans brought African slaves with them and spent a significant amount of time and effort in Gaul.

Phoenicians and other traders around the Mediterranean also traded along the coast of Europe; they are known to have traded with Cornwall, so they would easily have traded with France as well.

In each of these examples, some lineages would have spread from Africa into Europe (and vice versa).

Finally, U6a is not the most common haplogroup branch. More research will probably shed more light on what population groups it can be found in (both within Africa and outside of Africa) and possibilities for how it migrated and spread to these different areas. [49]

Based on this response from Eileen Krause, my U6a haplogroup result clearly shows that the maternal ancestors of Catherine and Edmée were European. Given that we know naught who their father was, there will never be a way of testing the male Y-DNA line as a means of comparison and cross-checking.

It also needs to be shared, herein, that my U6a result (which also happened to be *the very first test result* for the Lejeune sisters, specifically Edmée), has since been corroborated by 18 additional mtDNA test results. [50]

In summation, then, the Lejeune sisters confirm maternal ancestry to a European female, of a rare and ancient haplogroup. This DNA fact simply cannot be ignored.

---

[49] Response from Eileen Krause as shared on the mtDNA Origins page as maintained by Lucie LeBlanc Consentino at www.acadian-home.org/frames.html
[50] https://www.familytreedna.com/public/mothersofacadia/default.aspx?section=mtresults

In the explanatory words of Debra Katz, an mtDNA sister ......

A haplogroup involves a significantly large group of people, all of whom have a key mutation that sets them apart from the other haplogroups that exist.

The little band who left Africa around 70,000 years ago were all L3 (the haplogroup of the woman). Some mutations among them led to groups M and N. As the years went by, some N descendants split into R. Later, R split into U. What needs to be remembered is that these splits (mutation offshoots) happened on the scale of tens of thousands of years ago.

Within haplogroups exist subclades (which continue to be discovered as more and more genetic research is done); to put it simply, these are further divisions, due to mutations, into groups of more closely matched people, with the time scale being typically 10,000 years ago or less.

As a result, U split into U1, U2, etc. In turn, the U6 group had some dividing mutations and that led to U6a, U6b, etc.

While U6a is of North African origin, it must be remembered that this specific origin is close to 70,000 years old.

While this U6a branch ended up back in North Africa, approximately 25,000 years ago, some migration from there went to the Middle East, and then to Europe.

What does European mean in the case of U6a?

If it means descended from people who migrated to Europe first (around 50,000 years ago), then no, U6a is not European; however, a person of this haplogroup could easily have had ancestry in Europe for several thousand years, and perhaps even as much as 20,000 years.

Being in the same haplogroup subclade (as in U6a) means that individuals share a common ancestor within the last 2,000 to 5,000 years or so.

Being of the U6a7 subset, means that individuals share a common ancestor within the last 1,000 to 2,000 years or so.

Having become even further affiliated with U6a7a, an even more recent subset, means that a shared common ancestor lived within the last 500 to 800 years or so.

In addition, there are a group of us who are either exactly the same or almost exactly the same.

However, if one should be of the same haplogroup subclade, while also sharing the same haplotype (a specific string of genetic markers that are either exactly the same or almost exactly the same), this means that an individual is much more closely related.

There are many different haplotypes within one haplogroup. Those with the same haplotype may share an ancestor anywhere within a 200 to 1,500 year time frame.

Upon further DNA testing (and specifically the Full Genomic Sequence, or FGS), the Acadian cluster, meaning the Lejeune sisters, has since been identified as subclade U6a7a1. In addition, it is the FGS that determines a person's true haplotype.

According to Family Tree DNA, there is a 50% probability that our most recent common ancestor (MRCA) with Debra Katz (also U6a7a1), <u>with whom we share both a haplogroup subclade as well as a haplotype</u>, lived no longer than 24 generations ago (meaning about 600 years ago, presuming 4.5 generations per century), which gives us a time frame of about 1400 to 1500, around the time of the Spanish Inquisition, when many Jews converted to

Catholicism (a definite possibility for the maternal ancestor of the Lejeune sisters, given how closely we match markers with Debra, whose line is east European Jewish).

Clearly, this gives one much to ponder.

As a result, my mtDNA results (Kit 73923) are also posted within the mtDNA results segment of the Canadian Anusim Family Tree DNA Project. [51]

According to history, Sephardic Jews were forced to leave Spain and Portugal during the Spanish Inquisition. Many made their way to France, especially the southern part of France, known as Bayonne and Bordeaux. It was during the early 1600's that some of the Anusim (Jews forced to convert to Catholicism) who fled to France, ended up immigrating to New France, now known as Québec, seeking a life without religious persecution.

The objective of the Canadian Anusim Family Tree DNA Project is to prove this theory through the use of genetic means, thereby linking themselves through Canadian Anusim surnames, places of origin and DNA, to other Anusim and Jewish families, thus, re-establishing family ties that were lost during the Jewish diaspora.

Thanks must hereby be extended to Debra Katz, without whose words, shared in this segment, I would not have been able to glean a better understanding of my own mtDNA results.

In addition, Bernard Secher, [52] the administrator of the U6 mtDNA Family Tree DNA Project, does his best to keep everyone up-to-date with regards to the newest findings.

---

[51] https://www.familytreedna.com/public/canadiananusim/
[52] http://secher.bernard.free.fr/blog/

Generation 2

Family 1.1 [53] [54]

Marie Anne Doucet (born c. 1661), daughter of Pierre Doucet and Henriette Pelletret, married Jean Hébert (s/o Antoine Hébert and Geneviève Lefranc) c. 1676. She died in GP on November 3, 1710 and was buried on November 4, 1710.

1. Jacques (born c. 1677)

2. Pierre dit La Pradelle (born c. 1679)

3. Jean (born c. 1681)

4. Jeanne (born c. 1683)

5. Joseph (born c. November 1685)

6. Catherine (born c. 1688)

7. René dit Groc (born c. 1689)

8. Augustin (born after 1693 census)

9. Madeleine

10. daughter (born before 1701 census)

---

[53] White, Stephen A. (1999) <u>Dictionnaire Généalogique des Familles Acadiennes</u>, Volume A to G, page 529.
[54] White, Stephen A. (1999) <u>Dictionnaire Généalogique des Familles Acadiennes</u>, Volume H to Z, pages 798, 801 and 802.

11. daughter (born before 1701 census)

12. Anne (according to Stephen A. White)

13. François (according to Placide Gaudet)

14. son (born before 1707 census)

Family 1.2 [55]

Toussaint Doucet (born c. 1663), son of of Pierre Doucet and Henriette Pelletret, married Marie Caissie (d/o Roger Caissie and Marie Françoise Poirier) c. 1690. He died before August 11, 1733.

1. François (born c. 1691)

2. Marie (born c. 1692)

3. Michel (born c. 1694)

4. Anne (born c. 1697)

5. Pierre (according to 1714 census for Bbn)

6. Marguerite (according to 1714 census for Bbn)

7. son (born before 1707 census; died before 1714 census)

8. son (born before 1707 census; died before 1714 census)

9. son (born before 1707 census; died before 1714 census)

10. Madeleine (according to 1714 census for Bbn)

11. Marguerite (born c. 1717)

---

[55] White, Stephen A. (1999) <u>Dictionnaire Généalogique des Familles Acadiennes</u>, Volume A to G, pages 529, 535 and 536.

Family 1.3 [56]

Jean Doucet (born c. 1665), son of Pierre Doucet and Henriette Pelletret, married Françoise Blanchard (d/o Martin Blanchard and Françoise LeBlanc) c. 1692.

1. Madeleine (born c. 1693)

2. Marie Josèphe (born c. 1694)

3. Jean (born before 1701 census)

4. son (born before 1707 census)

5. Françoise (according to Archange Godbout)

6. Marguerite (born GP on September 24, 1708)

7. Claire (born c. 1712)

---

[56] White, Stephen A. (1999) <u>Dictionnaire Généalogique des Familles Acadiennes</u>, Volume A to G, pages 529, 538 and 539.

Family 1.4 [57]

Pierre Doucet (born c.1667), son of Pierre Doucet and Henriette Pelletret.

---

[57] White, Stephen A. (1999) <u>Dictionnaire Généalogique des Familles Acadiennes</u>, Volume A to G, page 529.

Family 1.5 [58]

Madeleine Doucet (born c. August 1671), daughter of Pierre Doucet and Henriette Pelletret, married (1) René Bernard c. 1689 and (2) Pierre Doiron (s/o Jean Doiron and Marie Anne Canol) c. 1709. She died before February 25, 1740.

Marriage 1

1. René dit Renochet (born c. 1690)

2. Joseph (born c. 1692)

3. Marie dite Renochet (born c. 1693)

4. Jean-Baptiste (born c. 1696)

5. Anne (according to 1714 census for Bbn)

6. Marguerite (according to 1714 census for Bbn)

7. Joseph (born after 1703 census)

8. Michel (born after 1703 census)

Marriage 2

9. Paul dit Grand Paul (born c. 1710)

10. Pierre dit Pitre (according to 1714 census for Bbn)

---

[58] White, Stephen A. (1999) Dictionnaire Généalogique des Familles Acadiennes, Volume A to G, pages 126, 513, 518 and 529.

Family 1.6 [59]

Louis Doucet (born c. 1674), son of Pierre Doucet and Henriette Pelletret, married Marguerite Girouard (d/o Jacques Girouard and Marguerite Gautrot) c. 1702.

1. Pierre (according to 1714 census for Bbn)

2. Louis (according to 1714 census for Bbn)

3. Marguerite (according to 1714 census for Bbn)

4. Madeleine (according to 1714 census for Bbn)

5. Marie (born c. 1714)

6. Joseph (according to Patrice Gallant)

7. Madeleine (born Bbn on August 9, 1722)

---

[59] White, Stephen A. (1999) <u>Dictionnaire Généalogique des Familles Acadiennes</u>, Volume A to G, pages 529, 543 and 720.

Family 1.7 [60]

Louise dite Jeanne Doucet (born c. 1675), daughter of Pierre Doucet and Henriette Pelletret, married Pierre Chênet, Sieur Dubreuil, c. 1691.

1. Pierre (born c. 1692)

2. François (born c. 1693)

3. Marie (born c. 1698)

---

[60] White, Stephen A. (1999) <u>Dictionnaire Généalogique des Familles Acadiennes</u>, Volume A to G, pages 339 and 529.

Family 1.8 [61]

René Doucet (born c. 1678), son of Pierre Doucet and Henriette Pelletret, married Marie Broussard (d/o François Broussard and Catherine Richard) c. 1702.

1. Pierre (born PR on December 24, 1703) [62] [63]

2. Anne-Marie (born PR on November 14, 1706) [64] [65]

3. Agathe (born PR on January 19, 1710) [66] [67]

4. Anne (also referenced as Jeanne) (born PR on March 23, 1713) [68]

5. François (born PR on May 1, 1715) [69] [70]

6. Catherine Josèphe (born PR on April 19, 1718) [71] [72]

7. Marguerite (born PR on February 5, 1721) [73] [74]

8. Charles (according to Placide Gaudet)

9. Jean (born PR on August 20, 1725) [75] [76]

---

[61] White, Stephen A. (1999) <u>Dictionnaire Généalogique des Familles Acadiennes</u>, Volume A to G, pages 285, 529, 544 and 545.
[62] https://novascotia.ca/archives/acadian/archives.asp?ID=40
[63] https://novascotia.ca/archives/acadian/archives.asp?ID=1040
[64] https://novascotia.ca/archives/acadian/archives.asp?ID=169
[65] https://novascotia.ca/archives/acadian/archives.asp?ID=1098
[66] https://novascotia.ca/archives/acadian/archives.asp?ID=311
[67] https://novascotia.ca/archives/acadian/archives.asp?ID=1150
[68] https://novascotia.ca/archives/acadian/archives.asp?ID=442
[69] https://novascotia.ca/archives/acadian/archives.asp?ID=549
[70] https://novascotia.ca/archives/acadian/archives.asp?ID=2513
[71] https://novascotia.ca/archives/acadian/archives.asp?ID=694
[72] https://novascotia.ca/archives/acadian/archives.asp?ID=1536
[73] https://novascotia.ca/archives/acadian/archives.asp?ID=843
[74] https://novascotia.ca/archives/acadian/archives.asp?ID=2729
[75] https://novascotia.ca/archives/acadian/archives.asp?ID=1035

10. Cécile (born PR on July 20, 1728) [77] [78]

---

[76] https://novascotia.ca/archives/acadian/archives.asp?ID=3026
[77] https://novascotia.ca/archives/acadian/archives.asp?ID=1667
[78] https://novascotia.ca/archives/acadian/archives.asp?ID=3301

Family 1.9 [79]

Marguerite Doucet (born c. 1680), daughter of Pierre Doucet and Henriette Pelletret, married Alexandre Comeau (s/o Étienne Comeau and Marie-Anne Lefebvre) c. 1700.

1. Françoise (born PR on January 20, 1703) [80] [81]

2. Marie-Anne (born PR on June 19, 1707) [82] [83]

3. Joseph (born PR on June 2, 1714) [84] [85]

4. Madeleine (born PR on March 7, 1716) [86] [87]

5. François (born PR on March 19, 1722) [88] [89]

6. Charles (born PR on October 19, 1725) [90]

---

[79] White, Stephen A. (1999) <u>Dictionnaire Généalogique des Familles Acadiennes</u>, Volume A to G, pages 371, 382 and 529.
[80] https://novascotia.ca/archives/acadian/archives.asp?ID=9
[81] https://novascotia.ca/archives/acadian/archives.asp?ID=1137
[82] https://novascotia.ca/archives/acadian/archives.asp?ID=188
[83] https://novascotia.ca/archives/acadian/archives.asp?ID=1622
[84] https://novascotia.ca/archives/acadian/archives.asp?ID=494
[85] https://novascotia.ca/archives/acadian/archives.asp?ID=2100
[86] https://novascotia.ca/archives/acadian/archives.asp?ID=578
[87] https://novascotia.ca/archives/acadian/archives.asp?ID=2101
[88] https://novascotia.ca/archives/acadian/archives.asp?ID=901
[89] https://novascotia.ca/archives/acadian/archives.asp?ID=3047
[90] https://novascotia.ca/archives/acadian/archives.asp?ID=1048

Family 1.10 [91][92][93]

Mathieu Doucet (born c. 1685), son of Pierre Doucet and Henriette Pelletret, married Anne Lord (d/o Julien Lord dit Lamontagne and Anne Charlotte Girouard) at PR on June 15, 1712.

1. Joseph (born PR on July 24, 1713) [94][95]

2. Pierre (born PR on January 28, 1715) [96][97]

3. Anne (born PR on September 14, 1717) [98]

4. Marguerite (born c. 1719)

5. Marie Josèphe (born PR on October 2, 1722) [99][100]

6. Élisabeth (also referenced as Isabelle) (born PR on December 31, 1725) [101]

7. Charles (born PR c. 1732, after the death of his father)

---

[91] White, Stephen A. (1999) <u>Dictionnaire Généalogique des Familles Acadiennes</u>, Volume A to G, pages 529, 548 and 549.
[92] White, Stephen A. (1999) <u>Dictionnaire Généalogique des Familles Acadiennes</u>, Volume H to Z, page 1101.
[93] https://novascotia.ca/archives/acadian/archives.asp?ID=1267
[94] https://novascotia.ca/archives/acadian/archives.asp?ID=458
[95] https://novascotia.ca/archives/acadian/archives.asp?ID=2103
[96] https://novascotia.ca/archives/acadian/archives.asp?ID=547
[97] https://novascotia.ca/archives/acadian/archives.asp?ID=2518
[98] https://novascotia.ca/archives/acadian/archives.asp?ID=667
[99] https://novascotia.ca/archives/acadian/archives.asp?ID=908
[100] https://novascotia.ca/archives/acadian/archives.asp?ID=2705
[101] https://novascotia.ca/archives/acadian/archives.asp?ID=1057

Family 2.1 [102] [103]

Marie Dugas (born c. 1648), daughter of Abraham Dugas and Marguerite Doucet, married Charles Melanson dit La Ramée (s/o Pierre Melanson dit LaVerdure and Priscilla ----------) c. 1663. She died at PR on July 7, 1737 and was buried on July 8, 1737.

1. Marie dite Laverdure (born c. 1664)

2. Marguerite (born c. 1666)

3. Anne (born c. 1668)

4. Cécile (born c. May 1671)

5. Élisabeth (also referenced as Isabelle) (born c. 1673)

6. Charles (born c. 1675)

7. Madeleine (born c. 1677)

8. Marie (born c.1680)

9. Françoise (born c. 1683)

10. Ambroise (born c. March 1685) twin

11. Pierre (born c. March 1685) twin

12. Claude (born c. 1688)

13. Jean dit Jani (born c. 1690)

14. Marguerite (born c. 1693)

---

[102] White, Stephen A. (1999) Dictionnaire Généalogique des Familles Acadiennes, Volume A to G, page 562.
[103] White, Stephen A. (1999) Dictionnaire Généalogique des Familles Acadiennes, Volume H to Z, page s 1146 and 1147.

Family 2.2 [104]

Claude Dugas (born c. 1649) son of Abraham Dugas and Marguerite Doucet, married (1) Françoise Bourgeois (d/o Jacques dit Jacob Bourgeois and Jeanne Trahan) c. 1763 and (2) Marguerite Bourg (d/o Bernard Bourg and Françoise Brun) c. 1697. He was buried at PR on October 16, 1732.

Marriage 1

1. Marie (born c. 1674)

2. Claude (born c. 1677)

3. Françoise (born c. 1679)

4. Joseph (born c. 1680)

5. Marguerite (baptized Bbn on March 19, 1681)

6. Anne (born c. 1683)

7. Jeanne (born c. 1684) [105]

8. Agnès (born c. 1686) [106]

9. François (born c. 1688) [107]

10. Madeleine (born c. 1689) [108]

11. Marie (born c. 1691) [109] [110]

---

[104] White, Stephen A. (1999) <u>Dictionnaire Généalogique des Familles Acadiennes</u>, Volume A to G, pages 226, 252, 562, 564, 565 and 567.
[105] https://novascotia.ca/archives/acadian/archives.asp?ID=1206
[106] https://novascotia.ca/archives/acadian/archives.asp?ID=1185
[107] https://novascotia.ca/archives/acadian/archives.asp?ID=1275
[108] https://novascotia.ca/archives/acadian/archives.asp?ID=1181
[109] https://novascotia.ca/archives/acadian/archives.asp?ID=1239
[110] https://novascotia.ca/archives/acadian/archives.asp?ID=3498

12. Cécile (born c. 1692) [111]

Marriage 2

13. Élisabeth (also referenced as Isabelle) (born c. 1698) [112]

14. Joseph dit le jeune (born c. 1699)

15. Marguerite (born c. 1703) [113]

16. Louis (born and baptized PR on November 12, 1703) [114] [115]

17. Claire (born PR on January 21, 1706 and baptized PR on March 19, 1706) [116]

18. Marie-Anne (born PR on April 16, 1707 and baptized PR on April 17, 1707) [117] [118]

19. Charles (born PR on February 18, 1709 and baptized PR on February 19, 1709) [119] [120]

20. Marie (born c. 1711)

21. Claude (born PR on May 28, 1712 and baptized PR on July 3, 1712) [121] [122]

22. Michel (born and baptized PR on November 13, 1715) [123] [124]

---

[111] https://novascotia.ca/archives/acadian/archives.asp?ID=1240
[112] https://novascotia.ca/archives/acadian/archives.asp?ID=1307
[113] https://novascotia.ca/archives/acadian/archives.asp?ID=1335
[114] https://novascotia.ca/archives/acadian/archives.asp?ID=36
[115] https://novascotia.ca/archives/acadian/archives.asp?ID=2017
[116] https://novascotia.ca/archives/acadian/archives.asp?ID=1119
[117] https://novascotia.ca/archives/acadian/archives.asp?ID=182
[118] https://novascotia.ca/archives/acadian/archives.asp?ID=1875
[119] https://novascotia.ca/archives/acadian/archives.asp?ID=263
[120] https://novascotia.ca/archives/acadian/archives.asp?ID=1856
[121] https://novascotia.ca/archives/acadian/archives.asp?ID=409
[122] https://novascotia.ca/archives/acadian/archives.asp?ID=2023
[123] https://novascotia.ca/archives/acadian/archives.asp?ID=571
[124] https://novascotia.ca/archives/acadian/archives.asp?ID=2604

Family 2.3 [125] [126]

Anne Dugas (born c. 1654), daughter of Abraham Dugas and Marguerite Doucet, married (1) Charles Bourgeois (s/o Jacques dit Jacob Bourgeois and Jeanne Trahan) c. 1668 and (2) Jean Aubin Mignot dit Châtillon (s/o Jean Mignot and Louise Cloutier of Beauport, Québec) at Bbn on April 26, 1679. She died at Bbn on November 4, 1740 and was buried on November 5, 1740.

Marriage 1

1. Marie (born c. 1670)

2. Charles (born c. 1673)

3. Claude (born c. 1674)

4. Anne (born c. 1678)

Marriage 2

5. Jean (born c. 1680)

6. Cécile dite Aubin (born and baptized Bbn on March 17, 1683)

7. Alexis (born and baptized Bbn on September 17, 1685)

8. Jacques (born c. 1689)

9. Louis Joseph dit Aubin (born c. 1692)

10. Pierre dit Châtillon (born c. 1695)

---

[125] White, Stephen A. (1999) <u>Dictionnaire Généalogique des Familles Acadiennes</u>, Volume A to G, pages 251, 253, 254 and 562.
[126] White, Stephen A. (1999) <u>Dictionnaire Généalogique des Familles Acadiennes</u>, Volume H to Z, pages 1188 and 1189.

Family 2.4 [127] [128]

Martin Dugas (born c. 1656), son of Abraham Dugas and Marguerite Doucet, married Marguerite Petitpas (d/o Claude Petitpas, Sieur de La Fleur, and Catherine Bugaret) c. 1677. He died c. 1680.

1. Abraham dit Grivois (born c. 1678)

2. Marguerite (born c. 1680)

---

[127] White, Stephen A. (1999) Dictionnaire Généalogique des Familles Acadiennes, Volume A to G, pages 562 and 568.
[128] White, Stephen A. (1999) Dictionnaire Généalogique des Familles Acadiennes, Volume H to Z, page 1295.

Family 2.5 [129]

Marguerite Dugas (born c. 1657), daughter of Abraham Dugas and Marguerite Doucet, married Pierre Arsenault c. 1675. She died before the census of 1686.

1. Pierre (born c. 1676)

2. Abraham (born c. 1678)

---

[129] White, Stephen A. (1999) <u>Dictionnaire Généalogique des Familles Acadiennes</u>, Volume A to G, pages 23 and 562.

Family 2.6 [130]

Abraham Dugas (born c. 1661), son of Abraham Dugas and Marguerite Doucet, married Jeanne Guilbeau (d/o Pierre Guilbeau and Catherine Thériot) c. 1685. He died after the census of 1734.

1. Anne (born c. 1686)

2. Joseph

3. Marguerite

4. Marie

5. Jeanne (born c. 1700)

6. son (born before 1714 census)

---

[130] White, Stephen A. (1999) <u>Dictionnaire Généalogique des Familles Acadiennes</u>, Volume A to G, pages 562, 569 and 780.

Family 2.7 [131]

Madeleine Dugas (born c. 1664), daughter of Abraham Dugas and Marguerite Doucet, married Germain Bourgeois (s/o Jacques dit Jacob Bourgeois and Jeanne Trahan) c. 1682. She died at PR on August 8, 1738 and was buried on August 9, 1738.

1. Madeleine (born c. 1683)

2. Agnès (born Bbn on January 10, 1686 and baptized Bbn on January 13, 1686)

3. Anne (born c. 1688) [132]

4. Joseph (born c. 1691) [133]

5. Marie Josèphe (born c. 1693) [134]

6. Claude (born c. 1695) [135]

7. Françoise (born c. 1698) [136]

8. Marguerite (born after 1701 census) [137]

9. Marie Madeleine (born PR on December 22, 1704 and baptized PR on March 9, 1705) [138] [139]

10. Jeanne (born PR on November 30, 1708 and baptized PR on March 30, 1709) [140] [141]

---

[131] White, Stephen A. (1999) <u>Dictionnaire Généalogique des Familles Acadiennes</u>, Volume A to G, pages 252, 255, 256 and 562.
[132] https://novascotia.ca/archives/acadian/archives.asp?ID=1215
[133] https://novascotia.ca/archives/acadian/archives.asp?ID=1322
[134] https://novascotia.ca/archives/acadian/archives.asp?ID=1271
[135] https://novascotia.ca/archives/acadian/archives.asp?ID=1337
[136] https://novascotia.ca/archives/acadian/archives.asp?ID=1323
[137] https://novascotia.ca/archives/acadian/archives.asp?ID=1334
[138] https://novascotia.ca/archives/acadian/archives.asp?ID=78
[139] https://novascotia.ca/archives/acadian/archives.asp?ID=1359
[140] https://novascotia.ca/archives/acadian/archives.asp?ID=269
[141] https://novascotia.ca/archives/acadian/archives.asp?ID=1706

Family 2.8 [142] [143]

Marie Dugas (born c. 1667), daughter of Abraham Dugas and Marguerite Doucet, married André LeBlanc (s/o Daniel LeBlanc and Françoise Gaudet) c. 1683. She died at GP on January 13, 1734 and was buried on January 14, 1734.

1. Jean (born c. 1684) [144]

2. Marie (born c. 1687)

3. Pierre (born c. 1689)

4. Anne (born c. 1692)

5. Jacques

6. Claude André (born c. 1696)

7. François (born c. 1698)

8. Joseph André (born between 1701 census and 1703 census)

9. Charles André (born and baptized GP on September 24, 1707)

10. Claire (born GP on June 1, 1710 and baptized GP on June 2, 1710)

---

[142] White, Stephen A. (1999) <u>Dictionnaire Généalogique des Familles Acadiennes</u>, Volume A to G, page 562.
[143] White, Stephen A. (1999) <u>Dictionnaire Généalogique des Familles Acadiennes</u>, Volume H to Z, pages 983, 991 and 992.
[144] https://novascotia.ca/archives/acadian/archives.asp?ID=1179

Family 3.1 [145]

Pierre LeJeune dit Briard (born c. 1656), son of Pierre LeJeune dit Briard and ---------- Doucet, married Marie Thibodeau (d/o Pierre Thibodeau and Jeanne Thériot) at PR before the 1678 census.

1. Marie Marguerite dite Briard (born c. 1687)

2. Pierre (born c. 1689)

3. Jeanne (born c. 1691)

4. Germain (born c. 1693)

5. Marguerite (born at PR c. 1695)

6. Jean (born c. 1697)

7. Anne (born c. 1699)

8. Catherine (born c. 1701)

9. Joseph (born PR on July 20, 1704 and baptized PR on September 8, 1705) [146]

---

[145] White, Stephen A. (1999) Dictionnaire Généalogique des Familles Acadiennes, Volume H to Z, pages 1049, 1051, 1052 and 1508.
[146] https://novascotia.ca/archives/acadian/archives.asp?ID=115

Family 3.2 [147] [148]

Martin LeJeune dit Briard (born c. 1661), son of Pierre LeJeune dit Briard and ---------- Doucet, married (1) Jeanne (Marie) Kagigconiac, a Mi'kmaq, c. 1684 and (2) Marie Gaudet (d/o Jean Gaudet and Jeanne Henry) c. 1699.

Marriage 1

1. Claude dit Briard (according to 1686 census for La Hève) [149]

2. daughter (born before 1686 census)

3. Anne dite Briard (born c. 1687)

4. Germain (born c. 1689)

5. Bernard (born c. 1693)

Marriage 2

6. Théodore (born c. 1700)

7. Paul dit Briard (born PR on October 9, 1702 and baptized PR on September 10, 1705) twin [150]

8. Martin (born PR on October 9, 1702 and baptized PR on September 10, 1705) twin [151]

9. Claire (born c. 1706)

10. Marguerite (born GP on July 9, 1710 and baptized GP on August 10, 1710)

11. Eustache dit Briard (born GP in August 1715 and baptized GP on June 15, 1717)

---

[147] White, Stephen A. (1999) <u>Dictionnaire Généalogique des Familles Acadiennes</u>, Volume H to Z, pages 881, 1049, 1054 and 1055.
[148] White, Stephen A. (1999) <u>Dictionnaire Généalogique des Familles Acadiennes</u>, Volume A to G, page 669.
[149] https://novascotia.ca/archives/acadian/archives.asp?ID=1193
[150] https://novascotia.ca/archives/acadian/archives.asp?ID=117
[151] https://novascotia.ca/archives/acadian/archives.asp?ID=118

12. Pierre (born c. 1719)

Family 4.1 [152]

Charles Doucet (born c. 1665), son of Germain Doucet and Marie Landry, married Huguette Guérin (d/o François Guérin and Anne Blanchard) c. 1684. He died at PR on May 7, 1739 and was buried on May 8, 1739.

1. Claude (born c. 1685)

2. Charles (born c. 1688)

3. Jean (born c. 1690) [153]

4. François (born c. 1692)

5. Madeleine (born c. 1695) [154]

6. Germain (born c. 1697) [155]

7. Joseph (born c. 1699) [156]

8. Michel (born PR on April 10, 1703 and baptized PR on April 11, 1703) [157] [158]

9. Louis (baptized PR on February 17, 1706) [159]

---

[152] White, Stephen A. (1999) <u>Dictionnaire Généalogique des Familles Acadiennes</u>, Volume A to G, pages 530, 532 and 776.
[153] https://novascotia.ca/archives/acadian/archives.asp?ID=1290
[154] https://novascotia.ca/archives/acadian/archives.asp?ID=1296
[155] https://novascotia.ca/archives/acadian/archives.asp?ID=1137
[156] https://novascotia.ca/archives/acadian/archives.asp?ID=1049
[157] https://novascotia.ca/archives/acadian/archives.asp?ID=14
[158] https://novascotia.ca/archives/acadian/archives.asp?ID=1890
[159] https://novascotia.ca/archives/acadian/archives.asp?ID=126

Family 4.2 [160]

Bernard Doucet dit Laverdure (born c. 1667), son of Germain Doucet and Marie Landry, married Madeleine Corporon (d/o Jean Corporon and Françoise Savoie) c. 1690. He was buried at PR on August 4, 1709.

1. Jean (born c. 1692)

2. Marie Marthe (born c. 1694) [161]

3. Agnès (born c. 1697)

4. Cécile (born c. 1698)

---

[160] White, Stephen A. (1999) <u>Dictionnaire Généalogique des Familles Acadiennes</u>, Volume A to G, pages 411, 530, 537 and 538.
[161] https://novascotia.ca/archives/acadian/archives.asp?ID=1264

Family 4.3 [162]

Laurent Doucet (born c. 1669), son of Germain Doucet and Marie Landry, married Jeanne Babin (d/o Antoine Babin and Marie Mercier), widow of Michel Richard, c.1689. He died before January 19, 1728.

1. Pierre (born c. 1690)

2. Jeanne (born c. 1692) [163]

3. Marie (born c. 1694) [164]

4. Laurent (born c. 1696) [165]

5. Marie (born c. 1698)

6. Jean (born c. 1699)

7. Madeleine (born c. 1700)

8. Pierre Paul dit Paul Laurent (born PR on March 23, 1704 and baptized PR on April 23, 1704) [166] [167]

9. Agnès (baptized PR on March 9, 1706) [168] [169]

10. Joseph (born PR on January 15, 1708 and baptized PR on February 5, 1708) [170]

---

[162] White, Stephen A. (1999) <u>Dictionnaire Généalogique des Familles Acadiennes</u>, Volume A to G, pages 57, 531, 533 and 534.
[163] https://novascotia.ca/archives/acadian/archives.asp?ID=1297
[164] https://novascotia.ca/archives/acadian/archives.asp?ID=1241
[165] https://novascotia.ca/archives/acadian/archives.asp?ID=1339
[166] https://novascotia.ca/archives/acadian/archives.asp?ID=54
[167] https://novascotia.ca/archives/acadian/archives.asp?ID=2235
[168] https://novascotia.ca/archives/acadian/archives.asp?ID=130
[169] https://novascotia.ca/archives/acadian/archives.asp?ID=1633
[170] https://novascotia.ca/archives/acadian/archives.asp?ID=167

11. Michel (born PR on October 12, 1710 and baptized PR on November 9, 1710) [171] [172]

12. Claude (born and baptized PR on July 13, 1713) [173] [174]

---

[171] https://novascotia.ca/archives/acadian/archives.asp?ID=344
[172] https://novascotia.ca/archives/acadian/archives.asp?ID=3002
[173] https://novascotia.ca/archives/acadian/archives.asp?ID=455
[174] https://novascotia.ca/archives/acadian/archives.asp?ID=2586

Family 4.4 [175] [176]

Jacques Doucet dit Maillard (born c. 1671), son of Germain Doucet and Marie Landry, married Marie Pellerin (d/o Étienne Pellerin and Jeanne Savoie) c. 1695.

1. Marie Josèphe (born c. 1696) [177]

2. Madeleine (born c. 1698)

3. Jean (born before 1703 census)

4. Alexis (born PR on October 18, 1704 and baptized PR on October 19, 1704) [178]

5. Pierre dit Maillard (baptized PR on February 20, 1707) [179] [180]

6. Marguerite (born and baptized PR on February 2, 1710) [181] [182]

7. Marguerite dite Maillard (born PR on November 24, 1711 and baptized PR on January 30, 1712) [183] [184]

8. Anne (born PR on February 10, 1715 and baptized PR on March 10, 1715) [185] [186]

9. Brigitte (born PR on May 30, 1716 and baptized PR on May 31, 1716) [187]

---

[175] White, Stephen A. (1999) Dictionnaire Généalogique des Familles Acadiennes, Volume A to G, pages 531, 539 and 540.

[176] White, Stephen A. (1999) Dictionnaire Généalogique des Familles Acadiennes, Volume H to Z, page 1278.

[177] https://novascotia.ca/archives/acadian/archives.asp?ID=1063

[178] https://novascotia.ca/archives/acadian/archives.asp?ID=67

[179] https://novascotia.ca/archives/acadian/archives.asp?ID=175

[180] https://novascotia.ca/archives/acadian/archives.asp?ID=3033

[181] https://novascotia.ca/archives/acadian/archives.asp?ID=315

[182] https://novascotia.ca/archives/acadian/archives.asp?ID=1457

[183] https://novascotia.ca/archives/acadian/archives.asp?ID=369

[184] https://novascotia.ca/archives/acadian/archives.asp?ID=2522

[185] https://novascotia.ca/archives/acadian/archives.asp?ID=537

[186] https://novascotia.ca/archives/acadian/archives.asp?ID=1502

[187] https://novascotia.ca/archives/acadian/archives.asp?ID=596

10. Ursule (born PR on March 27, 1720 and baptized PR on April 20, 1720) [188]

11. Euphrosine dite Maillard (born PR on January 5, 1723 and baptized PR on May 22, 1724) [189] [190]

---

[188] https://novascotia.ca/archives/acadian/archives.asp?ID=808
[189] https://novascotia.ca/archives/acadian/archives.asp?ID=979
[190] https://novascotia.ca/archives/acadian/archives.asp?ID=3269

Family 4.5 [191] [192]

Claude dit Maître Jean Doucet (born c. 1674), son of Germain Doucet and Marie Landry, married Marie Comeau (d/o Étienne Comeau and Marie-Anne Lefebvre) c. 1696. He died at PR on December 5, 1754 and was buried on December 6, 1754.

1. Charles (born c. 1697) [193]

2. Marie (born c. 1699)

3. Marguerite (born c. 1700)

4. Anne (born PR on August 26, 1703 and baptized PR on September 9, 1703) [194] [195]

5. Joseph (born PR on March 12, 1706 and baptized PR on March 13, 1706) [196] [197]

6. Louis (born PR on August 22, 1708 and baptized PR on August 26, 1708) [198] [199]

7. Pierre (born PR on November 2, 1709 and baptized PR on November 3, 1709) [200] [201]

8. Madeleine (born PR on March 15, 1712 and baptized PR on April 4, 1712) [202] [203]

9. Claude (born PR on November 13, 1714 and baptized PR on November 17, 1714) [204] [205]

---

[191] White, Stephen A. (1999) <u>Dictionnaire Généalogique des Familles Acadiennes</u>, Volume A to G, pages 371, 531, 541 and 542.
[192] https://novascotia.ca/archives/acadian/archives.asp?ID=3510
[193] https://novascotia.ca/archives/acadian/archives.asp?ID=1002
[194] https://novascotia.ca/archives/acadian/archives.asp?ID=25
[195] https://novascotia.ca/archives/acadian/archives.asp?ID=1347
[196] https://novascotia.ca/archives/acadian/archives.asp?ID=127
[197] https://novascotia.ca/archives/acadian/archives.asp?ID=1807
[198] https://novascotia.ca/archives/acadian/archives.asp?ID=237
[199] https://novascotia.ca/archives/acadian/archives.asp?ID=1424
[200] https://novascotia.ca/archives/acadian/archives.asp?ID=304
[201] https://novascotia.ca/archives/acadian/archives.asp?ID=1854
[202] https://novascotia.ca/archives/acadian/archives.asp?ID=392
[203] https://novascotia.ca/archives/acadian/archives.asp?ID=2602
[204] https://novascotia.ca/archives/acadian/archives.asp?ID=520

10. Cécile (born PR on October 22, 1719 and baptized PR on October 24, 1719) [206] [207]

11. Ursule (born PR on June 17, 1722 and baptized PR on July 19, 1722) [208]

---

[205] https://novascotia.ca/archives/acadian/archives.asp?ID=2363
[206] https://novascotia.ca/archives/acadian/archives.asp?ID=777
[207] https://novascotia.ca/archives/acadian/archives.asp?ID=3308
[208] https://novascotia.ca/archives/acadian/archives.asp?ID=902

Family 4.6 [209]

Marie Doucet (born c. 1678), daughter of Germain Doucet and Marie Landry.

---

[209] White, Stephen A. (1999) <u>Dictionnaire Généalogique des Familles Acadiennes</u>, Volume A to G, page 531.

Family 4.7 [210] [211]

Jeanne Doucet (born c. 1680), daughter of Germain Doucet and Marie Landry, married Jean Chrysostôme Loppinot c. 1702. She died before January 7, 1733.

1. Jean Chrysostôme Nicolas Sebastien (born PR on January 21, 1703 and baptized PR on February 1, 1703) [212]

2. Louis (baptized PR on June 20 1705) [213]

3. Louis dit La Frésillière (born and baptized PR on October 9, 1707) [214]

4. Jeanne (born PR on December 30, 1708 and baptized PR on January 1, 1708) [215]

5. Joseph (born PR on January 26, 1710 and baptized PR on January 27, 1710) [216] [217]

---

[210] White, Stephen A. (1999) Dictionnaire Généalogique des Familles Acadiennes, Volume A to G, page 531.
[211] White, Stephen A. (1999) Dictionnaire Généalogique des Familles Acadiennes, Volume H to Z, pages 1099 and 1100.
[212] https://novascotia.ca/archives/acadian/archives.asp?ID=10
[213] https://novascotia.ca/archives/acadian/archives.asp?ID=87
[214] https://novascotia.ca/archives/acadian/archives.asp?ID=201
[215] https://novascotia.ca/archives/acadian/archives.asp?ID=256
[216] https://novascotia.ca/archives/acadian/archives.asp?ID=313
[217] https://novascotia.ca/archives/acadian/archives.asp?ID=1454

Family 4.8 [218]

Alexis Doucet (born c. 1682), son of Germain Doucet and Marie Landry.

---

[218] White, Stephen A. (1999) <u>Dictionnaire Généalogique des Familles Acadiennes</u>, Volume A to G, page 531.

Family 4.9 [219]

Pierre Doucet (born c. 1685) son of Germain Doucet and Marie Landry.

---

[219] White, Stephen A. (1999) <u>Dictionnaire Généalogique des Familles Acadiennes</u>, Volume A to G, page 531.

Michele's Direct Lineage

GENERATION 1

Germain Doucet, Sieur de LaVerdure, and unknown.

GENERATION 2

Germain Doucet was born c. 1641. [220] He died before the PR census of 1698. [221] He married **Marie Landry** (d/o René Landry and Perrine Bourg) c. 1664. [222] [223] Marie Landry was born c. 1646. [224] [225] She died at PR, date unknown. [226] [227]

GENERATION 3

Claude dit Maître Jean Doucet was born c. 1674. [228] He died at PR on December 5, 1754 [229] [230] and was buried on December 6, 1754 in the Ste-Anne cemetery. [231] [232] He married **Marie**

---

[220] White, Stephen A. (1999) <u>Dictionnaire Généalogique des Familles Acadiennes</u>, Volume A to G, pages 526 and 530.
[221] Ibid.
[222] Ibid.
[223] White, Stephen A. (1999) <u>Dictionnaire Généalogique des Familles Acadiennes</u>, Volume H to Z, page 915.
[224] Ibid.
[225] White, Stephen A. (1999) <u>Dictionnaire Généalogique des Familles Acadiennes</u>, Volume A to G, page 530.
[226] White, Stephen A. (1999) <u>Dictionnaire Généalogique des Familles Acadiennes</u>, Volume H to Z, page 915.
[227] White, Stephen A. (1999) <u>Dictionnaire Généalogique des Familles Acadiennes</u>, Volume A to G, page 530.
[228] Ibid, pages 531 and 541.
[229] Ibid.
[230] https://novascotia.ca/archives/acadian/archives.asp?ID=3510

Comeau (d/o Étienne Comeau and Marie-Anne Lefebvre) c. 1696. [233] Marie was born c. 1676. [234]

Claude lived at the Cape (the section where the first road to Halifax starts from the main street of Annapolis). There were a total of 41 families living along that same road. [235]

Claude dit Maître Jean Doucet and Marie Comeau had the following children:

1. Charles (born c. 1697) [236] married Madeleine Préjean (d/o Jean Préjean and Andrée Savoie) on February 12, 1725 at PR. [237] [238] [239]

2. Marie (born c. 1699) [240] married Bernard dit Blèche Gaudet (s/o Pierre Gaudet le jeune and Marie Blanchard), widower of Marguerite Pellerin, about 1724. [241]

3. Marguerite (born c. 1700) [242] married Pierre Préjean dit l'aîné (s/o Jean Préjean and Andrée Savoie) on February 3, 1722 at Bbn. [243] [244] She died at PR on October 31, 1749 at about 48 years of age. [245] [246] She was buried on November 2, 1749. [247] [248]

---

[231] White, Stephen A. (1999) <u>Dictionnaire Généalogique des Familles Acadiennes</u>, Volume A to G, pages 531 and 541.
[232] https://novascotia.ca/archives/acadian/archives.asp?ID=3510
[233] White, Stephen A. (1999) <u>Dictionnaire Généalogique des Familles Acadiennes</u>, Volume A to G, pages 371, 531 and 541.
[234] Ibid, pages 371 and 541.
[235] Research of Wilfred Doucette, one of the Directors of the Acadian Heritage and Culture Foundation Incorporated in Erath, Louisiana, now deceased. Information shared with me through his nephew, Robert (Bob) Doucet.
[236] White, Stephen A. (1999) <u>Dictionnaire Généalogique des Familles Acadiennes</u>, Volume A to G, page 541.
[237] Ibid.
[238] White, Stephen A. (1999) <u>Dictionnaire Généalogique des Familles Acadiennes</u>, Volume H to Z, page 1351.
[239] https://novascotia.ca/archives/acadian/archives.asp?ID=1002
[240] White, Stephen A. (1999) <u>Dictionnaire Généalogique des Familles Acadiennes</u>, Volume A to G, page 541.
[241] Ibid, pages 541 and 673.

4. Anne (born at PR on August 26, 1703 and baptized on September 9, 1703) [249] [250] married François Chiasson (s/o Gabriel Chiasson and Marie Savoie) on November 3, 1722 at PR. [251] [252] According to the archives for St-Servan, Bretagne, France, she died at sea, during the 1758 deportation crossing to France. [253] François died on February 14, 1759 and was buried on February 15, 1759 at St-Servan, Bretagne, France. [254]

5. Joseph (born in PR on March 12, 1706 and baptized on March 13, 1706) [255] [256] married Anne Surette (d/o Pierre Surette and Jeanne Pellerin) on January 8, 1731 at PR. [257] [258] [259]

---

[242] White, Stephen A. (1999) Dictionnaire Généalogique des Familles Acadiennes, Volume A to G, page 541.
[243] Ibid.
[244] White, Stephen A. (1999) Dictionnaire Généalogique des Familles Acadiennes, Volume H to Z, page 1351.
[245] White, Stephen A. (1999) Dictionnaire Généalogique des Familles Acadiennes, Volume A to G, page 541.
[246] https://novascotia.ca/archives/acadian/archives.asp?ID=3096
[247] White, Stephen A. (1999) Dictionnaire Généalogique des Familles Acadiennes, Volume A to G, page 541.
[248] https://novascotia.ca/archives/acadian/archives.asp?ID=3096
[249] White, Stephen A. (1999) Dictionnaire Généalogique des Familles Acadiennes, Volume A to G, page 541.
[250] https://novascotia.ca/archives/acadian/archives.asp?ID=25
[251] White, Stephen A. (1999) Dictionnaire Généalogique des Familles Acadiennes, Volume A to G, pages 351 and 541.
[252] https://novascotia.ca/archives/acadian/archives.asp?ID=1347
[253] White, Stephen A. (1999) Dictionnaire Généalogique des Familles Acadiennes, Volume A to G, page 541.
[254] Ibid, page 351.
[255] Ibid, page 541.
[256] https://novascotia.ca/archives/acadian/archives.asp?ID=127
[257] White, Stephen A. (1999) Dictionnaire Généalogique des Familles Acadiennes, Volume A to G, page 541.
[258] White, Stephen A. (1999) Dictionnaire Généalogique des Familles Acadiennes, Volume H to Z, page 1476.
[259] https://novascotia.ca/archives/acadian/archives.asp?ID=1807

6. Louis (born in PR on August 22, 1708 and baptized on August 26, 1708) [260] [261] died on August 26, 1708 and was buried on August 27, 1708. [262] [263]

7. Pierre (born at PR on November 2, 1709 and baptized on November 3, 1709) [264] [265] married Marie Josèphe Robichaud (d/o Prudent Robichaud and Henriette Petitpas) on January 15, 1732 at PR. [266] [267] [268] He died on December 27, 1775 and was buried on December 28, 1775 as per the Notre-Dame parish register in Québec. [269] Marie Josèphe died on February 7, 1782 and was buried on February 8, 1782 as per the Notre-Dame parish register in Québec. [270]

8. Madeleine (born at PR on March 15, 1712 and baptized on April 4, 1712) [271] [272] married François Grosvalet (s/o Bertrand Grosvalet and Françoise Binard), widower of Angélique

---

[260] White, Stephen A. (1999) Dictionnaire Généalogique des Familles Acadiennes, Volume A to G, page 541.
[261] https://novascotia.ca/archives/acadian/archives.asp?ID=237
[262] White, Stephen A. (1999) Dictionnaire Généalogique des Familles Acadiennes, Volume A to G, page 541.
[263] https://novascotia.ca/archives/acadian/archives.asp?ID=1424
[264] White, Stephen A. (1999) Dictionnaire Généalogique des Familles Acadiennes, Volume A to G, page 542.
[265] https://novascotia.ca/archives/acadian/archives.asp?ID=304
[266] White, Stephen A. (1999) Dictionnaire Généalogique des Familles Acadiennes, Volume A to G, page 542.
[267] White, Stephen A. (1999) Dictionnaire Généalogique des Familles Acadiennes, Volume H to Z, page 1408.
[268] https://novascotia.ca/archives/acadian/archives.asp?ID=1854
[269] White, Stephen A. (1999) Dictionnaire Généalogique des Familles Acadiennes, Volume A to G, page 542.
[270] White, Stephen A. (1999) Dictionnaire Généalogique des Familles Acadiennes, Volume H to Z, page 1408.
[271] White, Stephen A. (1999) Dictionnaire Généalogique des Familles Acadiennes, Volume A to G, page 542.
[272] https://novascotia.ca/archives/acadian/archives.asp?ID=392

Mius, on February 6, 1743 at PR. [273] [274] She died on January 30, 1776 and was buried on January 31, 1776 as per the Notre-Dame parish register in Québec. [275]

9. Claude (born at PR on November 13, 1714 and baptized on November 17, 1714) [276] [277] married Marguerite Pellerin (d/o Jean Baptiste Pellerin and Marie Martin) on November 23, 1739 at PR. [278] [279] [280] He died before the census of 1763. [281] Marguerite was buried on December 14, 1762 at St-Pierre de Martinique. [282] St-Pierre is a town on the island of Martinique, owned by France, as located in the east Caribbean sea.

10. Cécile (born at PR on October 22, 1719 and baptized on October 24, 1719) [283] [284] married Jacques Le Borgne dit Cotte (s/o Jacques Le Borgne dit Cotte and Marie Anne Morise) on January 31, 1752 at PR. [285] [286] She was buried at St-François, Basse-Terre,

---

[273] White, Stephen A. (1999) <u>Dictionnaire Généalogique des Familles Acadiennes</u>, Volume A to G, page 542.
[274] https://novascotia.ca/archives/acadian/archives.asp?ID=2602
[275] White, Stephen A. (1999) <u>Dictionnaire Généalogique des Familles Acadiennes</u>, Volume A to G, page 542.
[276] Ibid.
[277] https://novascotia.ca/archives/acadian/archives.asp?ID=520
[278] White, Stephen A. (1999) <u>Dictionnaire Généalogique des Familles Acadiennes</u>, Volume A to G, page 542.
[279] White, Stephen A. (1999) <u>Dictionnaire Généalogique des Familles Acadiennes</u>, Volume H to Z, page 1280.
[280] https://novascotia.ca/archives/acadian/archives.asp?ID=2363
[281] White, Stephen A. (1999) <u>Dictionnaire Généalogique des Familles Acadiennes</u>, Volume A to G, page 542.
[282] White, Stephen A. (1999) <u>Dictionnaire Généalogique des Familles Acadiennes</u>, Volume H to Z, page 1280.
[283] White, Stephen A. (1999) <u>Dictionnaire Généalogique des Familles Acadiennes</u>, Volume A to G, page 542.
[284] https://novascotia.ca/archives/acadian/archives.asp?ID=777
[285] White, Stephen A. (1999) <u>Dictionnaire Généalogique des Familles Acadiennes</u>, Volume A to G, page 542.
[286] https://novascotia.ca/archives/acadian/archives.asp?ID=3308

Guadeloupe, on October 26, 1765. [287] Guadeloupe, an archipelago located in the eastern Caribbean Sea, has been a French possession since 1635, and is comprised of five islands; namely, Basse-Terre, Grande-Terre, La Désirade, Les Saintes and Marie-Galante.

12. Ursule was born at PR on June 17, 1722 and baptized on July 19, 1722. [288] [289]

GENERATION 4

Joseph Doucet was born at PR on March 12, 1706. [290] [291] He was baptized at PR on March 13, 1706. [292] [293] He married **Anne Surette** (d/o Pierre Surette and Jeanne Pellerin) on January 8, 1731 at PR. [294] [295] [296] Anne was born at PR on September 28, 1715. [297] [298] She was baptized at PR on September 30, 1715. [299] [300]

---

[287] White, Stephen A. (1999) <u>Dictionnaire Généalogique des Familles Acadiennes,</u> Volume A to G, page 542.
[288] Ibid.
[289] https://novascotia.ca/archives/acadian/archives.asp?ID=902
[290] White, Stephen A. (1999) <u>Dictionnaire Généalogique des Familles Acadiennes,</u> Volume A to G, page 541.
[291] https://novascotia.ca/archives/acadian/archives.asp?ID=127
[292] White, Stephen A. (1999) <u>Dictionnaire Généalogique des Familles Acadiennes,</u> Volume A to G, page 541.
[293] https://novascotia.ca/archives/acadian/archives.asp?ID=127
[294] White, Stephen A. (1999) <u>Dictionnaire Généalogique des Familles Acadiennes,</u> Volume A to G, page 541.
[295] White, Stephen A. (1999) <u>Dictionnaire Généalogique des Familles Acadiennes,</u> Volume H to Z, page 1476.
[296] https://novascotia.ca/archives/acadian/archives.asp?ID=1807
[297] White, Stephen A. (1999) <u>Dictionnaire Généalogique des Familles Acadiennes,</u> Volume H to Z, page 1476.
[298] https://novascotia.ca/archives/acadian/archives.asp?ID=562
[299] White, Stephen A. (1999) <u>Dictionnaire Généalogique des Familles Acadiennes,</u> Volume H to Z, page 1476.
[300] https://novascotia.ca/archives/acadian/archives.asp?ID=562

Father Clarence d'Entremont, author of <u>Histoire de Quinan, Nouvelle-Écosse</u>, now deceased, makes mention of the fact that all Doucet individuals living in the Yarmouth County area of Nova Scotia are direct descendants of Joseph Doucet and Anne Surette.

Joseph Doucet and Anne Surette had the following children:

1. Joseph Doucet was born at PR on December 6, 1731. [301] [302] He was baptized at PR on December 9, 1731. [303] [304] He married Ludivine Mius (d/o Jean Baptiste Mius and Marie Josèphe Surette) c. 1770. [305] Ludivine was born c. 1751. [306] Joseph died on November 16, 1809 [307] and was buried on November 18, 1809. [308] [309] Ludivine died on March 17, 1836 and was buried on March 19, 1836. [310] [311]

2. Isidore Doucet was born at PR on August 26, 1733. [312] He was baptized at PR on August 28, 1733, the first born twin. [313] [314] He married Rachel ---------- on November 22, 1760. [315]

---

[301] Information received from Kenneth Breau, cousin and archivist at the Université de Moncton.
[302] https://novascotia.ca/archives/acadian/archives.asp?ID=1852
[303] Information received from Kenneth Breau, cousin and archivist at the Université de Moncton.
[304] https://novascotia.ca/archives/acadian/archives.asp?ID=1852
[305] Information received from Kenneth Breau, cousin and archivist at the Université de Moncton.
[306] Ibid.
[307] Ibid.
[308] Ibid.
[309] https://novascotia.ca/archives/acadian/reborn/archives.asp?ID=883
[310] Information received from Kenneth Breau, cousin and archivist at the Université de Moncton.
[311] https://novascotia.ca/archives/acadian/reborn/archives.asp?ID=2686
[312] Information received from Kenneth Breau, cousin and archivist at the Université de Moncton.
[313] Ibid.
[314] https://novascotia.ca/archives/acadian/archives.asp?ID=1925

3. Dominique Doucet was born at PR on August 26, 1733. [316] [317] He was baptized at PR on August 28, 1733. [318] [319] He married Madeleine Modeste Mius (d/o Charles Amand Mius and Marie Marthe Hébert) c. 1761. [320] Madeleine was born at CS c. 1742. [321] Dominique died before January 16, 1772. [322] Madeleine Modeste Mius married John O'Bird (Hubbard) in Salem, Essex County, Massachusetts, on January 16, 1772. [323] [324] Madeleine died in Hubbard's Point, Yarmouth County, Nova Scotia, on February 10, 1826. [325] [326] She was buried in the SAR Cemetery in Eel Brook, Yarmouth County, Nova Scotia. [327]

4. Charles Doucet was born at PR on December 21, 1735. [328] [329] He was baptized at PR on January 22, 1736. [330] [331] He married Félicité Mius (d/o Charles Amand I and Marie Marthe

---

[315] Information received from Kenneth Breau, cousin and archivist at the Université de Moncton.
[316] Ibid.
[317] https://novascotia.ca/archives/acadian/archives.asp?ID=1926
[318] Information received from Kenneth Breau, cousin and archivist at the Université de Moncton.
[319] https://novascotia.ca/archives/acadian/archives.asp?ID=1926
[320] Information received from Kenneth Breau, cousin and archivist at the Université de Moncton.
[321] Ibid.
[322] Ibid.
[323] Ibid.
[324] Sheila Hubbard Macauley. (1996) The Hubbard Family of Nova Scotia, page 1. Baltimore, Maryland: Gateway Press Incorporated.
[325] Ibid.
[326] https://novascotia.ca/archives/acadian/reborn/archives.asp?ID=1650
[327] Information received from Kenneth Breau, cousin and archivist at the Université de Moncton.
[328] Ibid.
[329] https://novascotia.ca/archives/acadian/archives.asp?ID=2115
[330] Information received from Kenneth Breau, cousin and archivist at the Université de Moncton.
[331] https://novascotia.ca/archives/acadian/archives.asp?ID=2115

Hébert) c. 1775. [332] Félicité was born c. 1745. [333] Charles died on March 1, 1817 and was buried on March 3, 1817. [334] [335] Félicité died on February 7, 1828 and was buried on February 10, 1828. [336] [337]

5. François Doucet was born at PR on May 3, 1738. [338] [339] He was baptized at PR on May 4, 1738. [340] [341]

6. Anne Doucet was born at PR on January 6, 1740. [342] She was baptized at PR on January 6, 1740. [343] She died at PR on January 6, 1740. [344]

7. Paul Doucet was born at PR on January 27, 1741. [345] [346] He was baptized at PR on January 28, 1741. [347] [348]

---

[332] Information received from Kenneth Breau, cousin and archivist at the Université de Moncton.
[333] Ibid.
[334] Ibid.
[335] https://novascotia.ca/archives/acadian/reborn/archives.asp?ID=1333
[336] Information received from Kenneth Breau, cousin and archivist at the Université de Moncton.
[337] https://novascotia.ca/archives/acadian/reborn/archives.asp?ID=1881
[338] Information received from Kenneth Breau, cousin and archivist at the Université de Moncton.
[339] https://novascotia.ca/archives/acadian/archives.asp?ID=2253
[340] Information received from Kenneth Breau, cousin and archivist at the Université de Moncton.
[341] https://novascotia.ca/archives/acadian/archives.asp?ID=2253
[342] Information received from Kenneth Breau, cousin and archivist at the Université de Moncton.
[343] Ibid.
[344] https://novascotia.ca/archives/acadian/archives.asp?ID=2372
[345] Information received from Kenneth Breau, cousin and archivist at the Université de Moncton.
[346] https://novascotia.ca/archives/acadian/archives.asp?ID=2456

8. Marie Modeste Doucet was born at PR on January 13, 1743.[349][350] She was baptized at PR on January 13, 1743.[351][352] She married Jean Baptiste II Mius (s/o Jean Baptiste I and Marie Josèphe Surette) c. 1770.[353] Jean Baptiste II was born c. 1745.[354] Marie died on January 7, 1835 and was buried on January 9, 1835.[355][356] Jean Baptiste died on April 27, 1800 and was buried on April 28, 1800.[357][358]

9. Jean Magloire Doucet was born and baptized at PR on July 22, 1745.[359][360] He married Hélène Amirault dit Padène (d/o Charles Amirault and Claire Dugas) c. 1770.[361][362] Hélène was born c. 1745.[363] Jean Magloire died at Wedgeport, Yarmouth County, Nova Scotia, on

---

[347] Information received from Kenneth Breau, cousin and archivist at the Université de Moncton.
[348] https://novascotia.ca/archives/acadian/archives.asp?ID=2456
[349] Information received from Kenneth Breau, cousin and archivist at the Université de Moncton.
[350] htttps://novascotia.ca/archives/acadian/archives.asp?ID=2594
[351] Information received from Kenneth Breau, cousin and archivist at the Université de Moncton.
[352] https://novascotia.ca/archives/acadian/archives.asp?ID=2594
[353] Information received from Kenneth Breau, cousin and archivist at the Université de Moncton.
[354] Ibid.
[355] Ibid.
[356] https://novascotia.ca/archives/acadian/reborn/archives.asp?ID=2547
[357] Information received from Kenneth Breau, cousin and archivist at the Université de Moncton.
[358] https://novascotia.ca/archives/acadian/reborn/archives.asp?ID=201
[359] Information received from Kenneth Breau, cousin and archivist at the Université de Moncton.
[360] https://novascotia.ca/archives/acadian/archives.asp?ID=2768
[361] Information received from Kenneth Breau, cousin and archivist at the Université de Moncton.
[362] https://www.acadian-home.org/wedgeport.html
[363] Information received from Kenneth Breau, cousin and archivist at the Université de Moncton.

November 23, 1826 and was buried on November 24, 1826. [364] [365] Hélène died on April 9, 1812 and was buried on April 10, 1812. [366] [367]

10. Anne Doucet was born at PR on April 1, 1747. [368] [369] She was baptized at PR on April 2, 1747. [370] [371] She married Jean Pierre Mius (s/o François and Jeanne Duon) c. 1768. [372] Jean was born on February 2, 1743. [373] Anne was buried on January 4, 1838. [374] [375] Jean died on February 7, 1825 and was buried on February 8, 1825. [376] [377]

11. Laurent Doucet was born at PR on August 15, 1749. [378] [379] He was baptized at PR on August 17, 1749. [380] [381]

---

[364] Information received from Kenneth Breau, cousin and archivist at the Université de Moncton.
[365] https://novascotia.ca/archives/acadian/reborn/archives.asp?ID=1679
[366] Information received from Kenneth Breau, cousin and archivist at the Université de Moncton.
[367] https://novascotia.ca/archives/acadian/reborn/archives.asp?ID=952
[368] Information received from Kenneth Breau, cousin and archivist at the Université de Moncton.
[369] https://novascotia.ca/archives/acadian/archives.asp?ID=2893
[370] Information received from Kenneth Breau, cousin and archivist at the Université de Moncton.
[371] https://novascotia.ca/archives/acadian/archives.asp?ID=2893
[372] Information received from Kenneth Breau, cousin and archivist at the Université de Moncton.
[373] Ibid.
[374] Ibid.
[375] https://novascotia.ca/archives/acadian/reborn/archives.asp?ID=4262
[376] Information received from Kenneth Breau, cousin and archivist at the Université de Moncton.
[377] https://novascotia.ca/archives/acadian/reborn/archives.asp?ID=1512
[378] Information received from Kenneth Breau, cousin and archivist at the Université de Moncton.
[379] https://novascotia.ca/archives/acadian/archives.asp?ID=3078
[380] Information received from Kenneth Breau, cousin and archivist at the Université de Moncton.

12. Marie Osite Doucet was born at PR on March 18, 1752. [382] [383] She was baptized at PR on March 19, 1752. [384] [385] She married Joseph Moulaison (s/o Joseph Moulaison and Jeanne Comeau) c. 1780. [386] Joseph was born c. 1754. [387] Marie Osite died on August 9, 1827 and was buried on August 11, 1827. [388] [389] Joseph died on November 20, 1834 and was buried on November 22, 1834. [390]

13. Michel Doucet was born at PR on October 17, 1754. [391] [392] [393] He was baptized at PR on October 17, 1754. [394] [395] He married Marie Suzanne Mius (d/o François Mius and Jeanne Duon) c. 1778. [396] [397] Marie Suzanne was born in MA (exile) c. 1758. [398] Michel died on

---

[381] https://novascotia.ca/archives/acadian/archives.asp?ID=3078
[382] Information received from Kenneth Breau, cousin and archivist at the Université de Moncton.
[383] https://novascotia.ca/archives/acadian/archives.asp?ID=3322
[384] Information received from Kenneth Breau, cousin and archivist at the Université de Moncton.
[385] https://novascotia.ca/archives/acadian/archives.asp?ID=3322
[386] Information received from Kenneth Breau, cousin and archivist at the Université de Moncton.
[387] Ibid.
[388] Ibid.
[389] https://novascotia.ca/archives/acadian/reborn/archives.asp?ID=1728
[390] https://novascotia.ca/archives/acadian/reborn/archives.asp?ID=2565
[391] d'Entremont, Father Clarence Joseph. (1984) Histoire de Quinan, Nouvelle-Écosse, page 18.
[392] Information received from Kenneth Breau, cousin and archivist at the Université de Moncton.
[393] https://novascotia.ca/archives/acadian/archives.asp?ID=3522
[394] Information received from Kenneth Breau, cousin and archivist at the Université de Moncton.
[395] https://novascotia.ca/archives/acadian/archives.asp?ID=3522
[396] d'Entremont, Father Clarence Joseph. (1984) Histoire de Quinan, Nouvelle-Écosse, page 18.
[397] Information received from Kenneth Breau, cousin and archivist at the Université de Moncton.
[398] d'Entremont, Father Clarence Joseph. (1984) Histoire de Quinan, Nouvelle-Écosse, page 18.

April 19, 1830 [399] [400] at the age of 75 in Quinan, Yarmouth County, Nova Scotia. He was buried on April 30, 1830. [401] According to parish records, Marie Suzanne died after her husband at a date that is not registered.

14. Pierre Doucet was born in MA (exile) c. 1758. [402]

Joseph Doucet and his family, together with other Acadians living at Port Royal, Acadie, were deported to Massachusetts on December 4, 1755. It was after a few weeks in Boston, that Joseph and his family were assigned to the town of Gloucester in County Essex; the Massachusetts records show that he was on relief and received food and wood from the town for the period of January 17, 1756 to May 22, 1756. [403]

He is listed on a petition to the Governor of Massachusetts, dated August 24, 1763, with 179 families wanting permission to return to Old France (meaning the country of France); permission to leave was not granted. [404]

Several years later, a second attempt was made.

On February 8, 1766, 147 families (for a total of 890 souls), including Joseph Doucet, asked for permission to leave Massachusetts in order to return to Canada; as before, leave was not granted. [405]

---

[399] d'Entremont, Father Clarence Joseph. (1984) Histoire de Quinan, Nouvelle-Écosse, page 18.
[400] https://novascotia.ca/archives/acadian/reborn/archives.asp?ID=2031
[401] Ibid.
[402] Information received from Kenneth Breau, cousin and archivist at the Université de Moncton.
[403] Research of Wilfred Doucette, one of the Directors of the Acadian Heritage and Culture Foundation Incorporated in Erath, Louisiana, now deceased. Information shared with me through his nephew, Robert (Bob) Doucet.
[404] Ibid.

As they were all very poor and could get no help from either the government of Massachusetts or Canada, they were unable to leave. [406]

It was during the following year, 1767, that the poor Acadians petitioned Governor Franklin of Nova Scotia for land on which to settle. As they were Roman Catholic, they could not be granted land; however, on December 23, 1767, the Governor allotted them land along the shore of Baie Sainte-Marie, today known as St. Mary's Bay. [407]

Joseph Doucet spent the first winter at Annapolis Royal (the very town that was formerly known as Port Royal, his former Acadian home). [408]

The next year, 1768, the land was surveyed and the township of Clare was laid out along Baie Sainte-Marie. Joseph Doucet settled near what is today called Church Point. The records show that after completing the necessary requirements, he was granted title to Lot 58 (103 acres) in the township of Clare on May 18, 1775, whereby he lived there for the rest of his life as a fisherman and a farmer. [409]

GENERATION 5

Michel Doucet was born at PR on October 17, 1754. [410][411][412] He was baptized on October 17, 1754. [413][414] He married **Marie Suzanne Mius** (d/o François Mius and Jeanne Duon)

---

[405] Research of Wilfred Doucette, one of the Directors of the Acadian Heritage and Culture Foundation Incorporated in Erath, Louisiana, now deceased. Information shared with me through his nephew, Robert (Bob) Doucet.
[406] Ibid.
[407] Ibid.
[408] Ibid.
[409] Ibid.
[410] d'Entremont, Father Clarence Joseph. (1984) Histoire de Quinan, Nouvelle-Écosse, page 18.
[411] Information received from Kenneth Breau, cousin and archivist at the Université de Moncton.

c. 1778. [415] [416] Marie Suzanne was born in MA (exile) c. 1758. [417] Michel died on April 19, 1830 [418] [419] at the age of 75 in Quinan, Yarmouth County, Nova Scotia. He was buried on April 30, 1830. [420] According to parish records, Marie Suzanne died after her husband at a date that is not registered.

In Histoire de Quinan, Nouvelle-Écosse, Father Clarence d'Entremont writes that Doucet is the true spelling of this surname or family name. [421]

Given that the letter T on the end of the surname was emphasized in the past, as it is today in many areas, the English often wrote it as Doucett, as was the case of John Doucett, Lieutenant Governor of Acadia during the English occupation, who, although French by birth, became Protestant and English to which the Acadian Doucet are not linked in any way. [422]

It is for this very reason that members of this same family, in Yarmouth County in particular, have almost universally adopted the form Doucette that we find written, for the first time, in

---

[412] https://novascotia.ca/archives/acadian/archives.asp?ID=3522
[413] Information received from Kenneth Breau, cousin and archivist at the Université de Moncton.
[414] https://novascotia.ca/archives/acadian/archives.asp?ID=3522
[415] d'Entremont, Father Clarence Joseph. (1984) Histoire de Quinan, Nouvelle-Écosse, page 18.
[416] Information received from Kenneth Breau, cousin and archivist at the Université de Moncton.
[417] d'Entremont, Father Clarence Joseph. (1984) Histoire de Quinan, Nouvelle-Écosse, page 18.
[418] Ibid.
[419] https://novascotia.ca/archives/acadian/reborn/archives.asp?ID=2031
[420] Ibid.
[421] d'Entremont, Father Clarence Joseph. (1984) Histoire de Quinan, Nouvelle-Écosse, page 17.
[422] Ibid.

the registers of Sainte Anne du Ruisseau on May 1, 1856 as inscribed by Father Roles, Parish Priest. [423]

All Doucet persons with roots to Yarmouth County, Nova Scotia, share a common ancestor, namely; Joseph Doucet (born March 12, 1706), son of Claude (of Germain) and Marie Comeau. He was married at PR on the 8th of January 1731 to Anne Surette, daughter of Pierre and Jeanne Pellerin. The family was exiled to Massachusetts where they can be found as early as 1757, principally in Gloucester. [424]

At some unknown date the family settled in southwest Nova Scotia, some at Baie Sainte-Marie, the others in Yarmouth County.

[1] Joseph (born December 6, 1731) settled at Butte-des Doucet (Hubbard's Point) in Yarmouth County. [425]

[2] Charles (born on December 21, 1735) settled at Butte-Amirault (Amirault's Hill) in Yarmouth County. [426]

[3] Jean Magloire (born July 22, 1745) settled at Bas Tousquet (Wedgeport) in Yarmouth County. [427]

[4] Michel (born October 17, 1754) settled at Pointe-des-Ben (part of Sluice Point, referred to as Muise Point) in Yarmouth County before moving to La Fourches, later known as Quinan. Hence, Michel Doucet is the ancestor of the Doucet's of Quinan. [428]

---

[423] d'Entremont, Father Clarence Joseph. (1984) Histoire de Quinan, Nouvelle-Écosse, page 18.
[424] Ibid.
[425] Ibid.
[426] Ibid.
[427] Ibid.

La Fourches was also called The Forks.

Michel Doucet and Marie Suzanne Mius had a large family, of which fourteen are known. The family moved to "the Forks" a little after 1800. Before this date, those children who were already married had married persons from Point-des-Ben (part of Sluice Point, referred to as Muise Point) or close by. After this date, the children married persons from the region of Quinan. Four of their sons settled at "the Forks," with Michel and David settling there temporarily and the two younger, Jacques and Joseph Mathurin, settling there more permanently. [429]

The children of Michel Doucet and Marie Suzanne Mius are as follows:

1. Rosalie Doucet was married on April 14, 1807 in SAR to Jean Baptiste Thibault (s/o Yves dit Ephrem Thibault and Marguerite Anastasie Deveau). [430] [431]

2. Jeanne Geneviève Doucet was married on September 29, 1807 in SAR to Firmin Mius (s/o Louis Mius and Anne Josèphe Corporon). [432] [433]

3. Élisabeth (Isabelle) Doucet was married on August 19, 1806 in SAR to Augustin dit Justin Frontain (s/o Victor Frontain and Anne Marguerite Corporon). [434] [435] She died on January 7, 1864. [436]

---

[428] d'Entremont, Father Clarence Joseph. (1984) Histoire de Quinan, Nouvelle-Écosse, page 18.
[429] Ibid.
[430] Information received from Kenneth Breau, cousin and archivist at the Université de Moncton.
[431] https://novascotia.ca/archives/acadian/reborn/archives.asp?ID=709
[432] Information received from Kenneth Breau, cousin and archivist at the Université de Moncton.
[433] https://novascotia.ca/archives/acadian/reborn/archives.asp?ID=747

4. Lucie Ursule Doucet was married on September 7, 1810 in SAR to Jean Baptiste LeBlanc (s/o Charles LeBlanc and Marie Suzanne Mius). [437] [438]

5. Michel Doucet was married on September 29, 1807 in SAR to Marguerite Frontain (d/o Victor Frontain and Anne Marguerite Corporon). [439] [440]

6. Anne Marguerite Doucet was married on January 12, 1802 in SAR to Jean Boutier (s/o Jean Boutier and Marie Godreau from Saint-Malo, France). [441] [442] Today, the Boutier surname is known as Boucher.

7. Marie Anne Doucet married (1) Jean O'Bird (s/o John O'Bird and Madeleine Modeste Mius) on January 10, 1794 in SAR; [443] [444] (2) Jean Baptiste Comeau, widower of Modeste Thibaud, on June 28, 1826 in SAR. [445] [446] Jean died on August 12, 1817 [447] [448] and was buried on August 13, 1817. [449] Today, the common form of the O'Bird surname is Hubbard.

---

[434] Information received from Kenneth Breau, cousin and archivist at the Université de Moncton.
[435] https://novascotia.ca/archives/acadian/reborn/archives.asp?ID=670
[436] Information received from Kenneth Breau, cousin and archivist at the Université de Moncton.
[437] Ibid.
[438] https://novascotia.ca/archives/acadian/reborn/archives.asp?ID=915
[439] Information received from Kenneth Breau, cousin and archivist at the Université de Moncton.
[440] https://novascotia.ca/archives/acadian/reborn/archives.asp?ID=746
[441] Information received from Kenneth Breau, cousin and archivist at the Université de Moncton.
[442] https://novascotia.ca/archives/acadian/reborn/archives.asp?ID=275
[443] Information received from Kenneth Breau, cousin and archivist at the Université de Moncton.
[444] Sheila Hubbard Macauley. (1996) <u>The Hubbard Family of Nova Scotia</u>, page 5. Baltimore, Maryland: Gateway Press Incorporated.
[445] https://novascotia.ca/archives/acadian/reborn/archives.asp?ID=1637

8. Geneviève Doucet married Firmin Mius (s/o Louis Mius and Marie Josèphe Mius). [450]

9. François David Doucet was born c. 1781. [451] He was married on September 5, 1808 in SAR to Isabelle Mius (d/o Pierre Mius and Cécile Amirault). [452] [453]

10. Jacques Doucet was born c. 1790. [454] He married (1) Anne LeBlanc (d/o Charles LeBlanc and Marie Suzanne Mius) on April 28, 1812 in SAR; [455] [456] (2) Anne Théotiste Mius (d/o Nicolas Mius and Anastasie Doucet) on July 27, 1841 in SAR. [457] [458] He died on March 24, 1863. [459]

---

[446] Sheila Hubbard Macauley. (1996) The Hubbard Family of Nova Scotia, page 5. Baltimore, Maryland: Gateway Press Incorporated.
[447] Information received from Kenneth Breau, cousin and archivist at the Université de Moncton.
[448] Sigogne, Father Jean Mandé. Catalogue des Familles de Ste. Anne et de St. Pierre d'Argyle (1816 to 1824), page 46; a catalogue of families as taken by Father Jean Mandé Sigogne and edited by Father Clarence Joseph d'Entremont. Information obtained from Pauline d'Entremont in an email dated July 6, 2001.
[449] Ibid.
[450] Information received from Kenneth Breau, cousin and archivist at the Université de Moncton.
[451] Ibid.
[452] Ibid.
[453] https://novascotia.ca/archives/acadian/reborn/archives.asp?ID=809
[454] Information received from Kenneth Breau, cousin and archivist at the Université de Moncton.
[455] Ibid.
[456] https://novascotia.ca/archives/acadian/reborn/archives.asp?ID=979
[457] Information received from Kenneth Breau, cousin and archivist at the Université de Moncton.
[458] https://novascotia.ca/archives/acadian/reborn/archives.asp?ID=3384
[459] Information received from Kenneth Breau, cousin and archivist at the Université de Moncton.

11. Joseph Mathurin Doucet was born on May 7, 1795, probably at Pointe-des Ben (part of Sluice Point referred to as Muise Point). [460] [461] He was baptized on July 14, 1799 in SAR. [462] He was married on October 28, 1816 in SAR to Angélique Mathilde Mius (d/o Paul Mius and Marie LeBlanc). [463] [464] [465] Angélique was born on June 28, 1795 [466] [467] [468] and baptized on July 27, 1799. [469]

12. Marguerite Doucet was born on March 27, 1798. [470] [471] She was baptized on July 14, 1798. [472] [473] She was married on November 21, 1820 to Bernard Armagille LeBlanc (s/o Charles LeBlanc and Marie Suzanne Mius). [474] [475]

---

[460] d'Entremont, Father Clarence Joseph. (1984) Histoire de Quinan, Nouvelle-Écosse, pages 94 and 113.
[461] https://novascotia.ca/archives/acadian/reborn/archives.asp?ID=109
[462] Ibid.
[463] Information received from Kenneth Breau, cousin and archivist at the Université de Moncton.
[464] d'Entremont, Father Clarence Joseph. (1984) Histoire de Quinan, Nouvelle-Écosse, pages 94 and 113.
[465] https://novascotia.ca/archives/acadian/reborn/archives.asp?ID=1292
[466] Information received from Kenneth Breau, cousin and archivist at the Université de Moncton.
[467] d'Entremont, Father Clarence Joseph. (1984) Histoire de Quinan, Nouvelle-Écosse, page 94.
[468] https://novascotia.ca/archives/acadian/reborn/archives.asp?ID=90
[469] Ibid.
[470] Information received from Kenneth Breau, cousin and archivist at the Université de Moncton.
[471] https://novascotia.ca/archives/acadian/reborn/archives.asp?ID=110
[472] Information received from Kenneth Breau, cousin and archivist at the Université de Moncton.
[473] https://novascotia.ca/archives/acadian/reborn/archives.asp?ID=110
[474] Information received from Kenneth Breau, cousin and archivist at the Université de Moncton.
[475] https://novascotia.ca/archives/acadian/reborn/archives.asp?ID=1448

13. Édouard Doucet was born on September 13, 1800. [476] [477] He was baptized on September 14, 1800. [478] [479] He married (1) Marguerite LeBlanc (d/o Charles LeBlanc and Marie Suzanne Mius) on November 24, 1818 in SAR; [480] [481] (2) Monique Doucet (d/o Sylvain Doucet and Rosalie Cottereau). [482]

14. Henriette Concorde Doucet was born and baptized on August 12, 1812. [483] [484] She died on November 26, 1820 and never married. [485]

GENERATION 6

Joseph Mathurin Doucet was born on May 7, 1795, probably at Pointe-des Ben (part of Sluice Point, referred to as Muise Point), Yarmouth County, Nova Scotia. [486] [487] He was baptized on July 14, 1799 at SAR. [488] He was married on October 28, 1816 in SAR to

---

[476] Information received from Kenneth Breau, cousin and archivist at the Université de Moncton.
[477] https://novascotia.ca/archives/acadian/reborn/archives.asp?ID=206
[478] Information received from Kenneth Breau, cousin and archivist at the Université de Moncton.
[479] https://novascotia.ca/archives/acadian/reborn/archives.asp?ID=206
[480] Information received from Kenneth Breau, cousin and archivist at the Université de Moncton.
[481] https://novascotia.ca/archives/acadian/reborn/archives.asp?ID=1386
[482] Information received from Kenneth Breau, cousin and archivist at the Université de Moncton.
[483] Ibid.
[484] https://novascotia.ca/archives/acadian/reborn/archives.asp?ID=293
[485] Information received from Kenneth Breau, cousin and archivist at the Université de Moncton.
[486] d'Entremont, Father Clarence Joseph. (1984) Histoire de Quinan, Nouvelle-Écosse, page 113.
[487] https://novascotia.ca/archives/acadian/reborn/archives.asp?ID=109
[488] Ibid.

Angélique Mathilde Mius (d/o Paul Mius and Marie LeBlanc). [489] [490] [491] Angélique was born on June 28, 1795 [492] [493] [494] and baptized on July 27, 1799. [495] They established themselves at Koucougôke (part of Quinan), Yarmouth County, Nova Scotia. [496]

Joseph Mathurin and Angélique Mathilde had thirteen children.

1. Michel Patrice (called L'Anglais) Doucet was born on March 16, 1817 in Quinan, Yarmouth County, Nova Scotia. [497] He was baptized on March 16, 1817 in SAR. [498] He married Anne Anastasie Mius (d/o François Mius and Marie Osithe O'Bird) about 1838 (or 1839). [499] Anne Anastasie (called Nanette) Mius was born on December 25, 1817 in Quinan, Yarmouth County, Nova Scotia. [500] [501]

---

[489] Information received from Kenneth Breau, cousin and archivist at the Université de Moncton.
[490] d'Entremont, Father Clarence Joseph. (1984) Histoire de Quinan, Nouvelle-Écosse, pages 94 and 113.
[491] https://novascotia.ca/archives/acadian/reborn/archives.asp?ID=1292
[492] Information received from Kenneth Breau, cousin and archivist at the Université de Moncton.
[493] d'Entremont, Father Clarence Joseph. (1984) Histoire de Quinan, Nouvelle-Écosse, page 94.
[494] https://novascotia.ca/archives/acadian/reborn/archives.asp?ID=90
[495] Ibid.
[496] d'Entremont, Father Clarence Joseph. (1984) Histoire de Quinan, Nouvelle-Écosse, page 113.
[497] Ibid.
[498] https://novascotia.ca/archives/acadian/reborn/archives.asp?ID=1335
[499] d'Entremont, Father Clarence Joseph. (1984) Histoire de Quinan, Nouvelle-Écosse, page 113.
[500] Ibid, page 75.
[501] https://novascotia.ca/archives/acadian/reborn/archives.asp?ID=1362

2. François David (called Catoon) Doucet was born on June 14, 1818 at Quinan, Yarmouth County, Nova Scotia. [502] He married Madeleine Honorine (dite Honorme) Doucet (d/o Augustin Doucet and Marguerite LeBlanc). [503] Madeleine Honorine Doucet was born on December 15, 1826. [504] [505] They established themselves at Pointe-aux-Bouleaux (part of Sluice Point), Yarmouth County, Nova Scotia. [506]

3. Joseph Mathurin Doucet was born on June 27, 1820 at Quinan, Yarmouth County, Nova Scotia. [507] He married Anne Juliette (dite Julie) Moulaison (d/o Brigitte Moulaison) on November 23, 1840. [508] [509] He died on September 30, 1886 at the age of 66. [510] Anne Juliette was born on June 15, 1815 (out of wedlock) and baptized on October 4, 1815. [511] She died on April 9, 1895. [512]

4. Françoise Doucet (born between 1821 and 1823) died at a young age. [513]

---

[502] d'Entremont, Father Clarence Joseph. (1984) Histoire de Quinan, Nouvelle-Écosse, page 115.
[503] Ibid.
[504] d'Entremont, Father Clarence Joseph. (1984) Histoire de Quinan, Nouvelle-Écosse, page 115.
[505] https://novascotia.ca/archives/acadian/reborn/archives.asp?ID=1680
[506] d'Entremont, Father Clarence Joseph. (1984) Histoire de Quinan, Nouvelle-Écosse, page 115.
[507] Ibid, page 116.
[508] Ibid.
[509] https://novascotia.ca/archives/acadian/reborn/archives.asp?ID=2979
[510] d'Entremont, Father Clarence Joseph. (1984) Histoire de Quinan, Nouvelle-Écosse, page 116.
[511] https://novascotia.ca/archives/acadian/reborn/archives.asp?ID=1184
[512] d'Entremont, Father Clarence Joseph. (1984) Histoire de Quinan, Nouvelle-Écosse, page 116.
[513] Ibid, page 117.

5. Anne Rosalie (called both Rosalie Modèste as well as Rosalie Osithe) Doucet was married to Cyrille Baptiste (dit Weegeegane) Mius (s/o Jean Baptiste II Mius and Geneviève Moulaison) on November 15, 1842. [514] [515] They were the parents of 23 children.

6. Rosalie Ursule Doucet was born on October 15, 1824 at Quinan, Yarmouth County, Nova Scotia. [516] [517] She married Pierre Ambroise Doucet (s/o Charles (dit Tania) Doucet and Anne Mius) on November 20, 1844. [518] [519]

7. Anne Élisabeth Doucet was born on April 6, 1826 at Quinan, Yarmouth County, Nova Scotia. [520] [521] She married Sylvain (dit Senteur) Mius (s/o Frédéric Mius and Anne Moulaison) on January 14, 1847. [522] They established themselves at Buttes-Amirault (Amirault's Hill), Yarmouth County, Nova Scotia. [523]

8. Jean-Baptiste Toussaint Doucet was born November 1, 1829 at Quinan, Yarmouth County, Nova Scotia. [524] [525] He married Anne Julienne Mius (d/o Basile Mius and Anne

---

[514] d'Entremont, Father Clarence Joseph. (1984) Histoire de Quinan, Nouvelle-Écosse, page 117.
[515] https://novascotia.ca/archives/acadian/reborn/archives.asp?ID=3404
[516] d'Entremont, Father Clarence Joseph. (1984) Histoire de Quinan, Nouvelle-Écosse, page 117.
[517] https://novascotia.ca/archives/acadian/reborn/archives.asp?ID=1431
[518] d'Entremont, Father Clarence Joseph. (1984) Histoire de Quinan, Nouvelle-Écosse, page 117.
[519] https://novascotia.ca/archives/acadian/reborn/archives.asp?ID=3418
[520] d'Entremont, Father Clarence Joseph. (1984) Histoire de Quinan, Nouvelle-Écosse, page 117.
[521] https://novascotia.ca/archives/acadian/reborn/archives.asp?ID=1649
[522] d'Entremont, Father Clarence Joseph. (1984) Histoire de Quinan, Nouvelle-Écosse, page 117.
[523] Ibid.
[524] Ibid, page 118.
[525] https://novascotia.ca/archives/acadian/reborn/archives.asp?ID=2013

Françoise Dulain). [526] He died on May 13, 1885 at the age of 56. [527] Anne Julienne Mius died on May 5, 1921. [528]

9. Sophie Doucet was born on February 29, 1832 at Quinan, Yarmouth County, Nova Scotia. [529] [530] She married Mandé Doucet (s/o Charles dit Tania Doucet and Anne Mius) on November 12, 1851. [531]

10. Marie Anne Doucet, twin to Sophie, was born on February 29, 1832 at Quinan, Yarmouth County, Nova Scotia. [532] [533] She married Zacharie Mius (s/o Maximin Mius and Anne Hiltrude LeBlanc) on February 3, 1857. [534]

11. Jean Robert Doucet was born on April 13, 1834. [535] [536] He married (1) Anne Elisabeth (called Zabeth) Mius (d/o Frédéric Mius and Julie Moulaison) on February 23, 1868 and (2) Rosalie Frontain (d/o Marc Frontain and Anne Élisabeth Mius). [537] Anne Élisabeth Mius

---

[526] d'Entremont, Father Clarence Joseph. (1984) <u>Histoire de Quinan, Nouvelle-Écosse</u>, page 118.
[527] Ibid.
[528] Ibid.
[529] d'Entremont, Father Clarence Joseph. (1984) <u>Histoire de Quinan, Nouvelle-Écosse</u>, page 118.
[530] https://novascotia.ca/archives/acadian/reborn/archives.asp?ID=2226
[531] d'Entremont, Father Clarence Joseph. (1984) <u>Histoire de Quinan, Nouvelle-Écosse</u>, page 118.
[532] Ibid.
[533] https://novascotia.ca/archives/acadian/reborn/archives.asp?ID=2225
[534] d'Entremont, Father Clarence Joseph. (1984) <u>Histoire de Quinan, Nouvelle-Écosse</u>, page 118.
[535] Ibid.
[536] https://novascotia.ca/archives/acadian/reborn/archives.asp?ID=2454
[537] d'Entremont, Father Clarence Joseph. (1984) <u>Histoire de Quinan, Nouvelle-Écosse</u>, page 118.

died a short time after giving birth to a son, Moïse; more than likely a result of birth complications.[538] Rosalie Frontain was born on October 21, 1872.[539]

12. Anne Scholastique Doucet was born on May 15, 1836.[540] [541] She married Charles Charest (sometimes called David Charest), from the province of Québec, on January 29, 1856.[542]

13. Anne Julienne Doucet, twin to Anne Scholastique, was born on May 15, 1836.[543] [544] She married Simon Dulain (s/o Olivier Martin Dulain and Scholastique LeBlanc) on March 7, 1859.[545]

GENERATION 7

Michel Patrice (called L'Anglais) Doucet was born on March 16, 1817 in Quinan, Yarmouth County, Nova Scotia.[546] He was baptized on March 16, 1817 in SAR.[547] He married **Anne Anastasie Mius** (d/o François Mius and Marie Osithe O'Bird) about 1838 (or 1839).[548]

---

[538] d'Entremont, Father Clarence Joseph. (1984) Histoire de Quinan, Nouvelle-Écosse, page 118.
[539] Ibid.
[540] Ibid.
[541] https://novascotia.ca/archives/acadian/reborn/archives.asp?ID=2730
[542] d'Entremont, Father Clarence Joseph. (1984) Histoire de Quinan, Nouvelle-Écosse, page 118.
[543] Ibid, page 119.
[544] https://novascotia.ca/archives/acadian/reborn/archives.asp?ID=2731
[545] d'Entremont, Father Clarence Joseph. (1984) Histoire de Quinan, Nouvelle-Écosse, page 119.
[546] Ibid, page 113.
[547] https://novascotia.ca/archives/acadian/reborn/archives.asp?ID=1335
[548] d'Entremont, Father Clarence Joseph. (1984) Histoire de Quinan, Nouvelle-Écosse, page 113.

Anne Anastasie (called Nanette) Mius was born on December 25, 1817 in Quinan, Yarmouth County, Nova Scotia. [549] [550] She died on November 17, 1885 at the age of 62. [551]

Michel-Patrice and Anne Anastasie had eight children.

1. François David (called Quançois) Doucet was born on September 19, 1839. [552] He married Jeanne Cyprienne Dulain (d/o Louis (called Piflet) Dulain and Marie Julie Doucet). [553] They established themselves at Koucougôke (part of Quinan), Yarmouth County, Nova Scotia. [554] He died on March 25, 1904, at the age of 64. [555]

2. Michel Patrice Doucet was born on October 24, 1841. [556] [557] He married (1) Marie Elisabeth Frontain (d/o Pierre Frontain and Marie Élisabeth Corporon) on October 22, 1861, who died with child; (2) Anne Mius (d/o Florent Mius and Anne Élisabeth Dulain) on November 15, 1864; and (3) Rosalie LeBlanc (d/o Remi LeBlanc), widow of Gabriel Mius, on September 4, 1893. [558]

3. Rosalie Angélique Doucet was born on July 13, 1844. [559] [560]

---

[549] d'Entremont, Father Clarence Joseph. (1984) <u>Histoire de Quinan, Nouvelle-Écosse</u>, page 75.
[550] https://novascotia.ca/archives/acadian/reborn/archives.asp?ID=1362
[551] d'Entremont, Father Clarence Joseph. (1984) <u>Histoire de Quinan, Nouvelle-Écosse</u>, page 75.
[552] d'Entremont, Father Clarence Joseph. (1984) <u>Histoire de Quinan, Nouvelle-Écosse</u>, page 113.
[553] Ibid.
[554] Ibid.
[555] Ibid.
[556] Ibid.
[557] https://novascotia.ca/archives/acadian/reborn/archives.asp?ID=3027
[558] d'Entremont, Father Clarence Joseph. (1984) <u>Histoire de Quinan, Nouvelle-Écosse</u>, pages 113 and 114.
[559] Ibid, page 114.
[560] https://novascotia.ca/archives/acadian/reborn/archives.asp?ID=3167

4. Jean Émilien Doucet was baptized on September 18, 1857. [561] He married Anne Mathilde Mius (d/o Anselme Mius and Marguerite Mius) on November 26, 1887. [562]

5. Henri Adolphe Doucet was born on February 8, 1860. [563] He died on January 21, 1871. [564]

6. Jean Théophile (called Câlin) Doucet was baptized in April 1867. [565] He married (1) Rose Mius (d/o Jean (called Johnny Coco) Mius); (2) Adèle Dulain (d/o Louis Cyprien Dulain and Vitaline Mius) on January 10, 1893; and (3) Delphine Jacquard (d/o Jovite Jacquard and Geneviève Mius). [566]

---

[561] d'Entremont, Father Clarence Joseph. (1984) Histoire de Quinan, Nouvelle-Écosse, page 114.
[562] Ibid.
[563] Ibid, page 115.
[564] Ibid.
[565] Information obtained from Pauline d'Entremont in an email dated July 6, 2001.
[566] d'Entremont, Father Clarence Joseph. (1984) Histoire de Quinan, Nouvelle-Écosse, page 115.

Certificat de Baptême

Les présentes certifient que **Jean Théophile Doucet**
Fils ou fille de **Patrice Doucet** et de **Anne Mius**
Est né(e) à **Quinan, N.É.** le **avril 1867**
et a été baptisé(e) **le 8 avril 1867** par **Jean J. Quinan**
Parrain **Dominique Doucet** Marraine **Julia Frotten**
a été confirmé(e) le   à
a été marié(e) le   à
Extrait des registres de la paroisse de **Ste-Agnès**
Donné à **Quinan N.É.** le **5 mars 2002**

Sr Yvette Duguay
Agente de Pastorale

7. Avite Doucet (died on May 12, 1895) [567] married (1) Marie Jacquard (sister to Delphine, d/o Jovite Jacquard and Geneviève Mius); (2) Julienne Doucet (d/o Remi Doucet and Rosalie Mius). [568]

8. Vital Doucet [569]

---

[567] d'Entremont, Father Clarence Joseph. (1984) Histoire de Quinan, Nouvelle-Écosse, page 115.
[568] Ibid.
[569] Ibid.

GENERATION 8

Jean Théophile (called Câlin) Doucet (baptized April 1867 at Quinan, Yarmouth County, Nova Scotia) [570] was married a second time to **Adèle Dulain** on January 10, 1893. [571] Adèle Dulain (d/o Louis Cyprien Dulain and Vitaline Muise) was born in 1876. She died on March 5, 1903, after the birth of her last child, at the age of 27, in Quinan, Yarmouth County, Nova Scotia. [572] She was buried on March 10, 1903 in Quinan, Yarmouth County, Nova Scotia. [573]

Théophile and Adèle had five children.

1. Marie Rose Doucet was born on May 4, 1894 at East Quinan, Yarmouth County, Nova Scotia. [574] She was baptized on May 20, 1894 in Quinan, Yarmouth County, Nova Scotia. [575] Godfather was Ernest Frontin and Godmother was Anne Doucet. [576] Marie Rose died on September 15, 1913 at nineteen years of age. The cause of death was listed as Tuberculosis and the death registration (Registration Year: 1913, Book: 19, Page: 292, Number: 1721) can be accessed online. [577] She was buried at the Ste. Agnès RC Church in Quinan on September 17, 1913. [578]

---

[570] Information obtained from Pauline d'Entremont in an email dated July 6, 2001.
[571] d'Entremont, Father Clarence Joseph. (1984) Histoire de Quinan, Nouvelle-Écosse, page 115.
[572] Ste. Agnès RC Church records in Quinan, NS. Information obtained by Linda Joyce Campbell (first cousin once removed to my father) of Yarmouth, NS.
[573] Ibid.
[574] Ibid.
[575] Ibid.
[576] Ibid.
[577] https://www.novascotiagenealogy.com/ItemView.aspx?ImageFile=19-292&Event=death&ID=90207
[578] Ste. Agnès RC Church records in Quinan, NS. Information obtained by Linda Joyce Campbell (first cousin once removed to my father) of Yarmouth, NS.

Certificat de Baptême

Les présentes certifient que **Marie Rose Doucet**
Fils ou fille de **Théophile Doucet** et de **Marie Adèle Dulin**
Est né(e) à **Quinan N.É.** le **4 mai 1894**
et a été baptisé(e) **le 20 mai 1894** par **J. Crousier**
Parrain **Ernest Frontin** Marraine **Anne Doucet**
a été confirmé(e) le _____ à _____
a été marié(e) le _____ à _____
Extrait des registres de la paroisse de **Ste-Agnès**
Donné à **Quinan, N.É.** le **5 mars 2002**

Sr Yvette Duguay
Agente de Pastorale

DEATHS

District No. _____, _____ County of _____
(City, Town or Municipality)

	No. 1721	No. 1722	No. 1723
	Surname first	Surname first	Surname first Standlake
Name of Deceased	Doucet, Rose	Myers, Beulah Geraldine	Van Amburg, Carl
Sex	Female	Female	Male
Date of Death	Sep. 15, 1913	July 20, 1913	July 30, 1913
Age	19 yrs	2 yrs. 7 mos.	4 years
Residence, Street and No. or P.O. Address	Quinan	Argyle Sound, Yarmouth Co.	Lower Argyle, N.S.
Occupation			
Single, Married or Widowed	Single		
If Single give Name of Father / If Married give Name of Husband	Doucet, Theophile	Myers, Elijah	Van Amburg, Clifford E.
Where Born	Quinan	Argyle Sound, N.S.	Lower Argyle, N.S.
Cause of Death — Primary / Immediate	Tuberculosis	Burned	Ileo colitis / Exhaustion
Length of Illness	6 mos	2 days	8 days
Religious Denomination	R. Catholic		Baptist
Race of Deceased	White	White	White
Name of Physician in attendance	A. R. Melancon	Dr. J. W. Barton	Dr. Chas. J. Fox
Name of Undertaker		Jeremiah Goodwin	
Place of Burial — Cemetery / at	Quinan	Green Grove, Argyle Sound, N.S.	Mt. Pleasant, Argyle, N.S.
Name of Person making Return	A. R. Melancon	Mrs Ulysses Frost	Clifford E. Van Amburg
Date of Return		July 22, 1913	July 31, 1913
REMARKS	A. R. Melancon, Div. Reg. No. 5, Eel Brook		

2. Jean-Avite (called Harvey) Doucet was born on August 7, 1896 in East Quinan, Yarmouth County, Nova Scotia.[579] He was baptized on August 16, 1896 in Quinan, Yarmouth County, Nova Scotia.[580] Godfather was François Mius and Godmother was Eleanora Doucet.[581] He died on October 23, 1965, at the age of 69, in the hospital in Yarmouth, Yarmouth County, Nova Scotia.[582] He was buried on October 25, 1965 in the Our Lady of Calvary Cemetery, Yarmouth, Yarmouth County, Nova Scotia.[583] He died as a result of a stroke.

---

[579] Ste. Agnès RC Church records in Quinan, NS. Information obtained by Linda Joyce Campbell (cousin to Dad) of Yarmouth, NS.
[580] Ibid.
[581] Ibid.
[582] d'Entremont, Father Clarence Joseph. (1984) <u>Histoire de Quinan, Nouvelle-Écosse</u>, page 115.
[583] Gordon Grant, Caretaker (1999) of Our Lady of Calvary Cemetery (902-742-7386) on Forest Street in Yarmouth, NS.

3. Louis Théophile Doucet was born on December 28, 1898 in East Quinan, Yarmouth County, Nova Scotia. [584] He was baptized on January 15, 1899 in Quinan, Yarmouth County, Nova Scotia. [585] [586] Godfather was Enos Mius and Godmother was Rose Mius. [587] Louis Théophile married Alice Anne Boudreau of Wakefield, Massachusetts, on August 12, 1922, in a ceremony officiated by Reverend W. Flynn. [588]

---

[584] Ste. Agnès RC Church records in Quinan, NS. Information obtained by Linda Joyce Campbell (first cousin once removed to my father) of Yarmouth, NS.
[585] Sainte-Anne-du-Ruisseau (SAR) Church records.
[586] Ste. Agnès RC Church records in Quinan, NS. Information obtained by Linda Joyce Campbell (first cousin once removed to my father) of Yarmouth, NS.
[587] Ibid.
[588] Information obtained from Linda Joyce Campbell (first cousin once removed to my father) of Yarmouth, NS.

4. Joseph Harris Doucet was born on March 2, 1901 in East Quinan, Yarmouth County, Nova Scotia. [589] He was baptized on March 17, 1901 in Quinan, Yarmouth County, Nova Scotia. [590] Godfather was Jacques Doucet and Godmother was Emily Doucet. [591] Joseph Harris married Marie Sarah Surette of Surette's Island, Yarmouth County, Nova Scotia, on September 11, 1928 at St. Joseph's Church on Surette's Island. [592] [593]

---

[589] Ste. Agnès RC Church records in Quinan, NS. Information obtained by Linda Joyce Campbell (first cousin once removed to my father) of Yarmouth, NS.
[590] Ibid.
[591] Ibid.
[592] Information obtained from Barbara Atwood (first cousin to my father) of Yarmouth, NS, in 1989.
[593] https://www.novascotiagenealogy.com/ItemView.aspx?ImageFile=53-294&Event=marriage&ID=183464

5. Anne Vitaline Doucet was born on March 4, 1903 in East Quinan, Yarmouth County, Nova Scotia. [594] She was baptized on May 17, 1903 in Quinan, Yarmouth County, Nova Scotia. [595] Godfather was Joseph Mius and Godmother was Josephine Mius. [596]

Certificat de Baptême

Les présentes certifient que **Anne Vitaline Doucet**
Fils ou fille de **Théophile A. Doucet** et de **Adèle Dulin**
Est né(e) à **Quinan, N.E.** le **4 mars 1903**
et a été baptisé(e) **le 17 mai 1903** par **F. Crouzier**
Parrain **Joseph Mius** Marraine **Josephine Mius**
a été confirmé(e) le
a été marié(e) le
Extrait des registres de la paroisse de **Ste-Agnès**
Donné à **Quinan, N.E.** le **5 mars 2002**
Sr Yvette Duguay
Agente de Pastorale

---

[594] Ste. Agnès RC Church records in Quinan, NS. Information obtained by Linda Joyce Campbell (first cousin once removed to my father) of Yarmouth, NS.
[595] Ibid.
[596] Ibid.

Long has there existed a story in the family; a story that spoke about our actually being of the Colins surname and not Doucet(te).

As has been proven, herein, the birth mother of Jean-Avite (called Harvey) Doucet, my grandfather, was Adèle Dulain (d/o Louis Cyprien Dulain and Vitaline Muise). Born in 1876, she died on March 5, 1903, at the age of 27, in Quinan, Yarmouth County, Nova Scotia. [597] She was buried on March 10, 1903 in Quinan, Yarmouth County, Nova Scotia. [598]

Jean Théophile (called Câlin) Doucet, soon to turn 36, was now a widower with five children: Marie Rose, soon to be 9; Jean-Avite (called Harvey), soon to be 7; Louis Théophile, just turned 4; Joseph Harris, just turned 2; and Anne Vitaline, 1 day old.

Could it simply be that the nickname of their father, Câlin, was taken to mean Colin?

As it turns out, there *was* a Marcel II Colin (s/o Marcel I Colin and Léonice Gautreau), born about 1803 in Trois-Rivières, Québec, married to Marie Louise Cyr from Madawaska, New Brunswick, born about 1805, who settled in Quinan, Nova Scotia. [599]

Too young to have understood the implications of a nickname that sounded a great deal like Colin, it is quite conceivable that these young children simply thought they were adopted; hence, the confusion that has continued to persist, even into today.

Following the death of Adèle Dulain, Jean Théophile (called Câlin) Doucet was married a third time to Delphine Jacquard (d/o Jovite Jacquard and Geneviève Mius); so, too, was this a third marriage for Delphine. [600]

---

[597] Ste. Agnès RC Church records in Quinan, NS. Information obtained by Linda Joyce Campbell (first cousin once removed to my father) of Yarmouth, NS.
[598] Ibid.
[599] d'Entremont, Father Clarence Joseph. (1984) Histoire de Quinan, Nouvelle-Écosse, pages 23 and 132.

Unsure of the date of death for Jean Théophile (called Câlin) Doucet, Delphine was united in marriage, a fourth time, to Gervais Doucet (s/o Michel Patrice Doucet and Anne Mius) [601] on February 20, 1911. [602] Gervais, born c. 1886, was the nephew of Jean Théophile (called Câlin) Doucet, thereby making Delphine his aunt by marriage. At the time of the marriage, Gervais was aged 24 and Delphine was aged 54.

It was through the diligence of Linda Joyce Campbell, first cousin once removed to my father, that I was able to glean more. Listed in the 1911 Census for Belleville, Yarmouth County, [603] the three boys (Avite, born August 1896, aged 14, Louis Théophile, born December 1897, aged 13, and Joseph Harris, born March 1901, aged 10) were listed as *step sons* living with Jarvis (whom we now know to be Gervais), Doucette, age 25, head of household, and Delphine Doucette, age 53, wife.

In reference to the 1901 Census for Belleville, Yarmouth County, [604] Jean Théophile is listed as Tomas and Adèle is listed as Addie. The birthdate for Jean Théophile is listed as August 15, 1864. I have a date of baptism for him as being April 1867. [605] The birthdate for Adèle is listed as November 10, 1877. I have a birthdate of June 4, 1876, in keeping with the Ste. Agnès RC Church records in Quinan, NS.

Children listed on the 1901 Census are: [1] Sadie, born December 4, 1889, aged 12; [2] Rosea, born July 17, 1881 (but should read as 1891), aged 10; [3] Avite, born February 4, 1896, aged 5; [4] Louis, born February 2, 1898, aged 3; [5] Joe, born March 2, 1900, aged 1.

---

[600] d'Entremont, Father Clarence Joseph. (1984) Histoire de Quinan, Nouvelle-Écosse, page 115.
[601] Ibid, pages 91 and 114.
[602] https://www.novascotiagenealogy.com/ItemView.aspx?ImageFile=16-332&Event=marriage&ID=146434
[603] automatedgenealogy.com/census11/View.jsp?id=68015&highlight=15
[604] automatedgenealogy.com/census/DisplayHousehold.jsp?sdid=2107&household=208
[605] Information obtained from Pauline d'Entremont in an email dated July 6, 2001.

As you will be able to denote from the certificates located within this tome, while the 1901 Census dates are wrong, this *is* the correct family.

Back to the original story of confusion, there was only one family by the name of Collin living in the entire enumeration district; Anthony and Marguerite, who, in their 60s in 1911, were quite unlikely to have had anything to do with the raising of the Doucet(te) boys.

In essence, this whole concocted story was simply a rumor; nevertheless, it is funny, albeit in a sad way, how these things seem to get perpetuated when there is a perfectly rational explanation.

As already shared herein, I believe the explanation to be a simple one.

Jean Théophile was called Câlin and somehow the nickname got twisted around to there being a Colin(s) in the mix; a fact that has been disproven, courtesy of my research.

Ste Agnes Parish Records: 1859 - 1929

BAPTISMS

1894
DOUCET
Marie R.

May 20, I baptised Marie Rose, born the fourth, daughter of Theophile Doucet and Marie Adele Dulin. Godfather- Ernest Frontin; godmother- Anne Doucet

1896
DOUCET
Jean Avit

Aug. 16, I baptised Jean Avit, born the 7th, son of Theophile Doucet and Adele Dulin. Godfather- Francois Mius; godmother-Eleanore Doucet. (He was called "Harvey") [L.C.]

Married Nov. 15, 1918 to Beatrice Mius at Yarmouth by Rev. W.E.Young, pastor

1899
DOUCET
Louis T.

Jan. 15, I baptised Louis Theophile, born last Dec. 28, son of Theophile Doucet and Adele Frontin. Godfather- Enos Mius; godmother- Rose Mius. (The name "Frontin" is an error; her maiden name was "Dulin") [L.C.]

Married Aug. 12, 1922 to Alice Anne Boudreau of Wakefield by Rev. W. Flynn.

1901
DOUCET
Joseph

March 17, I baptised Joseph, born the 2nd, son of Theophile Doucet and Adele Dulin. Godfather- Jacques Doucet; godmother- Emily Doucet.

Married to Marie Seraphie Surette at St. Joseph's Church, Surette's Island, Sept. 11, 1928.

1903, May 17
DOUCET
Anne V.

This day I baptised Anne Vitaline, daughter of Theophile A. Doucet and Adele Dulin. Godfather- Joseph Mius; godmother- Josephine Mius. (She was probably born on March 4 or 5. The mother died March 5.) [L.C.]

DEATHS

1903
DOUCET
Adele

March 10, I buried Adele, deceased the 5th at the age of 27 years, daughter of Cyprien Dulin and Vitaline Mius. Wife of Theophile Doucet.

1913
DOUCET
Rose

Sept. 15, 1913, Rose Doucet deceased, aged 19 years, daughter of Theophile Doucet and Adele Dulin. Buried Sept. 17, 1913

Parish Records - Ste. Anne Du Ruisseau: 1867 - 1899.

BAPTISMS

Jacquard, Marie Eugenie   (Forks)
daughter of Zacharie Jacquard / Helene Doucet
born - 13 Sept, 1877; baptised 26 Sept., 1877
sponsors - Isaie Doucet, Marie Susanne Watkins

GENERATION 9

Jean-Avite (called Harvey) Doucet was born on August 7, 1896 in East Quinan, Yarmouth County, Nova Scotia.[606] He was baptized on August 16, 1896 in Quinan, Yarmouth County, Nova Scotia.[607] Godfather was François Mius and Godmother was Eleanora Doucet.[608]

He died on October 23, 1965, at the age of 69, in the hospital in Yarmouth, Yarmouth County, Nova Scotia.[609] He was buried on October 25, 1965 in the Our Lady of Calvary Cemetery, Yarmouth, Yarmouth County, Nova Scotia.[610] He died as a result of a stroke.

According to my father, Jean Avite (Harvey) was a man of small stature, standing at either 5 foot 2 inches or 5 foot 3 inches tall; roughly, my father's height as well.

In August 1999, Dad and I went to the Our Lady of Calvary Cemetery on Forest Street in an attempt to locate his grave. We were told that Jean-Avite was buried in the NEW SECTION of the cemetery (Row 9-31). However, we were not able to locate a stone.

Harvey was a very gifted carpenter. While family lore states that he made a crucifix for the St. Ambrose Catholic Church in Yarmouth, I have never been able to verify its authenticity.

Jean Avite (Harvey) Doucet married **Beatrice Muise** (d/o Peter Muise and Martha Roach of Yarmouth) on November 15, 1915 in Yarmouth, Yarmouth County, Nova Scotia.[611] They were married at St. Ambrose Catholic Church in Yarmouth by Reverend W. E. Young.

---

[606] Ste. Agnès RC Church records in Quinan, NS. Information obtained by Linda Joyce Campbell (first cousin once removed to my father) of Yarmouth, NS.
[607] Ibid.
[608] Ibid.
[609] d'Entremont, Father Clarence Joseph. (1984) Histoire de Quinan, Nouvelle-Écosse, page 115.
[610] Gordon Grant, Caretaker (1999) of Our Lady of Calvary Cemetery (902-742-7386) on Forest Street in Yarmouth, NS.

Beatrice was born on October 14, 1898. She died on May 20, 1954 at the age of 55, in Yarmouth, Yarmouth County, Nova Scotia. [612] Cause of death was Coronary Thrombosis. Her death was registered on June 7, 1954 (and can be located on page 4332 of the registration book for 1954). [613] She was buried on May 22, 1954 in the Our Lady of Calvary Cemetery, Yarmouth, Nova Scotia.

In August 1999, Dad and I went to Our Lady of Calvary Cemetery on Forest Street in an attempt to locate her grave. In the early days, no records were kept. At some point, there was also a fire and records were lost. It appears as if she was buried on the lower end of the cemetery, just down over the hill to the right as soon as you drive through the gate.

According to my father, Beatrice was a woman of petite stature, standing at about 5 foot 1 inch tall.

Jean-Avite and Beatrice had sixteen children, with only eight living to adulthood. These eight names have been underlined.

When I first began sleuthing, I had eight names. It was through the diligent assistance of two female cousins living in the United States, Jane Doucette Barber and Pauline Moulaison Kimball, both with ties to Yarmouth County area, as well as Linda Joyce Campbell, of Yarmouth, Nova Scotia, that I was successful in identifying an additional seven children, thereby bringing the new total to fifteen; a process that spanned many years.

---

[611] https://www.novascotiagenealogy.com/ItemView.aspx?ImageFile=16-992&Event=marriage&ID=147091
[612] Sweeney's Funeral Home (information denoted in ledger 14 on page 152). Information obtained by Linda Joyce Campbell (first cousin once removed to my father) of Yarmouth, NS.
[613] https://www.novascotiagenealogy.com/ItemView.aspx?ImageFile=1954-4332&Event=death&ID=367794

There was a sole sibling who managed to evade me, at every turn, for countless years; that is, until the summer of 2011, when I was perusing the Nova Scotia Historical Vital Statistics website.

1. Mary May Doucette was born on December 1, 1916 in Yarmouth, Yarmouth County, Nova Scotia. [614] She died on December 23, 1916 in Yarmouth, Yarmouth County, Nova Scotia, at three weeks of age. Death was registered the same day (Registration Year: 1916, Book: 50, Page: 317, Number: 1013). [615]

2. John Doucette was born on October 14, 1918 in Yarmouth, Yarmouth County, Nova Scotia. [616] He died on November 14, 1918 in Yarmouth, Yarmouth County, Nova Scotia, at four weeks of age. Death was registered the same day (Registration Year: 1918, Book: 51, Page: 111, Number: 349). [617]

3. Peter Doucette was born on January 28, 1920 in Yarmouth, Yarmouth County, Nova Scotia. Peter died of a heart attack on December 27, 1978 in Prince Rupert, British Columbia. [618] He is buried in the Fairview Cemetery in Prince Rupert, British Columbia.

---

[614] Email dated Tuesday, March 5, 2002, from Linda Joyce Campbell (first cousin once removed to my father) of Yarmouth, NS. This information was located in an old birth register in Yarmouth (page 247). Registration was filed by Mrs. George P. Muise, of Yarmouth South, on December 7, 1916.

[615] https://www.novascotiagenealogy.com/ItemView.aspx?ImageFile=50-317&Event=death&ID=138703

[616] Email dated Tuesday, March 5, 2002, from Linda Joyce Campbell (first cousin once removed to my father) of Yarmouth, NS. This information was located in an old birth register in Yarmouth (page 304). Registration was filed by Harvey Doucette on October 21, 1918.

[617] https://www.novascotiagenealogy.com/ItemView.aspx?ImageFile=51-111&Event=death&ID=139421

[618] Email dated September 24, 2004, from Tina Prokopsky (first cousin once removed to me). Her father, Nelson, was the son of Peter, my father's brother.

4. <u>Helen</u> Doucette was born on May 7, 1921 in Yarmouth, Yarmouth County, Nova Scotia. She died on August 2, 1998 at the Yarmouth Regional Hospital in Yarmouth, Yarmouth County, Nova Scotia.

Halifax Herald Obituary Listing denoted on the following page.

DOUCETTE CROSBY, Mary Helen (age 77) of Wyman Road, Yarmouth Co., died August 2, 1998 in Yarmouth Regional Hospital. Born in Yarmouth, she was the daughter of the late Harvey and Beatrice (Muise) Doucette. She was a member of Notre Dame of Fatima Church. She was a homemaker all her life. Surviving are her husband, St. Clair; daughter, Louise Muise, Plymouth; sons, Brian, Bob, Brooklyn, Yarmouth Co., brothers, Anthony, Prince Rupert, B.C., Albert, Truro; sister Martha Surette, Arcadia, Yarmouth Co.; 6 grandchildren; 5 ggchildren. She was predeceased by her first husband, Louis F. Doucette; brothers, Peter, John, Percy, Harvey Jr., several brothers and sisters in infancy. Body can be viewed at Sweeney's Funeral Home in Yarmouth. Funeral will take place on Wednesday, August 5, at Notre Dame of Fatima Church with Reverend Gerard MacInnis officiating. Burial will be at Our Lady of Cavalry Cemetary.

5. <u>David Percy</u> (called Popeye) Doucette was born on February 26, 1923 in Reading, Massachusetts.[619] Percy died at home, on May 3, 1977, in Yarmouth, Yarmouth County, Nova Scotia, the cause of death being cardiac related. He is buried in the Our Lady of Cavalry Cemetery in Yarmouth.

---

[619] Information received from Jane Doucette Barber of Lynn, Massachusetts, who visited the Reading Town Hall during the summer of 1998.

6. George Harvey (called Harvey) Doucette was born on May 29, 1924 in Wakefield, Massachusetts. [620] Harvey died on January 27, 1948 in Yarmouth, Yarmouth County, Nova Scotia. [621] The cause of death is listed as Leukemia. Death was registered on March 10, 1948 (Registration Year: 1948, Page: 2051). [622]

In August 1999, Dad and I went to Our Lady of Calvary Cemetery on Forest Street in an attempt to locate his grave. In the early days, there were no records kept. At some point, there was also a fire and records were lost. It appears as if he was buried on the lower end of the cemetery just down over the hill to the right as soon as you drive through the gate.

7. William Doucette was born on March 19, 1926 in Wakefield, Massachusetts. [623]

8. Raymond L Doucette, twin to William, was born on March 19, 1926 in Wakefield, Massachusetts. [624] He died on March 19, 1926 in Wakefield, Massachusetts.

9. William Henry Doucette was born on June 26, 1927 in Reading, Massachusetts. [625] He died on August 29, 1927 in Reading, Massachusetts. [626] Cause of death was Gastro Enteritis. This information was acquired through Theresa Bond at the Reading Public Library.

---

[620] Information received from Pauline Moulaison Kimball of Saugus, Massachusetts, who visited the Wakefield Town Hall during the summer of 1998.
[621] Sweeney's Funeral Home (information denoted in ledger 14 on page 152). Information obtained by Linda Joyce Campbell (first cousin once removed to my father) of Yarmouth, NS.
[622] https://www.novascotiagenealogy.com/ItemView.aspx?ImageFile=1948-2051&Event=death&ID=329939
[623] Information received from Pauline Moulaison Kimball of Saugus, Massachusetts, who visited the Wakefield Town Hall during the summer of 1998.
[624] Ibid.
[625] Information received from Jane Doucette Barber of Lynn, Massachusetts, who visited the Reading Town Hall during the summer of 1998.
[626] Information received from Theresa Bond, Librarian of the Reading Public Library in Reading, Massachusetts.

10. Beatrice Martha Doucette was born on July 10, 1928 in Reading, Massachusetts.[627] She died on June 20, 1933 in Yarmouth, Yarmouth County, Nova Scotia.[628] Cause of death was Coronary Thrombosis. Death was registered on July 6, 1933 (Registration Year: 1933, Book: 156, Page: 152).[629]

From Sweeny records: Beatrice Martha Doucette; died 20 June, 1933 at Regent Street (born 10 July, 1928 in Reading, Mass.) aged 4 years, 11 months, 9 days; daughter of Harvey (born in Quinan) and Beatrice (born in Yarmouth) (Muise) Doucette. Buried June 22, 1933 in Poor lot and charged to Poor Board. No cause of death given.

From St. Ambrose records: Most of the same information as Sweeny's, except that the cause of death is given as "neuralgia." (Fr. LeBlanc)

11. Jean Theresa Doucette was born on February 16, 1931 in Yarmouth, Yarmouth County, Nova Scotia. She died on December 28, 1931 at the age of 10 months in Yarmouth, Yarmouth County, Nova Scotia.[630] Cause of death was Convulsions. Death was registered on December 31, 1931 (Registration Year: 1931, Book: 133, Number: 1430).[631]

From Sweeny records: Jean E. Doucett (resident of Regent Street) died 28 December, 1931, aged 10 months; no cause of death given. Parents names not given. Burial was ordered and paid by the Poor Board.

---

[627] Information received from Jane Doucette Barber of Lynn, Massachusetts, who visited the Reading Town Hall during the summer of 1998.
[628] Email dated July 12, 2001 from Linda Joyce Campbell (first cousin once removed to my father) of Yarmouth, NS.
[629] https://www.novascotiagenealogy.com/ItemView.aspx?ImageFile=156-152&Event=death&ID=245832
[630] Sweeney's Funeral Home (information denoted in ledger 14 on page 152). Information obtained by Linda Joyce Campbell (first cousin once removed to my father) of Yarmouth, NS.
[631] https://www.novascotiagenealogy.com/ItemView.aspx?ImageFile=133-1430&Event=death&ID=222554

From St Ambrose records: It seems rather apparent that the priest of the day, Father Young, did not approve of the name this child was given at birth, so he saw fit to enter it as something more to his liking (or so it would seem).

Genevieve Therese Doucet: died 28 December, 1931, aged 1 year. This is another thing they did (they rounded the ages up to the next year). No cause of death listed. No parent's names listed. Buried in Poor lot.

Since this was the only death recorded on that day in St. Ambrose records, there is no doubt that it has to be the same child.

12. <u>John Doucette</u>, twin to Jean Theresa, was born on February 16, 1931 in Yarmouth, Yarmouth County, Nova Scotia. He died of cancer on April 15, 1989 in Yarmouth, Yarmouth County, Nova Scotia, spending his days comfortably at home.

13. <u>Martha Doucette</u> was born on August 22, 1932 in Yarmouth, Yarmouth County, Nova Scotia (*the only living sibling at the time of this publication*).

14. Female Doucette was born premature (stillborn) on November 4, 1933 in Yarmouth, Yarmouth County, Nova Scotia. Death was registered the same day (Registration Year: 1933, Book: 156, Page 262). [632]

---

[632] https://www.novascotiagenealogy.com/ItemView.aspx?ImageFile=156-262&Event=death&ID=245941

15. <u>Thomas Anthony</u> called "Anthony" Doucette was born on March 2, 1935 in Yarmouth, Yarmouth County, Nova Scotia. He died of a massive heart attack on August 7, 2005 while at home in Prince Rupert, British Columbia. [633] The Doctor said that he went quickly and did not suffer.

16. <u>Albert</u> called "Al" Doucette was born on May 3, 1936 in Yarmouth, Yarmouth County, Nova Scotia.

In 1923, Jean Avite (Harvey) and Beatrice lived at 4 Maple Street in Reading, Massachusetts. During the years 1924 to 1926, they lived in Wakefield, Massachusetts. By 1927, they were living at 25 Haven Street in Reading, having moved back from Wakefield. During the years 1929 and 1930, they were living at 8 Pleasant Street in Reading.

In 1947, George Harvey Doucette was living at 50 Village Street in Reading, Massachusetts.

Upon returning to Yarmouth, Jean Avite (Harvey) and Beatrice lived at 95 Regent Street in a house that Jean Avite (Harvey) had built himself.

His in-laws (Peter Muise and Martha Roach) lived at 16 Regent Street. Dad's first cousin, Fred Muise (and spouse Rose Moulaison) lives in the original house today.

Jean Avite (Harvey) also built the house at 25 Regent Street. A first cousin by the name of Jeanette Muise lives there. It was the home of her parents, Peter Muise (brother to Beatrice) and Doris Muise.

---

[633] Information received from Leona Doucette Walsh (first cousin once removed to me). Her mother, Linda, was the daughter of Peter, my father's brother.

Province of Nova Scotia
MARRIAGE REGISTER

Date of Marriage	November 15th 1915
Place of Marriage	Yarmouth NS
County	Yarmouth
How Married; by License or Banns	Banns
Dates of Publication, if by Banns	3 preceeding Sundays
Full name of Groom	Harvé Doucette
Age	19
Condition (Bachelor or Widower)	Bachelor
Religious Denomination	Catholic
Occupation	Labourer
Residence	Yarmouth NS
Where Born	Quinan NS
Names of Parents	Theophilus & Adele Doucette
Occupation of Parent	Labourer
Full name of Bride	Beatrice Muise
Age	17
Condition (Spinster or Widow)	Spinster
Religious Denomination	Catholic
Her Place of Residence	Yarmouth NS
Where Born	"
Names of Parents	Peter & Martha Muise
Occupation of Parent	Laborer
Names of Witnesses	William H. Doucette / Lillian Titus
Signature of Parties Married	Harvé Doucette / Beatrice Muise
Officiating Clergyman	H. E. Young
Denomination of Clergyman	Catholic Priest

I Certify, That the marriage of the persons above named was duly celebrated by me at the time and place and in the manner stated in this Register.

H. E. Young
Officiating Clergyman.

St. Ambrose Cathedral

65 Green Street
Yarmouth, Nova Scotia
B5A 1Z6
(902) 742-7151
Fax: (902) 742-7152
E-mail: ycc@ns.aliantzinc.ca

Certificate of Baptism

++

Name:	Mary Mae Doucette
Father:	Harvey Doucette
Mother:	Beatrice Muise
Date of Birth:	Dec. 1, 1916
Place of Birth:	
Date of Baptism:	Dec. 3, 1916
Sponsors:	Mrs. George Muise
	Fred Muise
Presider:	Rev. W. E. Young
Confirmation:	
Marriage:	
Issued by:	*Mary Sweeney*
Date:	25 August 2011

DEATHS

District No. 1, Town of Yarmouth, County of Yarmouth

	No. 1011	No. 1012	No. 1013
Name of Deceased	Smith, Mary Rose	Dick Adam	Doucette Mary May
Sex	Female	Male	Female
Date of Death	December 13, 1916	December 22, 1916	December 23, 1916
Age	5 minutes	76 years	3 weeks
Residence	Yarmouth, N.S.	Yarmouth, N.S.	Regent St, Yarmouth, N.S.
Occupation			
Single, Married or Widowed		Married	
If Single give Name of Father / If Married give Name of Husband	Smith Edward		Doucette Harvey
Where Born	Yarmouth	Scotland	Yarmouth
Cause of Death		Myocarditis	Heart trouble
Length of Illness		11 days	3 days
Religious Denomination	Roman Catholic	Plymouth Brethren	Roman Catholic
Race of Deceased	white	white	white
Name of Physician in attendance	Farish G.W.T.	Perrin A.M.	Farish G.W.T.
Name of Undertaker	Van Norse A.X.	Sweeny V.S.	None
Place of Burial	St. Ambrose, Yarmouth, N.S.	Mountain, Yarmouth, N.S.	St. Ambrose, Yarmouth, N.S.
Name of Person making Return	Smith Edward	Dick Mrs. A.	Muise Mrs. Geo. P.
Date of Return	Dec. 13, 1916	Dec. 23, 1916	Dec. 23, 1916
Remarks			

St. Ambrose Cathedral

65 Green Street
Yarmouth, Nova Scotia
B5A 1Z6
(902) 742-7151
Fax: (902) 742-7152
E-mail: ycc@ns.aliantzinc.ca

Certificate of Baptism

++

Name: John Doucette

Father: Harvey Doucette

Mother: Beatrice Muise

Date of Birth: Oct. 14, 1918

Place of Birth:

Date of Baptism: Oct. 20, 1918

Sponsors: Peter Muise

Martha Muise

Presider: Rev. W. E. Young

Confirmation:

Marriage:

Issued by: *Mary Sweeney*

Date: 25 August 2011

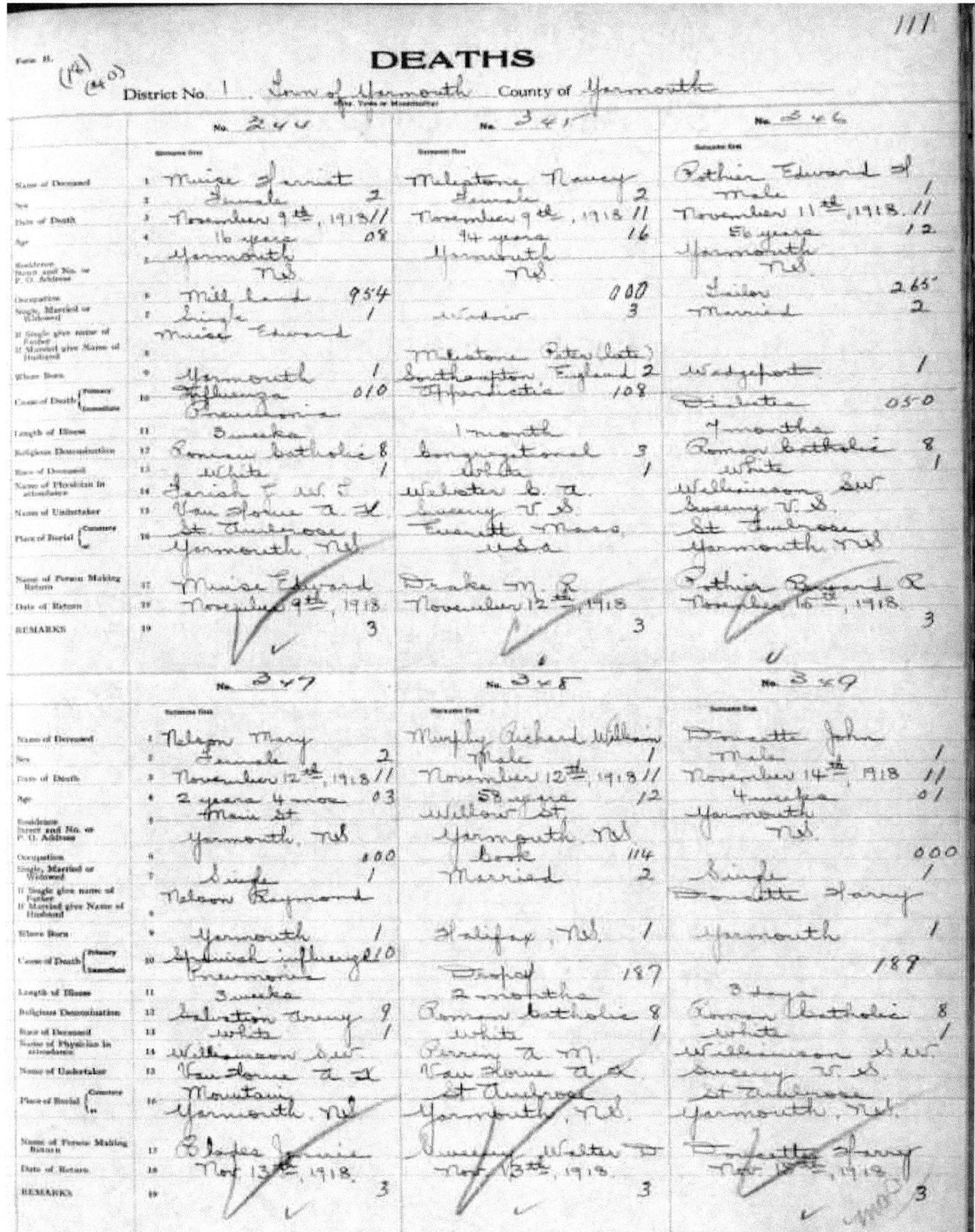

St. Ambrose Cathedral

65 Green Street
Yarmouth, Nova Scotia
B5A 1Z6
(902) 742-7151
Fax: (902) 742-7152
E-mail: ycc@ns.aliantzinc.ca

Certificate of Baptism

++

Name:	Peter Patrick Doucette
Father:	Harvé Doucette
Mother:	Beatrice Muise
Date of Birth:	28 January 1920
Place of Birth:	
Date of Baptism:	1 February 1920
Sponsors:	George Muise
	Theresa Muise
Presider:	Rev. W.E.Young
Confirmation:	
Marriage:	Dorothy LeBlanc 9 July 1941

Issued by: *Mary Sweeney*

Date: 25 August 2011

St. Ambrose Cathedral

65 Green Street
Yarmouth, Nova Scotia
B5A 1Z6
(902) 742-7151
Fax: (902) 742-7152
E-mail: ycc@ns.aliantzinc.ca

Certificate of Baptism

++

Name:	Mary Helena Doucette
Father:	Harvé Doucette
Mother:	Beatrice Muise
Date of Birth:	7 May 1921
Place of Birth:	
Date of Baptism:	8 May 1921
Sponsors:	Edward Gaudet
	Theresa Muise
Presider:	Rev. W. E. Young
Confirmation:	August 14, 1938
Marriage:	St. Clair Crosby 3 Sept. 1983

Issued by: *Mary Sweeney*

Date: 25 August 2011

The Commonwealth of Massachusetts
United States of America

Registered No. 30

Town of Reading

CERTIFICATE OF BIRTH

FROM THE RECORDS OF BIRTHS IN THE TOWN OF READING, MASSACHUSETTS, U.S.A.

Date of Birth:	February 26, 1923	Time:	- - -
Name of Child:	David Percy Doucette		
Sex:	Male	Color:	White
Place of Birth:	Reading		
Residence of Parents:	4 Maple Street		
	Reading, MA		
Name of Father:	Harvey Doucette		
Father's Age:	26		
Birthplace of Father:	Yarmouth, N.S.		
Occupation of Father:	Mover		
Name of Mother (Maiden):	Beatrice Doucette (Muse)		
Mother's Age:	24		
Birthplace of Mother:	N.S.		
Occupation of Mother:	- - -		
Date Recorded:	March 20, 1923		
Record No./Book/Page:	#30/BK. 1923/PG. 1		

I, Laura A. Gemme, depose and say that I hold the office of Town Clerk of the Town of Reading, Massachusetts, U.S.A.; that the records of Births, Marriages and Deaths in said town are in my custody; and that the above is a true extract from said records, as certified by me.

WITNESS my hand and the Seal of the Town of Reading, on this 6th day of September 2011

Laura A. Gemme, Town Clerk

READING BIRTHS - 1923.

DONAHUE, Margaret Mary, d. of
　　Joseph Donahue, b. in Woburn, and
　　Irene F. Halloran, b. in Reading.
　　Residence of parents, Reading.
　　Feb. 17, 1923, in Reading.

BABINE, Louis Cornelius, s. of
　　Louis C. Babine, b. in Nova Scotia, and
　　Mary Meuse, b. in Reading.
　　Residence of parents, Reading.
　　Feb. 21, 1923, in Reading.

FIELD, Shirley Eleanor, d. of
　　Charles H. Field, b. in Chelsea, and
　　Emma M. Keefe, b. in Malden.
　　Residence of parents, Reading.
　　Feb. 21, 1923, in Stoneham.

GONNAM, Barbara, d. of
　　Harold E. Gonnam, b. in Lynn, and
　　Elizabeth P. Higgins, b. in No. Andover.
　　Residence of parents, Reading.
　　Feb. 24, 1923, in Andover.

RATHBUN, Marjorie Lillian, d. of
　　Lloyd E. Rathbun, b. in Bridgeport, Conn., &
　　Lillian G. Heselton, b. in Reading.
　　Residence of parents, Reading.
　　Feb. 26, 1923, in Winchester.

DOUCETTE, David Percy, s. of
　　Harvey Doucette, b. in Yarmouth, N. S., &
　　Beatrice Muse, b. in Nova Scotia.
　　Residence of parents, Reading.
　　Feb. 26, 1923, in Reading.

TOWN OF WAKEFIELD

Copy of records of the Town of Wakefield, County of Middlesex and Commonwealth of Massachusetts, U.S.A., relating to Births.

No. 147

Date of Birth MAY 29, 1924

Name GEORGE HARVEY DOUCETTE

Sex MALE

Color (if other than white) ---

Place of Birth WAKEFIELD

Informant HARVEY DOUCETTE

Name of Father HARVEY DOUCETTE

Birthplace of Father EAST QUINAN, NOVA SCOTI

Maiden Name of Mother BEATRICE MUISE

Birthplace of Mother YARMOUTH, NOVA SCOTIA

Occupation of Father ---

Occupation of Mother HOUSEWIFE

Residence of Parents WAKEFIELD

Date of Record MAY 31, 1924

I, MARY K. GALVIN depose and say, that I hold the office of Town Clerk of the Town of Wakefield, County of Middlesex and Commonwealth of Massachusetts, U.S.A.; that records of Births, Marriages, and Deaths in said Town are in my custody, and the above is a true extract from the Records of Births in said Town, as certified by me.

WITNESS, my hand and the Seal of said Town on the TWENTY-FIFTH day of JULY 2006

Mary K. Galvin
TOWN CLERK

NOTE: The town of South Reading was set off from Reading and incorporated as a separate town in 1812 and the name "South Reading" was changed to Wakefield in 1868.

PROVINCE OF NOVA SCOTIA—CERTIFICATE OF REGISTRATION OF DEATH

No. 02051

1. **PLACE OF DEATH**: County of Yarmouth, Municipality of Yarmouth, City or Town of Yarmouth, Street: Hay Hospital
2. **LENGTH OF STAY**: (a) In City, Town or Rural Division where death occurred: 8 hrs. (b) In Province: Lifetime (c) In Canada (if immigrant): —
3. **NAME OF DECEASED**: Doucette, George Harvey
4. **RESIDENCE**: No. 2 Street: Regent, City/Town: Yarmouth, Province: N.S.

4. Sex	5. Nationality	6. Racial Origin	7. Single, Married, Widowed or Divorced
Male	Canadian	French	Single

8. **BIRTHPLACE**: Yarmouth, N.S.
9. **DATE OF BIRTH**: May 28, 1924
10. **AGE**: Years 23, Months 7, Days 30

11. **Trade, profession or kind of work**: Labour
12. **Kind of industry or business**: —
13. **Date deceased last worked at this occupation**: —
14. **Total yrs. spent in this occupation**: —
15. **If married give name of wife or husband of deceased**: —

FATHER
16. Name: Harvey Doucette
17. Birthplace: East Quinan, N.S.

MOTHER
18. Maiden Name: Beatrice Muise
19. Birthplace: Yarmouth, N.S.

20. **Signature of Informant**: Harvey Doucette
    Address: Wyman Rd, Yar Co.
    Relationship to deceased: Father

21. **Place of burial**: St. Ambrose, N.S.
    Date of burial: January 30/48
22. **Undertaker**: H. Sweeney

MEDICAL CERTIFICATE OF DEATH

23. **DATE OF DEATH**: Jan. 27, 1948
24. I HEREBY CERTIFY that I attended deceased from ___ to ___, and last saw him alive on ___

CAUSE OF DEATH
I
(a) Immediate cause: Uraemia
due to (b):
due to (c):

II Other morbid conditions: —

25. If a woman, was the death associated with pregnancy? —
26. Was there a surgical operation? No. Date of operation: —
    Was there an autopsy? No
27. If death was due to external causes (violence) fill in also the following—
    Accident, suicide or homicide: —
    Manner of injury: —
    Nature of injury: —

Signed by: M. R. Sutherland, M.D.
Address: Yarmouth, N.S.
Date: 9 March 1948

28. Registrar's Record Number: —
29. Filed Mar 10, 1948, Freeland R. Smith, Division Registrar

Dr. Brien Sutherland

Birth of William (1926) twin

Death of Raymond L (1926) twin

The Commonwealth of Massachusetts
United States of America

Registered No. 63

Town of Reading

CERTIFICATE OF BIRTH

FROM THE RECORDS OF BIRTHS IN THE TOWN OF READING, MASSACHUSETTS, U.S.A.

Date of Birth:	June 26, 1927
Name of Child:	William Henry Doucette
Sex:	Male Color: White
Place of Birth:	Reading
Residence of Parents:	25 Haven Street
	Reading, MA
Name of Father:	Harvey Doucette
Father's Age:	30
Birthplace of Father:	E. Quinnan, N.S.
Occupation of Father:	Millhand
Name of Mother (Maiden):	Beatrice Doucette
Mother's Age:	29
Birthplace of Mother:	Yarmouth, N.S.
Occupation of Mother:	Housewife
Date Recorded:	July 13, 1927
Record No./Book/Page:	#63/BK. 1927/PG. 19

I, Laura A. Gemme, depose and say that I hold the office of Town Clerk of the Town of Reading, Massachusetts, U.S.A.; that the records of Births, Marriages and Deaths in said town are in my custody; and that the above is a true extract from said records, as certified by me.

WITNESS my hand and the Seal of the Town of Reading, on this 6th day of September 2011

Laura A. Gemme, Town Clerk

1203.

READING BIRTHS - 1927.

RIESSLE, Margaret Patricia, d. of
   Frederick L. Riessle, b. in Everett, and
   Margaret I. Turner, b. in Reading.
   Residence of parents, Reading.
   June 13, 1927, in Winchester.

POST, Jerome Dermon, s. of
   Frank S. Post, b. in Rugby, Tenn., and
   Elise G. Dermon, b. in Watertown.
   Residence of parents, Reading.
   June 16, 1927, in Marlboro.

CLOUGH, Donald Robert, s. of
   Robert M. Clough, b. in Reading, and
   Mabelle M. Burditt, b. in No. Reading.
   Residence of parents, Reading.
   June 20, 1927, in Reading.

DOUCETTE, William Henry, s. of
   Harvey Doucette, b. in E. Quinan, N. S., &
   Beatrice Muse, b. in Yarmouth, N. S.
   Residence of parents, Reading.
   June 26, 1927, in Reading.

MALING, John Cushman, Jr., s. of
   John C. Maling, b. in Kennebunkport, Me., &
   Katherine C. Sullivan, b. in Boston.
   Residence of parents, Reading.
   June 26, 1927, in Winchester.

D'ENTREMONT, Leonard Joseph, s. of
   Pius L. D' Entremont, b. in Nova Scotia, and
   Esther I. D'Entremont, b. in Nova Scotia.
   Residence of parents, Reading.
   June 27, 1927, in Winchester.

The Commonwealth of Massachusetts
United States of America

Registered No. 77

Town of Reading

CERTIFICATE OF DEATH

FROM THE RECORDS OF DEATHS IN THE TOWN OF READING, MASSACHUSETTS, U.S.A.

Name:	William Henry Doucette	Occupation:	---
Date of Death:	August 29, 1927	Place of Birth:	Reading, Mass
Place of Death:	Reading	Place of Burial:	Stoneham
Residence:	25 Haven Street, Reading, Mass	Name of Cemetery:	St. Patrick's
Age:	2 Months	Veteran:	---
Sex:	Male	Specifiy War:	---
Color:	White	Name of Father:	Harvey Doucette
Social Security #:	---	Birthplace of Father:	Nova Scotia
Marital Status:	Single	Name of Mother:	Beatrice Muese
Name of Spouse:	---	Birthplace of Mother:	Nova Scotia
Cause of Death:	Gastro Enteritis		

Year/Page: 1927/27

I, Laura A. Gemme, depose and say that I hold the office of Town Clerk of the Town of Reading, Massachusetts, U.S.A.; that the records of Births, Marriages and Deaths in said town are in my custody; and that the above is a true extract from said records, as certified by me.

WITNESS my hand and the Seal of the Town of Reading, on this 6th day of September 2011

Laura A. Gemme, Town Clerk

The Commonwealth of Massachusetts
United States of America

Registered No. 93

Town of Reading

CERTIFICATE OF BIRTH

FROM THE RECORDS OF BIRTHS IN THE TOWN OF READING, MASSACHUSETTS, U.S.A.

Date of Birth:	July 10, 1928
Name of Child:	Beatrice Doucette
Sex:	Female Color: White
Place of Birth:	Reading
Residence of Parents:	25 Haven Street
	Reading, MA
Name of Father:	Harvey Doucette
Father's Age:	31
Birthplace of Father:	Quinnan, N.S.
Occupation of Father:	Rubber Worker
Name of Mother (Maiden):	Beatrice Muse
Mother's Age:	29
Birthplace of Mother:	Yarmouth, N.S.
Occupation of Mother:	Housewife
Date Recorded:	July 23, 1928
Record No./Book/Page:	#93/BK. 1928/PG. 24

I, Laura A. Gemme, depose and say that I hold the office of Town Clerk of the Town of Reading, Massachusetts, U.S.A.; that the records of Births, Marriages and Deaths in said town are in my custody; and that the above is a true extract from said records, as certified by me.

WITNESS my hand and the Seal of the Town of Reading, on this 6th day of September 2011

Laura A. Gemme, Town Clerk

READING BIRTHS - 1928.

SMALLEY, Caroline Frances, d. of
   James J. Smalley, b. in Wisconsin, and
   Elizabeth F. Hickey, b. in Reading.
   Residence of parents, Reading.
   June 30, 1928, in Winchester.

NEWBURY, -, (Stillborn), s. of
   - -, b. in -, and
   Marie Newbury, b. in Prince Ed. Isle.
   Residence of parents, Reading.
   July 3, 1928, in Reading.

TOWER, Richard Earle, s. of
   Lorne W. Tower, b. in Nova Scotia, and
   Christine Stonehouse, b. in Nova Scotia.
   Residence of parents, Reading.
   July 3, 1928, in Stoneham.

BURBANK, Eleanor Johnston, d. of
   Thomas H. Burbank, b. in East Milton, and
   Euphemia E. Johnston, b. in Belfast, Ireland.
   Residence of parents, Reading.
   July 6, 1928, in Winchester.

DOUCETTE, Catherine Mary, d. of
   Jeffrey Doucette, b. in Nova Scotia, and
   Catherine Le Fave, b. in Nova Scotia.
   Residence of parents, Reading.
   July 7, 1928, in Reading.

DOUCETTE, Beatrice, d. of
   Harvey Doucette, b. in Quinan, N. S., and
   Beatrice Muse, b. in Yarmouth, N. S.
   Residence of parents, Reading.
   July 10, 1928, in Reading.

FORM 6.   PROVINCE OF NOVA SCOTIA

CERTIFICATE OF REGISTRATION OF DEATH

1 PLACE OF DEATH—
County of Yarmouth   Municipality of Yarmouth   Registered No. 157
City or Town Yarmouth   Street   House No.
If in hospital or institution, give name Yarmouth Hospital

2 NAME OF DECEASED Beatrice Martha Doucette
Residence Yarmouth, Nova Scotia

PERSONAL AND STATISTICAL INFORMATION

- **3 SEX:** Female
- **4 RACIAL ORIGIN:** French
- **5 Single, Married, Widowed or Divorced:** Single
- **6 BIRTHPLACE:** Reading, Mass.
- **7 DATE OF BIRTH:** July 10, 1928
- **8 AGE IN:** Years 4, Months 11, Days 9
- **9 OCCUPATION OF DECEASED:** (a) Childhood
- **10 LENGTH OF RESIDENCE:**
  - (a) At place of death: Lifetime
  - (b) In province:
  - (c) In Canada (if an immigrant):
- **11 Name of father:** Harry Doucette
- **12 Birthplace of father:** East Quinan, N.S.
- **13 Maiden name of mother:** Beatrice Muise
- **14 Birthplace of mother:** Yarmouth, N.S.
- **15 Informant's name:** Harry Doucette   Address: Yarmouth, N.S.
- **16 Relationship to deceased:** Father
- **17 Place of burial, cremation or removal:** St. Ambrose   Date of burial: June 22, 1933
- **18 Undertaker:** Sweeney

MEDICAL CERTIFICATE OF DEATH

- **19 Date of death:** June 20, 1933
- **20** I HEREBY CERTIFY that I attended deceased from May 10, 1933 to June 20, 1933, that I last saw her alive on June 20, 1933, and that death occurred on the date stated above, at ___ m.

The CAUSE of DEATH was as follows:—
Tuberculosis Meningitis
Generalized Tuberculosis
(duration) yrs mos dys
CONTRIBUTORY: Tuberculosis Hip
(duration) yrs 2 mos dys

- **21 Where was disease contracted if not at place of death?** at home - Yarmouth
- Did an operation precede death? 0   Date of 0
- Nature of operation: 0
- Was there an autopsy? 0

(Signed) D.J. Macdonald, M.D.
Address: Yarmouth
Date: 7/5/33

- **22 Registrar's Record Number:**
- **23 Filed** July 6, 1933   Harry McKinlay (Division Registrar)

Dr. Macdonald

St. Ambrose Cathedral

65 Green Street
Yarmouth, Nova Scotia
B5A 1Z6
(902) 742-7151
Fax: (902) 742-7152
E-mail: ycc@ns.aliantzinc.ca

Certificate of Baptism

++

Name:	Genevieve Theresa Doucette
Father:	Harvé Doucette
Mother:	Beatrice Muise
Date of Birth:	16 February 1931
Place of Birth:	
Date of Baptism:	March 1. 1931
Sponsors:	James Saulnier
	Frances Muise
Presider:	Rev. A.LeBlanc
~~Confirmation~~	Died: Dec. 28,1931
Marriage:	

Issued by: *Mary Sweeney*

Date: 25 August 2011

FORM 6.

PROVINCE OF NOVA SCOTIA

Conn + Locate Birth

CERTIFICATE OF REGISTRATION OF DEATH

1 PLACE OF DEATH—
County of Yarmouth Municipality of Yarmouth Registered No. 1430
City or Town Yarmouth Street Regent House No.
If in hospital or institution, give name

2 NAME OF DECEASED Jean Theresa Doucette
Residence Regent St. - Yarmouth N.S.

PERSONAL AND STATISTICAL INFORMATION

3 SEX Female **4 RACIAL ORIGIN** French **5** Single

6 BIRTHPLACE Yarmouth

7 DATE OF BIRTH Feb. 16 - 1931

8 AGE IN — Years —, Months 10, Days 17

9 OCCUPATION OF DECEASED
(a)
(b)

10 LENGTH OF RESIDENCE
(a) At place of death
(b) In province
(c) In Canada (if an immigrant)

11 Name of father Harvey Doucette
12 Birthplace of father East Quinan
13 Maiden name of mother Beatrice Muise
14 Birthplace of mother Yarmouth
15 Informant's name Harvey Doucette
Address Yarmouth
16 Relationship to deceased Father

17 Place of burial St. Ambrose Date of burial Dec 29 1931

18 Undertaker Harvey Doucette, Yarmouth

MEDICAL CERTIFICATE OF DEATH

19 Date of death Dec 28 1931

20 I HEREBY CERTIFY that I attended deceased from Dec 28 1931 to Dec 28 1931 that I last saw her alive on Dec 28 1931 and that death occurred on the date stated above, at ___ m.

The CAUSE of DEATH was as follows:—

Convulsions

(duration) yrs mos 2 dys
CONTRIBUTORY
(duration) yrs mos dys

21 Where was disease contracted if not at place of death?
Did an operation precede death? Date of
Nature of operation
Was there an autopsy? no
(Signed) D W Williamson M.D.
Address Yarmouth
Date Dec 31st 1931

22 Registrar's Record Number

23 Filed December 31 1931 Harry McKinlay

St. Ambrose Cathedral

65 Green Street
Yarmouth, Nova Scotia
B5A 1Z6
(902) 742-7151
Fax: (902) 742-7152
E-mail: ycc@ns.aliantzinc.ca

Certificate of Baptism

++

Name:	John Thomas Doucette
Father:	Harvé Doucette
Mother:	Beatrice Muise
Date of Birth:	16 Feb 1931
Place of Birth:	
Date of Baptism:	March 1, 1931
Sponsors:	Peter Muise
	Martha Muise
Presider:	Rev. A. LeBlanc
Confirmation:	
Marriage:	
Issued by:	*Mary Sweeny*
Date:	25 August 2011

St. Ambrose Cathedral

65 Green Street
Yarmouth, Nova Scotia
B5A 1Z6
(902) 742-7151
Fax: (902) 742-7152
E-mail: ycc@ns.aliantzinc.ca

Certificate of Baptism

++

Name:	Martha Veronica Doucette
Father:	Harvé Doucette
Mother:	Beatrice Muise
Date of Birth:	22 August 1932
Place of Birth:	
Date of Baptism:	28 August 1932
Sponsors:	Peter Muise
	Dorothy Muise
Presider:	Rev. A. LeBlanc
Confirmation:	June 17, 1956
Marriage:	Thomas H. Surette July 31, 1951
	Comeau's Hill

Issued by: *Mary Sweeney*

Date: 25 August 2011

FORM 6.
PROVINCE OF NOVA SCOTIA
CERTIFICATE OF REGISTRATION OF DEATH

b1933.254.977

1 PLACE OF DEATH—
County of Yarmouth Municipality of Yarmouth Registered No. 267
City or Town Yarmouth Street Regent House No.
If in hospital or institution, give name

2 NAME OF DECEASED Stillborn Doucette
Residence Yarmouth N.S.

PERSONAL AND STATISTICAL INFORMATION

3 SEX: Female
4 RACIAL ORIGIN: French
5 Single, Married, Widowed or Divorced: Single
6 BIRTHPLACE: Yarmouth
7 DATE OF BIRTH: November 4, 1933
8 AGE IN: Years / Months / Days — If less than one day, hrs. or min.
9 OCCUPATION OF DECEASED: (a) — (b) —
10 LENGTH OF RESIDENCE:
 (a) At place of death
 (b) In province
 (c) In Canada (if an immigrant)
11 Name of father: Harvey Doucette
12 Birthplace of father: East Quinan
13 Maiden name of mother: Beatrice Muise
14 Birthplace of mother: Yarmouth
15 Informant's name: Harvey Doucette
 Address: Yarmouth
16 Relationship to deceased: Father
17 Place of burial, cremation or removal: St Ambrose Date of burial: Nov. 4, 1933
18 Undertaker: Harvey Doucette

MEDICAL CERTIFICATE OF DEATH

19 Date of death: November 4, 1933
20 I HEREBY CERTIFY that I attended deceased from Stillborn 19 to 19 that I last saw h_ alive Nov 4 1933 and that death occurred on the date stated above, at m.

The CAUSE of DEATH was as follows:—
Stillborn (Premature)
(duration) yrs mos dys

CONTRIBUTORY
(duration) yrs mos dys

21 Where was disease contracted if not at place of death?
Did an operation precede death? no Date of
Nature of operation
Was there an autopsy? no
(Signed) L. M. Morton M.D.
Address Yarmouth N.S.
Date Nov 4/33

22 Registrar's Record Number
23 Filed November 1933 Harry McKinley

St. Ambrose Cathedral

65 Green Street
Yarmouth, Nova Scotia
B5A 1Z6
(902) 742-7151
Fax: (902) 742-7152
E-mail: ycc@ns.aliantzinc.ca

Certificate of Baptism

++

Name:	Thomas Anthony Doucet
Father:	Harvé Doucet
Mother:	Beatrice Muise
Date of Birth:	2 March 1935
Place of Birth:	
Date of Baptism:	19 March 1935
Sponsors:	Frederick Muise
	Elizabeth Muise
Presider:	Rev.N. Theriault
Confirmation:	June 8, 1950
Marriage:	

Issued by: *Mary Sweeney*

Date: 25 August 2011

Baptismal Certificate

✝

On the 10th day of May 1936

I Baptized Albert , the legitimate child

of Herme Doucet and Beatrice Muise

Born in Yarmouth on May 3rd 1936

Sponsors were Leo Muise and Mrs Elizabeth Muise

Signed A. LeBlanc

I Hereby Certify that the above is a correct extract from the Baptismal Register of St. Ambrose Church, Yarmouth, N. S.

January 4, 1946   Dellie Comeau

Certificate of Death

No 005236

Name of Deceased Person:	JOHN AVITE DOUCET
Sex:	MALE
Date of Death:	Oct 23, 1965
Place of Death:	YARMOUTH
Date of Birth:	Aug 07, 1896
Age:	69 YRS
Place of Birth:	EAST QUINAN, NOVA SCOTIA
Residence:	YARMOUTH, NOVA SCOTIA
Occupation:	CARPENTER
Marital Status:	WIDOWED
Name of Spouse:	NOT STATED
Name of Father:	THEOPHILE DOUCET
Name of Mother:	ADELE DULAIN
Name of Attending Physician:	M. O'BRIEN
Name of Funeral Director:	HUSKILSON'S FUNERAL HOME
Disposition:	NOT STATED
Place of Disposition:	MT. CALVARY CEMETERY
At:	NOT STATED
Name of Informant:	MRS. HENRY ATKINS
Address:	3 JENKINS ST. YARMOUTH, NS
Relationship:	NONE
Date of Registration:	Oct 25, 1965
Registration No:	1965-02-006284

This is to certify that the record herein contained is from a Record of Death on file in the office of the REGISTRAR GENERAL of NOVA SCOTIA.

Given under my hand and the SEAL of the DEPUTY REGISTRAR GENERAL at Halifax, THIS 7th DAY OF September 2001

Deputy Registrar General

Certificate of Death

№ 005766

Name of Deceased Person:	BEATRICE DOUCETTE
Sex:	FEMALE
Date of Death:	May 20, 1954
Place of Death:	YARMOUTH
Date of Birth:	Oct 14, 1898
Age:	55 YRS
Place of Birth:	YARMOUTH, NOVA SCOTIA
Residence:	YARMOUTH, NOVA SCOTIA
Occupation:	HOUSEWIFE
Marital Status:	MARRIED
Name of Spouse:	HARVEY MUISE
Name of Father:	PETER P. MUISE
Name of Mother:	MARTHA ROACH
Name of Attending Physician:	M.C. O'BRIEN
Name of Funeral Director:	V.S. SWEENY
Disposition:	NOT STATED
Place of Disposition:	ST. AMBROSE
At:	YARMOUTH
Name of Informant:	HARVEY DOUCETTE
Address:	REGENT ST.
Relationship:	HUSBAND
Date of Registration:	Jul 09, 1954
Registration No:	1954-02-004332

This is to certify that the record herein contained is from a Record of Death on file in the office of the REGISTRAR GENERAL of NOVA SCOTIA.

Given under my hand and the SEAL of the DEPUTY REGISTRAR GENERAL at Halifax, THIS 13th DAY OF June 2002

Deputy Registrar General

PROVINCE OF NOVA SCOTIA—REGISTRATION OF DEATH

02- 004332

1. PLACE OF DEATH: County of Yarmouth, Municipality of Yarmouth, City/Town Yarmouth, Street Regent, House No. At Home
2. LENGTH OF STAY: (a) Life (b) Life (c) —
3. PRINT NAME OF DECEASED: Doucette, Beatrice
   RESIDENCE: Regent St., Yarmouth, N.S.
4. Sex: Female
5. Citizenship: Canadian
6. Racial Origin: French
7. Married
8. Birthplace: Yarmouth, N.S.
9. Date of Birth: October 14, 1898
10. Age: 55 years, 7 months, 6 days
11. Occupation: Housewife
15. Husband: Harvey Muise [Doucette]
16. Father: Peter P. Muise
17. Birthplace: Nova Scotia
18. Mother Maiden Name: Martha Peach
19. Birthplace: Nova Scotia
20. Signature of Informant: Harvey Doucette, Regent St., Yarmouth — Husband
21. Place of Burial: Yarmouth, St. Ambrose; Date of burial: May 22/54
22. Undertaker: V.S. Sweeny

MEDICAL CERTIFICATE OF DEATH

21. Date of Death: May 20, 1954
24. Attended deceased from May 17, 1954 to May 20, 1954; last saw alive May 20, 1954

CAUSE OF DEATH:
(a) Coronary Thrombosis — 3 days
(b) Hypertension

25. Was death associated with pregnancy? No
26. Surgical operation? No
27. External causes? No

Signed by: McQuinn M.D., Yarmouth, Date Jun 7, 1954
29. Filed July 9th, 1954

July 20, 1953

Wedding Day for John Doucet and Betty Hayes

John Doucet (age 22), Beatrice (Muise) Doucet (age 56), Albert Doucette (age 17)

GENERATION 10

Albert Doucette was born on May 3, 1936 in Yarmouth, Yarmouth County, Nova Scotia. He died at the Colchester Regional Hospital in Truro, Colchester County, Nova Scotia on July 24, 2000.

He married **Anne Elizabeth Feeley** (d/o James Henry (Harry) Feeley and Marie Catherine (Kay) Breau of Wentworth, Cumberland County, Nova Scotia) on November 11, 1961. Anne was born on May 15, 1939 in Amherst, Cumberland County, Nova Scotia.

Albert and Anne had five daughters.

1. Michele Anne Doucette (born on August 13, 1962) in Truro, Colchester County, Nova Scotia

2. Catherine Beatrice Doucette (born on July 3, 1963) in Truro, Colchester County, Nova Scotia

3. Lynette Marie Doucette (born on September 19, 1964) in Truro, Colchester County, Nova Scotia

4. Denise Helen Doucette (born on April 25, 1966) in Truro, Colchester County, Nova Scotia

5. Andrea Jean Doucette (born in November 9, 1967) in Truro, Colchester County, Nova Scotia

Mom and Dad (August 1961) Wentworth, Nova Scotia

Mom's Wedding Dress

November 11, 1961

Dad's Wedding Suit

November 11, 1961

Mom and Dad (November 11, 1961)

Immaculate Conception Church, Truro, Nova Scotia

Mom and Dad (November 11, 1961)

Immaculate Conception Church, Truro, Nova Scotia

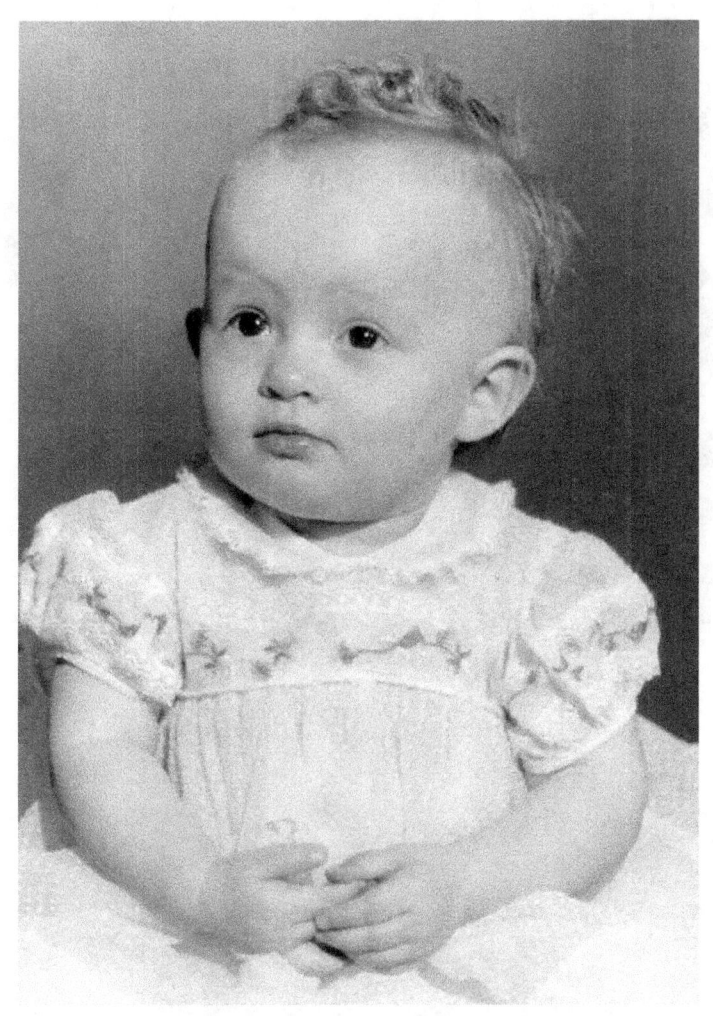

Michele (age 1)

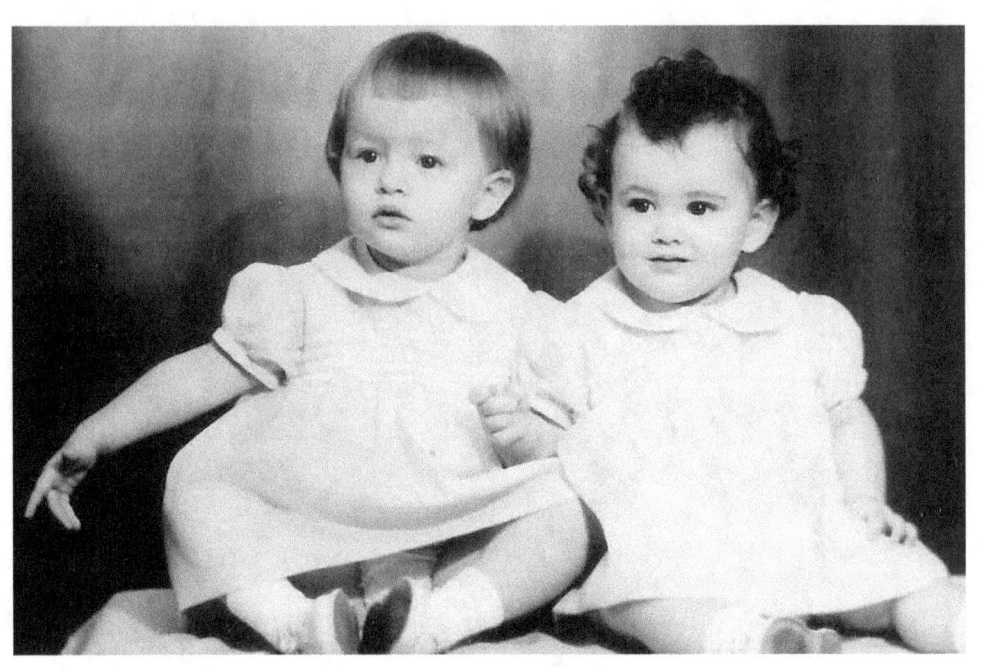

Michele (age 2), Cathy (age 1)

Family Photo (1965)

Michele (age 3), Lynette (age 1), Cathy (age 2)

Family Picture (August 1965) Wentworth, Nova Scotia

Back (left to right): Mom holding Lynette (almost 1)

Front (left to right): Cathy (age 2), Michele (age 3)

Dad loved to build things, just like his father.

Family Picture (1971)

Middle (left to right): Cathy (age 8), Lynette (age 7), Michele (age 9)

Front (left to right): Denise (age 5), Andrea (age 4)

Michele (Grade Primary)   Michele (Grade 12)

1967   1980

Michele (Grade 12)   Michele (MSVU Graduation)

1980   1985

Dad with new guitar

1994

July 2013 Addendum to Doucet DNA

I published Germain Doucet (Sieur de LaVerdure): My Paternal Ancestry on June 27, 2012; a culmination of twenty-three years of research. A few years previous to the publication, I took over the duties as administrator of the Doucet Surname Project with Family Tree DNA.

I now have a better understanding of the inner workings of Y-DNA, courtesy of Al Aburto (admin of the J-L24 Family Tree DNA Project), Jacques Beaugrand (cousin and co-admin of the French Heritage DNA Project), Lucie LeBlanc Consentino, David Dugas, Steve St. Clair (admin of the Sinclair/St. Clair DNA Study) and Stephen White (Université de Moncton).

In reviewing what the documents tell us, researcher genealogist F. René Perron of Sèvres, France, instructs us to begin with the January 20, 1649 will of Charles de Menou d'Aulnay de Charnizay. When he makes note of Germain Doucet being from *the parish of Couperans-en-Brie*, he hardly gives any supplementary indication. [634] The will also references the wife of Germain Doucet, without ever mentioning her family name. In keeping, her given name is also unaccounted for.

Perron also shares that Charles de Menou d'Aulnay de Charnizay was extremely generous, in spite of the enormous debts that he had incurred, his will stating that Germain Doucet would be given "only 200 pounds, but the assistance which I render to his *nephews and nieces and to all who concern him*, amounts to 100 pounds. One does not choose so precisely; he well deserves 100 crowns per year for his salary and his food and that of *his wife*." [635]

---

[634] Perron, F. René. *De La Verdure aux Ant-Isles et Vice-Versa* article.
[635] Ibid.

In truth, Perron wonders if this Doucet couple really had children, or if Germain Doucet and his wife were, in fact, raising as their own children ... their nieces and nephews ... a supposition that author Maurice Caillebeau, from Poitiers, also adheres to.

As Perron further asserts, historians tell us that Germain Doucet, Sieur de LaVerdure, returned to France.

Of course, this merits further questioning: did he return alone or did he return with his wife? Unfortunately, we do not have an answer to either question.

The only thing we *can* be sure of is that "his children" remained in Acadie, an act that Perron sees as outside the boundaries of what would constitute normal behavior with regards to family.

In addition, Stephen White (French Acadian genealogist, researcher and historian) has also shared that *there is no proof that Henriette Pelletret's husband, Pierre Doucet, was a son of Germain Doucet de La Verdure. That supposed connection always depended upon the belief that all the Doucets in Acadia were nearly related,* [636] a fact that the DNA results of this study appear to be disproving.

He further states that *it takes a number of tests to establish an ancestor's genetic signature. More tests are required where there are inconsistencies in the initial results.*

The first three sets of results for Michele Doucette's so-called cousins were all different. That situation has since been clarified.

We have enough results to establish that the true male-line descendants of Germain Doucet and Marie Landry carry the C3b Y-DNA signature.

---

[636] Email response dated June 28, 2012.

Moreover, it has been shown that this C3b Y-DNA carries down through the Claude Doucet who married Marie Comeau and the Joseph Doucet who married Anne Surette.

We can thus be sure that Claude was Germain's son, and Joseph was Claude's son. An additional test, for Kit 194117, extends the C3b results to the Michel Doucet who married Marie Susanne Mius, so we can thus be sure that any Doucets or Doucettes whose Y-DNA is not C3b do not descend from Michel Doucet and Marie Susanne Mius in the male line.

This is the same paper trail, claimed by two Doucet(te) males, as represented by Kit 203487 and Kit 206660, and yet their DNA results are *not* C3b.

Stephen explains that *the only way to find out where the two R1b lineages diverge from the C3b Doucets is to secure more males for additional testing. It is clear that there are two separate and distinct divergences here.*

As there is no family recollection of an adoption or other disconnect, it seems likely that these divergences are not recent.

There is a possible clue as to where one of the divergences may have occurred in the nickname of Michel Patrice Doucet. It may be that he was called L'Anglais because it was known that his father wasn't one of the C3b Doucets. On the other hand, there could be many other possible explanations for his nickname. Only the results of more Y-DNA tests can provide proof of the matter.

STEP 1

Charting the male Doucet(te)s who claim to descend from Joseph Mathurin Doucet and Angélique Mathilde Mius (the parents of the aforementioned Michel Patrice); of course, I merely have access to the names of the children, *not* their direct line descendants.

Before doing so, however, it is important that the following point be established.

Joseph Mathurin Doucet (born on May 7, 1795, probably at Pointe-des Ben (part of Sluice Point referred to as Muise Point). He was baptized on July 14, 1799 in Ste-Anne-du-Ruisseau. He was married on October 28, 1816 in Ste-Anne-du-Ruisseau to Angélique Mathilde Mius (d/o Paul Mius and Marie LeBlanc). Angélique was born on June 28, 1795 and baptized on July 27, 1799.

François David Doucet (born c. 1781), <u>brother to Joseph Mathurin Doucet</u>, was married on September 5, 1808 in Ste-Anne-du-Ruisseau to Isabelle Mius (d/o Pierre Mius and Cécile Amirault). This line has been shown to be C3b in accordance with Kit 194117.

Joseph Mathurin Doucet and Angélique Mathilde Mius had thirteen children, six of whom were male.

° Michel Patrice (called L'Anglais) Doucet was born on March 16, 1817 in Quinan, Yarmouth County, Nova Scotia. He was baptized on March 16, 1817 in Ste-Anne-du-Ruisseau. He married Anne Anastasie Mius (d/o François Mius and Marie Osithe O'Bird) about 1838 (or 1839). Anne Anastasie (called Nanette) Mius was born on December 25, 1817 in Quinan, Yarmouth County, Nova Scotia.

This is the same paper trail, claimed by two Doucet(te) males, as represented by Kit 203487 and Kit 206660, and yet their DNA results are *not* C3b.

As a result, *definitive* Y-DNA results are currently unknown.

° François David (called Catoon) Doucet was born on June 14, 1818 at Quinan, Yarmouth County, Nova Scotia. He married Madeleine Honorine (dite Honorme) Doucet (d/o Augustin Doucet and Marguerite LeBlanc). Madeleine Honorine Doucet was born on December 15, 1826. They established themselves at Pointe-aux-Bouleaux (part of Sluice Point), Yarmouth County, Nova Scotia.

° Joseph Mathurin Doucet was born on June 27, 1820 at Quinan, Yarmouth County, Nova Scotia. He married Anne Juliette (dite Julie) Moulaison (d/o Brigitte Moulaison) on November 23, 1840. He died on September 30, 1886 at the age of 66. Anne Juliette was born on June 15, 1815 (out of wedlock) and baptized on October 4, 1815. She died on April 9, 1895.

° Françoise Doucet (born between 1821 and 1823) died at a young age.

° Jean-Baptiste Toussaint Doucet was born November 1, 1829 at Quinan, Yarmouth County, Nova Scotia. He married Anne Julienne Mius (d/o Basile Mius and Anne Françoise Dulain). He died on May 13, 1885 at the age of 56. Anne Julienne Mius died on May 5, 1921.

° Jean Robert Doucet was born on April 13, 1834. He married (1) Anne Elisabeth (called Zabeth) Mius (d/o Frédéric Mius and Julie Moulaison) on February 23, 1868 and (2) Rosalie Frontain (d/o Marc Frontain and Anne Élisabeth Mius). Anne Élisabeth Mius died a short time after giving birth to a son, Moïse; more than likely a result of birth complications. Rosalie Frontain was born on October 21, 1872.

Stephen has also shared that he would then begin to *look for a male-line descendant of another son of Michel Patrice Doucet, if one could be found who would agree to be tested. If the results from his test matched either Kit 206660 or Kit 203487, then it would be clear which of the R1b lineages was really a descendant of Michel Patrice; on the other hand, if the results from this new testee came back with the C3b signature, then we would know that Michel Patrice's nickname had nothing to do with his paternal lineage, and there would be no need to further test a descendant of Joseph Mathurin Doucet, as his C3b Y-DNA would be likewise proved. Of course there is always a risk with these Y-DNA tests that they will produce results that do not match anyone else's. Another big problem with all this is that one has to await the results of each individual test before one can see what needs to be done next. Getting to the bottom of all the issues is thus sure to be a long and costly process.*

STEP 2

Outlining the male children born to Michel Patrice Doucet and Anne Anastasie Mius, and, as stated previously, I merely have access to the names of the children, *not* their direct line descendants.

Michel-Patrice Doucet and Anne Anastasie Mius had eight children, seven of whom were male.

° François David (called Quançois) Doucet was born on September 19, 1839. He married Jeanne Cyprienne Dulain (d/o Louis (called Piflet) Dulain and Marie Julie Doucet). They established themselves at Koucougôke (part of Quinan), Yarmouth County, Nova Scotia. He died on March 25, 1904, at the age of 64.

This represents a possible line for testing.

° Michel Patrice Doucet was born on October 24, 1841. He married (1) Marie Elisabeth Frontain (d/o Pierre Frontain and Marie Élisabeth Corporon) on October 22, 1861, who died with child; (2) Anne Mius (d/o Florent Mius and Anne Élisabeth Dulain) on November 15, 1864; and (3) Rosalie LeBlanc (d/o Remi LeBlanc), widow of Gabriel Mius, on September 4, 1893.

This represents a possible line for testing.

° Jean Émilien Doucet was baptized on September 18, 1857. He married Anne Mathilde Mius (d/o Anselme Mius and Marguerite Mius) on November 26, 1887.

This represents a possible line for testing.

° Henri Adolphe Doucet was born on February 8, 1860. He died on January 21, 1871.

This represents a possible line for testing.

° Jean Théophile (called Câlin) Doucet was baptized in April 1867. He married (1) Rose Mius (d/o Jean (called Johnny Coco) Mius); (2) Adèle Dulain (d/o Louis Cyprien Dulain and Vitaline Mius) on January 10, 1893; and (3) Delphine Jacquard (d/o Jovite Jacquard and Geneviève Mius).

Kit 206660 shows this line to be R1b1a2a1a1b.

° Avite Doucet (died on May 12, 1895) married (1) Marie Jacquard (sister to Delphine, d/o Jovite Jacquard and Geneviève Mius); (2) Julienne Doucet (d/o Remi Doucet and Rosalie Mius).

Kit 203487 shows this line to be R1b1a2a1a1b4.

What is so very interesting about these two siblings is that the R1b test results show that they only match on 17 out of 37 markers (with 20 mismatches), denoting a mere a 46% match. With so many marker mismatches, this means that they are not even closely related.

° Vitale Doucet

Nothing cited about this child; perhaps he died young, without issue.

STEP 3

If there are any Doucet or Doucette males who, after reading this segment, would be willing to have their DNA tested, I would like for them to make email contact.

Based on the R1b results that seemingly go back to Germain Doucet (born about 1641), which is also the paper trail that I lay claim to, there appears to have been a non-paternal event (adoption, silent assimilation, infidelity and/or the like) that took place, primarily because the Y-DNA results were *not* C3b.

While I am a Doucette on paper (birth certificate, school entry registration, report cards, High School diploma, University transcripts, University degrees, marriage certificate, birth certificates for my children, Social Insurance card, all bank paperwork, credit cards), and will continue to remain a Doucette, it has become clear that I must now embark on a new adventure; one based on genetic genealogy. In essence, it will probably take many years to solve this DNA mystery, if we are able to solve it at all.

In summation, there is a paper well worth reading; namely, Germain Doucet and Haplogroup C3b.[637]

In keeping with Germain Doucet and Haplogroup C3b, there are several key possibilities that have presented themselves; namely, [1] Germain Doucet SR and his wife adopted an Indian child, naming him Germain Doucet, [2] one of Germain Doucet SR's daughter's had an illegitimate child, naming him Germain Doucet, in honor of her father, [3] Germain Doucet SR's wife became pregnant by a Native man, [4] a Native person adopted Germain Doucet's name out of respect; when Native people were baptized in the Catholic faith, they were given non-Native names. All of them are plausible.

The aforementioned theory of F. René Perron of Sèvres, France, one also believed true by author Maurice Caillebeau, from Poitiers, France, is most assuredly plausible as well.

Michele Doucette, M. Ed.   July 3, 2013

michele.doucette@nf.sympatico.ca

---

[637] https://dna-explained.com/2012/09/18/germain-doucet-and-haplogroup-c3b/

May 2016 Addendum to Doucet DNA

Based on the Y-DNA STR Matches chart [638] summation that follows.

	Y-DNA12	Y-DNA25	Y-DNA37	Y-DNA67	Y-DNA111	Interpretation
Not Related	3	4	6	>7	>10	You are not related on your Y-chromosome lineage within recent or distant genealogical times (one to 15 generations).

This chart, then, serves to illustrate my point in the previous July 2013 Addendum to Doucet DNA chapter.

° Jean Théophile (called Câlin) Doucet was baptized in April 1867. He married (1) Rose Mius (d/o Jean (called Johnny Coco) Mius); (2) Adèle Dulain (d/o Louis Cyprien Dulain and Vitaline Mius) on January 10, 1893; and (3) Delphine Jacquard (d/o Jovite Jacquard and Geneviève Mius). Kit 206660 (my first cousin) shows this line to be R1b1a2a1a1b.

° Avite Doucet (died on May 12, 1895) married (1) Marie Jacquard (sister to Delphine, d/o Jovite Jacquard and Geneviève Mius); (2) Julienne Doucet (d/o Remi Doucet and Rosalie Mius). Kit 203487 (a third cousin on paper) shows this line to be R1b1a2a1a1b4.

What was so very interesting about these two *supposed* siblings is that they only match on 17 out of 37 markers (with 20 mismatches), denoting a mere a 46% match. With so many marker mismatches, this means that they are not even closely related.

---

[638] https://www.familytreedna.com/learn/y-dna-testing/y-str/expected-relationship-match/

Expected Relationships with Y-DNA STR Matches [639]

The expected relationship between you and your Y-chromosome DNA (Y-DNA) match is dependent on both the number of markers you have tested and the genetic distance. For example, if you and your match have both tested at the Y-DNA37 level and are a 36/37 match, this is a genetic distance of one. You are then considered tightly related.

	Y-DNA12	Y-DNA25	Y-DNA37	Y-DNA67	Y-DNA111	Interpretation
Very Tightly Related	N/A	N/A	0	0	0	Your exact match means your relatedness is extremely close. Few people achieve this close level of a match. All confidence levels are well within the time frame that surnames were adopted in Western Europe.
Tightly Related	N/A	N/A	1	1-2	1-2	Few people achieve this close level of a match. All confidence levels are well within the time frame that surnames were adopted in Western Europe.
Related	0	0-1	2-3	3-4	3-5	Your degree of matching is within the range of most well-established surname lineages in Western Europe. If you have tested with the Y-DNA12 or Y-DNA25 test, you should consider upgrading to additional STR markers. Doing so will improve your time to common ancestor calculations.
Probably Related	1	2	4	5-6	6-7	Without additional evidence, it is unlikely that you share a common ancestor in recent genealogical times (one to six generations). You may have a connection in more distant genealogical times (less than 15 generations). If you have traditional genealogy records that indicate a relationship, then by testing additional individuals you will either prove or disprove the connection.
Only Possibly	2	3	5	7	8-10	It is unlikely that you share a common ancestor in genealogical times (one to 15

---

[639] https://www.familytreedna.com/learn/y-dna-testing/y-str/expected-relationship-match/

Related						generations). Should you have traditional genealogy records that indicate a relationship, then by testing additional individuals you will either prove or disprove the connection. A careful review of your genealogical records is also recommended.
Not Related	3	4	6	>7	>10	You are not related on your Y-chromosome lineage within recent or distant genealogical times (one to 15 generations).

Kit 473459 is a 37/37 marker match with my first cousin (Kit 206660). With a genetic distance of zero, they are considered <u>very tightly related</u>. Few people achieve this close level of a match.

Kit 473459 is a 66/67 marker match with my first cousin (Kit 206660). With a genetic distance of one, they are considered <u>tightly related</u>. Few people achieve this close level of a match.

The closeness of the match tells us that there is a definite connection between his biological father and the gentleman involved in our NPE event.

The test results for Kit 473459 were completed on May 16, 2017. The test results for my first cousin (Kit 206660) were completed on February 2, 2012. This is the *only match*, to date, within the Family Tree DNA database.

Kit 473459 was adopted. He knows that his father was French with a dark complexion. He also knows that he was either in Toronto or Kingston in early 1953. However, due to confidentiality restraints, the adoption agency cannot provide him with his name until 2026. This means that his birth father was born in 1925 because of the mandatory 100 year wait. While he was able to find his birth mother, she had already passed.

June 2018 Addendum to Doucet DNA

Jean Théophile (called Câlin) Doucet, my great grandfather, was baptized in April 1867. I am beginning to suspect that *he* may be the NPE link, based on the information presented herein. [640]

On the issue of the Doucette family line, I think I have found something that will help to clarify the Théophile conundrum. As it turns out, Théophile was not "adopted" as suggested by Denis Beauregard. He was brought up by Michel Patrice Doucet and Anne Anastasie Mius because he was their grandson; the child of their daughter, Rosalie.

Stephen White has speculated that one of the R1b lineage *divergences may have occurred in the nickname of Michel Patrice Doucet. It may be that he was called L'Anglais because it was known that his father wasn't one of the C3b Doucets. On the other hand, there could be many other possible explanations for his nickname. Only the results of more Y-DNA tests can provide proof of the matter.*

It may also be possible that Rosalie's father was called L'Anglais because he spoke English; something that few people were able to do at that time.

In taking the time to revisit pages 118 to 120, long has there existed a story in the family; a story that spoke about our actually being of the Colin surname and not Doucet(te).

---

[640] Information obtained from Linda Joyce Campbell (first cousin once removed to my father) of Yarmouth, NS, dated June 4, 2018.

In reference to the 1901 Census for Belleville, Yarmouth County, [641] Jean Théophile is listed as Tomas and Adèle is listed as Addie. The birthdate for Jean Théophile is listed as August 15, 1864. I have a date of baptism for him as being April 1867. [642]

Rosalie Angélique Doucet [643] was born on July 13, 1844 and baptized on July 15, 1844.

If Jean Théophile was born in August 1864, Rosalie would have been 20 years of age. If Jean Théophile was born in 1867, but before his baptism in April 1867, Rosalie would have been 22 years of age.

It is highly probable that Jean Théophile was nicknamed "Câlin" because his father *might have been* a Colin.

---

[641] automatedgenealogy.com/census/DisplayHousehold.jsp?sdid=2107&household=208
[642] Information obtained from Pauline d'Entremont in an email dated July 6, 2001.
[643] https://novascotia.ca/archives/acadian/reborn/archives.asp?ID=3167

As it turns out, there *was* a Marcel II Colin (s/o Marcel I Colin and Léonice Gautreau), born about 1803 in Trois-Rivières, Québec, married to Marie Louise Cyr (from Madawaska, New Brunswick, born about 1805) who settled in Quinan, Nova Scotia. [644]

At the time Jean Théophile was born, there were three Colin brothers living in the Quinan area.

[1] Théophile Colin, born March 8, 1832, who married Marguerite Thériault from Meteghan on July 28, 1851. They had one child; a daughter named Natalie (born July 28, 1852). They separated. Marguerite went to Meteghan and Théophile, who was a carpenter, built a little house at Church Point.

If Jean Théophile was born in August 1864, Théophile would have been 32 years of age. If Jean Théophile was born in 1867, Théophile would have been 35 years of age.

[2] Marcel Colin III, born September 9, 1841 (Madawaska, New Brunswick), who married firstly Rosalie Mius (d/o Basile dit Tâchine Mius and Anne Françoise Dulain) in Ste. Anne du Ruisseau on November 15, 1864. Rosalie died in Quinan on June 2, 1884 at the age of 38 years. They had 8 children; namely, Joseph (born about 1866), Bénonie Émile (born July 8, 1869), Louise (born March 24, 1871), Solomon (born March 24, 1873), Françoise (born November 11, 1874), Rose Déline (born December 21, 1876), Job Marcel (born May 24 or May 29, 1879), Marie Bibiane (born July 16, 1881). He married secondly Joséphine Mius (d/o Charles Henri dit P'tit Coco Mius and Henriette Doucet) on June 29, 1884; four weeks after the death of his first wife. They had 3 children; namely, Louise Justine (born September 26, 1888), Anne Rosalie (born August 15, 1890) and Jacob (born February 28, 1893).

---

[644] d'Entremont, Father Clarence Joseph. (1984) Histoire de Quinan, Nouvelle-Écosse, pages 23 and 132.

If Jean Théophile was born in August 1864, Marcel III would have been 22 years of age. If Jean Théophile was born in 1867, Marcel III would have been 25 years of age.

[3] Antoine Colin, born in Madawaska, New Brunswick, about the beginning of November 1845. He married Marguerite Frontain (d/o Jean Maurice Frontain and Anne Catherine Doucet) in Ste. Anne du Ruisseau on May 24, 1874. They had 2 children; namely, Catherine (born about 1877) and Maurice Wenceslaus (born July 23, 1883).

If Jean Théophile was born in August 1864, Antoine would have been 18 years of age. If Jean Théophile was born in 1867, Antoine would have been 20 years of age.

Kit 473459 is a 37/37 marker match with my first cousin (Kit 206660). With a genetic distance of zero, they are considered very tightly related. Few people achieve this close level of a match.

Kit 473459 is also a 66/67 marker match with my first cousin (Kit 206660). With a genetic distance of one, they are considered tightly related. Few people achieve this close level of a match.

What is so fascinating is that Kit 473459 has no other matches other than my first cousin (Kit 206660) and vice versa, which makes this DNA signature unique; clearly, it serves to distinguish only our line.

The closeness of the match tells us that there is a definite connection between his biological father and the gentleman involved in our NPE event.

I shared this picture with an Acadian cousin, Leland Surette, who lives on Morris Island in Yarmouth County, Nova Scotia, about 25 minutes from Quinan, Nova Scotia. Upon showing his mother-in-law, her immediate response was, *Oh, yes, those look like Colin ears alright*. This physical confirmation is rather fascinating, to be sure.

OUR PAPER TRAIL	DNA BASED EVIDENCE
Germain Doucet Marie Landry	Germain Doucet Marie Landry
Claude dit Maître Jean Doucet Marie Comeau	Claude dit Maître Jean Doucet Marie Comeau
Joseph Doucet Anne Surette	Joseph Doucet Anne Surette
Michel Doucet Marie Suzanne Mius	Michel Doucet Marie Suzanne Mius
Joseph Mathurin Doucet Angélique Mathilde Mius	Joseph Mathurin Doucet Angélique Mathilde Mius
Michel Patrice (L'Anglais) Doucet Anne Anastasie Mius	Michel Patrice (L'Anglais) Doucet Anne Anastasie Mius
Jean Théophile (Câlin) Doucet Adèle Dulain	Rosalie Angélique Doucet ???? Colin
Jean-Avite (called Harvey) Doucet Beatrice Muise	Jean Théophile (Câlin) Doucet NPE Adèle Dulain
Albert Doucette Anne Elizabeth Feeley	Jean-Avite (called Harvey) Doucet Beatrice Muise
Michele Doucette	Albert Doucette Anne Elizabeth Feeley
	Michele Doucette

This updated genealogy chart is based on information obtained from Linda Joyce Campbell (first cousin once removed to my father) of Yarmouth, NS, dated June 4, 2018.

It is quite possible that Rosalie was reluctant to give the father's name when Théophile was born; naming him after the father would have been an admission. Of course, it may have been common knowledge anyway.

April 2019 Addendum to Doucet DNA

I have been most fortunate to be making email contact with Gayle Bouchard Collin. My Acadian cousin, Leland Surette, knows her well, mainly because he has a daughter with Alström Syndrome.

Gayle had worked with Jan Marshall, Genetics Coordinator at the Jackson Laboratory in Bar Harbor, Maine. She now works with Jüergen Naggert. [645] He tells me that she is still the heart of their lab.

The reason they stopped work directly with human patients (Alström Syndrome) was that the regulations are very extensive and they had problems meeting them. However, they still conduct research on the disease. They recently finished a drug study on their mouse models and are still are working to determine the function of the ALMS 1 protein. I am told that this type of research lends itself far better to mice.

Given her work in genetics, I am hoping that she made be able to assist me with regards to my search for links back to the family of Marcel II Colin (s/o Marcel I Colin and Léonice Gautreau), born about 1803 in Trois-Rivières, Québec, married to Marie Louise Cyr (from Madawaska, New Brunswick, born about 1805) who settled in Quinan, Nova Scotia.

---

[645] https://www.jax.org/research-and-faculty/faculty/juergen-naggert

Alström Syndrome

I first learned about Jan Marshall, Genetics Coordinator at the Jackson Laboratory in Bar Harbor, Maine, when I first began researching my family tree in the 1990s; at that time, she was wanting to make contact with direct descendants of Michel Doucet and Marie Suzanne Mius.

At that time, Alström Syndrome was thought to be a disease affecting only French Acadians; this ultra-rare, genetic syndrome, which affects many different organ systems in the body (vision, hearing, endocrine function, cardiac function, hepatic function, obesity and growth, as well as urological and renal function) is now known to be in 58 countries and amongst many ethnicities.

Although Alström Syndrome is extremely rare, chances that a child will inherit the double dose of the gene are increased in culturally isolated populations. A point of interest is that there *is* a higher frequency of reported cases in French Acadian history.

The Jackson Laboratory is no longer doing human studies on Alström Syndrome, in large part because the gene (ALMS1) was finally identified.

For those who wish a detailed information on the syndrome, please visit the denoted website [646] where you will find a link to the full text of the Alström Syndrome Handbook.

If you suspect a member of your family may have the syndrome, please visit the Alström Syndrome International website.

---

[646] https://www.alstrom.org/

ADDENDUM

May 15, 2017

While I am sad to share that Jan passed away in September 2016, I am pleased to be able to share that her research continues to live on.

Jan was eventually successful in having traced the disease back to a couple from the early 1600's; namely, Joseph Mius dit d'Azy (son of Philippe Mius dit d'Azy and his first Amérindien wife, name unknown) and Marie Amirault (daughter of François Amirault dit Tourangeau and Marie Pitre). What I find shocking about this newest revelation is that it is this very same couple (Joseph Mius dit d'Azy and Marie Amirault) to which the fatal Niemann-Pick disease (variant D) of Yarmouth, County, Nova Scotia, has been linked. [647]

I was blessed to have known Lesley Anne Doucet, a dear Acadian cousin, from Yarmouth, albeit for too short a time. Continuing to remain brave in her battle with Neimann-Pick disease, she transitioned on January 15, 2003, at the tender age of eighteen years.

Robert (Robin) P. Marshall, Executive Director, Alstrom Syndrome International

14 Whitney Farm Road

Mt. Desert, ME 04660 USA

Phone: (207) 244-7043

FAX: (207) 244-7678

EMAIL: robin.marshall@alstrom.org

---

[647] https://www.ncbi.nlm.nih.gov/pmc/articles/PMC1685594/pdf/ajhg00203-0078.pdf

Michele's Letter to F. René Perron

July 31, 2006

Mr. Perron,

In past correspondence with a cousin of mine, Florian Bernard of Québec, I was told that you are very well informed about the European roots of Acadian families.

I have also been in regular email correspondence with Paul Pierre Bourgeois of Grand Digue, NB, author of À la recherche des Bourgeois d'Acadie (1641 - 1800), hence my reason for writing to you.

I am a direct descendant of Germain Doucet, Sieur de LaVerdure.

A major find for France has clearly been the discovery of the St. Jehan passenger list of April 1636, a ship which left La Rochelle, France, for Port Royal, Acadie.

Has the passenger list of the initial voyage of the St. Jehan (July 4, 1632) ever surfaced?

Following the St-Germain-en-Laye treaty of March 1632, Commander Isaac de Razilly departed La Rochelle, France, for Acadie, disembarking at La Hève on September 8, 1632, with 300 hand-picked men. While there were a total of three vessels, the only names known to us are that of the L'Espérance à Dieu and the St. Jehan.

It was courtesy of this voyage that my ancestor, Germain Doucet, Sieur de LaVerdure, came to Acadie. I have always wondered if the spouse of Germain, mother of Pierre (1621) and Marguerite (1625), accompanied them; likewise for the children.

I am aware that Jacques (dit Jacob) Bourgeois was a known brother-in-law to Germain Doucet. In keeping with the mystery, and possible illegitimacy, surrounding the birth of Jacques Bourgeois, courtesy of your article entitled *De Germain Doucet à Jacob Bourgeois* followed by *Bourgeois & Doucet: À Basseville, des suites surprenantes*, both of which were published by La Société Historique Acadienne, there are many unanswered questions.

Paul Pierre Bourgeois cites your research in his book; namely, you were able to provide him with the names of Jacques' siblings: [1] Johannis, born December 1614, [2] Charola, born November 1615, [3] Nicolas, born January 1617, [4] Catharina, born September 1618, and [5] Barbara, born January 1620. In addition, you stated that all were born to Nicolas Grandjehan and Marguerite Bourgeois.

Given the names of the three identified daughters, it never ceases to amaze me that many people researching our shared genealogical roots still cite Marie Bourgeois (surmised sister to Jacques Bourgeois) as having been the wife of Germain Doucet.

As further quoted by Paul Pierre Bourgeois, you also make mention of the possibility that an Isaac Le Gendre may have been the birth father of Jacques (dit Jacob) Bourgeois. When baptized, he was given his mother's surname; it appears, then, that he may have been born out of wedlock.

Setting this difficulty aside, how might one discover more about [1] the Grandjehan line that Nicolas descended from, as well as [2] the Bourgeois line that Marguerite descended from?

In conjunction with your articles, you state that Marguerite Doucet, daughter of Germain Doucet, Sieur de LaVerdure, was born in 1634. Most of the information that I have come across, in my 15+ years of research, states her birth year as having been about 1625.

To my mind, the 1625 date would have meant that she was born in France, whereas a date of 1634 could only imply that she was born in Acadie. Please correct me if I am wrong.

Have you ever been successful in securing a baptismal record for Pierre Doucet, born about 1621? Any possible idea(s) as to where he may have been born?

More importantly, have you ever been successful in securing a baptismal record for Germain Doucet? It is generally felt that he was born about 1595.

Your discovery of the Commandery of the Hospitaliers, found at Coutran, interestingly enough, also connects to the Order of Malta. Am I correct in surmising that Germain Doucet was from the fiefdom (hamlet) of LaVerdure, 12 km north of La Ferté-Gaucher, in the municipality of St. Cyr-sur-Morin?

Given Germain Doucet's position as a soldier, has material ever surfaced pertaining to the Order of Malta? Is it possible that Germain might have had a role to play within the order? Might this somehow connect him to Commander Isaac de Razilly, thereby leading to his arrival in Acadie in 1632?

Is there anything known pertaining to the whereabouts of Germain Doucet following his return to France in 1654? I have been told that he was known to have been alive in 1660. Apparently, there was a letter dated October 13, 1660, posted from Villy, France, that is now in the archives. Have you ever come across such information?

Thank you so much for your time.

Ms. Michele Doucette

Letter from F. René Perron

F. René Perron

Les Amitiés Acadiennes

www.lesamitiesacadiennes.org

Sèvres, France

March 6, 2007

Hello cousin,

I am not very fond in English language: so, I prefer, for many reasons, to return to french. You will excuse me.

Tout d'abord, je vous joins photocopies de trois articles sur Germain DOUCET, parus il y a quelques années dans ma brochure de recherches "Suite N° 7". Ce sera déjà un "canevas" qui vous servira de base. Il y a quelques rectifications à y faire depuis:

• La célèbre "Lettre de Villy" mentionnée dans un arrêt du Conseil d'Etat de 1703 n'a pas été expédiée de Sedan, mais d'un autre Villy situé dans le Département de l'Yonne, à 150 km au sud-est de Paris (Commune de Ligny-le-Châtel). Or ce Villy avait appartenu à César de VENDOME, le fils naturel d'HENRI IV, qui, à la mort de Charles d'AULNAY, a essayé de devenir propriétaire (pour moité) avec la veuve de Gouverneur, Jeanne MOTIN. Un de mes articles, en ma "Suite N° 9" est consacré à cette affaire, avec photocopies de documents historiques. (Mes brochures sont disponibles au Centre d'Etudes Acadiennes de l'Université de Moncton N.B., et mon fonds d'archives du Centre). A mon avis, Germain DOUCET reveneu en France après 1654, a du rencontrer César de VENDOME pour être "conseillé" sur son avenir.

• Le lien de parenté avec Jacob BOURGEOIS doit se comprendre à travers le second mariage de Germain DOUCET, mariage fort probable (je n'en ai pa las preuve) avec une fille de Guillaume TRAHAN, et non avec une GRANDJEHAN. Plusieurs chercheurs, en France, sont aussi de cet avis.

A propos de Jacob BOURGEOIS, j'avais pensé que son père naturel pouvait être sont parrain, Isaac LE GENDRE. Depuis, d'autres indices me font croire, pour cette paternité naturelle, à un parent par alliance d'Isaac LE GENDRE, un des Mâitres-Chirurgiens de Coutran. Mais je ne peux pas l'affirmer (et pour cause!) et encore moins l'écrire dans mes articles. J'en ai toutefois fait part à mon cousin Paul-Pierre (qui se meurt d'un cancer, hélas), sans garantie bien entendu. Je n'ai en effet que les indices ...

Le patronyme DOUCET est toujours présent à Bassevelle (don't dépend le hameau de "La Verdure"). Il figure bien sur une tombe de cimetière, et un élève de l'école porte ce nom. Je vous rapelle que c'est aux "Groseilliers" (une ancienne ferme toujours debout) que résidait Médard CHOUART "des Groseilliers", commensal de Pierre-Esprit RADISSON, à la Baie d'Hudson.

Bassevelle était alors "en censive" de dame Henriette de LORRAINE, une des soeurs de Charles II de LORRAINE, Duc d'Elbeuf, époux en 1619 de Catherine Henriette de FRANCE, fille d'HENRI IV et de Gabrielle d'ESTRÉES, et cousine par alliance de César de VENDOME. "Tout se tient" avec ce personnage. De plus, c'est Charles II de LORRAINE qui fut le parrain de Christine (Chrestienne) de FRANCE, fille d'HENRI IV et future Duchesse de SAVOIE. Et cette grand Dame est venue aux moins deux fois à Sallenoves (un hameau de Bassevelle), rencontrer le Grand-Veneur de SALLENOVES qui fui le beau-frère de René LE COQ, celui que Mme de GUERCHEVILLE envoya en 1613 coloniser les Monts-Desert. "Tout se tient" encore. J'ajoute qu'Antoinette de PONS, marquise de Guercheville, était alliée des de LANNOY (Anne Elisabeth de LANNOY, première épouse de Charles III de LORRAINE, Duc d'Elbeuf, aprés son père). "Tout se tient" une fois encore.

Mais revenons aux embarquements de 1632 et 1636. Aucun rôle pour celui n'a été retrouvé, et les "Hommes d'Elite" qu'il mentionne étaient fort probablement des soldats venus avec le Commandeur de RAZILLY (qui devait connaître la Commanderie de Coutran à La Ferté-Gaucher). Celui de 1636, que j'ai longuement éudié pour maintes raisons, ne mentionne pas Germain DOUCET.

A Bassevelle, le registre paroissial rescapé de toutes les guerres, invasions, dents de souris, etc, ne débute que bien après 1595. Il ne peut donc nous donner le baptême de Germain DOUCET (en supposant qu'il soit bien né en ce village avant d'y devenir SIEUR de La Verdure).

Stephen WHITE, avec qui j'ai eu de nombreux contacts directs lors de mes séjours à Moncton, est resté prudent sur les épouses du Commandant d'Armes de Port-Royal. Excellent généalogiste, il n'a toutefois guère fait de recherches en France, comme j'ai pu le faire pendant des années.

Bien de choses lui ont échappé sur ce terrain : il est en encore à douter du baptême de 1621 à La Ferté-Gaucher, pour Jacob BOURGEOIS. Cela est un peu navrant. En ce qui concern les GRANDJEHAN alliées du pionnier (si l'on peut dire), mes recherches me font croire qu'ils étaient plus ou moins liés à Nicolas HARLAY de Sancy, le Recruteur des soldats Suisses des Rois de France, et qu'ils ont participé à ce recrutement. Un des GRANDJEHAN que j'ai pu retrouver était justement de Genève. Hasard seulement?

Qui sait d'ailleurs si notre Germain DOUCET n'était pas mêlé lui aussi, à ce recrutement, pour être, par la suite, "Commandant d'Armes"? Je suis tenté de le croire.

Je ne pouvais pas, à La Ferté-Gaucher, retrouver les ancêtres de Nicolas GRANDJEHAN, ni ceux de Marguerite BOURGEOIS. Pour ces derniers, j'ai donné à Paul-Pierre BOURGEOIS beaucoup d'indications sur l'origine des BOURGEOIS, avec le village de Cressy-sur-Somme (Morvan/Charolais) où il y avait un Grenier à Sel dirigé par Guillaume BOURGEOIS, lié à Madame de MONTAFFIÉ pour cela (épouse de Charles de BOURBON, cousin d'HENRI IV, Vice-Roi de la Nouvelle-France en 1612). En effet, cette grande Dame avait des intérêts (financiers) dans les Greniers à Sel du Royaume, où l'on retrouve ... Louis MOTIN (MOTTIN), le beau-frère de Charles d'AULNAY. Bien d'autres personnages fréquentant la Cour de France était impliqués dans ces Greniers à Sel, et j'en ai cités plusieurs dans mes brochures.

Ces brochures (10 en tout), mettent en évidence les alliances de la famille BOURGEOIS, souvent de "haut-niveau". De plus, Louis BOURGEOIS, ancêtre direct du pionnier, était le Premier Médecin du Roi François 1er. Il coiffait à ce titre un d'AILEBOUST, dont un descendant fut Gouverneur de la Nouvelle-France. Encore, une coincidence!

Sur internet circulent malheureusement des notions fausses sur Jacob BOURGEOIS, et c'est souvent que j'ai eu à écrire aux auteurs un peu trop inventifs. Il en est de même dans le Dictionnaire Biographique du Canada, où un "père" imaginaire de Jacob, du "même prénom" serait venu avec lui à Port-Royal. L'auteur, malheureusement, fut en de mes meilleurs amis à Moncton: le Père Clément CORMIER.

Voilà ce que je peux vous écrire sur Germain DOUCET (dont je ne suis pas descendant). Un dossier sur les DOUCET aurait existé aux Archives de la ville de Paris, mais je n'ai pas pu le retrouver.

Les recherches aux 16è et 17è siècles ne sont pas faciles. J'ai eu une certaine chance en fouillant les Archives Nationales de France, et beaucoup de dépôts d'Archives des villes de France. Mais "à l'impossible, nul n'est tenu" et je ne peux guère vous en donner plus sur ce personnage important de notre Histoire Acadienne. Je le regrette vivement.

Avec mes meilleurs sentiments acadiens,

L'Acadien Dispersé de Belle-Île-en-Mer

F. René Perron

P.S. Mes brochures de recherches portent la mention suivant, REPRODUCTION AUTORISEE, en CITANT L'AUTEUR ET SES SOURCES.

Translation of Letter from F. René Perron

F. René Perron

Les Amitiés Acadiennes

www.lesamitiesacadiennes.org

Sèvres, France

March 6, 2007

Hello cousin,

I am not very fond of the English language: so, I prefer, for many reasons, to return to french. You will excuse me.

First of all, I am attaching photocopies of three articles about Germain DOUCET which were published several years ago in my research document "Suite N° 7. These will serve as an outline forming a base. There have since been some corrections:

• The famous "Lettre de Villy" mentioned in a 1703 ruling of the State Council was not sent from Sedan, but from another Villy situated in the Yonne Department, 150 kilometres south-east of Paris (Commune of Ligny-le-Châtel). This Villy had belonged to César de VENDOME, illegitimate son of HENRI IV, who, upon the death of Charles d'AULNAY, tried to assert a claim, in half, with the Governor's wife, Jeanne MOTIN. One of my articles in "Suite N° 9 is dedicated to this affair, with photocopies of historical documents. My documents are available in my archival file at the Centre d'Etudes Acadiennes of the

University of Moncton, New Brunswick. In my opinion, Germain DOUCET, after his return to France in 1654, must have met with César de VENDOME for advice about his future.

• The marriage link with Jacob BOURGEOIS must be through *a second marriage* of Germain DOUCET, most likely (although I don't have any proof) with a daughter of Guillaume TRAHAN, and not with a GRANDJEHAN. Several researchers in France concur with this theory.

Regarding Jacob BOURGEOIS, I originally thought that his biological father might have been his godfather, Isaac LE GENDRE. Since then, however, several clues have led me to believe, regarding his paternity, that he is a relative through marriage of Isaac LE GENDRE, one of the Master Surgeons of Coutran, but I cannot confirm this (for good reason) and certainly cannot write about it in my articles. I have, however, shared this theory with my cousin Paul-Pierre (who, unfortunately, is dying of cancer). But I only have clues suggesting this speculation.

The surname DOUCET still exists in Bassevelle (where the hamlet of "La Verdure" is located). It can be found on a tombstone and one student from the local school bears the name. May I remind you that at "Groseilliers (an old farmhouse which is still standing) resided Médard CHOUART 'des Groseilliers", an acquaintance of Pierre-Esprit RADISSON of Hudson's Bay.

At that time, Bassevelle was a fiefdom of Dame Henriette de LORRAINE, one of the sisters of Charles II de LORRAINE, Duke of Elbeuf, who in 1619 married Catherine-Henriette de FRANCE, daughter of HENRI IV and Gabrielle d'ESTRÉES, and…a cousin through marriage of César de VENDOME! This all fits with this individual. Moreover, it was Charles II de LORRAINE who was the godfather of Christine (Chrestiennne) de FRANCE, daughter of HENRI IV and the future Duchess of SAVOIE. This woman of high birth came at least twice to Sallenoves (a small village in Bassevelle) to meet the Master of the Hunt de

SALLENOVES, the father-in-law of René LE COCQ whom Mme de GUERCHEVILLE sent to colonize Monts-Déserts in 1613! This all fits again. I might add that Antoinette de PONS, the marquise of Guercheville had ties with the de LANNOYS (Anne-Elisabeth de LANNOY, first wife of Charles III de LORRAINE, heir to the title of Duc d'Elbeuf). Once again, this all fits.

But let's talk about the sailings of 1632 and 1636. No passenger list has been found for the 1632 trip and the "Hommes d'Elite" that he mentions were most likely soldiers who arrived with the Commander de RAZILLY (who must have been familiar with the Commandery of Coutran in La Ferté-Gaucher). Regarding the 1636 list, I have studied it at length for numerous reasons and there is no mention of Germain DOUCET.

In Bassevelle, the parish register, which has survived all the wars, invasions, rodent bites, etc., dates from well after 1595. Therefore, it cannot provide us with a record of Germain DOUCET's baptism (presuming that he was born in this village before becoming SIEUR de La Verdure).

Stephen WHITE, whom I contacted a number of times during my stays in Moncton, remains very cautious regarding the wives of the Commander-at-Arms of Port-Royal. Although he is an excellent genealogist, he has done little research in France, something which I have been able to do over many years.

Many things have eluded him regarding this area: there is still some question about the 1621 baptism of Jacob BOURGEOIS in La Ferté-Gaucher. This is somewhat unnerving. As for the GRANDJEHANS having ties with the pioneer (if one can say this), my research leads me to believe that they were more or less linked to Nicolas de HARLAY from Sancy, recruiter of the Swiss soldiers of the Kings of France, and that they aided in this recruitment. Indeed, one of the GRANDJEHANS that I have found came from Geneva. Is this just chance?

Who knows if our Germain DOUCET didn't also help in this recruiting, leading to the position of "Commander-at-Arms"? I am tempted to believe this.

At La Ferté-Gaucher, I couldn't find the forefathers of Nicolas GRANDJEHAN, nor those of Marguerite BOURGEOIS. Concerning the latter, I gave Paul-Pierre BOURGEOIS many clues about the origin of the BOURGEOIS, with the village of Cressy-sur-Somme (Morvan/Charolais) where there was a salt cellar managed by Guillaume BOURGEOIS, who was associated with Madame de MONTAFFLÉ (wife of Charles de BOURBON, cousin of HENRI IV, Vice-Regent of New France in 1612). Indeed this aristocratic lady had interests (financial) in the royal salt cellars where we find Louis MOTIN (Mottin), the father-in-law of Charles d'AULNAY. Many other individuals who frequented the French Court were involved in these salt cellars, and I have mentioned several in my articles.

These articles (10 in all) outline the alliances of the BOURGEOIS family, often with the "upper classes". Moreover, Louis BOURGEOIS, a direct ancestor of the pioneer, was the Primary Doctor of King François I. He was above a certain d'AILLEBOUST, whose descendant was Governor of New France. Another coincidence?

Unfortunately, there are many misconceptions floating about the Internet concerning Jacob BOURGEOIS, and I often have to write to authors who are overly imaginative. This has even happened in the Dictionnaire Biographique du Canada where an imaginary "father" of Jacob, with the same given name, supposedly came to Port Royal with him; the author, unfortunately, was one of my best friends in Moncton: le Père Clément CORMIER.

This is all I can write to you about Germain DOUCET (because I am not a descendant). A file about the DOUCETS would have existed in the Paris archives, but I have been unable to find one.

Research in the 16th and 17th centuries is not easy.

I've had a certain amount of luck going through the National Archives of France and those of many French towns. But "Never give up…" I can't give you any more information about this important person in our Acadian history. I regret this very much.

With Best Acadian Wishes,

The Acadian Expelled to Belle-Ile-en-Mer

F. René Perron

PS. My research articles bear the following directive: REPRODUCTION IS AUTHORIZED IF THE AUTHOR AND SOURCES ARE CITED. If you use these papers on the Internet, please include the directive. THANK YOU. I am only an explorer, and not a historian; therefore my research only suggests paths to follow. Do not consider them historical facts!

Origin Maps

F. René Perron identifies these maps as pertaining to the possible area that Germain Doucet came from. [648]

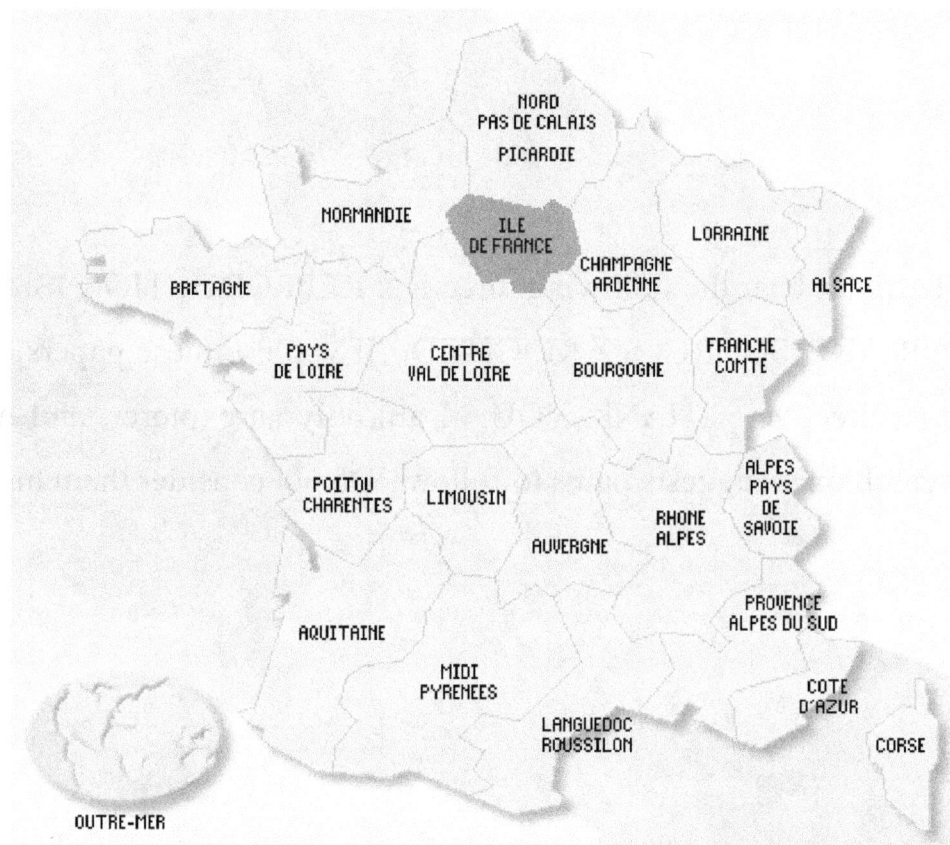

---
[648] www.doucetfamily.org/Genealogy/GemainOriginMaps.htm

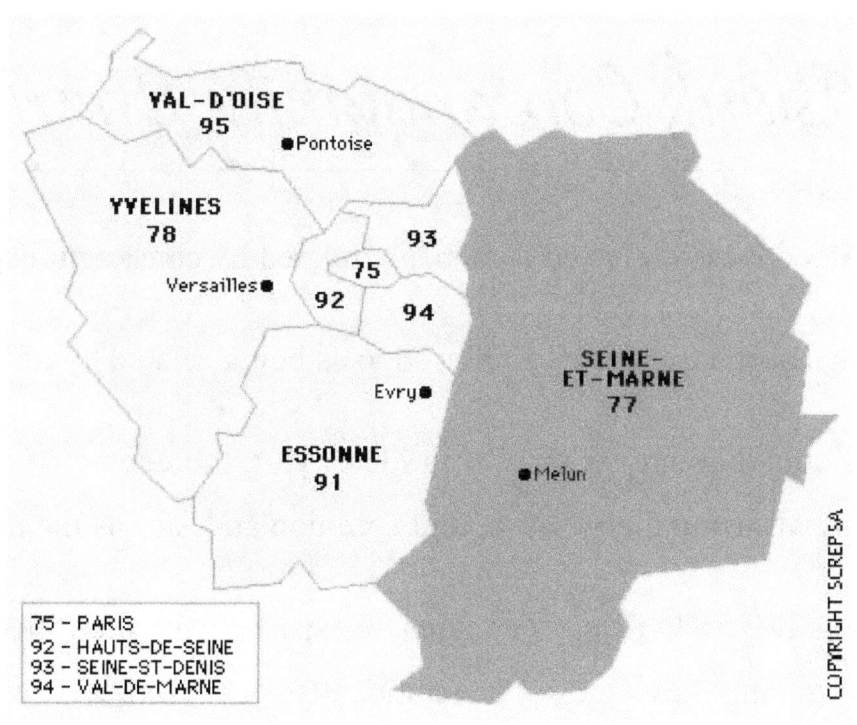

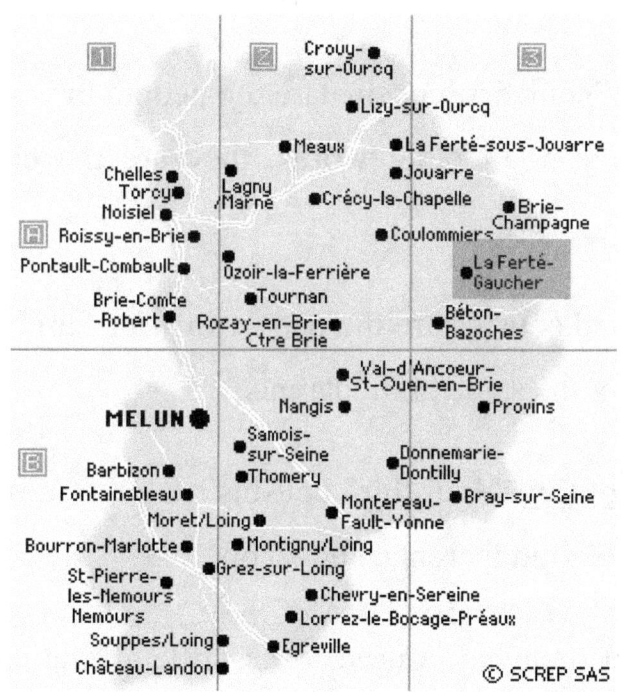

Blank Consanguinity Chart

A relationship by blood is also referred to as being related by consanguinity.

A relationship by marriage is sometimes referred to as being related by affinity.

A table or chart of consanguinity is helpful in identifying the degree of cousin relationship between two individuals using their most recent common ancestor as the reference point.

Cousinship between two individuals can then be specifically identified, in degrees and removals, by determining how close, generationally, the common ancestor is to each individual.

Cousin (aka First Cousin): Your first cousins are the people in your family who have two of the same grandparents as you. In other words, they are the children of your aunts and uncles.

Second Cousin: Your second cousins are the people in your family who have the same great grandparents as you, but not the same grandparents.

Third, Fourth, and Fifth Cousins: Your third cousins have the same GG grandparents, fourth cousins have the same GGG grandparents, and so on.

Removed: When the word removed is used to describe a relationship, it indicates that the two people are from different generations. Given that you and your first cousins are in the same generation (two generations younger than your grandparents), the word removed is not used to describe your relationship.

The words *once removed* mean that there is a difference of one generation. For example, your mother's first cousin is your first cousin, once removed. This is because your mother's first cousin is one generation younger than your grandparents and you are two generations younger than your grandparents. This one-generation difference equals once removed. A two-generation difference equates to *twice removed* means that there is a two-generation difference. In this case, you are two generations younger than a first cousin of your grandmother, so you and your grandmother's first cousin are first cousins, twice removed.

Consanguinity Chart [649]

Table of Consanguinity [650]

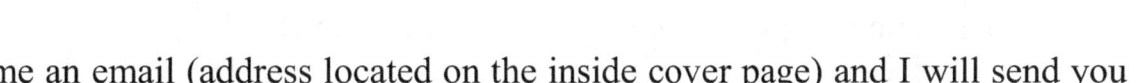

Feel free to send me an email (address located on the inside cover page) and I will send you a consanguinity chart that can easily be used for plotting purposes.

---

[649] www.thegordondnaproject.com/Gordon_Consanguinity_Chart.html
[650] www.alanddavis.com/Chart.pdf

In order to ascertain the definitive relationship that exists between two people, begin by plotting the shared ancestor in the top left hand corner.

	Brother Sister	Aunt Uncle Nephew Niece	Great Aunt Uncle Nephew Niece	GG Aunt Uncle Nephew Niece	GGG Aunt Uncle Nephew Niece	GGGG Aunt Uncle Nephew Niece	GGGGG Aunt Uncle Nephew Niece
	Aunt Uncle Nephew Niece	FIRST Cousin	First Cousin Once Removed	First Cousin Twice Removed	First Cousin 3 Times Removed	First Cousin 4 Times Removed	First Cousin 5 Times Removed
	Great Aunt Uncle Nephew Niece	First Cousin Once Removed	SECOND Cousin	Second Cousin Once Removed	Second Cousin Twice Removed	Second Cousin 3 Times Removed	Second Cousin 4 Times Removed
	GG Aunt Uncle Nephew Niece	First Cousin Twice Removed	Second Cousin Once Removed	THIRD Cousin	Third Cousin Once Removed	Third Cousin Twice Removed	Third Cousin 3 Times Removed
	GGG Aunt Uncle Nephew Niece	First Cousin 3 Times Removed	Second Cousin Twice Removed	Third Cousin Once Removed	FOURTH Cousin	Fourth Cousin Once Removed	Fourth Cousin Twice Removed
	GGGG Aunt Uncle Nephew Niece	First Cousin 4 Times Removed	Second Cousin 3 Times Removed	Third Cousin Twice Removed	Fourth Cousin Once Removed	FIFTH Cousin	Fifth Cousin Once Removed
	GGGGG Aunt Uncle Nephew Niece	First Cousin 5 Times Removed	Second Cousin 4 Times Removed	Third Cousin 3 Times Removed	Fourth Cousin Twice Removed	Fifth Cousin Once Removed	SIXTH Cousin

Charts: Jean-Avite Doucet

Charts of consanguinity are included here to show the direct relationships that existed between the ancestors of my paternal grandfather, Jean-Avite (Harvey) Doucet.

Given the close nature of some of the relationships that existed, the reader will also be able to see how my grandfather was related to my grandmother.

Jean Avite (Harvey) Doucet and Beatrice Muise (grandparents)

François Mius 1770	Anne Anastasie Mius 1822	Jean Théophile Doucet 1867	Jean Avite Doucet 1896				
Charles Séraphin Mius 1803	Brother Sister	Aunt Uncle Nephew Niece	Great Aunt Uncle Nephew Niece	GG Aunt Uncle Nephew Niece	GGG Aunt Uncle Nephew Niece	GGGG Aunt Uncle Nephew Niece	GGGGG Aunt Uncle Nephew Niece
Rosalie Angèle Mius 1834	Aunt Uncle Nephew Niece	FIRST Cousin	First Cousin Once Removed	First Cousin Twice Removed	First Cousin 3 Times Removed	First Cousin 4 Times Removed	First Cousin 5 Times Removed
Peter Muise 1852	Great Aunt Uncle Nephew Niece	First Cousin Once Removed	SECOND Cousin	Second Cousin Once Removed	Second Cousin Twice Removed	Second Cousin 3 Times Removed	Second Cousin 4 Times Removed
Beatrice Muise 1898	GG Aunt Uncle Nephew Niece	First Cousin Twice Removed	**Second Cousin Once Removed**	THIRD Cousin	Third Cousin Once Removed	Third Cousin Twice Removed	Third Cousin 3 Times Removed
	GGG Aunt Uncle Nephew Niece	First Cousin 3 Times Removed	Second Cousin Twice Removed	Third Cousin Once Removed	FOURTH Cousin	Fourth Cousin Once Removed	Fourth Cousin Twice Removed
	GGGG Aunt Uncle Nephew Niece	First Cousin 4 Times Removed	Second Cousin 3 Times Removed	Third Cousin Twice Removed	Fourth Cousin Once Removed	FIFTH Cousin	Fifth Cousin Once Removed
	GGGGG Aunt Uncle Nephew Niece	First Cousin 5 Times Removed	Second Cousin 4 Times Removed	Third Cousin 3 Times Removed	Fourth Cousin Twice Removed	Fifth Cousin Once Removed	SIXTH Cousin

Jean Théophile (dit Câlin) Doucet and Adèle Dulain (G grandparents)

François Mius 1703	Marie Suzanne Mius 1758	Joseph Mathurin Doucet 1795	Michel Patrice Doucet 1817	Jean Théophile Doucet 1867			
Anne Mius 1736	Brother Sister	Aunt Uncle Nephew Niece	Great Aunt Uncle Nephew Niece	GG Aunt Uncle Nephew Niece	GGG Aunt Uncle Nephew Niece	GGGG Aunt Uncle Nephew Niece	GGGGG Aunt Uncle Nephew Niece
Marie Apoline Frontain 1770	Aunt Uncle Nephew Niece	FIRST Cousin	First Cousin Once Removed	First Cousin Twice Removed	First Cousin 3 Times Removed	First Cousin 4 Times Removed	First Cousin 5 Times Removed
Louis Cyprien Dulain 1806	Great Aunt Uncle Nephew Niece	First Cousin Once Removed	SECOND Cousin	Second Cousin Once Removed	Second Cousin Twice Removed	Second Cousin 3 Times Removed	Second Cousin 4 Times Removed
Adèle Dulain 1876	GG Aunt Uncle Nephew Niece	First Cousin Twice Removed	Second Cousin Once Removed	**THIRD Cousin**	Third Cousin Once Removed	Third Cousin Twice Removed	Third Cousin 3 Times Removed
	GGG Aunt Uncle Nephew Niece	First Cousin 3 Times Removed	Second Cousin Twice Removed	Third Cousin Once Removed	FOURTH Cousin	Fourth Cousin Once Removed	Fourth Cousin Twice Removed
	GGGG Aunt Uncle Nephew Niece	First Cousin 4 Times Removed	Second Cousin 3 Times Removed	Third Cousin Twice Removed	Fourth Cousin Once Removed	FIFTH Cousin	Fifth Cousin Once Removed
	GGGGG Aunt Uncle Nephew Niece	First Cousin 5 Times Removed	Second Cousin 4 Times Removed	Third Cousin 3 Times Removed	Fourth Cousin Twice Removed	Fifth Cousin Once Removed	SIXTH Cousin

Louis Cyprien Dulain and Anne Vitaline Mius (GG grandparents)

Joseph Mius d'Azy 1679	François Mius 1703	Anne Mius 1736	Marie Apoline Frontain 1770	Louis Cyprien Dulain 1806			
Jean Baptiste I Mius 1713	Brother Sister	Aunt Uncle Nephew Niece	Great Aunt Uncle Nephew Niece	GG Aunt Uncle Nephew Niece	GGG Aunt Uncle Nephew Niece	GGGG Aunt Uncle Nephew Niece	GGGGG Aunt Uncle Nephew Niece
Paul Mius 1755 or 1756	Aunt Uncle Nephew Niece	FIRST Cousin	First Cousin Once Removed	First Cousin Twice Removed	First Cousin 3 Times Removed	First Cousin 4 Times Removed	First Cousin 5 Times Removed
Anselme Mius	Great Aunt Uncle Nephew Niece	First Cousin Once Removed	SECOND Cousin	Second Cousin Once Removed	Second Cousin Twice Removed	Second Cousin 3 Times Removed	Second Cousin 4 Times Removed
Jean Cyrille Mius 1812	GG Aunt Uncle Nephew Niece	First Cousin Twice Removed	Second Cousin Once Removed	THIRD Cousin	Third Cousin Once Removed	Third Cousin Twice Removed	Third Cousin 3 Times Removed
Anne Vitaline Mius 1833	GGG Aunt Uncle Nephew Niece	First Cousin 3 Times Removed	Second Cousin Twice Removed	**Third Cousin Once Removed**	FOURTH Cousin	Fourth Cousin Once Removed	Fourth Cousin Twice Removed
	GGGG Aunt Uncle Nephew Niece	First Cousin 4 Times Removed	Second Cousin 3 Times Removed	Third Cousin Twice Removed	Fourth Cousin Once Removed	FIFTH Cousin	Fifth Cousin Once Removed
	GGGGG Aunt Uncle Nephew Niece	First Cousin 5 Times Removed	Second Cousin 4 Times Removed	Third Cousin 3 Times Removed	Fourth Cousin Twice Removed	Fifth Cousin Once Removed	SIXTH Cousin

Michel Patrice Doucet and Anne Anastasie Mius (GG grandparents)

François Mius 1703	Marie Suzanne Mius 1758	Joseph Mathurin Doucet 1795	Michel Patrice Doucet 1817				
Jean Pierre Mius 1743	Brother Sister	Aunt Uncle Nephew Niece	Great Aunt Uncle Nephew Niece	GG Aunt Uncle Nephew Niece	GGG Aunt Uncle Nephew Niece	GGGG Aunt Uncle Nephew Niece	GGGGG Aunt Uncle Nephew Niece
François Mius 1770	Aunt Uncle Nephew Niece	FIRST Cousin	First Cousin Once Removed	First Cousin Twice Removed	First Cousin 3 Times Removed	First Cousin 4 Times Removed	First Cousin 5 Times Removed
Anne Anastasie Mius 1822	Great Aunt Uncle Nephew Niece	First Cousin Once Removed	**SECOND Cousin**	Second Cousin Once Removed	Second Cousin Twice Removed	Second Cousin 3 Times Removed	Second Cousin 4 Times Removed
	GG Aunt Uncle Nephew Niece	First Cousin Twice Removed	Second Cousin Once Removed	THIRD Cousin	Third Cousin Once Removed	Third Cousin Twice Removed	Third Cousin 3 Times Removed
	GGG Aunt Uncle Nephew Niece	First Cousin 3 Times Removed	Second Cousin Twice Removed	Third Cousin Once Removed	FOURTH Cousin	Fourth Cousin Once Removed	Fourth Cousin Twice Removed
	GGGG Aunt Uncle Nephew Niece	First Cousin 4 Times Removed	Second Cousin 3 Times Removed	Third Cousin Twice Removed	Fourth Cousin Once Removed	FIFTH Cousin	Fifth Cousin Once Removed
	GGGGG Aunt Uncle Nephew Niece	First Cousin 5 Times Removed	Second Cousin 4 Times Removed	Third Cousin 3 Times Removed	Fourth Cousin Twice Removed	Fifth Cousin Once Removed	SIXTH Cousin

Jean Cyrille (dit Coco) Mius and Scholastique Doucet (GGG grandparents)

Joseph Mius d'Azy 1679	Jean Baptiste I Mius 1713	Paul Mius 1755 or 1756	Anselme Mius	Jean Cyrille Mius 1812			
Joseph Mius 1700	Brother Sister	Aunt Uncle Nephew Niece	Great Aunt Uncle Nephew Niece	GG Aunt Uncle Nephew Niece	GGG Aunt Uncle Nephew Niece	GGGG Aunt Uncle Nephew Niece	GGGGG Aunt Uncle Nephew Niece
Louis Mius 1746	Aunt Uncle Nephew Niece	FIRST Cousin	First Cousin Once Removed	First Cousin Twice Removed	First Cousin 3 Times Removed	First Cousin 4 Times Removed	First Cousin 5 Times Removed
Anne Mius 1792	Great Aunt Uncle Nephew Niece	First Cousin Once Removed	SECOND Cousin	Second Cousin Once Removed	Second Cousin Twice Removed	Second Cousin 3 Times Removed	Second Cousin 4 Times Removed
Scholastique Doucet 1812	GG Aunt Uncle Nephew Niece	First Cousin Twice Removed	Second Cousin Once Removed	**THIRD Cousin**	Third Cousin Once Removed	Third Cousin Twice Removed	Third Cousin 3 Times Removed
	GGG Aunt Uncle Nephew Niece	First Cousin 3 Times Removed	Second Cousin Twice Removed	Third Cousin Once Removed	FOURTH Cousin	Fourth Cousin Once Removed	Fourth Cousin Twice Removed
	GGGG Aunt Uncle Nephew Niece	First Cousin 4 Times Removed	Second Cousin 3 Times Removed	Third Cousin Twice Removed	Fourth Cousin Once Removed	FIFTH Cousin	Fifth Cousin Once Removed
	GGGGG Aunt Uncle Nephew Niece	First Cousin 5 Times Removed	Second Cousin 4 Times Removed	Third Cousin 3 Times Removed	Fourth Cousin Twice Removed	Fifth Cousin Once Removed	SIXTH Cousin

Joseph Mathurin Doucet and Angélique Mathilde Mius (GGG grandparents)

Joseph Mius d'Azy 1679	François Mius 1703	Marie Suzanne Mius 1758	Joseph Mathurin Doucet 1795				
Jean Baptiste I Mius 1713	Brother Sister	Aunt Uncle Nephew Niece	Great Aunt Uncle Nephew Niece	GG Aunt Uncle Nephew Niece	GGG Aunt Uncle Nephew Niece	GGGG Aunt Uncle Nephew Niece	GGGGG Aunt Uncle Nephew Niece
Paul Mius 1755 or 1756	Aunt Uncle Nephew Niece	FIRST Cousin	First Cousin Once Removed	First Cousin Twice Removed	First Cousin 3 Times Removed	First Cousin 4 Times Removed	First Cousin 5 Times Removed
Angélique Mathilde Mius 1795	Great Aunt Uncle Nephew Niece	First Cousin Once Removed	**SECOND Cousin**	Second Cousin Once Removed	Second Cousin Twice Removed	Second Cousin 3 Times Removed	Second Cousin 4 Times Removed
	GG Aunt Uncle Nephew Niece	First Cousin Twice Removed	Second Cousin Once Removed	THIRD Cousin	Third Cousin Once Removed	Third Cousin Twice Removed	Third Cousin 3 Times Removed
	GGG Aunt Uncle Nephew Niece	First Cousin 3 Times Removed	Second Cousin Twice Removed	Third Cousin Once Removed	FOURTH Cousin	Fourth Cousin Once Removed	Fourth Cousin Twice Removed
	GGGG Aunt Uncle Nephew Niece	First Cousin 4 Times Removed	Second Cousin 3 Times Removed	Third Cousin Twice Removed	Fourth Cousin Once Removed	FIFTH Cousin	Fifth Cousin Once Removed
	GGGGG Aunt Uncle Nephew Niece	First Cousin 5 Times Removed	Second Cousin 4 Times Removed	Third Cousin 3 Times Removed	Fourth Cousin Twice Removed	Fifth Cousin Once Removed	SIXTH Cousin

François Mius and Marie Osithe O'Bird (Hubbard) (GGG grandparents)

Joseph Mius d'Azy 1679	François Mius 1703	Jean Pierre Mius 1743	François Mius 1770				
Charles Amand I Mius 1702	Brother Sister	Aunt Uncle Nephew Niece	Great Aunt Uncle Nephew Niece	GG Aunt Uncle Nephew Niece	GGG Aunt Uncle Nephew Niece	GGGG Aunt Uncle Nephew Niece	GGGGG Aunt Uncle Nephew Niece
Madeleine Modeste Mius 1742	Aunt Uncle Nephew Niece	FIRST Cousin	First Cousin Once Removed	First Cousin Twice Removed	First Cousin 3 Times Removed	First Cousin 4 Times Removed	First Cousin 5 Times Removed
Marie Osithe O'Bird 1775	Great Aunt Uncle Nephew Niece	First Cousin Once Removed	**SECOND Cousin**	Second Cousin Once Removed	Second Cousin Twice Removed	Second Cousin 3 Times Removed	Second Cousin 4 Times Removed
	GG Aunt Uncle Nephew Niece	First Cousin Twice Removed	Second Cousin Once Removed	THIRD Cousin	Third Cousin Once Removed	Third Cousin Twice Removed	Third Cousin 3 Times Removed
	GGG Aunt Uncle Nephew Niece	First Cousin 3 Times Removed	Second Cousin Twice Removed	Third Cousin Once Removed	FOURTH Cousin	Fourth Cousin Once Removed	Fourth Cousin Twice Removed
	GGGG Aunt Uncle Nephew Niece	First Cousin 4 Times Removed	Second Cousin 3 Times Removed	Third Cousin Twice Removed	Fourth Cousin Once Removed	FIFTH Cousin	Fifth Cousin Once Removed
	GGGGG Aunt Uncle Nephew Niece	First Cousin 5 Times Removed	Second Cousin 4 Times Removed	Third Cousin 3 Times Removed	Fourth Cousin Twice Removed	Fifth Cousin Once Removed	SIXTH Cousin

Anselme Mius and Marguerite Mius (GGGG grandparents)

Joseph Mius d'Azy 1679	Jean Baptiste I Mius 1713	Paul Mius 1755 or 1756	Anselme Mius				
François Mius 1703	Brother Sister	Aunt Uncle Nephew Niece	Great Aunt Uncle Nephew Niece	GG Aunt Uncle Nephew Niece	GGG Aunt Uncle Nephew Niece	GGGG Aunt Uncle Nephew Niece	GGGGG Aunt Uncle Nephew Niece
Jean Pierre Mius 1743	Aunt Uncle Nephew Niece	FIRST Cousin	First Cousin Once Removed	First Cousin Twice Removed	First Cousin 3 Times Removed	First Cousin 4 Times Removed	First Cousin 5 Times Removed
Marguerite Mius	Great Aunt Uncle Nephew Niece	First Cousin Once Removed	**SECOND Cousin**	Second Cousin Once Removed	Second Cousin Twice Removed	Second Cousin 3 Times Removed	Second Cousin 4 Times Removed
	GG Aunt Uncle Nephew Niece	First Cousin Twice Removed	Second Cousin Once Removed	THIRD Cousin	Third Cousin Once Removed	Third Cousin Twice Removed	Third Cousin 3 Times Removed
	GGG Aunt Uncle Nephew Niece	First Cousin 3 Times Removed	Second Cousin Twice Removed	Third Cousin Once Removed	FOURTH Cousin	Fourth Cousin Once Removed	Fourth Cousin Twice Removed
	GGGG Aunt Uncle Nephew Niece	First Cousin 4 Times Removed	Second Cousin 3 Times Removed	Third Cousin Twice Removed	Fourth Cousin Once Removed	FIFTH Cousin	Fifth Cousin Once Removed
	GGGGG Aunt Uncle Nephew Niece	First Cousin 5 Times Removed	Second Cousin 4 Times Removed	Third Cousin 3 Times Removed	Fourth Cousin Twice Removed	Fifth Cousin Once Removed	SIXTH Cousin

Charles (dit Tania) Doucet and Anne Mius (GGGG grandparents)

Joseph Mius d'Azy 1679	Charles Amand I Mius 1702	Félicité Mius 1745	Charles (Tania) Doucet 1788				
Joseph Mius 1700	Brother Sister	Aunt Uncle Nephew Niece	Great Aunt Uncle Nephew Niece	GG Aunt Uncle Nephew Niece	GGG Aunt Uncle Nephew Niece	GGGG Aunt Uncle Nephew Niece	GGGGG Aunt Uncle Nephew Niece
Louis Mius 1746	Aunt Uncle Nephew Niece	FIRST Cousin	First Cousin Once Removed	First Cousin Twice Removed	First Cousin 3 Times Removed	First Cousin 4 Times Removed	First Cousin 5 Times Removed
Anne Mius 1792	Great Aunt Uncle Nephew Niece	First Cousin Once Removed	**SECOND Cousin**	Second Cousin Once Removed	Second Cousin Twice Removed	Second Cousin 3 Times Removed	Second Cousin 4 Times Removed
	GG Aunt Uncle Nephew Niece	First Cousin Twice Removed	Second Cousin Once Removed	THIRD Cousin	Third Cousin Once Removed	Third Cousin Twice Removed	Third Cousin 3 Times Removed
	GGG Aunt Uncle Nephew Niece	First Cousin 3 Times Removed	Second Cousin Twice Removed	Third Cousin Once Removed	FOURTH Cousin	Fourth Cousin Once Removed	Fourth Cousin Twice Removed
	GGGG Aunt Uncle Nephew Niece	First Cousin 4 Times Removed	Second Cousin 3 Times Removed	Third Cousin Twice Removed	Fourth Cousin Once Removed	FIFTH Cousin	Fifth Cousin Once Removed
	GGGGG Aunt Uncle Nephew Niece	First Cousin 5 Times Removed	Second Cousin 4 Times Removed	Third Cousin 3 Times Removed	Fourth Cousin Twice Removed	Fifth Cousin Once Removed	SIXTH Cousin

Charts: Beatrice Muise

Charts of consanguinity are included here to show the direct relationships that existed between the ancestors of my paternal grandmother, Beatrice Muise.

Given the close nature of some of the relationships that existed, the reader will also be able to see how my grandmother was related to my grandfather.

Beatrice Muise and Jean Avite (Harvey) Doucet (grandparents)

François Mius 1770	Anne Anastasie Mius 1822	Jean Théophile Doucet 1867	Jean Avite Doucet 1896				
Charles Séraphin Mius 1803	Brother Sister	Aunt Uncle Nephew Niece	Great Aunt Uncle Nephew Niece	GG Aunt Uncle Nephew Niece	GGG Aunt Uncle Nephew Niece	GGGG Aunt Uncle Nephew Niece	GGGGG Aunt Uncle Nephew Niece
Rosalie Angèle Mius 1834	Aunt Uncle Nephew Niece	FIRST Cousin	First Cousin Once Removed	First Cousin Twice Removed	First Cousin 3 Times Removed	First Cousin 4 Times Removed	First Cousin 5 Times Removed
Peter Muise 1852	Great Aunt Uncle Nephew Niece	First Cousin Once Removed	SECOND Cousin	Second Cousin Once Removed	Second Cousin Twice Removed	Second Cousin 3 Times Removed	Second Cousin 4 Times Removed
Beatrice Muise 1898	GG Aunt Uncle Nephew Niece	First Cousin Twice Removed	**Second Cousin Once Removed**	THIRD Cousin	Third Cousin Once Removed	Third Cousin Twice Removed	Third Cousin 3 Times Removed
	GGG Aunt Uncle Nephew Niece	First Cousin 3 Times Removed	Second Cousin Twice Removed	Third Cousin Once Removed	FOURTH Cousin	Fourth Cousin Once Removed	Fourth Cousin Twice Removed
	GGGG Aunt Uncle Nephew Niece	First Cousin 4 Times Removed	Second Cousin 3 Times Removed	Third Cousin Twice Removed	Fourth Cousin Once Removed	FIFTH Cousin	Fifth Cousin Once Removed
	GGGGG Aunt Uncle Nephew Niece	First Cousin 5 Times Removed	Second Cousin 4 Times Removed	Third Cousin 3 Times Removed	Fourth Cousin Twice Removed	Fifth Cousin Once Removed	SIXTH Cousin

Peter Muise and Martha Roach (G grandparents)

Jean Pierre Mius 1743	Jean Baptiste Mius	Pierre Eusèbe Mius 1801	Vital Mius 1828	Peter Muise 1852			
Cécile Mius	Brother Sister	Aunt Uncle Nephew Niece	Great Aunt Uncle Nephew Niece	GG Aunt Uncle Nephew Niece	GGG Aunt Uncle Nephew Niece	GGGG Aunt Uncle Nephew Niece	GGGGG Aunt Uncle Nephew Niece
Jean Séraphin Deveau 1799	Aunt Uncle Nephew Niece	FIRST Cousin	First Cousin Once Removed	First Cousin Twice Removed	First Cousin 3 Times Removed	First Cousin 4 Times Removed	First Cousin 5 Times Removed
Marie Elizabeth Deveau 1830	Great Aunt Uncle Nephew Niece	First Cousin Once Removed	SECOND Cousin	Second Cousin Once Removed	Second Cousin Twice Removed	Second Cousin 3 Times Removed	Second Cousin 4 Times Removed
Martha Roach 1862	GG Aunt Uncle Nephew Niece	First Cousin Twice Removed	Second Cousin Once Removed	**THIRD Cousin**	Third Cousin Once Removed	Third Cousin Twice Removed	Third Cousin 3 Times Removed
	GGG Aunt Uncle Nephew Niece	First Cousin 3 Times Removed	Second Cousin Twice Removed	Third Cousin Once Removed	FOURTH Cousin	Fourth Cousin Once Removed	Fourth Cousin Twice Removed
	GGGG Aunt Uncle Nephew Niece	First Cousin 4 Times Removed	Second Cousin 3 Times Removed	Third Cousin Twice Removed	Fourth Cousin Once Removed	FIFTH Cousin	Fifth Cousin Once Removed
	GGGGG Aunt Uncle Nephew Niece	First Cousin 5 Times Removed	Second Cousin 4 Times Removed	Third Cousin 3 Times Removed	Fourth Cousin Twice Removed	Fifth Cousin Once Removed	SIXTH Cousin

Vital Mius and Rosalie Angèle Mius (GG grandparents)

Jean Pierre Mius 1743	Jean Baptiste Mius	Pierre Eusèbe Mius 1801	Vital Mius 1828				
François Mius 1770	Brother Sister	Aunt Uncle Nephew Niece	Great Aunt Uncle Nephew Niece	GG Aunt Uncle Nephew Niece	GGG Aunt Uncle Nephew Niece	GGGG Aunt Uncle Nephew Niece	GGGGG Aunt Uncle Nephew Niece
Charles Séraphin Mius 1803	Aunt Uncle Nephew Niece	FIRST Cousin	First Cousin Once Removed	First Cousin Twice Removed	First Cousin 3 Times Removed	First Cousin 4 Times Removed	First Cousin 5 Times Removed
Rosalie Angèle Mius 1834	Great Aunt Uncle Nephew Niece	First Cousin Once Removed	**SECOND Cousin**	Second Cousin Once Removed	Second Cousin Twice Removed	Second Cousin 3 Times Removed	Second Cousin 4 Times Removed
	GG Aunt Uncle Nephew Niece	First Cousin Twice Removed	Second Cousin Once Removed	THIRD Cousin	Third Cousin Once Removed	Third Cousin Twice Removed	Third Cousin 3 Times Removed
	GGG Aunt Uncle Nephew Niece	First Cousin 3 Times Removed	Second Cousin Twice Removed	Third Cousin Once Removed	FOURTH Cousin	Fourth Cousin Once Removed	Fourth Cousin Twice Removed
	GGGG Aunt Uncle Nephew Niece	First Cousin 4 Times Removed	Second Cousin 3 Times Removed	Third Cousin Twice Removed	Fourth Cousin Once Removed	FIFTH Cousin	Fifth Cousin Once Removed
	GGGGG Aunt Uncle Nephew Niece	First Cousin 5 Times Removed	Second Cousin 4 Times Removed	Third Cousin 3 Times Removed	Fourth Cousin Twice Removed	Fifth Cousin Once Removed	SIXTH Cousin

Pierre Eusèbe Mius and Scholastique Boutier (GGG grandparents)

François Mius 1703	Jean Pierre Mius 1743	Jean Baptiste Mius	Pierre Eusèbe Mius				
Marie Suzanne Mius 1758	Brother Sister	Aunt Uncle Nephew Niece	Great Aunt Uncle Nephew Niece	GG Aunt Uncle Nephew Niece	GGG Aunt Uncle Nephew Niece	GGGG Aunt Uncle Nephew Niece	GGGGG Aunt Uncle Nephew Niece
Anne Marguerite Doucet	Aunt Uncle Nephew Niece	FIRST Cousin	First Cousin Once Removed	First Cousin Twice Removed	First Cousin 3 Times Removed	First Cousin 4 Times Removed	First Cousin 5 Times Removed
Scholastique Boutier	Great Aunt Uncle Nephew Niece	First Cousin Once Removed	**SECOND Cousin**	Second Cousin Once Removed	Second Cousin Twice Removed	Second Cousin 3 Times Removed	Second Cousin 4 Times Removed
	GG Aunt Uncle Nephew Niece	First Cousin Twice Removed	Second Cousin Once Removed	THIRD Cousin	Third Cousin Once Removed	Third Cousin Twice Removed	Third Cousin 3 Times Removed
	GGG Aunt Uncle Nephew Niece	First Cousin 3 Times Removed	Second Cousin Twice Removed	Third Cousin Once Removed	FOURTH Cousin	Fourth Cousin Once Removed	Fourth Cousin Twice Removed
	GGGG Aunt Uncle Nephew Niece	First Cousin 4 Times Removed	Second Cousin 3 Times Removed	Third Cousin Twice Removed	Fourth Cousin Once Removed	FIFTH Cousin	Fifth Cousin Once Removed
	GGGGG Aunt Uncle Nephew Niece	First Cousin 5 Times Removed	Second Cousin 4 Times Removed	Third Cousin 3 Times Removed	Fourth Cousin Twice Removed	Fifth Cousin Once Removed	SIXTH Cousin

Jean Séraphin Deveau and Marie Madeleine O'Bird (Hubbard) (GGG grandparents)

François Mius 1703	Jean Pierre Mius 1743	Cécile Mius	Jean Séraphin Deveau 1799				
Marie Suzanne Mius 1758	Brother Sister	Aunt Uncle Nephew Niece	Great Aunt Uncle Nephew Niece	GG Aunt Uncle Nephew Niece	GGG Aunt Uncle Nephew Niece	GGGG Aunt Uncle Nephew Niece	GGGGG Aunt Uncle Nephew Niece
Marie Anne Doucet	Aunt Uncle Nephew Niece	FIRST Cousin	First Cousin Once Removed	First Cousin Twice Removed	First Cousin 3 Times Removed	First Cousin 4 Times Removed	First Cousin 5 Times Removed
Marie Madeleine O'Bird 1802	Great Aunt Uncle Nephew Niece	First Cousin Once Removed	**SECOND Cousin**	Second Cousin Once Removed	Second Cousin Twice Removed	Second Cousin 3 Times Removed	Second Cousin 4 Times Removed
	GG Aunt Uncle Nephew Niece	First Cousin Twice Removed	Second Cousin Once Removed	THIRD Cousin	Third Cousin Once Removed	Third Cousin Twice Removed	Third Cousin 3 Times Removed
	GGG Aunt Uncle Nephew Niece	First Cousin 3 Times Removed	Second Cousin Twice Removed	Third Cousin Once Removed	FOURTH Cousin	Fourth Cousin Once Removed	Fourth Cousin Twice Removed
	GGGG Aunt Uncle Nephew Niece	First Cousin 4 Times Removed	Second Cousin 3 Times Removed	Third Cousin Twice Removed	Fourth Cousin Once Removed	FIFTH Cousin	Fifth Cousin Once Removed
	GGGGG Aunt Uncle Nephew Niece	First Cousin 5 Times Removed	Second Cousin 4 Times Removed	Third Cousin 3 Times Removed	Fourth Cousin Twice Removed	Fifth Cousin Once Removed	SIXTH Cousin

Charles Séraphin Mius and Marguerite Mius (GGG grandparents)

Joseph Mius d'Azy 1679	François Mius 1703	Jean Pierre Mius 1743	François Mius 1770	Charles Séraphin Mius 1803			
Jean Baptiste I Mius 1713	Brother Sister	Aunt Uncle Nephew Niece	Great Aunt Uncle Nephew Niece	GG Aunt Uncle Nephew Niece	GGG Aunt Uncle Nephew Niece	GGGG Aunt Uncle Nephew Niece	GGGGG Aunt Uncle Nephew Niece
Paul Mius 1755 or 1756	Aunt Uncle Nephew Niece	FIRST Cousin	First Cousin Once Removed	First Cousin Twice Removed	First Cousin 3 Times Removed	First Cousin 4 Times Removed	First Cousin 5 Times Removed
Marguerite Mius 1801	Great Aunt Uncle Nephew Niece	First Cousin Once Removed	SECOND Cousin	**Second Cousin Once Removed**	Second Cousin Twice Removed	Second Cousin 3 Times Removed	Second Cousin 4 Times Removed
	GG Aunt Uncle Nephew Niece	First Cousin Twice Removed	Second Cousin Once Removed	THIRD Cousin	Third Cousin Once Removed	Third Cousin Twice Removed	Third Cousin 3 Times Removed
	GGG Aunt Uncle Nephew Niece	First Cousin 3 Times Removed	Second Cousin Twice Removed	Third Cousin Once Removed	FOURTH Cousin	Fourth Cousin Once Removed	Fourth Cousin Twice Removed
	GGGG Aunt Uncle Nephew Niece	First Cousin 4 Times Removed	Second Cousin 3 Times Removed	Third Cousin Twice Removed	Fourth Cousin Once Removed	FIFTH Cousin	Fifth Cousin Once Removed
	GGGGG Aunt Uncle Nephew Niece	First Cousin 5 Times Removed	Second Cousin 4 Times Removed	Third Cousin 3 Times Removed	Fourth Cousin Twice Removed	Fifth Cousin Once Removed	SIXTH Cousin

Jean O'Bird (Hubbard) and Marie Anne Doucet (GGGG grandparents)

Joseph Mius d'Azy 1679	Charles Amand I Mius 1702	Madeleine Modeste Mius 1742	Jean O'Bird 1774				
François Mius 1703	Brother Sister	Aunt Uncle Nephew Niece	Great Aunt Uncle Nephew Niece	GG Aunt Uncle Nephew Niece	GGG Aunt Uncle Nephew Niece	GGGG Aunt Uncle Nephew Niece	GGGGG Aunt Uncle Nephew Niece
Marie Suzanne Mius 1758	Aunt Uncle Nephew Niece	FIRST Cousin	First Cousin Once Removed	First Cousin Twice Removed	First Cousin 3 Times Removed	First Cousin 4 Times Removed	First Cousin 5 Times Removed
Marie Anne Doucet	Great Aunt Uncle Nephew Niece	First Cousin Once Removed	**SECOND Cousin**	Second Cousin Once Removed	Second Cousin Twice Removed	Second Cousin 3 Times Removed	Second Cousin 4 Times Removed
	GG Aunt Uncle Nephew Niece	First Cousin Twice Removed	Second Cousin Once Removed	THIRD Cousin	Third Cousin Once Removed	Third Cousin Twice Removed	Third Cousin 3 Times Removed
	GGG Aunt Uncle Nephew Niece	First Cousin 3 Times Removed	Second Cousin Twice Removed	Third Cousin Once Removed	FOURTH Cousin	Fourth Cousin Once Removed	Fourth Cousin Twice Removed
	GGGG Aunt Uncle Nephew Niece	First Cousin 4 Times Removed	Second Cousin 3 Times Removed	Third Cousin Twice Removed	Fourth Cousin Once Removed	FIFTH Cousin	Fifth Cousin Once Removed
	GGGGG Aunt Uncle Nephew Niece	First Cousin 5 Times Removed	Second Cousin 4 Times Removed	Third Cousin 3 Times Removed	Fourth Cousin Twice Removed	Fifth Cousin Once Removed	SIXTH Cousin

François Mius and Marie Osithe O'Bird (Hubbard) (GGGG grandparents)

Joseph Mius d'Azy 1679	François Mius 1703	Jean Pierre Mius 1743	François Mius 1770				
Charles Amand I Mius 1702	Brother Sister	Aunt Uncle Nephew Niece	Great Aunt Uncle Nephew Niece	GG Aunt Uncle Nephew Niece	GGG Aunt Uncle Nephew Niece	GGGG Aunt Uncle Nephew Niece	GGGGG Aunt Uncle Nephew Niece
Madeleine Modeste Mius 1742	Aunt Uncle Nephew Niece	FIRST Cousin	First Cousin Once Removed	First Cousin Twice Removed	First Cousin 3 Times Removed	First Cousin 4 Times Removed	First Cousin 5 Times Removed
Marie Osithe O'Bird 1775	Great Aunt Uncle Nephew Niece	First Cousin Once Removed	**SECOND Cousin**	Second Cousin Once Removed	Second Cousin Twice Removed	Second Cousin 3 Times Removed	Second Cousin 4 Times Removed
	GG Aunt Uncle Nephew Niece	First Cousin Twice Removed	Second Cousin Once Removed	THIRD Cousin	Third Cousin Once Removed	Third Cousin Twice Removed	Third Cousin 3 Times Removed
	GGG Aunt Uncle Nephew Niece	First Cousin 3 Times Removed	Second Cousin Twice Removed	Third Cousin Once Removed	FOURTH Cousin	Fourth Cousin Once Removed	Fourth Cousin Twice Removed
	GGGG Aunt Uncle Nephew Niece	First Cousin 4 Times Removed	Second Cousin 3 Times Removed	Third Cousin Twice Removed	Fourth Cousin Once Removed	FIFTH Cousin	Fifth Cousin Once Removed
	GGGGG Aunt Uncle Nephew Niece	First Cousin 5 Times Removed	Second Cousin 4 Times Removed	Third Cousin 3 Times Removed	Fourth Cousin Twice Removed	Fifth Cousin Once Removed	SIXTH Cousin

Aboriginal Ancestry

PATERNAL 1
Courtesy of mtDNA testing, this unidentified first Mi'kmaq spouse of Philippe Mius dit d'Azy shows as belonging to HAPLOGROUP A2f [651] which is a native haplogroup.

1. Philippe Mius dit d'Azy and first Amérindien wife

2. Joseph Mius dit d'Azy and Marie Amirault

This couple has been genetically traced to the fatal Niemann-Pick (variant C) disease as per the French Acadian population of Yarmouth County, Nova Scotia.

Further lines of descent continue from 4 of the 5 sons of Joseph and Marie, namely

* François Mius and Jeanne Duon

* Jean Baptiste I Mius and Marie Josèphe Surette

* Charles Amand I Mius and Marie Marthe Hébert

* Joseph Mius and Marie Josèphe Préjean

The irony of my Doucet ancestry is that I have far more Mius/Muise individuals than I have Doucet, and yet they are all related.

The only son that I do not descend from is the youngest, Charles Benjamin Mius, who, along with his wife, Marie Josèphe Guédry, died at sea (1758-1759).

---

[651] https://www.familytreedna.com/public/mothersofacadia/default.aspx?section=mtresults

PATERNAL 1A

Courtesy of mtDNA Testing, this unidentified first Mi'kmaq spouse of Philippe Mius dit d'Azy shows as belonging to HAPLOGROUP A2f [652] which is a native haplogroup.

1. Philippe Mius dit d'Azy and first Amérindien wife

2. Joseph Mius dit d'Azy and Marie Amirault

This couple has been genetically traced to the fatal Niemann-Pick (variant C) disease as per the French Acadian population of Yarmouth County, Nova Scotia.

3. François Mius and Jeanne Duon

4. Marie Suzanne Mius and Michel Doucet

This couple has been genetically traced to Alström Syndrome as per the French Acadian population of Yarmouth County, Nova Scotia.

5. Joseph Mathurin Doucet and Angélique Mathilde Mius

6. Michel Patrice (dit L'Anglais) Doucet and Anne Anastasie (dite Nanette) Mius

7. Théophile (dit Câlin) Doucet and Adèle Dulain

8. Jean Avite (called Harvey) Doucette and Beatrice Muise

9. Albert Doucette and Anne Elizabeth Feeley

10. Michele Anne Doucette

---

[652] https://www.familytreedna.com/public/mothersofacadia/default.aspx?section=mtresults

PATERNAL 1A
Courtesy of mtDNA testing, this unidentified first Mi'kmaq spouse of Philippe Mius dit d'Azy shows as belonging to HAPLOGROUP A2f [653] which is a native haplogroup.
1. Philippe Mius dit d'Azy and first Amérindien wife
2. Joseph Mius dit d'Azy and Marie Amirault
This couple has been genetically traced to the fatal Niemann-Pick (variant C) disease as per the French Acadian population of Yarmouth County, Nova Scotia.
3. François Mius and Jeanne Duon
4. Anne Mius and Julien Alexandre Frontain
5. Marie Apoline (dite Pauline) Frontain and Louis Dulain
6. Louis Cyprien Dulain and Anne Vitaline Mius
7. Adèle Dulain and Théophile (dit Câlin) Doucet
8. Jean Avite (called Harvey) Doucette and Beatrice Muise
9. Albert Doucette and Anne Elizabeth Feeley
10. Michele Anne Doucette

---

[653] https://www.familytreedna.com/public/mothersofacadia/default.aspx?section=mtresults

PATERNAL 1A
Courtesy of mtDNA testing, this unidentified first Mi'kmaq spouse of Philippe Mius dit d'Azy shows as belonging to **HAPLOGROUP A2f** [654] which is a native haplogroup.

1. Philippe Mius dit d'Azy and first Amérindien wife

2. Joseph Mius dit d'Azy and Marie Amirault

This couple has been genetically traced to the fatal Niemann-Pick (variant C) disease as per the French Acadian population of Yarmouth County, Nova Scotia.

3. François Mius and Jeanne Duon

4. Jean Pierre Mius and Anne Doucet

5. François Mius and Marie O'Bird (Hubbard)

6. Anne Anastasie (dite Nanette) Mius and Michel Patrice (dit L'Anglais) Doucet

7. Théophile (dit Câlin) Doucet and Adèle Dulain

8. Jean Avite (called Harvey) Doucette and Beatrice Muise

9. Albert Doucette and Anne Elizabeth Feeley

10. Michele Anne Doucette

---

[654] https://www.familytreedna.com/public/mothersofacadia/default.aspx?section=mtresults

PATERNAL 1A
Courtesy of mtDNA testing, this unidentified first Mi'kmaq spouse of Philippe Mius dit d'Azy shows as belonging to **HAPLOGROUP A2f** [655] which is a native haplogroup.

1. Philippe Mius dit d'Azy and first Amérindien wife

2. Joseph Mius dit d'Azy and Marie Amirault

This couple has been genetically traced to the fatal Niemann-Pick (variant C) disease as per the French Acadian population of Yarmouth County, Nova Scotia.

3. François Mius and Jeanne Duon

4. Jean Pierre Mius and Anne Doucet

5. François Mius and Marie O'Bird (Hubbard)

6. Charles Séraphin Mius and Marguerite Mius

7. Rosalie Angèle (dite Angélique) Mius and Vital Mius

8. Peter Muise and Martha Roach

9. Beatrice Muise and Jean-Avite (called Harvey) Doucette

10. Albert Doucette and Anne Elizabeth Feeley

11. Michele Anne Doucette

---

[655] https://www.familytreedna.com/public/mothersofacadia/default.aspx?section=mtresults

PATERNAL 1A

Courtesy of mtDNA testing, this unidentified first Mi'kmaq spouse of Philippe Mius dit d'Azy shows as belonging to HAPLOGROUP A2f [656] which is a native haplogroup.

1. Philippe Mius dit d'Azy and first Amérindien wife

2. Joseph Mius dit d'Azy and Marie Amirault

This couple has been genetically traced to the fatal Niemann-Pick (variant C) disease as per the French Acadian population of Yarmouth County, Nova Scotia.

3. François Mius and Jeanne Duon

4. Jean Pierre Mius and Anne Doucet

5. Cécile Mius and François Christophe (dit Couchique) Deveau

6. Jean Séraphin Deveau and Marie Madeleine O'Bird (Hubbard)

7. Marie Elizabeth Deveau and John William Henry Roach

8. Martha Roach and Peter Muise

9. Beatrice Muise and Jean-Avite (called Harvey) Doucette

10. Albert Doucette and Anne Elizabeth Feeley

11. Michele Anne Doucette

---

[656] https://www.familytreedna.com/public/mothersofacadia/default.aspx?section=mtresults

PATERNAL 1A

Courtesy of mtDNA testing, this unidentified first Mi'kmaq spouse of Philippe Mius dit d'Azy shows as belonging to HAPLOGROUP A2f [657] which is a native haplogroup.

1. Philippe Mius dit d'Azy and first Amérindien wife

2. Joseph Mius dit d'Azy and Marie Amirault

This couple has been genetically traced to the fatal Niemann-Pick (variant C) disease as per the French Acadian population of Yarmouth County, Nova Scotia.

3. François Mius and Jeanne Duon

4. Jean Pierre Mius and Anne Doucet

5. Jean Baptiste (dit Petit John) Mius and Marguerite Robichaud

6. Pierre Eusèbe (dit Petit John) Mius and Scholastique Boutier

7. Vital Mius and Rosalie Angèle (dite Angélique) Mius

8. Peter Muise and Martha Roach

9. Beatrice Muise and Jean-Avite (called Harvey) Doucette

10. Albert Doucette and Anne Elizabeth Feeley

11. Michele Anne Doucette

---

[657] https://www.familytreedna.com/public/mothersofacadia/default.aspx?section=mtresults

PATERNAL 1A Courtesy of mtDNA testing, this unidentified first Mi'kmaq spouse of Philippe Mius dit d'Azy shows as belonging to HAPLOGROUP A2f [658] which is a native haplogroup.
1. Philippe Mius dit d'Azy and first Amérindien wife 2. Joseph Mius dit d'Azy and Marie Amirault This couple has been genetically traced to the fatal Niemann-Pick (variant C) disease as per the French Acadian population of Yarmouth County, Nova Scotia. 3. François Mius and Jeanne Duon 4. Jean Pierre Mius and Anne Doucet 5. Marguerite Mius and Anselme Mius 6. Jean Cyrille (dit Coco) Mius and Scholastique Doucet 7. Anne Vitaline Mius and Louis Cyprien Dulain 8. Adèle Dulain and Théophile (dit Câlin) Doucet 9. Jean Avite (called Harvey) Doucette and Beatrice Muise 10. Albert Doucette and Anne Elizabeth Feeley 11. Michele Anne Doucette

---

[658] https://www.familytreedna.com/public/mothersofacadia/default.aspx?section=mtresults

PATERNAL 1B

Courtesy of mtDNA testing, this unidentified first Mi'kmaq spouse of Philippe Mius dit d'Azy shows as belonging to HAPLOGROUP A2f [659] which is a native haplogroup.

1. Philippe Mius dit d'Azy and first Amérindien wife

2. Joseph Mius dit d'Azy and Marie Amirault

This couple has been genetically traced to the fatal Niemann-Pick (variant C) disease as per the French Acadian population of Yarmouth County, Nova Scotia.

3. Jean Baptiste I Mius and Marie Josèphe Surette

4. Paul Mius and Marie LeBlanc

5. Angélique Mathilde Mius and Joseph Mathurin Doucet

6. Michel Patrice (dit L'Anglais) Doucet and Anne Anastasie (dite Nanette) Mius

7. Théophile (dit Câlin) Doucet and Adèle Dulain

8. Jean Avite (called Harvey) Doucette and Beatrice Muise

9. Albert Doucette and Anne Elizabeth Feeley

10. Michele Anne Doucette

---

[659] https://www.familytreedna.com/public/mothersofacadia/default.aspx?section=mtresults

PATERNAL 1B

Courtesy of mtDNA testing, this unidentified first Mi'kmaq spouse of Philippe Mius dit d'Azy shows as belonging to HAPLOGROUP A2f [660] which is a native haplogroup.

1. Philippe Mius dit d'Azy and first Amérindien wife

2. Joseph Mius dit d'Azy and Marie Amirault

This couple has been genetically traced to the fatal Niemann-Pick (variant C) disease as per the French Acadian population of Yarmouth County, Nova Scotia.

3. Jean Baptiste I Mius and Marie Josèphe Surette

4. Paul Mius and Marie LeBlanc

5. Anselme Mius and Marguerite Mius

6. Jean Cyrille (dit Coco) Mius and Scholastique Doucet

7. Anne Vitaline Mius and Louis Cyprien Dulain

8. Adèle Dulain and Théophile (dit Câlin) Doucet

9. Jean Avite (called Harvey) Doucette and Beatrice Muise

10. Albert Doucette and Anne Elizabeth Feeley

11. Michele Anne Doucette

---

[660] https://www.familytreedna.com/public/mothersofacadia/default.aspx?section=mtresults

PATERNAL 1B

Courtesy of mtDNA testing, this unidentified first Mi'kmaq spouse of Philippe Mius dit d'Azy shows as belonging to HAPLOGROUP A2f [661] which is a native haplogroup.

1. Philippe Mius dit d'Azy and first Amérindien wife

2. Joseph Mius dit d'Azy and Marie Amirault

This couple has been genetically traced to the fatal Niemann-Pick (variant C) disease as per the French Acadian population of Yarmouth County, Nova Scotia.

3. Jean Baptiste I Mius and Marie Josèphe Surette

4. Paul Mius and Marie LeBlanc

5. Marguerite Mius and Charles Séraphin Mius

6. Rosalie Angèle (dite Angélique) Mius and Vital Mius

7. Peter Muise and Martha Roach

8. Beatrice Muise and Jean-Avite (called Harvey) Doucette

9. Albert Doucette and Anne Elizabeth Feeley

10. Michele Anne Doucette

---

[661] https://www.familytreedna.com/public/mothersofacadia/default.aspx?section=mtresults

PATERNAL 1C
Courtesy of mtDNA testing, this unidentified first Mi'kmaq spouse of Philippe Mius dit d'Azy shows as belonging to HAPLOGROUP A2f [662] which is a native haplogroup.
1. Philippe Mius dit d'Azy and first Amérindien wife
2. Joseph Mius dit d'Azy and Marie Amirault
This couple has been genetically traced to the fatal Niemann-Pick (variant C) disease as per the French Acadian population of Yarmouth County, Nova Scotia.
3. Charles Amand I Mius and Marie Marthe Hébert
4. Félicité Mius and Charles Doucet
5. Charles (dit Tania) Doucet and Anne Mius
6. Scholastique Doucet and Jean Cyrille (dit Coco) Mius
7. Anne Vitaline Mius and Louis Cyprien Dulain
8. Adèle Dulain and Théophile (dit Câlin) Doucet
9. Jean Avite (called Harvey) Doucette and Beatrice Muise
10. Albert Doucette and Anne Elizabeth Feeley
11. Michele Anne Doucette

---

[662] https://www.familytreedna.com/public/mothersofacadia/default.aspx?section=mtresults

PATERNAL 1C

Courtesy of mtDNA testing, this unidentified first Mi'kmaq spouse of Philippe Mius dit d'Azy shows as belonging to HAPLOGROUP A2f [663] which is a native haplogroup.

1. Philippe Mius dit d'Azy and first Amérindien wife

2. Joseph Mius dit d'Azy and Marie Amirault

This couple has been genetically traced to the fatal Niemann-Pick (variant C) disease as per the French Acadian population of Yarmouth County, Nova Scotia.

3. Charles Amand I Mius and Marie Marthe Hébert

4. Madeleine Modeste Mius and John O'Bird (Hubbard)

5. Jean O'Bird (Hubbard) JR and Marie Anne Doucet

6. Marie Madeleine O'Bird (Hubbard) and Jean Séraphin Deveau

7. Marie Elizabeth Deveau and John William Henry Roach

8. Martha Roach and Peter Muise

9. Beatrice Muise and Jean-Avite (called Harvey) Doucette

10. Albert Doucette and Anne Elizabeth Feeley

11. Michele Anne Doucette

---

[663] https://www.familytreedna.com/public/mothersofacadia/default.aspx?section=mtresults

PATERNAL 1C
Courtesy of mtDNA testing, this unidentified first Mi'kmaq spouse of Philippe Mius dit d'Azy shows as belonging to HAPLOGROUP A2f [664] which is a native haplogroup.
1. Philippe Mius dit d'Azy and first Amérindien wife
2. Joseph Mius dit d'Azy and Marie Amirault
This couple has been genetically traced to the fatal Niemann-Pick (variant C) disease as per the French Acadian population of Yarmouth County, Nova Scotia.
3. Charles Amand I Mius and Marie Marthe Hébert
4. Madeleine Modeste Mius and John O'Bird (Hubbard)
5. Marie Osithe O' Bird (Hubbard) and François Mius
6. Anne Anastasie (dite Nanette) Mius and Michel Patrice (dit L'Anglais) Doucet
7. Théophile (dit Câlin) Doucet and Adèle Dulain
8. Jean Avite (called Harvey) Doucette and Beatrice Muise
9. Albert Doucette and Anne Elizabeth Feeley
10. Michele Anne Doucette

---

[664] https://www.familytreedna.com/public/mothersofacadia/default.aspx?section=mtresults

PATERNAL 1C

Courtesy of mtDNA testing, this unidentified first Mi'kmaq spouse of Philippe Mius dit d'Azy shows as belonging to HAPLOGROUP A2f [665] which is a native haplogroup.

1. Philippe Mius dit d'Azy and first Amérindien wife

2. Joseph Mius dit d'Azy and Marie Amirault

This couple has been genetically traced to the fatal Niemann-Pick (variant C) disease as per the French Acadian population of Yarmouth County, Nova Scotia.

3. Charles Amand I Mius and Marie Marthe Hébert

4. Madeleine Modeste Mius and John O'Bird (Hubbard)

5. Marie Osithe O' Bird (Hubbard) and François Mius

6. Charles Séraphin Mius and Marguerite Mius

7. Rosalie Angèle (dite Angélique) Mius and Vital Mius

8. Peter Muise and Martha Roach

9. Beatrice Muise and Jean-Avite (called Harvey) Doucette

10. Albert Doucette and Anne Elizabeth Feeley

11. Michele Anne Doucette

---

[665] https://www.familytreedna.com/public/mothersofacadia/default.aspx?section=mtresults

PATERNAL 1D
Courtesy of mtDNA testing, this unidentified first Mi'kmaq spouse of Philippe Mius dit d'Azy shows as belonging to HAPLOGROUP A2f [666] which is a native haplogroup.
1. Philippe Mius dit d'Azy and first Amérindien wife
2. Joseph Mius dit d'Azy and Marie Amirault
This couple has been genetically traced to the fatal Niemann-Pick (variant C) disease as per the French Acadian population of Yarmouth County, Nova Scotia.
3. Joseph Mius and Marie Josèphe Préjean
4. Louis Mius and Anne Josèphe Corporon
5. Anne Mius and Charles (dit Tania) Doucet
6. Scholastique Doucet and Jean Cyrille (dit Coco) Mius
7. Anne Vitaline Mius and Louis Cyprien Dulain
8. Adèle Dulain and Théophile (dit Câlin) Doucet
9. Jean Avite (called Harvey) Doucette and Beatrice Muise
10. Albert Doucette and Anne Elizabeth Feeley
11. Michele Anne Doucette

---

[666] https://www.familytreedna.com/public/mothersofacadia/default.aspx?section=mtresults

Joseph Mius, son of Philippe Mius dit d'Azy and an Amérindienne, was married to Marie Amirault, an Acadian woman. I descend from four sons of this couple; namely, Joseph (born June 27, 1700), Charles dit Charles Amand I (born December 17, 1702), François (born March 19, 1703) and Jean-Baptiste (born about 1713).

Brothers to Joseph Mius dit d'Azy (Marriage 1 to unknown Amérindienne about 1678) were

[1] Mathieu Mius, born c. 1682, married Marie-Madeleine, an Amérindienne, c. 1706; they were living in the region of CS, according to the census of 1708.

[2] Maurice Mius, born c. 1682, twin to Mathieu, married Marguerite, an Amérindienne, c. 1702; they were living at Mouscoudabouet, north of Halifax, according to the census of 1708.

Brothers to Joseph Mius dit d'Azy (Marriage 2 to Marie, an Amérindienne, about 1687) were

[3] Jacques Mius, born c. 1688, married c. 1715 to a woman whose name is unknown to us; they were living at La Hève, according to the census of 1708.

[4] Pierre Mius dit Dasy, born c. 1691, married Marguerite LaPierre c. 1718.

[5] Jean-Baptiste was married c. 1720 to Marie ----------.

[6] François Mius, born c. 1700, Mi'kmaq chief of the La Hève nation, married Marie ---------- c. 1726.

[7] Philippe Mius, born c. 1703.

There was a Treaty of Peace and Friendship signed between Jonathan Belcher and François Mius; a treaty that constitutes the La Hève Treaty of 1761.

As per the Nova Scotia Archives, the Treaty of Peace and Friendship, dated 1761, is part of the Indians series: NSARM RG 1 vol. 430 no. 20a [667]

Chief Francis Mius of the LaHeve Tribe, a key treaty signator, was the son of Philippe Mius dit d'Azy; a brother to Joseph Mius dit d'Azy, my key ancestor.

Philippe Mius dit d'Azy	Joseph Mius	François Mius	Jean Pierre Mius	Jean Baptiste Mius	Pierre Eusèbe Mius	Vital Mius	Peter Muise	Beatrice Muise	Albert Doucette	Michele Doucette
CHIEF François Mius	Brother	Uncle	Great Uncle	GG Uncle	GGG Uncle	GGGG Uncle	G5 Uncle	G6 Uncle	G7 Uncle	**G8 Uncle**

In keeping with the 37th Parliament, 2nd session [668] (dated Friday, November 1, 2002), the following information is freely available.

Mr. John Cummins

With regard to specific treaties with the crown and the following aboriginal bands or communities in the Maritimes; Abegweit, Lennox Island, Big Cove, Buctouche, Burnt Church, Eel Ground, Eel River, Fort Folly, Indian Island, Kingsclear, Madawaska, Red Bank, Oromocto, Pabineau, Saint Mary's, Tobique, Woodstock, Acadia, Afton, Annapolis Valley, Bear River, Chapel Island, Eskasoni, Glooscap, Membertou, Millbrook, Pictou Landing, Shubenacadie, Wagmatcook, Waycocomagh: (a) what is the specific treaty that covers each of these bands or communities; (b) when was each of these specific treaties

---

[667] https://novascotia.ca/archives/mikmaq/archives.asp?ID=627
[668] http://www.wabanaki.com/british_crown_treaties.htm

signed; (c) where was each of these specific treaties signed; (d) which of these bands or communities are covered by the so-called Marshall or Halifax treaties; (e) which of these bands or communities are covered by treaties signed after the so-called Marshall or Halifax treaties; (f) which of these bands or communities are covered by the Miramichi Treaty of 1779; and (g) which of these bands or communities are not covered by treaties?

Hon. Robert Nault (Minister of Indian Affairs and Northern Development, Liberal)

With regard to specific treaties being made between the crown and aboriginal bands or communities in the Maritimes, the British crown signed a number of historical documents with the Mi'kmaq, Maliseet and Passamaquoddy people between 1725 and 1779. These historical documents are commonly referred to as treaties, *but only three of them*, the two LaHeve treaties of 1760-61 and the Cope treaty of 1752, *have been formally recognized by the Supreme Court of Canada as having the constitutional status of treaties*.

In response to part (a) of the question, it is important to consider the geographical boundaries and political structures of the Maritimes in the 1700s. In the Marshall decision, the Supreme Court of Canada noted that "...the British signed a series of agreements with individual Mi'kmaq communities in 1760 and 1761 intending to have them consolidated into a comprehensive Mi'kmaq treaty that was never, in fact, brought into existence. The trial judge found that by the end of 1761 all of the Mi'kmaq villages in Nova Scotia had entered into separate but similar treaties." It is important to note that during the colonial period, Nova Scotia was considered to include modern day New Brunswick.

Regarding parts (b) and (c) as they relate to the Supreme Court of Canada decision on Marshall, *only the 1760-61 treaties were recognized by the Supreme Court of Canada as treaties* under section 35 of the Constitution Act, 1982. The 1760 LaHeve treaty was signed on March 10, 1760 in Halifax. The 1761 LaHeve treaty was signed on November 9, 1761 in Halifax.

In addition, the other "historical documents" that have been identified from various archival sources are virtually identical to the LaHeve treaty of 1760 with the exception of the February 23, 1760 agreement with the Saint John (Maliseet) and Passamaquoddy Indians, which contained similar promises, but also renewed previous peace and friendship treaties with the crown.

Copies of the following 1760-61 documents were provided to the House of Commons Standing Committee on Fisheries and Oceans, by the Department of Fisheries and Oceans in May 2001:

Renewal of 1725 Articles and 1749 Articles, with the delegates of the Saint John and Passamaquoddy, at Chebucto (Halifax) Harbour, 23 February 1760; Treaty dated 10 March 1760 with Chief Michael Augustine of the Richebuctou Tribe; Treaty with Chief Paul of LaHeve Tribe at Halifax, 10 March 1760; Treaty with Claude René, Chief of Chibennacadie and Muscadoboit, concluded at Halifax, 10 March 1760; Treaty with the Merimichi Tribe, concluded 25 June 1761; Treaty with Chief Claude Atouash of the Jedaick Tribe, concluded at Halifax, 25 June 1761; Treaty with Etiene Apshobon of the Pogmouch Tribe, Halifax, 25 June 1761; Treaty with Joseph Argimaut, Chief of Mesiguash Indians, Halifax, 8 July 1761; Treaty with Chief Jeannot Picklougawash on behalf of the Pictouk and Malegomich Tribes, 12 October 1761; and **Treaty with Chief François Mius of the LaHeve Tribe**, concluded at Halifax, 9 November 1761.

In part (d) reference is made to "Marshall or Halifax treaties." It is assumed this is in reference to the LaHeve treaties of 1760-61, which were considered by the Supreme Court of Canada in the Marshall decision. Therefore, with respect to which bands or communities are covered by these treaties, the *Government of Canada is of the view that while modern day first nations are the most likely successor groups of the original signatory groups, it is impossible to determine a direct correlation between the application of treaties to modern day first nations.*

It is important to keep in mind that the passage of time has meant that there have been changes to the composition of some of the signatory groups. *We recognize the difficulty in connecting the signatories of historic treaties to particular contemporary first nation communities.* This may be due in part to migration of first nations, intermarriage, government policies creating bands and other initiatives such as the centralization of reserves. *However, since the court found that all Mi'kmaq communities participated in the treaties, members of modern communities are likely beneficiaries of these treaty rights.*

For these reasons, the Government of Canada has determined that the most appropriate course of action is to enter into a dialogue with the 34 Mi'kmaq and Maliseet first nations in present day Nova Scotia, New Brunswick, Prince Edward Island and Quebec to consider the implications of the Marshall decision.

Parts (e) and (f) of the question are unanswerable since only the two LaHeve treaties of 1760-61 and the Cope treaty of 1752 have been formally recognized by the Supreme Court of Canada as having the constitutional status of treaties. In addition, the Government of Canada maintains that while modern day first nations are the most likely successor groups to the original collectives that signed the treaties, it is impossible to determine a direct correlation between the application of treaties to contemporary first nations. As for which bands are not covered by treaties, part (g), the question is unanswerable due to changes in the composition of some of the signatory groups over the years. Nonetheless, the Government of Canada has drawn from the observations of the Supreme Court of Canada in its decision on Marshall and has determined that working with the 34 Mi'kmaq and Maliseet first nations on the implications of this decision is the most appropriate course of action.

Reprinted with Permission

© Parks Canada, Fort Anne National Historic Site

Molly Muise (the name was originally Mius and is now spelled Meuse and Muse as well) is wearing a peaked cap with double curve beadwork, a dark shirt, a short jacket with darker cuffs, over which she apparently has draped a second short jacket, its sleeves pulled inside, as a capelet. Her traditional dress with the large fold at the top is held up by suspenders with ornamental tabs. In her hands, she seems to be clutching a white handkerchief.

In keeping with the 1832 Mi'kmaw Census [669] of Bear River, Molly Muise is listed, aged 3, with her parents, Joseph Muise and Nancy Magalash; she was born in 1829. The date of her death is not known.

Mi'kmaw census Bear River 1832

Names of Mi'kmaq Settled at Bear River, living in 1832, taken by Peleg Wiswall:

Andrew James Meuse, Chief, on a voyage to England
Magdalen Tony, his wife
Francis Christopher Meuse- 18
Louis Noel Meuse- 14, with his father
Mary Anne Meuse, girl
Adelah Meuse, boy
James Meuse, boy
Betsey Meuse, girl
of this family the Whole No.————— 8
Joseph Meuse
Nancy Magalash
Daughter Molly—————————— 3

Molly Muise is the subject of a large mural, that was painted on the Lafrance building, the tallest building on campus at the University of Moncton. The mural was painted in July 2017 by British artist Wasp Elder during Festival Inspire.

She is best known as the subject of one of the oldest known photographs of a Mi'kmaq woman. To shed light on her background, Acadian historian Maurice Basque gave a presentation titled *Who is Molly Muise* [670] at the university's Champlain Library.

---

[669] annapolisheritagesociety.com/genealogy/census-records/mikmaw-census-bear-river-1832/
[670] https://www.youtube.com/watch?v=HmX_tIVjmDw

According to Maurice Basque, Molly Muise was well-respected for her wisdom and advice, not only in her small Mi'kmaq community in Nova Scotia, but by non-Indigenous people as well, which was "exceptional" for her time. "If we believe in 2018 we have problems with racism, you can imagine what was going on in the 19th century," he said.[671] She was so highly regarded, the white community of Beaver River built a funerary monument to her when she died, Basque said.

Beaver River is a small rural community that straddles the Digby County and Yarmouth County line, located on the southwest coast of Nova Scotia, Canada, near the town of Yarmouth.

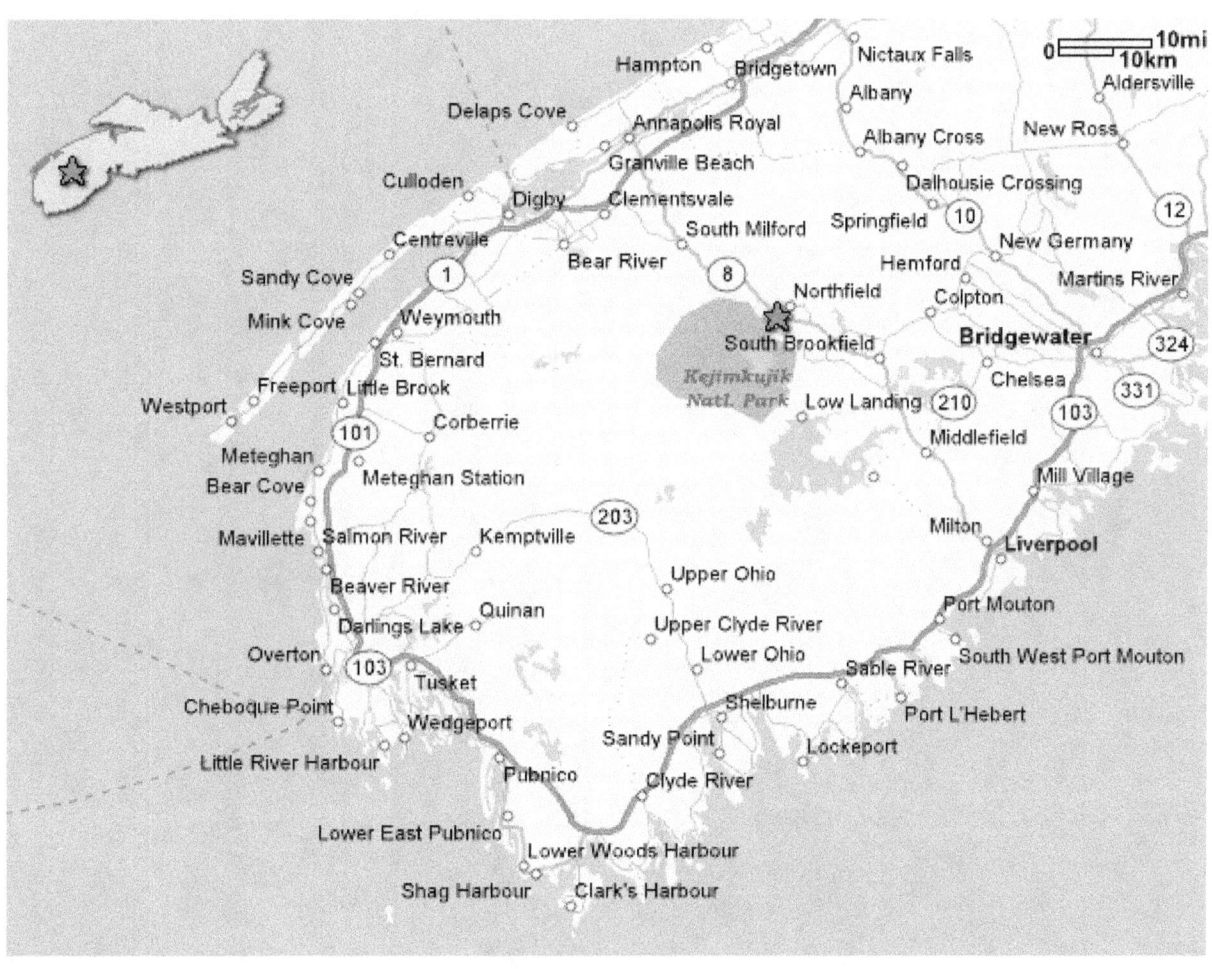

---

[671] https://www.cbc.ca/news/canada/new-brunswick/molly-muise-universite-de-moncton-mural-1.4537525

My paternal -------- grandmother, Mary Elizabeth Deveau, lived in the community of Beaver River, Nova Scotia.

For many thousands of years, the Mi'kmaq people made their home in Mi'kma'ki.

Mi'kma'ki is a vast area; its diverse landscapes, seascapes, rivers, plants, animals, fish, rocks, and islands are inseparable from Mi'kmaw people, language, stories, history and spirit. [672]

The earliest traces of the culture of the Mi'kmaq people have been found in Debert, Nova Scotia; a site is being excavated that dates back some 11,000 years. [673] [674]

The area continues to reveal new evidence of people living in what was an ice-age landscape; the oldest directly-dated archaeological sites in Canada, they are among the largest and best preserved archaeological sites of this age in North America. [675]

Contact with Europeans did not surprise the Mi'kmaq. An old legend in which one of their spritual beings traveled across the Atlantic to "discover" Europe taught that blue-eyes people would arrive from the east to disrupt their lives. [676] The people also knew the story of a Mi'kmaq woman who had a vision of an island floating toward their lands; the island was covered with tall trees on which were living beings that she thought were bears. [677] The Mi'kmaq recognized the validation of her vision; when the first ships appeared, they were prepared to greet the newcomers as friends. [678]

The Mi'kmaq developed a good relationship with the French settlers; these newcomers tended towards a commercial economy which encouraged trade with the Mi'kmaq. Eventually, there were marriages between the French colonists in Acadia and the Mi'kmaq; the children from these unions were welcome in both cultures, further cementing the relationship.

---

[672] www.mikmaweydebert.ca/home/ancestors-live-here/
[673] www.mikmaweydebert.ca/home/ancestors-live-here/debert/
[674] www.muiniskw.org/pgHistory0.htm
[675] www.mikmaweydebert.ca/home/ancestors-live-here/debert/
[676] www.muiniskw.org/pgHistory0.htm
[677] Ibid.
[678] Ibid.

Relations with outsiders grew more when the Mi'kmaq began converting to Catholicism. This process spanned a period of 70 years, beginning with the conversion of Grand Chief Membertou in 1610.

A stamp commemorating Chief Membertou

who welcomed the first French to arrive in Nova Scotia

https://liatris52.wordpress.com/more-art-about-mikmaq-people-of-earlier-days/

The Mi'kmaw nation's first treaty with a European nation was an agreement with the Vatican and the Holy See; a treaty that was recorded on a wampum belt, with symbols representing the incorporation of Mi'kmaw spirituality within the context of Roman Catholicism.[679]

The growing rivalry between France and England meant increasing trouble for the Mi'kmaw population; in 1746, they were devastated by epidemic disease brought by European ships. The lowest point in Mi'kmaw-British relations was the 1749 scalp bounty that the governor placed on Mi'kmaq rebels.[680]

---

[679] www.muiniskw.org/pgHistory0.htm
[680] Ibid.

After a long period of conflict, as the British battled the French and their Mi'kmaw allies, the Mi'kmaq eventually established a series of treaties with the British Crown that gave Britain an alliance with the Wabanaki Confederacy and security across the region.

It was during this time that the eight-pointed star design was created; seven of the points represented the seven districts of Mi'kma'ki, with the eighth point standing for Great Britain and the Crown. [681]

http://thehiddenrecords.com/oak-island.php

The Bedford Barrens [682] is the name attached to the **Mi'kmaq petroglyph discovered in 1983**; it is located a short distance from Oak Island, Nova Scotia.

---

[681] www.muiniskw.org/pgHistory0.htm
[682] https://rodneymackay.com/fun2017/Golden%20spiral/doomsday.html

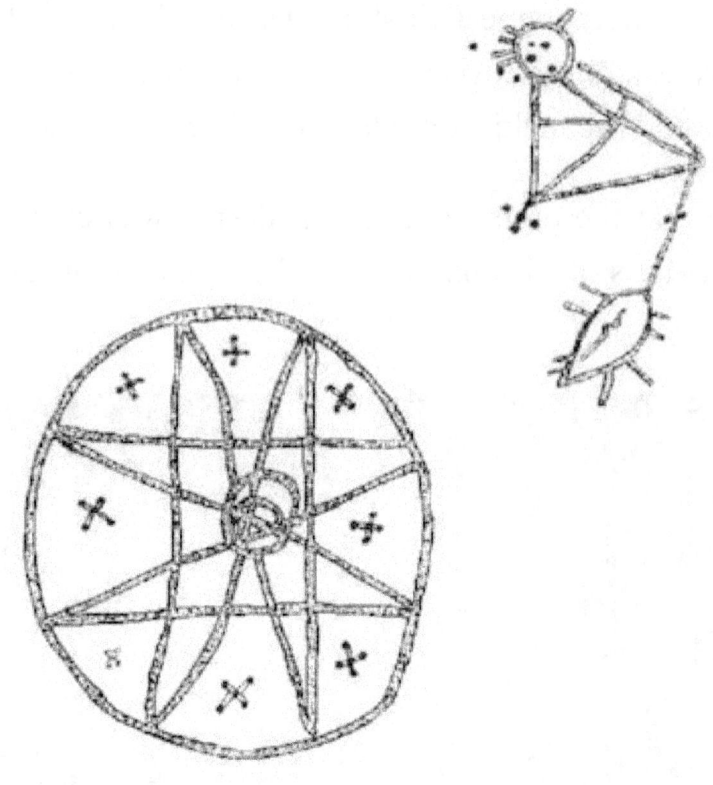

Taken from <u>Speaking About Our Land: NM'TGINEN</u> [683]

The Mi'kmaq have an eight-pointed star that is significant to them.

In 1983, a man in Bedford, Nova Scotia, came across a Mi'kmaq petroglyph in a wooded area.

A petroglyph is a symbol or design carved into the rock on the ground. This petroglyph was an eight-point star. It is believed that this eight-point petroglyph is over 500 years old.

The eight-point star is believed to be an updated version of the seven-point star; which the Mi'kmaq used to represent the seven districts of their nation. The Mi'kmaq nation grew to eight districts with the addition of Taqmkuk (Newfoundland). The Mi'kmaq updated the star to eight-points to welcome their brothers and sisters from Newfoundland.

---

[683] http://www.aboutourland.ca/resources/migmaq-stories/migmaq-star-0

Today, the eight-pointed star is often seen in four different colors: red, black, white and yellow. These four colors together represent harmony and unity between the four races of people. The four colors also represent the four directions: white represents north, black represents south, red represents east and yellow represent west.

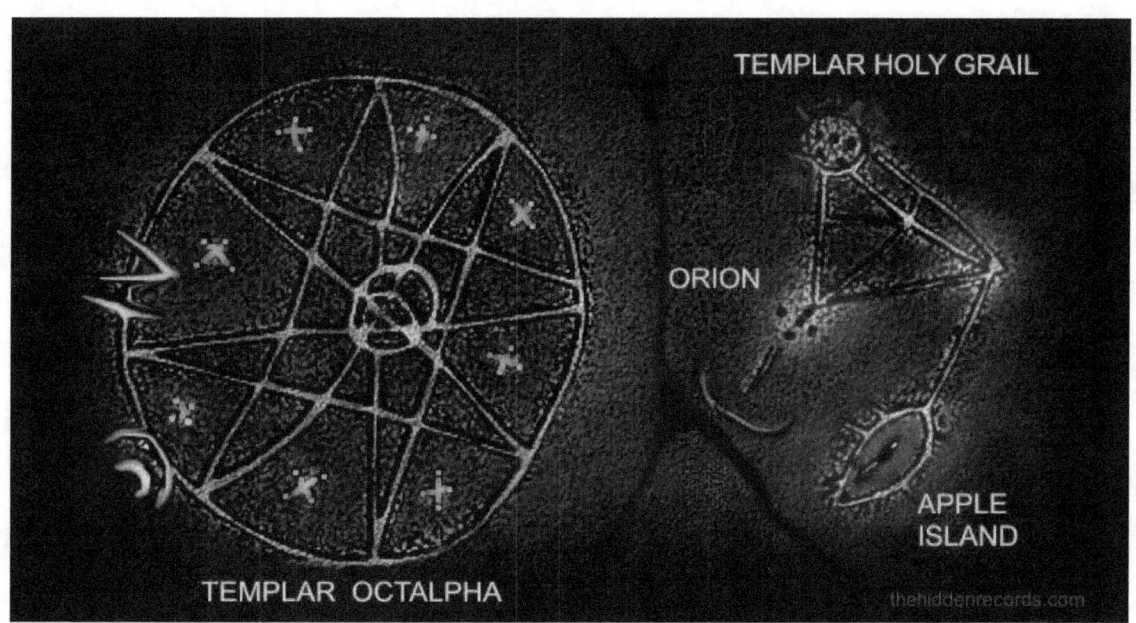

http://thehiddenrecords.com/oak-island.php

Could it be that the 8 pointed star pattern on a rock carving (as above) in Bedford, Nova Scotia, is Templar sourced? It also shares a marked similarity to an ancient Melchizedek reference. [684]

---

[684] sealofmelchizedek.com/wp-content/uploads/2011/05/Euclid.jpg

PATERNAL 2

Courtesy of mtDNA testing, this unidentified first Mi'kmaq spouse of Philippe Mius dit d'Azy shows as belonging to HAPLOGROUP A2f [685] which is a native haplogroup.

1. Philippe Mius dit d'Azy and first Amérindien wife

2. Marie Mius and François Viger

3. François Viger and Clair Lejeune

4. Angélique Viger (dit Brigeau) and Eustache Corporon

5. Marie Rose Corporon and Pierre Robichaud (dit Cadet)

6. Marguerite Robichaud and Jean Baptiste (dit Petit John) Mius

7. Pierre Eusèbe (dit Petit John) Mius and Scholastique Boutier

8. Vital Mius and Rosalie Angèle (dite Angélique) Mius

9. Peter Muise and Martha Roach

10. Beatrice Muise and Jean-Avite (called Harvey) Doucette

11. Albert Doucette and Anne Elizabeth Feeley

12. Michele Anne Doucette

---

[685] https://www.familytreedna.com/public/mothersofacadia/default.aspx?section=mtresults

PATERNAL 3
Courtesy of mtDNA testing, Anne Marie ----------, wife of ---------- Pinet, shows as belonging to **HAPLOGROUP A2f**[686] which is an Amerindian haplogroup.

1. ---------- Pinet and Anne Marie ----------

2. Philippe Pinet and Catherine Hébert

3. Marie Pinet and Jean (Baptiste) Corporon (dit l'aîné)

4. Eustache Corporon and Angélique Viger (dit Brigeau)

5. Marie Rose Corporon and Pierre Robichaud (dit Cadet)

6. Marguerite Robichaud and Jean Baptiste (dit Petit John) Mius

7. Pierre Eusèbe (dit Petit John) Mius and Scholastique Boutier

8. Vital Mius and Rosalie Angèle (dite Angélique) Mius

9. Peter Muise and Martha Roach

10. Beatrice Muise and Jean-Avite (called Harvey) Doucette

11. Albert Doucette and Anne Elizabeth Feeley

12. Michele Anne Doucette

---

[686] https://www.familytreedna.com/public/mothersofacadia/default.aspx?section=mtresults

Acadian Family Names

In the course of my research, I was quick to identify with the adage *all Acadians are related* as shared by Janet Jehn of AGE (Acadian Genealogy Exchange). After all, there were fewer women living in Acadie in comparison to men. Just taking a look at the consanguinity charts in the previous chapters can also attest to this understanding.

I have attempted, in this segment, to identify the individual key surnames (male progenitors) that figure into my paternal line, Acadian and/or otherwise, as they all culminate in the totality of my French Acadian ancestry.

The following surnames are noted herein;

Amirault

Bajolet, Bernard, Bornstra, Boudrot, Bourg, Bourgeois, Boutier (known today as Boucher), Brassaud, Brun

Chebrat, Clémenson, Comeau, Corporon

Deveau, Doucet(te), DuFosset, Dugas, Dulain (present day derivatives are Dulin and Dulong), Duon

de Forest, Frontain (known today as Frotten)

Gaudet

Hébert, Housseau

Lafleur, de La Grange, Landry, LeBlanc, Lefebvre, Lejeune

Maillard, Martin, Meunier, Mius d'Entremont (present day derivatives are d'Entremont, Mius, Meuse, Muise)

O'Bird (known today as Hubbard)

Pellerin, Pesseley, Pinet, Pitre, Poirier, Pothier, Préjean

Roach, Robichaud

Savoie, Surette

Thériot, Thibodeau, Trahan

Viger, Vigneau

Happy connecting!

Amirault 1A

François Amireau was originally from Tours or Touraine, hence his nickname. He resided at Cap-de-Sable, Acadie (Cape Sable, Nova Scotia). All children, except the two oldest and the youngest, were privately baptized at birth with the full religious ceremonies being supplied on May 22 and 23, 1705, by Father Félix Pain; the entry in the register of Port Royal is dated October 23, 1705. [687]

[1] François Amirault dit Tourangeau, born c. 1644, [688] married Marie Pitre (d/o Jean Pitre and Marie Pesseley) c. 1683. [689] [690] Marie was born c. 1666. [691] [692]

[2] Marie Amirault, born at CS c. 1684, [693] [694] married **Joseph Mius dit d'Azy** (s/o Philippe Mius dit d'Azy and Mi'kmaq woman) c. 1699. [695] [696] Joseph was born c. 1679. [697]

---

[687] White, Stephen A. (2000) English Supplement to the Dictionnaire Généalogique des Familles Acadiennes (page 5). Montréal, Québec: AGMV Marquis Imprimeur Inc.
[688] White, Stephen A. (1999) Dictionnaire Généalogique des Familles Acadiennes, Volume A to G, page 17.
[689] Ibid.
[690] White, Stephen A. (1999) Dictionnaire Généalogique des Familles Acadiennes, Volume H to Z, page 1318.
[691] Ibid.
[692] White, Stephen A. (1999) Dictionnaire Généalogique des Familles Acadiennes, Volume A to G, page 17.
[693] Ibid.
[694] White, Stephen A. (1999) Dictionnaire Généalogique des Familles Acadiennes, Volume H to Z, page 1207.
[695] Ibid, pages 1206 and 1207.
[696] White, Stephen A. (1999) Dictionnaire Généalogique des Familles Acadiennes, Volume A to G, page 17.
[697] White, Stephen A. (1999) Dictionnaire Généalogique des Familles Acadiennes, Volume H to Z, pages 1206 and 1207.

This is the couple has been genetically traced to the fatal Niemann-Pick (variant C) disease as per the French Acadian population of Yarmouth County, Nova Scotia.

Further lines of descent continue from <u>4 of the 5 sons</u> of Joseph and Marie, namely

■ François Mius and Jeanne Duon (Refer to Mius d'Entrement 1A for line continuation)

■ Jean Baptiste I Mius and Marie Josèphe Surette (Refer to Mius d'Entrement 1B for line continuation)

■ Charles Amand I Mius and Marie Marthe Hébert (Refer to Mius d'Entrement 1C for line continuation)

■ Joseph Mius and Marie Josèphe Préjean (Refer to Mius d'Entrement 1D for line continuation)

The irony of my Doucet ancestry is that I have <u>far more Mius/Muise</u> individuals than I have Doucet, and yet they are all related.

The only son that I do not descend from is Charles Benjamin Mius, the youngest, who, along with his wife Marie Josèphe Guédry, died at sea (1758-1759), a result of the Deportation.

Amirault 1B

François Amireau was originally from Tours or Touraine, hence his nickname. He resided at Cap-de-Sable, Acadie (today, Cape Sable, Nova Scotia). All children, except the two oldest and the youngest, were privately baptized at birth with the full religious ceremonies being supplied on May 22 and 23, 1705, by Father Félix Pain; the entry in the register of Port Royal is dated October 23, 1705. [698]

[1] François Amirault dit Tourangeau, born c. 1644, [699] married Marie Pitre (d/o Jean Pitre and Marie Pesseley) c. 1683. [700] [701] Marie was born c. 1666. [702] [703]

[2] Charles Amirault, born June 14, 1700, [704] and baptized at PR on May 22, 1705, [705] married Claire Dugas (d/o Claude Dugas and Marguerite Bourg) on August 28, 1726 at PR. [706] [707] [708] Claire was born January 21, 1706 at PR. [709]

---

[698] White, Stephen A. (2000) English Supplement to the Dictionnaire Généalogique des Familles Acadiennes (page 5). Montréal, Québec: AGMV Marquis Imprimeur Inc.
[699] White, Stephen A. (1999) Dictionnaire Généalogique des Familles Acadiennes, Volume A to G, page 17.
[700] Ibid.
[701] White, Stephen A. (1999) Dictionnaire Généalogique des Familles Acadiennes, Volume H to Z, page 1318.
[702] Ibid.
[703] White, Stephen A. (1999) Dictionnaire Généalogique des Familles Acadiennes, Volume A to G, page 17.
[704] Ibid, page 18.
[705] Ibid.
[706] https://novascotia.ca/archives/acadian/archives.asp?ID=1119
[707] White, Stephen A. (1999) Dictionnaire Généalogique des Familles Acadiennes, Volume A to G, page 18.
[708] Ibid, page 566.
[709] Ibid.

[3] Marguerite Amirault, born March 13, 1732 at CS, [710] married **Pierre LeBlanc** (s/o Pierre LeBlanc and Claire Boudrot). [711] Pierre was born c. 1741 at GP. [712] On August 16, 1769, Father Bailly blessed the marriage that had taken place in MA (exile), as no priests were allowed to go near the Acadians while in exile. If they did, imprisonment or death awaited them. [713] This couple is among some of the first settlers at SAR.

---

[710] http://novascotia.ca/archives/acadian/archives.asp?ID=1884
[711] d'Entremont, Father Clarence Joseph. (1984) Histoire de Quinan, Nouvelle-Écosse, page 89.
[712] www.acadian-home.org/ste-anne-du-ruisseau.html
[713] Ibid.

Bajolet 1

Antoine Bajolet was the main coachman for Queen Marie de Médicis.

[1] Antoine Bajolet was married to Jeanne Baudinet. [714]

[2] Barbe Bajolet was born on May 22, 1608, according to the Parish Register of Piney in the department of Champagne. [715] [716] She married **Isaac Pesseley**, her first husband, a merchant from Piney, three miles from Troyes, in the department of Champagne, c. 1629. [717] [718] Isaac arrived in Acadie on the *Saint-Jehan* in 1636. [719] [720] Isaac's death was probably due to the assault on Fort Saint Jean (located in present-day St. John, NewBrunswick) where d'Aulnay lost many men on April 16, 1645. [721] [722]

---

[714] White, Stephen A. (1999) Dictionnaire Généalogique des Familles Acadiennes, Volume A to G, page 70.
[715] Ibid.
[716] White, Stephen A. (1999) Dictionnaire Généalogique des Familles Acadiennes, Volume H to Z, page 1288.
[717] Ibid.
[718] White, Stephen A. (1999) Dictionnaire Généalogique des Familles Acadiennes, Volume A to G, page 70.
[719] http://acadian-cajun.com/stjehan.htm
[720] http://www.pitretrail.com/
[721] White, Stephen A. (1999) Dictionnaire Généalogique des Familles Acadiennes, Volume H to Z, page 1288.
[722] http://www.pitretrail.com/

Bajolet 2

Antoine Bajolet was the main coachman for Queen Marie de Médicis.

[1] Antoine Bajolet was married to Jeanne Baudinet. [723]

[2] Barbe Bajolet was born on May 22, 1608, according to the Parish Register of Piney in the department of Champagne. [724] [725] She married **Martin Lefebvre de Montespy**, her second husband, at the St-Barthélemy de La Rochelle parish, in Aunis, France, on January 10, 1647. [726] [727] In addition to being Sieur de Montespy, Martin was also the Ordinary Secretary to the Money Chamber of King Louis XIV. [728] Martin was born at St. Symphorien de Reims, France, and died on November 15, 1651 at St. Jean du Perrot, La Rochelle, France. [729]

The marriage contract made by Martin and Barbe indicates that he had *but shortly returned from the country of Canada*, when he became engaged to Barbe Bajolet, widow of Isaac Pesseley, adjutant of the garrison at Port Royal, *whence she had also but shortly returned.* [730]

---

[723] White, Stephen A. (1999) Dictionnaire Généalogique des Familles Acadiennes, Volume A to G, page 70.
[724] Ibid.
[725] White, Stephen A. (1999) Dictionnaire Généalogique des Familles Acadiennes, Volume H to Z, page 1034.
[726] Ibid.
[727] White, Stephen A. (1999) Dictionnaire Généalogique des Familles Acadiennes, Volume A to G, page 70.
[728] White, Stephen A. (1999) Dictionnaire Généalogique des Familles Acadiennes, Volume H to Z, page 1034.
[729] Ibid.
[730] White, Stephen A. (2000) English Supplement to the Dictionnaire Généalogique des Familles Acadiennes (page 220). Montréal, Québec: AGMV Marquis Imprimeur Inc.

Bernard

[1] ---------- Bernard married Andrée Guyon c. 1644. [731] Andrée was born c. 1615. [732]

[2] Marie Bernard, born c. 1645, [733] [734] was married to **René Landry dit lejeune** c. 1659. [735] [736] René was born c. 1634. [737] Marie was buried at PR on January 11, 1719. [738] [739] [740] René died at PR, sometime before the census of 1693. [741]

---

[731] White, Stephen A. (1999) <u>Dictionnaire Généalogique des Familles Acadiennes</u>, Volume A to G, pages 125 and 786.
[732] Ibid.
[733] Ibid, page 125.
[734] White, Stephen A. (1999) <u>Dictionnaire Généalogique des Familles Acadiennes</u>, Volume H to Z, page 916.
[735] Ibid.
[736] White, Stephen A. (1999) <u>Dictionnaire Généalogique des Familles Acadiennes</u>, Volume A to G, page 125.
[737] White, Stephen A. (1999) <u>Dictionnaire Généalogique des Familles Acadiennes</u>, Volume H to Z, page 916.
[738] Ibid.
[739] White, Stephen A. (1999) <u>Dictionnaire Généalogique des Familles Acadiennes</u>, Volume A to G, page 125.
[740] https://novascotia.ca/archives/acadian/archives.asp?ID=1533
[741] White, Stephen A. (1999) <u>Dictionnaire Généalogique des Familles Acadiennes</u>, Volume H to Z, page 916.

Bornstra

[1] Wybrant-Andriesz Bornstra was married to unknown. [742]

[2] Marguerite Bornstra was married to **Crispin de Forest** (s/o Gérard de Forest and Esther de La Grange) on July 1, 1636 (Leyde, Wallon's church, Amsterdam, the Netherlands). [743] Crispin was baptized on December 9, 1612 in Leyde, Wallon's church, Amsterdam, the Netherlands. [744]

---

[742] White, Stephen A. (1999) <u>Dictionnaire Généalogique des Familles Acadiennes</u>, Volume A to G, page 628.
[743] Ibid.
[744] Ibid.

Boudrot 1A

It is on September 21, 1639 that Michel Boudrot is mentioned as one of the first syndics at PR. [745] A general representative of the King in civil and criminal matters at PR, he gave up his post on August 20, 1688 due to advanced age. [746] December 2, 1705 records the expropriation of a lot *adjoining the side of the old fort*, belonging to Michel Boudrot, who had since been dead for over twelve years, for an extension of the fort at PR; one must, therefore, suppose that his heirs were the actual owners of this land in 1705. [747]

In 1999, the Association des Boudreau Inc. made a request to the Heraldry Authority of Canada to be granted a concession for a Coat of Arms. This request was accepted by her Excellence, the Right Honorable Adrienne Clarkson, Governor General of Canada, who presented them to the Boudreau (ot, ault, eaux) family during the ceremony on February 20, 2000 in Chéticamp, Nova Scotia. [748]

[1] Michel Boudrot, born c. 1600, [749] married Michelle Aucoin c. 1641. [750] Michelle was born c. 1621. [751] Michel died between August 20, 1688 and the census of 1693. [752] Michelle

---

[745] White, Stephen A. (2000) English Supplement to the Dictionnaire Généalogique des Familles Acadiennes (page 38). Montréal, Québec: AGMV Marquis Imprimeur Inc.
[746] Ibid.
[747] Ibid.
[748] webteque.net/Boudreauweb2/Boudreauweb2/Coat%20of%20Arms.html
[749] White, Stephen A. (1999) Dictionnaire Généalogique des Familles Acadiennes, Volume A to G, page 184.
[750] Ibid, pages 40 and 184.
[751] Ibid.
[752] Ibid, page 184.

died at PR on December 17, 1706 and was buried on December 18, 1706. [753] [754] Michelle was the sister of Jeanne Aucoin, wife of François Girouard. [755]

[2] Françoise Boudrot, born c. 1642, [756] [757] married **Étienne Robichaud** c. 1663. [758] [759] Étienne was born c. 1640. [760] Françoise died after the census of 1714. [761] Étienne died at PR, before the census of 1686. [762]

---

[753] White, Stephen A. (1999) <u>Dictionnaire Généalogique des Familles Acadiennes</u>, Volume A to G, pages 40 and 184.
[754] https://novascotia.ca/archives/acadian/archives.asp?ID=1401
[755] White, Stephen A. (1999) <u>Dictionnaire Généalogique des Familles Acadiennes</u>, Volume A to G, page 40.
[756] Ibid, page 184.
[757] White, Stephen A. (1999) <u>Dictionnaire Généalogique des Familles Acadiennes</u>, Volume H to Z, page 1403.
[758] Ibid.
[759] White, Stephen A. (1999) <u>Dictionnaire Généalogique des Familles Acadiennes</u>, Volume A to G, page 184.
[760] White, Stephen A. (1999) <u>Dictionnaire Généalogique des Familles Acadiennes</u>, Volume H to Z, page 1403.
[761] White, Stephen A. (1999) <u>Dictionnaire Généalogique des Familles Acadiennes</u>, Volume A to G, page 184.
[762] White, Stephen A. (1999) <u>Dictionnaire Généalogique des Familles Acadiennes</u>, Volume H to Z, page 1403.

Boudrot 1B

It is on September 21, 1639 that Michel Boudrot is mentioned as one of the first syndics at PR. [763] A general representative of the King in civil and criminal matters at PR, he gave up his post on August 20, 1688 due to advanced age. [764] December 2, 1705 records the expropriation of a lot *adjoining the side of the old fort*, belonging to Michel Boudrot, who had since been dead for over twelve years, for an extension of the fort at PR; one must, therefore, suppose that his heirs were the actual owners of this land in 1705. [765]

In 1999, the Association des Boudreau Inc. made a request to the Heraldry Authority of Canada to be granted a concession for a Coat of Arms. This request was accepted by her Excellency, the Right Honorable Adrienne Clarkson, Governor General of Canada who presented them to the Boudreau (ot, ault, eaux) family during the ceremony on February 20, 2000 in Chéticamp, Nova Scotia. [766]

[1] Michel Boudrot, born c. 1600, [767] married Michelle Aucoin c. 1641. [768] Michelle was born c. 1621. [769] Michel died between August 20, 1688 and the census of 1693. [770] Michelle

---

[763] White, Stephen A. (2000) English Supplement to the Dictionnaire Généalogique des Familles Acadiennes (page 38). Montréal, Québec: AGMV Marquis Imprimeur Inc.
[764] Ibid.
[765] Ibid.
[766] webteque.net/Boudreauweb2/Boudreauweb2/Coat%20of%20Arms.html
[767] White, Stephen A. (1999) Dictionnaire Généalogique des Familles Acadiennes, Volume A to G, page 184.
[768] Ibid, pages 40 and 184.
[769] Ibid.
[770] Ibid, page 184.

died at PR on December 17, 1706 and was buried on December 18, 1706. [771] [772] Michelle was the sister of Jeanne Aucoin, wife of François Girouard. [773]

[2] Marie Boudrot, born c. 1650, [774] [775] married **Michel Poirier** (s/o Jean Poirier and Jeanne Chebrat) c. 1673. [776] [777] Michel was born c. 1650. [778] Michel died at Bbn. [779]

---

[771] White, Stephen A. (1999) Dictionnaire Généalogique des Familles Acadiennes, Volume A to G, pages 40 and 184.
[772] https://novascotia.ca/archives/acadian/archives.asp?ID=1401
[773] White, Stephen A. (1999) Dictionnaire Généalogique des Familles Acadiennes, Volume A to G, page 40.
[774] Ibid, page 185.
[775] White, Stephen A. (1999) Dictionnaire Généalogique des Familles Acadiennes, Volume H to Z, page 1328.
[776] Ibid, pages 1327 and 1328.
[777] White, Stephen A. (1999) Dictionnaire Généalogique des Familles Acadiennes, Volume A to G, page 185.
[778] White, Stephen A. (1999) Dictionnaire Généalogique des Familles Acadiennes, Volume H to Z, pages 1327 and 1328.
[779] Ibid.

Boudrot 1C

It is on September 21, 1639 that Michel Boudrot is mentioned as one of the first syndics at PR.[780] A general representative of the King in civil and criminal matters at PR, he gave up his post on August 20, 1688 due to advanced age.[781] December 2, 1705 records the expropriation of a lot *adjoining the side of the old fort*, belonging to Michel Boudrot, who had since been dead for over twelve years, for an extension of the fort at PR; one must, therefore, suppose that his heirs were the actual owners of this land in 1705.[782]

In 1999, the Association des Boudreau Inc. made a request to the Heraldry Authority of Canada to be granted a concession for a Coat of Arms. This request was accepted by her Excellence, the Right Honorable Adrienne Clarkson, Governor General of Canada who presented them to the Boudreau (ot, ault, eaux) family during the ceremony on February 20, 2000 in Chéticamp, Nova Scotia.[783]

[1] Michel Boudrot, born c. 1600,[784] married Michelle Aucoin c. 1641.[785] Michelle was born c. 1621.[786] Michel died between August 20, 1688 and the census of 1693.[787] Michelle

---

[780] White, Stephen A. (2000) <u>English Supplement to the Dictionnaire Généalogique des Familles Acadiennes</u> (page 38). Montréal, Québec: AGMV Marquis Imprimeur Inc.
[781] Ibid.
[782] Ibid.
[783] webteque.net/Boudreauweb2/Boudreauweb2/Coat%20of%20Arms.html
[784] White, Stephen A. (1999) <u>Dictionnaire Généalogique des Familles Acadiennes</u>, Volume A to G, page 184.
[785] Ibid, pages 40 and 184.
[786] Ibid.
[787] Ibid, page 184.

died at PR on December 17, 1706 and was buried on December 18, 1706. [788] [789] Michelle was the sister of Jeanne Aucoin, wife of François Girouard. [790]

[2] Claude Boudrot, born about 1663, [791] [792] married Catherine Meunier (d/o Jean Meunier and Marguerite Housseau) c. 1700. [793] [794] Catherine was his second wife. Claude was buried at GP on March 7, 1740. [795]

[3] Claire Boudrot, born December 27, 1719 at GP, [796] [797] married **Pierre LeBlanc** (s/o René LeBlanc and Jeanne Landry), on October 24, 1740 at GP. [798] [799] Pierre was born and

---

[788] White, Stephen A. (1999) Dictionnaire Généalogique des Familles Acadiennes, Volume A to G, pages 40 and 184.
[789] https://novascotia.ca/archives/acadian/archives.asp?ID=1401
[790] White, Stephen A. (1999) Dictionnaire Généalogique des Familles Acadiennes, Volume A to G, page 40.
[791] Ibid, page 185.
[792] White, Stephen A. (1999) Dictionnaire Généalogique des Familles Acadiennes, Volume H to Z, page 1179.
[793] White, Stephen A. (1999) Dictionnaire Généalogique des Familles Acadiennes, Volume A to G, pages 185 and 191.
[794] White, Stephen A. (1999) Dictionnaire Généalogique des Familles Acadiennes, Volume H to Z, page 1179.
[795] White, Stephen A. (1999) Dictionnaire Généalogique des Familles Acadiennes, Volume A to G, pages 185 and 191.
[796] Ibid, page 192.
[797] White, Stephen A. (1999) Dictionnaire Généalogique des Familles Acadiennes, Volume H to Z, page 1007.
[798] Ibid.
[799] White, Stephen A. (1999) Dictionnaire Généalogique des Familles Acadiennes, Volume A to G, page 192.

baptized on August 21, 1718 at GP. [800] Claire died on November 1, 1741 at GP at the age of 22 years [801] and was buried on November 2, 1741. [802]

---

[800] White, Stephen A. (1999) <u>Dictionnaire Généalogique des Familles Acadiennes</u>, Volume H to Z, page 1007.
[801] White, Stephen A. (1999) <u>Dictionnaire Généalogique des Familles Acadiennes</u>, Volume A to G, page 192.
[802] Ibid.

Bourg 1A

On October 5, 1687, Antoine Bourg signed an attestation in favour of the accomplishments of Governor d'Aulnay; he had thus arrived in Acadie before 1650, the year of d'Aulnay's death. [803]

While Antoinette Landry is the sister of René Landry dit l'aîné, meaning *the elder*, husband of Perrine Bourg, it has not been possible to determine whether there was a family relationship between Perrine Bourg and Antoine Bourg, given the absence of any dispensation for kindred marriages.

[1] Antoine Bourg, born c. 1609, [804] married Antoinette Landry c. 1642. [805] [806] Antoinette was born c. 1618. [807] [808]

[2] Jean Bourg, born c. 1646, [809] married Marguerite Martin (d/o Pierre Martin and Catherine Vigneau) c. 1667. [810] [811] Marguerite was born c. 1644. [812] [813]

---

[803] White, Stephen A. (2000) English Supplement to the Dictionnaire Généalogique des Familles Acadiennes (page 48). Montréal, Québec: AGMV Marquis Imprimeur Inc.
[804] White, Stephen A. (1999) Dictionnaire Généalogique des Familles Acadiennes, Volume A to G, page 221.
[805] Ibid.
[806] White, Stephen A. (1999) Dictionnaire Généalogique des Familles Acadiennes, Volume H to Z, page 915.
[807] Ibid.
[808] White, Stephen A. (1999) Dictionnaire Généalogique des Familles Acadiennes, Volume A to G, page 221.
[809] Ibid, pages 221 and 224.
[810] Ibid.
[811] White, Stephen A. (1999) Dictionnaire Généalogique des Familles Acadiennes, Volume H to Z, page 1125.

[3] Marie Bourg, born c. 1673,[814][815] married **Charles Robichaud dit Cadet** (s/o Étienne Robichaud and Françoise Boudrot) on June 18, 1703 in PR.[816][817][818] Marie was his second wife. Charles was born c. 1667.[819]

---

[812] White, Stephen A. (1999) <u>Dictionnaire Généalogique des Familles Acadiennes</u>, Volume H to Z, page 1125.
[813] White, Stephen A. (1999) <u>Dictionnaire Généalogique des Familles Acadiennes</u>, Volume A to G, page 224.
[814] Ibid.
[815] White, Stephen A. (1999) <u>Dictionnaire Généalogique des Familles Acadiennes</u>, Volume H to Z, page 1405.
[816] White, Stephen A. (1999) <u>Dictionnaire Généalogique des Familles Acadiennes</u>, Volume A to G, page 224.
[817] White, Stephen A. (1999) <u>Dictionnaire Généalogique des Familles Acadiennes</u>, Volume H to Z, pages 1403 and 1405.
[818] https://novascotia.ca/archives/acadian/archives.asp?ID=1170
[819] White, Stephen A. (1999) <u>Dictionnaire Généalogique des Familles Acadiennes</u>, Volume H to Z, pages 1403 and 1405.

Bourg 1B

On October 5, 1687, Antoine Bourg signed an attestation in favour of the accomplishments of Governor d'Aulnay; he had thus arrived in Acadie before 1650, the year of d'Aulnay's death. [820]

While Antoinette Landry is the sister of René Landry dit l'aîné, meaning *the elder*, husband of Perrine Bourg, it has not been possible to determine whether there was a family relationship between Perrine Bourg and Antoine Bourg, given the absence of any dispensation for kindred marriages.

[1] Antoine Bourg, born c. 1609, [821] married to Antoinette Landry c. 1642. [822] [823] Antoinette was born c. 1618. [824] [825]

[2] Bernard Bourg, born c. 1648, [826] married Françoise Brun (d/o Vincent Brun and Renée Breau) c. 1670. [827] Françoise was born c. 1653. [828] Françoise died at PR on May 23, 1725 and was buried on May 24, 1725. [829] [830]

---

[820] White, Stephen A. (2000) English Supplement to the Dictionnaire Généalogique des Familles Acadiennes (page 48). Montréal, Québec: AGMV Marquis Imprimeur Inc.
[821] White, Stephen A. (1999) Dictionnaire Généalogique des Familles Acadiennes, Volume A to G, page 221.
[822] Ibid.
[823] White, Stephen A. (1999) Dictionnaire Généalogique des Familles Acadiennes, Volume H to Z, page 915.
[824] Ibid.
[825] White, Stephen A. (1999) Dictionnaire Généalogique des Familles Acadiennes, Volume A to G, page 221.
[826] Ibid, pages 221 and 225.
[827] Ibid, pages 221, 225 and 289.
[828] Ibid, pages 225 and 289.

[3] Marguerite Bourg, born c. 1674, [831] married **Claude Dugas** (s/o Abraham Dugas and Marguerite Doucet), widower of Françoise Bourgeois, c. 1697. [832] Claude was buried at PR on October 16, 1732. [833] [834] Marguerite died at PR on May 27, 1747 and was buried on May 28, 1747. [835] [836]

---

[829] White, Stephen A. (1999) Dictionnaire Généalogique des Familles Acadiennes, Volume A to G, pages 225 and 289.
[830] http://novascotia.ca/archives/acadian/archives.asp?ID=1023
[831] White, Stephen A. (1999) Dictionnaire Généalogique des Familles Acadiennes, Volume A to G, pages 226 and 565.
[832] Ibid.
[833] Ibid, pages 562 and 564.
[834] https://novascotia.ca/archives/virtual/acadian/archives.asp?ID=1876
[835] White, Stephen A. (1999) Dictionnaire Généalogique des Familles Acadiennes, Volume A to G, pages 226 and 565.
[836] https://novascotia.ca/archives/acadian/archives.asp?ID=2902

Bourgeois

Jacques (dit Jacob) Bourgeois was the surgeon (*chirugien*) at PR. [837] According to a deposition of July 31, 1699, Jacques Bourgeois had come to Acadia during the year 1642 to "settle there and practice surgery." [838]

Jacques (dit Jacob) Bourgeois was baptized on January 8, 1621 in the church of Saint-Romain in La Ferté-Gaucher, France; a town located some fifty kilometers to the east of Paris, [839] married **Jeanne Trahan** (d/o Guillaume Trahan and Françoise Corbineau) c. 1643. [840] [841]

Given the August 16, 1654 capitulation of Port Royal, we know that Germain left his brother-in-law, Jacques Bourgeois, surgeon, as both Lieutenant of Port Royal and a witness to see that the conditions of the treaty were carried out.

It is quite possible that Germain Doucet married a second time before 1654. No children have been traced to this marriage.

While Jacques (dit Jacob) Bourgeois does not figure into my ancestry per sé, he does figure into the history of the Doucet family, as so noted above; hence, his placement herein.

---

[837] Bujold, Nicole T. and Caillebeau, Maurice. (1979) Les origins françaises des premières familles acadiennes (page 15). Poitiers, France: Imprimerie l'Union.
[838] White, Stephen A. (2000) English Supplement to the Dictionnaire Généalogique des Familles Acadiennes (page 56). Montréal, Québec: AGMV Marquis Imprimeur Inc.
[839] Bourgeois, Paul-Pierre. (1994) À la recherche des Bourgeois d'Acadie (1641 à 1800) (pages 13 and 14). Sackville, NB: Tribune Press Ltée.
[840] White, Stephen A. (1999) Dictionnaire Généalogique des Familles Acadiennes, Volume H to Z, page 1536.
[841] White, Stephen A. (1999) Dictionnaire Généalogique des Familles Acadiennes, Volume A to G, page 251.

Even though the wife and/or wives of Germain Doucet have never been identified, it is important to make note of the words shared by Stephen A. White in the <u>Dictionnaire Généalogique des Familles Acadiennes</u>, Volume A to G, page 527.

[i]. It is not possible that the mother of the children of Germain Doucet is a sister of Jacques Bourgeois' wife, as certain authors have proposed, given that the in-laws of Jacques Bourgeois did not get married until 1627. There exists the possibility that Germain Doucet nevertheless married, in second nuptials, to a daughter of Guillaume Trahan who gave him no surviving children; but it is as possible that such a second wife is the sister of Jacques Bourgeois and not the sister of his wife. (Refer to *La Société Généalogique Canadienne Française*, Volume VI, 1955, page 372).

According to Father Archange Godbout, the second child who came to Acadie with Guillaume Trahan might well have been a daughter who was to marry, sometime before 1654, Germain Doucet, Sieur de LaVerdure. [842]

---

[842] White, Stephen A. (2000) <u>English Supplement to the Dictionnaire Généalogique des Familles Acadiennes</u> (page 139). Montréal, Québec: AGMV Marquis Imprimeur Inc.

Boutier

[1] Jean Boutier was married to Marie Godreau. [843] [844]

[2] Jean Boutier, born at St-Malo, Bretagne, France, married Anne Marguerite Doucet (d/o Michel Doucet and Marie Suzanne Mius) on January 12, 1802 at SAR. [845] Today, the Boutier surname is known as Boucher.

Certificat de Mariage

Les présentes certifient que Jean Boutier
fils de Jean Boutier et de Marie Godreaux
et
Marguerite Doucet
fille de Michel Doucet et de Marie Mius
ont contracté mariage le 12 janv. 1802
Témoins François Gilles et Pierre Mius
Prêtre officiant Rév. Sigogne
Extrait des registres de la paroisse de Ste-Anne-du-Ruisseau
Donné à Ste-Anne-du-Ruisseau le 10 oct. 2003
Rév. Crépin Khonde
Curé

---

[843] Information received from Kenneth Breau, cousin and archivist at the Université de Moncton.
[844] https://novascotia.ca/archives/acadian/reborn/archives.asp?ID=275
[845] Ibid.

[3] Scholastique Boutier, born November 22, 1806 and baptized April 5, 1807,[846] married **Pierre Eusèbe Mius (dit Petit Mius)** (s/o Pierre Baptiste dit Petit Jean Mius and Marguerite Robichaud) on October 25, 1825.[847] Pierre Eusèbe was born on June 28, 1801.[848]

Certificat de Baptême

Les présentes certifient que **Scholastique Boutier**
Fils ou fille de **Jean Boutier** et de **Anne Marguerite Doucet**
Est né(e) à _____ le **22 nov. 1806**
et a été baptisé(e) **6 avril 1807** par **Amable Boudreau**
Parrain **Simon d'Entremont** Marraine **Ursule Doucet**
a été confirmé(e) le _____ à _____
a été marié(e) le _____ à _____
Extrait des registres de la paroisse de **Ste Anne-du-Ruisseau**
Donné à **Ste-Anne-du-ruisseau** le **10 oct. 2003**

---

[846] https://novascotia.ca/archives/acadian/reborn/archives.asp?ID=701
[847] https://novascotia.ca/archives/acadian/reborn/archives.asp?ID=1605
[848] https://novascotia.ca/archives/acadian/reborn/archives.asp?ID=261

Certificat de Mariage

Les présentes certifient que **Pierre Eusebe Mius**

fils de **Jean Mius** et de **Marguerite Robicheau**

et

Scholastique Boutier

fille de **Jean Boutier** et de **Anne Marguerite Doucette**

ont contracté mariage le **25 oct. 1825**

Témoins **Joseph Mathurin**

Prêtre officiant **Rév. Sigogne**

Extrait des registres de la paroisse de **Ste-Anne-du-Ruisseau**

Donné à Ste-Anne-du-Ruisseau le **10 oct. 2003**

Rév. Crépin Khonde
Curé

Brassaud

[1] Pierre Brassaud, born c. 1663, [849] married Gabrielle Forest dit Michel (d/o Michel (dit Gereyt) de Forest and Marie Hébert) c. 1691 in PR. [850] Gabrielle was born c. 1673. [851] Pierre died before October 18, 1729. [852] Gabrielle died at GP on November 9, 1710 and was buried on November 10, 1710. [853]

[2] Susanne Brassaud, born c. 1707, [854] married **Pierre Robichaud dit Cadet** (s/o Charles Robichaud dit Cadet and Marie Bourg) c. 1730. [855] [856] Pierre was born April 25, 1707 at PR. [857] [858]

---

[849] White, Stephen A. (1999) <u>Dictionnaire Généalogique des Familles Acadiennes</u>, Volume A to G, page 267.
[850] Ibid.
[851] Ibid, pages 267 and 631.
[852] Ibid, page 267.
[853] Ibid, pages 267 and 631.
[854] Ibid, page 267.
[855] Ibid.
[856] White, Stephen A. (1999) <u>Dictionnaire Généalogique des Familles Acadiennes</u>, Volume H to Z, page 1405.
[857] Ibid.
[858] https://novascotia.ca/archives/acadian/archives.asp?ID=184

Brun

[1] Vincent Brun, born c. 1611, married Renée Breau c. 1644. [859] Renée was born c. 1616. [860] Vincent died at PR. [861] Renée died at PR, before the sensus of 1678. [862]

[2] Françoise Brun, born c. 1653, [863] married **Bernard Bourg** (s/o Antoine Bourg and Antoinette Landry) c. 1670. [864] Bernard was born c. 1648. [865] Françoise died at PR on May 23, 1725 and was buried on May 24, 1725. [866] Bernard died at PR. [867]

---

[859] White, Stephen A. (1999) <u>Dictionnaire Généalogique des Familles Acadiennes</u>, Volume A to G, pages 270 and 289.
[860] Ibid, page 270.
[861] Ibid, page 289.
[862] Ibid, pages 270 and 289.
[863] Ibid, pages 225 and 289.
[864] Ibid, pages 221, 225 and 289.
[865] Ibid.
[866] Ibid, pages 225 and 289
[867] Ibid, pages 221 and 225.

Chebrat

There is no proof that the same Jeanne Chebrat who was baptized at La Chaussée in 1627 was, in fact, the wife of Jean Poirier and Antoine Gougeon. It is, all the same, quite possible that this was the same person, considering that the Brun family in Acadie was originally from the same parish. [868] Furthermore, the Chebrat and Brun families were possibly connected by marriage, because Vincent Brun's wife was a Breau and Jeanne Chebrat's sister Philippe married the widower of a Breau. [869]

[1] Antoine Chebrat was married to Françoise Chaumoret. [870] Antoine died before January 15, 1662. [871]

[2] Jeanne Chebrat, baptized on February 5, 1627 in La Chaussée, Poitou, France, [872] [873] married **Jean Poirier** c. 1647. [874] [875] Jeanne died after the census of 1678. [876] [877] Jean died before 1654. [878]

---

[868] White, Stephen A. (2000) English Supplement to the Dictionnaire Généalogique des Familles Acadiennes (page 75). Montréal, Québec: AGMV Marquis Imprimeur Inc.
[869] Ibid.
[870] White, Stephen A. (1999) Dictionnaire Généalogique des Familles Acadiennes, Volume A to G, page 338.
[871] Ibid.
[872] Ibid.
[873] White, Stephen A. (1999) Dictionnaire Généalogique des Familles Acadiennes, Volume H to Z, page 1327.
[874] White, Stephen A. (1999) Dictionnaire Généalogique des Familles Acadiennes, Volume A to G, page 338.
[875] White, Stephen A. (1999) Dictionnaire Généalogique des Familles Acadiennes, Volume H to Z, page 1327.
[876] White, Stephen A. (1999) Dictionnaire Généalogique des Familles Acadiennes, Volume A to G, page 338.

---

[877] White, Stephen A. (1999) Dictionnaire Généalogique des Familles Acadiennes, Volume H to Z, page 1327.
[878] Ibid.

Clémenson

[1] Mathieu Clémenson was married to Antoinette Soland. [879]

[2] Jeanne Clémenson married **Jean Louis Duon** on June 22, 1683 at the St-Nizier de Lyon parish, in Lyonnais, France. [880] [881]

---

[879] White, Stephen A. (1999) <u>Dictionnaire Généalogique des Familles Acadiennes</u>, Volume A to G, page 581.
[880] Ibid.
[881] https://novascotia.ca/archives/acadian/archives.asp?ID=1272

Comeau

The origin of Pierre Comeau is unknown.

According to the research of Father James Comeau, the ancestor of the Acadian Comeau's would have been the son of Jean de Comeau de Créancy, seigneur of Chassenay, and Marguerite Ocquidem of La Choselle.[882] There is, however, no proof of this claim. Father Comeau only found this: that a Pierre de Comeau, born in 1606, was the son of Jean de Comeau de Créancy; the similarity of names does not constitute, by itself, a proof of identity.[883]

All things considered, it would seem most unlikely for this to have been one and the same person, for the following reasons: (a) one never finds the particle (de) in any documentation concerning the Comeau family in Acadie; (b) according to the censuses, the Acadian Pierre Comeau was at least eight years older than the similarly named Pierre de Comeau; (c) the trade of the Acadian Pierre Comeau was hardly the type of employment to which a member of a noble family would have been destined in the seventeenth century; one never sees the titles *esquire* and *barrelmaker* attributed to the same person in documents from that time period.[884]

---

[882] White, Stephen A. (2000) <u>English Supplement to the Dictionnaire Généalogique des Familles Acadiennes</u> (page 83). Montréal, Québec: AGMV Marquis Imprimeur Inc.
[883] Ibid.
[884] Ibid, pages 83 and 84.

The French term *tonnelier* means barrel maker or cooper. Pierre Comeau was a *tonnelier*. [885] [886]

[1] Pierre Comeau, born c. 1598, [887] married Rose Bayon c. 1649. [888] Rose Bayon was born c. 1631. [889] Pierre died at PR. [890] Rose died at PR, before the census of 1678. [891]

[2] Étienne Comeau, born c. 1650, [892] married Marie-Anne Lefebvre (d/o Martin Lefebvre and Barbe Bajolet) c. 1670. [893] [894] Marie-Anne Lefebvre was born on October 10, 1649, at the St-Jean de LaRochelle parish, in Aunis, France, and baptized on April 18, 1650. [895] [896] Étienne was buried at PR on January 22, 1723. [897] [898] Marie-Anne died before the census of 1693. [899] [900]

---

[885] Bujold, Nicole T. and Caillebeau, Maurice. (1979) Les origins françaises des premières familles acadiennes (page 15). Poitiers, France: Imprimerie l'Union.
[886] https://en.wikipedia.org/wiki/Cooper_(profession)
[887] White, Stephen A. (1999) Dictionnaire Généalogique des Familles Acadiennes, Volume A to G, page 369.
[888] Ibid, pages 93 and 369.
[889] Ibid.
[890] Ibid, page 569.
[891] Ibid, pages 93 and 569.
[892] Ibid, pages 369 and 371.
[893] Ibid.
[894] White, Stephen A. (1999) Dictionnaire Généalogique des Familles Acadiennes, Volume H to Z, page 1034.
[895] Ibid.
[896] White, Stephen A. (1999) Dictionnaire Généalogique des Familles Acadiennes, Volume A to G, page 371.
[897] Ibid, pages 369 and 371.
[898] https://novascotia.ca/archives/acadian/archives.asp?ID=1555
[899] White, Stephen A. (1999) Dictionnaire Généalogique des Familles Acadiennes, Volume H to Z, page 1034.
[900] White, Stephen A. (1999) Dictionnaire Généalogique des Familles Acadiennes, Volume A to G, page 371.

[3] Marie Comeau, born c. 1676, [901] married **Claude dit Maître Jean Doucet** (s/o Germain Doucet and Marie Landry) c. 1696. [902] Claude died at PR on December 5, 1754 and was buried on December 6, 1754. [903] [904]

---

[901] White, Stephen A. (1999) <u>Dictionnaire Généalogique des Familles Acadiennes</u>, Volume A to G, pages 371 and 541.
[902] Ibid, pages 371, 531 and 541.
[903] Ibid, pages 531 and 541.
[904] https://novascotia.ca/archives/acadian/archives.asp?ID=3510

Corporon

[1] Jean Corporon, born c. 1647, [905] married Françoise Savoie (d/o François Savoie and Catherine Lejeune) c. 1670. [906] [907] Françoise was born c. 1652. [908] [909] Jean died at PR on February 12, 1713 and was buried on the same day. [910] [911] He died during the English rule. Françoise was buried at PR on December 27, 1711. [912] [913] [914]

[2] Jean (Baptiste) Corporon dit l'aîné, born c. 1677, [915] married Marie Pinet (d/o Philippe Pinet and Catherine Hébert) c. 1702. [916] [917] Marie Pinet was born on October 8, 1685 at LM and baptized on May 13, 1686 at Bbn. [918] Jean died on March 16, 1741 at Lbg and was

---

[905] White, Stephen A. (1999) Dictionnaire Généalogique des Familles Acadiennes, Volume A to G, page 411.
[906] Ibid.
[907] White, Stephen A. (1999) Dictionnaire Généalogique des Familles Acadiennes, Volume H to Z, page 1456.
[908] Ibid.
[909] White, Stephen A. (1999) Dictionnaire Généalogique des Familles Acadiennes, Volume A to G, page 411.
[910] Ibid.
[911] https://novascotia.ca/archives/acadian/archives.asp?ID=1480
[912] White, Stephen A. (1999) Dictionnaire Généalogique des Familles Acadiennes, Volume H to Z, page 1456.
[913] White, Stephen A. (1999) Dictionnaire Généalogique des Familles Acadiennes, Volume A to G, page 411.
[914] https://novascotia.ca/archives/acadian/archives.asp?ID=1470
[915] White, Stephen A. (1999) Dictionnaire Généalogique des Familles Acadiennes, Volume A to G, pages 411 and 413.
[916] Ibid.
[917] White, Stephen A. (1999) Dictionnaire Généalogique des Familles Acadiennes, Volume H to Z, page 1311.
[918] Ibid.

buried on March 17, 1741. [919] Marie died on December 15, 1732 at Lbg and was buried on December 16, 1732. [920] [921]

[3] Eustache Corporon married Angélique Viger dit Brigeau (d/o François Viger and Clair Lejeune) c. 1749. [922] [923]

[4] Marie Rose Corporon, born c. 1752, married **Pierre Robichaud dit Cadet** (s/o Pierre Robichaud dit Cadet and Susanne Brassaud) c. 1763. [924] Their marriage was ratified by Father Bailly on October 1, 1770 at Pointe-de-l'Est (Eastern Passage, Nova Scotia). [925] This family settled in Wedgeport, Nova Scotia, sometime after the baptism of their daughter Agnès on December 1, 1771. [926]

This Pierre Robichaud would come to be known, at Bas-de-Tousquet (Wedgeport) as Pierre Cadet. He settled on land left by Joseph and Benjamin Robichaud, sons of Maximin Robichaud (à Pierre à Pierre). [927]

Pierre was among the 200 young Acadians and Natives of Villejouin recruited on Île-Saint-Jean to defend the French fort at Louisbourg. He was taken prisoner there in 1758. Nothing is known as to the lot of this family during the Deportation. [928]

---

[919] White, Stephen A. (1999) Dictionnaire Généalogique des Familles Acadiennes, Volume A to G, pages 411 and 413.
[920] Ibid, page 413.
[921] White, Stephen A. (1999) Dictionnaire Généalogique des Familles Acadiennes, Volume H to Z, page 1311.
[922] White, Stephen A. (1999) Dictionnaire Généalogique des Familles Acadiennes, Volume A to G, page 413.
[923] www.acadian-home.org/wedgeport.html
[924] Ibid.
[925] Ibid.
[926] Ibid.
[927] Ibid.
[928] Ibid.

Deveau

Deveau, a very old French name, pre-dating the Norman Conquest, is derived, as are many surnames, from topography; the very old French plural of valleys was vaux and thus *de Vaux* may be understood to be *people of the valleys* and the expression *par mon et par vaux*, meaning up hill and down dale is evidence of its meaning. [929]

It is said that a Robert deVaux, son of Harold deVaux, Lord of Vaux in Normandy made the 1066 voyage with William the Conqueror. [930] [931] [932] [933] While the immediate origin (in France) of the Acadian family cannot be established, the suggested area from which progenitor Michel may have come is not Normandy, but the old province of Dauphiné, thus no suggestion of kinship with Robert is implied, nor should any be inferred, from the above. [934]

The earliest record in Acadia of Michel (the census of 1698) gives his name as DeVaux (in France, likely deVaux); it must also be denoted that the early church registers used an au or aux ending as well, but later church and civil records came up with the misspelling DeVeau, or later, more commonly, Deveau. [935]

---

[929] Colonel John B. Devoe. (2000) <u>Devoe-deVaux Family History 1691 to 1991</u> (a self published work shared with the author in email correspondence).
[930] Ibid.
[931] fmg.ac/Projects/MedLands/ENGLISHNOBILITYMEDIEVAL3T-Z.htm#_Toc389115901
[932] racineshistoire.free.fr/LGN/PDF/Vaux.pdf
[933] <u>Reports and Papers of the Architectural and Archaeological Socities of the Counties of Lincoln and Northampton</u> (Volume 15, Google e-book, page 29).
[934] Colonel John B. Devoe. (2000) <u>Devoe-deVaux Family History 1691 to 1991</u> (a self published work shared with the author in email correspondence).
[935] Ibid.

The most common spelling today is likely Deveau; the most common anglicized version being Devoe or DeVoe.

The reason for the decades of the misspelling of names was because all spelling was held with some indifference and, of course, most individuals were not literate, depending upon the officials to spell their names; many of these scribes lacked both accuracy and consistency, as we all have observed in our search of records. [936]

In keeping with the progenitor of this Acadian family, Michel is referred to, in some records, as Michel DeVaux dit Dauphiné or simply Dauphiné. This sobriquet or nickname may hold a clue as to his origin in France, as there had been a province of that name in the 17th century. [937]

I have seen no evidence that refutes the generally held view that Michel came directly to Acadie from France and was not a resident, elsewhere, in New France, placing his arrival between 1698 and 1691, a time when few new colonists were arriving, thus suspect he may have been one of the thirty soldiers arriving at Port Royal aboard the frigate *La Frippone*. [938]

A number of sources suggest that a *dit* name associated with a French province betrays a military background; thus Michel could well have been a disbanded soldier; I have no knowledge of a list of the names of the soldiers aboard the frigate. [939]

Virtually every male between the ages of 15 and 80 (sic) in France was subject to a draft during the French and Indian War, and, by decree, every military man was required to carry a *dit* name and it most often indicated the province from which he came. [940]

---

[936] Colonel John B. Devoe. (2000) <u>Devoe-deVaux Family History 1691 to 1991</u> (a self published work shared with the author in email correspondence).
[937] Ibid.
[938] Ibid.
[939] Ibid.

Michel's ancestry presents a problem which is not likely to be solved, for there are no Beaubassin marriage records extant for the time period; also, he had no known siblings this side of the Atlantic, which might furnish other clues as to his parentage. [941]

In addition, finding a Michel born in the Dauphine province in 1663 would prove nothing.

Any researcher dealing with this family should be aware that prior to the arrival of Michel at Beaubassin, there were at least two families of the name established in the Québec area some thirty years before, but nothing in the available information on these contain any possibility of a kinship to the Acadian family. [942]

One should be aware, as well, that during the Deportation members of the Acadian DeVaux family escaped to the Québec area and remained there; many 18th century records from that province identify them as Acadian. [943]

[1] Michel Deveau dit Dauphiné, born c. 1663, [944] [945] married Marie Madeleine Martin (d/o Pierre Martin and Joachine Lafleur) c. 1693. [946] [947] [948] [949] Marie Madeleine was baptized on June 29, 1666 in Sillery, Québec. [950] [951]

---

[940] Colonel John B. Devoe. (2000) Devoe-deVaux Family History 1691 to 1991 (a self published work shared with the author in email correspondence).
[941] Ibid.
[942] Ibid.
[943] Ibid.
[944] White, Stephen A. (1999) Dictionnaire Généalogique des Familles Acadiennes, Volume A to G, page 508.
[945] csapstaff.ednet.ns.ca/jldeveau/deveau1.html
[946] White, Stephen A. (1999) Dictionnaire Généalogique des Familles Acadiennes, Volume A to G, page 508.
[947] http://www.francogene.com/genealogie-quebec-genealogy/084/084606.php
[948] Colonel John B. Devoe. (2000) Devoe-deVaux Family History 1691 to 1991 (a self published work shared with the author in email correspondence).
[949] csapstaff.ednet.ns.ca/jldeveau/deveau1.html

[2] Jacques Deveau, born c. 1699, [952] [953] married Marie Pothier (d/o Jean Pothier and Anne Poirier) on October 17, 1719 in Bbn. [954] [955] [956] Marie was born c. 1701. [957] [958] Both died before August 12, 1760. [959] [960]

[3] Jacques Deveau, born c. 1726 in the Tintamarre area (near the border of Nova Scotia and New Brunswick, close to Aulac), married Marie Madeleine Robichaud dit Cadet, (d/o Pierre Robichaud dit Cadet and Susanne Brassaud) on November 22, 1751 in PLJ. [961] [962] Marie Madeleine was born c. 1731 in Cbd. [963] [964]

---

[950] White, Stephen A. (1999) Dictionnaire Généalogique des Familles Acadiennes, Volume A to G, page 508.
[951] Tanguay, Mgr Cyprien. (1975) Dictionnaire Généalogique des Familles Canadiennes, Volume 1, page 89.
bibnum2.banq.qc.ca/bna/dicoGenealogie/src/0002/0022/0047/0048/3957-1-456.pdf
[952] White, Stephen A. (1999) Dictionnaire Généalogique des Familles Acadiennes, Volume A to G, page 508.
[953] csapstaff.ednet.ns.ca/jldeveau/deveau2.html
[954] White, Stephen A. (1999) Dictionnaire Généalogique des Familles Acadiennes, Volume H to Z, page 1346.
[955] White, Stephen A. (1999) Dictionnaire Généalogique des Familles Acadiennes, Volume A to G, page 508.
[956] csapstaff.ednet.ns.ca/jldeveau/deveau2.html
[957] White, Stephen A. (1999) Dictionnaire Généalogique des Familles Acadiennes, Volume H to Z, page 1346.
[958] csapstaff.ednet.ns.ca/jldeveau/deveau2.html
[959] White, Stephen A. (1999) Dictionnaire Généalogique des Familles Acadiennes, Volume H to Z, page 1346.
[960] White, Stephen A. (1999) Dictionnaire Généalogique des Familles Acadiennes, Volume A to G, page 508.
[961] Information received in an email from Fred Chandler Union III, dated July 2, 2001 (based on the research of Nova Scotia Acadian historian, J. Alphonse Deveau).
[962] csapstaff.ednet.ns.ca/jldeveau/deveau3.html
[963] Information received in an email from Fred Chandler Union III, dated July 2, 2001 (based on the research of Nova Scotia Acadian historian, J. Alphonse Deveau).
[964] csapstaff.ednet.ns.ca/jldeveau/deveau3.html

According to J. Alphonse Deveau, Jacques Deveau and his family were migrating from place to place between 1758 and 1786, and yet they survived. [965]

Jacques lived to a *very advanced age* according to historians Placide Gaudet and J. Alexandre Deveau. [966]

While some sources claim that Jacques died, April 1770, in Salmon River, Digby County, Nova Scotia, [967] there is documentary evidence that Jacques Deveau was still alive in Salmon River as late as 1813. [968]

We know that Jacques was still living in Salmon River in 1813 because *François Lambert Bourneuf mentions that he slept at Jacques Deveau's house that year, and he says it was Jacques himself who invited him to stay at his house until the tide permitted him to cross the river.* [969]

At that time, there was no bridge across the river and it could only be crossed at low tide. [970]

[4] François Chrysostôme (dit Couchique) Deveau, born May 1764 in Pointe du Diable, near Halifax, Nova Scotia, [971] [972] married Cécile Mius (d/o Jean Pierre Mius and Anne

---

[965] Deveau, J. Alphonse. (1989) The Deveau Family of Nova Scotia (page 58).
[966] Ibid.
[967] Information obtained from David A. Mallet.
[968] Deveau, J. Alphonse. (1989) The Deveau Family of Nova Scotia (page 58).
[969] Ibid
[970] Ibid.
[971] Information received from Kenneth Breau, cousin and archivist at the Université de Moncton.
[972] Information received in an email from Fred Chandler Union III, dated July 2, 2001 (based on the research of Nova Scotia Acadian historian, J. Alphonse Deveau).

Doucet) c. 1791. [973] [974] [975] [976] Françoise Chrysostôme (dit Couchique) died on November 25, 1842 in Salmon River, Digby County, Nova Scotia. [977] [978]

[5] Jean Séraphin Deveau, born March 27, 1799 in Salmon River, Nova Scotia, [979] [980] married Marie Madeleine O'Bird (Hubbard) (d/o Jean O'Bird and Marie Anne Doucet) c. about 1821. [981] [982] Marie Madeleine was born on October 31, 1802. [983] [984] Jean died at Lake Doucet, Digby County, Nova Scotia. [985] Marie Anne died at Lake Doucet, Digby County, Nova Scotia, sometime after 1843. [986]

---

[973] d'Entremont, Father Clarence Joseph. (1984) Histoire de Quinan, Nouvelle-Écosse, page 75.
[974] Information received from Kenneth Breau, cousin and archivist at the Université de Moncton.
[975] Information received in an email from Fred Chandler Union III, dated July 2, 2001 (based on the research of Nova Scotia Acadian historian, J. Alphonse Deveau).
[976] csapstaff.ednet.ns.ca/jldeveau/deveau3.html
[977] Information received from Kenneth Breau, cousin and archivist at the Université de Moncton.
[978] csapstaff.ednet.ns.ca/jldeveau/deveau3.html
[979] Sigogne, Father Jean Mandé. St. Mary's Bay Catalogue of Familles (1818 to 1829). Information received in an email from Fred Chandler Union III, dated July 2, 2001.
[980] Information received in an email from Sheila Hubbard Macauley, dated July 2, 2001.
[981] Macauley, Sheila Hubbard. (1996) The Hubbard Family of Nova Scotia, page 10. Baltimore, MD: Gateway Press, Inc.
[982] Sigogne, Father Jean Mandé. St. Mary's Bay Catalogue of Familles (1818 to 1829). Information received in an email from Fred Chandler Union III, dated July 2, 2001.
[983] Macauley, Sheila Hubbard. (1996) The Hubbard Family of Nova Scotia, page 10. Baltimore, MD: Gateway Press, Inc.
[984] Sigogne, Father Jean Mandé. Cape Sable Vital Statistics Catalogue of Families (1799 to 1841). Information received in an email from Fred Chandler Union III, dated July 2, 2001.
[985] Information obtained from David A. Mallet.
[986] Macauley, Sheila Hubbard. (1996) The Hubbard Family of Nova Scotia, page 10. Baltimore, MD: Gateway Press, Inc.

[6] Marie Elizabeth Deveau, born March 30, 1830 in Digby County, Nova Scotia, [987] [988] married **John William Henry Roach** on September 5, 1853. [989]

---

[987] Macauley, Sheila Hubbard. (1996) The Hubbard Family of Nova Scotia, page 10. Baltimore, MD: Gateway Press, Inc.
[988] Sigogne, Father Jean Mandé. St. Mary's Bay Catalogue of Familles (1840 to 1844). Information received in an email from Fred Chandler Union III, dated July 2, 2001.
[989] Parish of the Holy Trinity (Reel 2, Page 1, Number 2) located at the Argyle Courthouse in Tusket, NS.

Doucet 1A

August 16, 1654: Capitulation of Port Royal

Result of all the articles presented by M. Doucet de Le Verdure, on the one hand as captain commanding for the King in Port Royal, and on the other as surrogate guardian of the minor children of the late M. d'Aulnay, to Mr. Robert Sedqwick, general of the squadron and Commander-in-chief on all the coast of New England in America … and to better ensure the keeping of the above articles the said Sr de La Verdure has left as hostage M. Jacques Bourgeois, his brother-in-law and the lieutenant of the place, as well as the bearer of his power of attorney with respect to the present treaty. [990]

Having previously detailed my direct (unbroken) line of male descent from Germain Doucet, Sieur de La Verdure, in the beginning of this book, the line(s) that follow herein are other noted ancestral lines.

In essence, I am a direct line descendent of Michel Doucet, son of Joseph Doucet and Anne Surette. I also descend from several other siblings of Michel; namely, [1] Charles, who married Félicité Mius; [2] Anne, who married Jean Pierre Mius.

While my direct line then follows through to Joseph Mathurin Doucet, son of Michel Doucet and Marie Suzanne Mius, I also descend from Anne Marguerite, sister to Joseph Mathurin, as further denoted here.

---

[990] White, Stephen A. (2000) <u>English Supplement to the Dictionnaire Généalogique des Familles Acadiennes</u> (page 113). Montréal, Québec: AGMV Marquis Imprimeur Inc.

[1] Germain Doucet, Sieur de LaVerdure, was married to a woman whose name is not known to us. [991]

[2] Germain Doucet was born c. 1641. [992] He died before the census of 1698. [993] He married Marie Landry (d/o René Landry and Perrine Bourg) c. 1664. [994] [995] Marie Landry was born c. 1646. [996] [997] She died at PR, date unknown. [998] [999]

[3] Claude dit Maître Jean Doucet was born c. 1674. [1000] He died at PR on December 5, 1754 [1001] and was buried on December 6, 1754 in the Ste-Anne cemetery. [1002] [1003] He married Marie Comeau (d/o Étienne Comeau and Marie-Anne Lefebvre) c. 1696. [1004] Marie was born c. 1676. [1005]

---

[991] White, Stephen A. (1999) Dictionnaire Généalogique des Familles Acadiennes, Volume A to G, page 526.
[992] Ibid, pages 526 and 530.
[993] Ibid.
[994] Ibid.
[995] White, Stephen A. (1999) Dictionnaire Généalogique des Familles Acadiennes, Volume H to Z, page 915.
[996] Ibid.
[997] White, Stephen A. (1999) Dictionnaire Généalogique des Familles Acadiennes, Volume A to G, page 530.
[998] White, Stephen A. (1999) Dictionnaire Généalogique des Familles Acadiennes, Volume H to Z, page 915.
[999] White, Stephen A. (1999) Dictionnaire Généalogique des Familles Acadiennes, Volume A to G, page 530.
[1000] Ibid, pages 531 and 541.
[1001] https://novascotia.ca/archives/acadian/archives.asp?ID=3510
[1002] White, Stephen A. (1999) Dictionnaire Généalogique des Familles Acadiennes, Volume A to G, pages 531 and 541.
[1003] https://novascotia.ca/archives/acadian/archives.asp?ID=3510
[1004] White, Stephen A. (1999) Dictionnaire Généalogique des Familles Acadiennes, Volume A to G, pages 371, 531 and 541.
[1005] Ibid, pages 371 and 541.

[4] Joseph Doucet was born at PR on March 12, 1706. [1006] [1007] He was baptized on March 13, 1706. [1008] [1009] He married Anne Surette (d/o Pierre Surette and Jeanne Pellerin) on January 8, 1731. [1010] [1011] [1012] Anne was born at PR on May 22, 1712. [1013] [1014] She was baptized at PR on September 30, 1715. [1015] [1016]

[5] Charles Doucet was born at PR on December 21, 1735. [1017] [1018] He was baptized at PR on January 22, 1736. [1019] [1020] He married Félicité Mius (d/o Charles Amand I and Marie Marthe Hébert) c. 1775. [1021] Félicité was born c. 1745. [1022] Charles died on March 1, 1817

[1006] White, Stephen A. (1999) Dictionnaire Généalogique des Familles Acadiennes, Volume A to G, page 541.
[1007] https://novascotia.ca/archives/acadian/archives.asp?ID=127
[1008] White, Stephen A. (1999) Dictionnaire Généalogique des Familles Acadiennes, Volume A to G, page 541.
[1009] https://novascotia.ca/archives/acadian/archives.asp?ID=127
[1010] White, Stephen A. (1999) Dictionnaire Généalogique des Familles Acadiennes, Volume A to G, page 541.
[1011] White, Stephen A. (1999) Dictionnaire Généalogique des Familles Acadiennes, Volume H to Z, page 1476.
[1012] https://novascotia.ca/archives/acadian/archives.asp?ID=1807
[1013] White, Stephen A. (1999) Dictionnaire Généalogique des Familles Acadiennes, Volume H to Z, page 1476.
[1014] https://novascotia.ca/archives/acadian/archives.asp?ID=562
[1015] White, Stephen A. (1999) Dictionnaire Généalogique des Familles Acadiennes, Volume H to Z, page 1476.
[1016] https://novascotia.ca/archives/acadian/archives.asp?ID=562
[1017] Information received from Kenneth Breau, cousin and archivist at the Université de Moncton.
[1018] https://novascotia.ca/archives/acadian/archives.asp?ID=2115
[1019] Information received from Kenneth Breau, cousin and archivist at the Université de Moncton.
[1020] https://novascotia.ca/archives/acadian/archives.asp?ID=2115
[1021] Information received from Kenneth Breau, cousin and archivist at the Université de Moncton.
[1022] Ibid.

and was buried on March 3, 1817. [1023] [1024] Félicité died on February 8, 1828 and was buried on February 10, 1828. [1025] [1026]

[6] Charles (dit Tania) Doucet, born c. 1788, married Anne Mius (d/o Louis Mius and Anne Josèphe Corporon) on April 29, 1811. [1027] [1028] [1029] [1030] Anne was born c. 1792. [1031]

[7] Scholastique Doucet, born April 23, 1812, [1032] [1033] married **Jean Cyrille (dit Coco) Mius** (s/o Anselme Mius and Marguerite Mius) on October 29, 1832. [1034] [1035]

[1023] Information received from Kenneth Breau, cousin and archivist at the Université de Moncton.
[1024] https://novascotia.ca/archives/acadian/reborn/archives.asp?ID=1333
[1025] Information received from Kenneth Breau, cousin and archivist at the Université de Moncton.
[1026] https://novascotia.ca/archives/acadian/reborn/archives.asp?ID=1881
[1027] d'Entremont, Father Clarence Joseph. Histoire de Saint-Anne-du-Ruisseau, Belleville et Rivière Abram, page 21.
[1028] Information received from Kenneth Breau, cousin and archivist at the Université de Moncton.
[1029] Information received in an email from Pauline d'Entremont, dated July 6, 2001.
[1030] https://novascotia.ca/archives/acadian/reborn/archives.asp?ID=948
[1031] Information received from Kenneth Breau, cousin and archivist at the Université de Moncton.
[1032] d'Entremont, Father Clarence Joseph. (1984) Histoire de Quinan, Nouvelle-Écosse, page 89.
[1033] https://novascotia.ca/archives/acadian/reborn/archives.asp?ID=971
[1034] d'Entremont, Father Clarence Joseph. (1984) Histoire de Quinan, Nouvelle-Écosse, page 89.
[1035] https://novascotia.ca/archives/acadian/reborn/archives.asp?ID=2290

[1] Germain Doucet, Sieur de LaVerdure, was married to a woman whose name is not known to us. [1036]

[2] Germain Doucet was born c. 1641. [1037] He died before the census of 1698. [1038] He married Marie Landry (d/o René Landry and Perrine Bourg) c. 1664. [1039] [1040] Marie Landry was born c. 1646. [1041] [1042] She died at PR, date unknown. [1043] [1044]

[3] Claude dit Maître Jean Doucet was born c. 1674. [1045] He died at PR on December 5, 1754 [1046] and was buried on December 6, 1754 in the Ste-Anne cemetery. [1047] [1048] He married Marie Comeau (d/o Étienne Comeau and Marie-Anne Lefebvre) c. 1696. [1049] Marie was born c. 1676. [1050]

[1036] White, Stephen A. (1999) Dictionnaire Généalogique des Familles Acadiennes, Volume A to G, page 526.
[1037] Ibid, pages 526 and 530.
[1038] Ibid.
[1039] Ibid.
[1040] White, Stephen A. (1999) Dictionnaire Généalogique des Familles Acadiennes, Volume H to Z, page 915.
[1041] Ibid.
[1042] White, Stephen A. (1999) Dictionnaire Généalogique des Familles Acadiennes, Volume A to G, page 530.
[1043] White, Stephen A. (1999) Dictionnaire Généalogique des Familles Acadiennes, Volume H to Z, page 915.
[1044] White, Stephen A. (1999) Dictionnaire Généalogique des Familles Acadiennes, Volume A to G, page 530.
[1045] Ibid, pages 531 and 541.
[1046] https://novascotia.ca/archives/acadian/archives.asp?ID=3510
[1047] White, Stephen A. (1999) Dictionnaire Généalogique des Familles Acadiennes, Volume A to G, pages 531 and 541.
[1048] https://novascotia.ca/archives/acadian/archives.asp?ID=3510
[1049] White, Stephen A. (1999) Dictionnaire Généalogique des Familles Acadiennes, Volume A to G, pages 371, 531 and 541.
[1050] Ibid, pages 371 and 541.

[4] Joseph Doucet was born at PR on March 12, 1706. [1051] [1052] He was baptized at PR on March 13, 1706. [1053] [1054] He married Anne Surette (d/o Pierre Surette and Jeanne Pellerin) on January 8, 1731. [1055] [1056] [1057] Anne was born at PR on May 22, 1712. [1058] [1059] She was baptized on September 30, 1715. [1060] [1061]

[5] Michel Doucet was born at PR on October 17, 1754. [1062] [1063] [1064] He was baptized at PR on October 17, 1754. [1065] [1066] He married Marie Suzanne Mius (d/o François Mius and Jeanne Duon) c. 1778. [1067] [1068] Marie Suzanne was born c. 1758. [1069] Michel died on April

---

[1051] White, Stephen A. (1999) Dictionnaire Généalogique des Familles Acadiennes, Volume A to G, page 541.
[1052] https://novascotia.ca/archives/acadian/archives.asp?ID=127
[1053] White, Stephen A. (1999) Dictionnaire Généalogique des Familles Acadiennes, Volume A to G, page 541.
[1054] https://novascotia.ca/archives/acadian/archives.asp?ID=127
[1055] White, Stephen A. (1999) Dictionnaire Généalogique des Familles Acadiennes, Volume A to G, page 541.
[1056] White, Stephen A. (1999) Dictionnaire Généalogique des Familles Acadiennes, Volume H to Z, page 1476.
[1057] https://novascotia.ca/archives/acadian/archives.asp?ID=1807
[1058] White, Stephen A. (1999) Dictionnaire Généalogique des Familles Acadiennes, Volume H to Z, page 1476.
[1059] https://novascotia.ca/archives/acadian/archives.asp?ID=562
[1060] White, Stephen A. (1999) Dictionnaire Généalogique des Familles Acadiennes, Volume H to Z, page 1476.
[1061] https://novascotia.ca/archives/acadian/archives.asp?ID=562
[1062] d'Entremont, Father Clarence Joseph. (1984) Histoire de Quinan, Nouvelle-Écosse, page 18.
[1063] Information received from Kenneth Breau, cousin and archivist at the Université de Moncton.
[1064] https://novascotia.ca/archives/acadian/archives.asp?ID=3522
[1065] Information received from Kenneth Breau, cousin and archivist at the Université de Moncton.
[1066] https://novascotia.ca/archives/acadian/archives.asp?ID=3522
[1067] d'Entremont, Father Clarence Joseph. (1984) Histoire de Quinan, Nouvelle-Écosse, page 18.

19, 1830 [1070] [1071] at the age of 75 in Quinan, Yarmouth County, Nova Scotia. He was buried on April 30, 1830. [1072] According to parish records, Marie Suzanne died after her husband at a date that is not registered.

NOTE: This couple has been genetically traced to Alström Syndrome as per the French Acadian population of Yarmouth County, Nova Scotia.

[6] Anne Marguerite Doucet was married on January 12, 1802 in SAR to **Jean Boutier** (s/o Jean Boutier and Marie Godreau from Saint-Malo, France). [1073] [1074] Today, the Boutier surname is known as Boucher.

[1068] Information received from Kenneth Breau, cousin and archivist at the Université de Moncton.
[1069] d'Entremont, Father Clarence Joseph. (1984) Histoire de Quinan, Nouvelle-Écosse, page 18.
[1070] Ibid.
[1071] https://novascotia.ca/archives/acadian/reborn/archives.asp?ID=2031
[1072] Information received from Kenneth Breau, cousin and archivist at the Université de Moncton.
[1073] Ibid.
[1074] https://novascotia.ca/archives/acadian/reborn/archives.asp?ID=275

Certificat de Mariage

Les présentes certifient que **Jean Boutier**

fils de **Jean Boutier** et de **Marie Godreaux**

et

Marguerite Doucet

fille de **Michel Doucet** et de **Marie Mius**

ont contracté mariage le **12 janv. 1802**

Témoins **François Gilles et Pierre Mius**

Prêtre officiant **Rév. Sigogne**

Extrait des registres de la paroisse de **Ste-Anne-du-Ruisseau**

Donné à **Ste-Anne-du-Ruisseau** le **10 oct. 2003**

Rév. Crépin Khonde
Curé

[1] Germain Doucet, Sieur de LaVerdure, was married to a woman whose name is not known to us. [1075]

[2] Germain Doucet was born c. 1641. [1076] He died before the census of 1698. [1077] He married Marie Landry (d/o René Landry and Perrine Bourg) c. 1664. [1078] [1079] Marie Landry was born c. 1646. [1080] [1081] She died at PR, date unknown. [1082] [1083]

[3] Claude dit Maître Jean Doucet was born c. 1674. [1084] He died at PR on December 5, 1754 [1085] and was buried on December 6, 1754 in the Ste-Anne cemetery. [1086] [1087] He married Marie Comeau (d/o Étienne Comeau and Marie-Anne Lefebvre) c. 1696. [1088] Marie was born c. 1676. [1089]

[1075] White, Stephen A. (1999) Dictionnaire Généalogique des Familles Acadiennes, Volume A to G, page 526.
[1076] Ibid, pages 526 and 530.
[1077] Ibid.
[1078] Ibid.
[1079] White, Stephen A. (1999) Dictionnaire Généalogique des Familles Acadiennes, Volume H to Z, page 915.
[1080] Ibid.
[1081] White, Stephen A. (1999) Dictionnaire Généalogique des Familles Acadiennes, Volume A to G, page 530.
[1082] White, Stephen A. (1999) Dictionnaire Généalogique des Familles Acadiennes, Volume H to Z, page 915.
[1083] White, Stephen A. (1999) Dictionnaire Généalogique des Familles Acadiennes, Volume A to G, page 530.
[1084] Ibid, pages 531 and 541.
[1085] https://novascotia.ca/archives/acadian/archives.asp?ID=3510
[1086] White, Stephen A. (1999) Dictionnaire Généalogique des Familles Acadiennes, Volume A to G, pages 531 and 541.
[1087] https://novascotia.ca/archives/acadian/archives.asp?ID=3510
[1088] White, Stephen A. (1999) Dictionnaire Généalogique des Familles Acadiennes, Volume A to G, pages 371, 531 and 541.
[1089] Ibid, pages 371 and 541.

[4] Joseph Doucet was born at PR on March 12, 1706. [1090] [1091] He was baptized on March 13, 1706. [1092] [1093] He married Anne Surette (d/o Pierre Surette and Jeanne Pellerin) on January 8, 1731. [1094] [1095] [1096] Anne was born at PR on May 22, 1712. [1097] [1098] She was baptized on September 30, 1715. [1099] [1100]

[5] Anne Doucet was born at PR on April 1, 1747 and baptized on April 2, 1747. [1101] [1102] She married **Jean Pierre Mius** (s/o François and Jeanne Duon) c. 1768. [1103] Jean was born

---

[1090] White, Stephen A. (1999) <u>Dictionnaire Généalogique des Familles Acadiennes</u>, Volume A to G, page 541.
[1091] https://novascotia.ca/archives/acadian/archives.asp?ID=127
[1092] White, Stephen A. (1999) <u>Dictionnaire Généalogique des Familles Acadiennes</u>, Volume A to G, page 541.
[1093] https://novascotia.ca/archives/acadian/archives.asp?ID=127
[1094] White, Stephen A. (1999) <u>Dictionnaire Généalogique des Familles Acadiennes</u>, Volume A to G, page 541.
[1095] White, Stephen A. (1999) <u>Dictionnaire Généalogique des Familles Acadiennes</u>, Volume H to Z, page 1476.
[1096] https://novascotia.ca/archives/acadian/archives.asp?ID=1807
[1097] White, Stephen A. (1999) <u>Dictionnaire Généalogique des Familles Acadiennes</u>, Volume H to Z, page 1476.
[1098] https://novascotia.ca/archives/acadian/archives.asp?ID=562
[1099] White, Stephen A. (1999) <u>Dictionnaire Généalogique des Familles Acadiennes</u>, Volume H to Z, page 1476.
[1100] https://novascotia.ca/archives/acadian/archives.asp?ID=562
[1101] Information received from Kenneth Breau, cousin and archivist at the Université de Moncton.
[1102] https://novascotia.ca/archives/acadian/archives.asp?ID=2893
[1103] Information received from Kenneth Breau, cousin and archivist at the Université de Moncton.

on February 2, 1743. [1104] Anne was buried on January 4, 1838. [1105] [1106] Jean died on February 7, 1825 and was buried on February 8, 1825. [1107] [1108]

[1104] Information received from Kenneth Breau, cousin and archivist at the Université de Moncton.
[1105] Ibid.
[1106] https://novascotia.ca/archives/acadian/reborn/archives.asp?ID=4262
[1107] Information received from Kenneth Breau, cousin and archivist at the Université de Moncton.
[1108] https://novascotia.ca/archives/acadian/reborn/archives.asp?ID=1512

Doucet 1B

August 16, 1654: Capitulation of Port Royal

Result of all the articles presented by M. Doucet de Le Verdure, on the one hand as captain commanding for the King in Port Royal, and on the other as surrogate guardian of the minor children of the late M. d'Aulnay, to Mr. Robert Sedqwick, general of the squadron and Commander-in-chief on all the coast of New England in America … and to better ensure the keeping of the above articles the said Sr de La Verdure has left as hostage M. Jacques Bourgeois, his brother-in-law and the lieutenant of the place, as well as the bearer of his power of attorney with respect to the present treaty. [1109]

Having previously detailed my direct (unbroken) line of male descent from Germain Doucet, Sieur de La Verdure, in the beginning of this book, the line(s) that follow herein are other noted ancestral lines.

[1] Germain Doucet, Sieur de LaVerdure, was married to a woman whose name is not known to us. [1110]

[2] Marguerite Doucet, born c. 1625, [1111] was married to **Abraham Dugas** c. 1647. [1112] Abraham was born c. 1616. [1113]

[1109] White, Stephen A. (2000) English Supplement to the Dictionnaire Généalogique des Familles Acadiennes (page 113). Montréal, Québec: AGMV Marquis Imprimeur Inc.
[1110] White, Stephen A. (1999) Dictionnaire Généalogique des Familles Acadiennes, Volume A to G, page 526.
[1111] Ibid, pages 526 and 562.
[1112] Ibid.
[1113] Ibid, page 562.

Doucet 1C

August 16, 1654: Capitulation of Port Royal

Result of all the articles presented by M. Doucet de Le Verdure, on the one hand as captain commanding for the King in Port Royal, and on the other as surrogate guardian of the minor children of the late M. d'Aulnay, to Mr. Robert Sedqwick, general of the squadron and Commander-in-chief on all the coast of New England in America … and to better ensure the keeping of the above articles the said Sr de La Verdure has left as hostage M. Jacques Bourgeois, his brother-in-law and the lieutenant of the place, as well as the bearer of his power of attorney with respect to the present treaty. [1114]

Having previously detailed my direct (unbroken) line of male descent from Germain Doucet, Sieur de La Verdure, in the beginning of this book, the line(s) that follow herein are other noted ancestral lines.

[1] Germain Doucet, Sieur de LaVerdure, was married to a woman whose name is not known to us. [1115]

[2] ---------- Doucet was married to **Pierre Lejeune dit Briard**, c. 1650, according to the declarations given at Belle-Île-en-Mer. [1116] [1117]

[1114] White, Stephen A. (2000) English Supplement to the Dictionnaire Généalogique des Familles Acadiennes (page 113). Montréal, Québec: AGMV Marquis Imprimeur Inc.
[1115] White, Stephen A. (1999) Dictionnaire Généalogique des Familles Acadiennes, Volume A to G, page 526.
[1116] Ibid.
[1117] White, Stephen A. (1999) Dictionnaire Généalogique des Familles Acadiennes, Volume H to Z, page 1048.

DuFosset

[1] Antoine DuFosset was married to Isabeau Resteau. [1118]

[2] Catherine DuFosset married **Melchior de Forest** after the 4th Sunday of April 1533. [1119]

[1118] White, Stephen A. (1999) <u>Dictionnaire Généalogique des Familles Acadiennes</u>, Volume A to G, page 624.
[1119] Ibid.

Dugas

Tanguay mentions a Vincent Dugast, son of a physician named Vincent Dugast and Perrine Babin of Chouppes, in the diocese of Poitiers. [1120] N. Bujold and M. Caillebeau in Les Orinines françaises des premières familles acadiennes (pages 24 to 25) suggest that Chouppes could be the place of origin of certain Acadian families. [1121] Might it be there, that one might be able to discover the origin of this Acadian family?

December 2, 1705 records the expropriation of two lots *adjoining and drawing towards the old fort*, belonging to Abraham Dugas, who had since been dead for over five years, for an extension of the fort at PR; one must, therefore, suppose that his heirs were the actual owners of this land in 1705. [1122]

Abraham Dugas was a gunsmith (*armurier*), someone who repairs firearms. [1123]

[1] Abraham Dugas, born c. 1616, [1124] married Marguerite Doucet (d/o Germain Doucet and unknown) c. 1647. [1125] Marguerite was born c. 1625. [1126]

[2] Claude Dugas, born about 1649, [1127] married Marguerite Bourg (d/o Bernard Bourg and Françoise Brun) c. 1697. [1128] Marguerite was born c. 1674. [1129]

[1120] White, Stephen A. (2000) English Supplement to the Dictionnaire Généalogique des Familles Acadiennes (page 119). Montréal, Québec: AGMV Marquis Imprimeur Inc.
[1121] Ibid.
[1122] Ibid, page 120.
[1123] Bujold, Nicole T. and Caillebeau, Maurice. (1979) Les origins françaises des premières familles acadiennes (page15). Poitiers, France: Imprimerie l'Union.
[1124] White, Stephen A. (1999) Dictionnaire Généalogique des Familles Acadiennes, Volume A to G, page 562.
[1125] Ibid.
[1126] Ibid, pages 526 and 562.

[3] Claire Dugas, born January 21, 1706 in PR, [1130] married **Charles Amirault** (s/o François Amirault dit Tourangeau and Marie Pitre) on August 28, 1726 in PR. [1131] [1132] Charles was born June 14, 1700 in CS. [1133]

[1127] White, Stephen A. (1999) <u>Dictionnaire Généalogique des Familles Acadiennes</u>, Volume A to G, pages 562 and 564.
[1128] Ibid.
[1129] Ibid, pages 226 and 565.
[1130] Ibid, page 566.
[1131] Ibid, pages 18 and 566.
[1132] https://novascotia.ca/archives/acadian/archives.asp?ID=1119
[1133] White, Stephen A. (1999) <u>Dictionnaire Généalogique des Familles Acadiennes</u>, Volume A to G, page 18.

Dulain

When is a Dulong not a Dulong … when he is a Dulin, naturally!

For several decades I have dedicated some effort to trace the numerous descendants of Richard Dulong across North America; ironically, nine out of ten people who contact me about a possible connection to Richard Dulong are not even Dulongs and most of them are from the area around Woburn, Massachusetts, and have roots going back to Yarmouth, Nova Scotia. [1134] Most, if not all, the Dulongs from eastern Massachusetts and Nova Scotia are really Dulins.

According to a letter I received from Rev. Clarence J. d'Entremont, a leading Acadian genealogist (dated 10 July 1983) … *the ancestor of those who, in Yarmouth county [Nova Scotia], now call themselves DULONG, with relatives in the U.S., mostly in Massachusetts, was Louis DULIN, written also in the church registers DULAIN. He was from the parish of Minidray, of the diocese of Coutances, (Normandy, France). His father's name was also Louis Dulin, his mother Jeanne Gauthier. He arrived in Nova Scotia in the early 1790's, during the French Revolution. He married in Yarmouth county, most probably in Quinan (formerly The Forks), from where lived his wife, Marie Frontain, (now spelled Frotten), daughter of Julien Frontain and of Anne Mius, (now spelled Muise). This marriage took place before witnesses, as there were no priests available at the time. It was blessed at Sainte-Anne-du-Ruisseau, (formerly Eel Brook), Yarmouth county, September 30 of the same year [1799] by Father Sigogne.* [1135]

[1134] The Dulin Family website belonging to John P. Dulong located at habitant.org/dulong/dulin.htm
[1135] Ibid.

Rev. Clarence J. d'Entremont gives this couple the following children:

[1] Eudes, called Walter, born 15 October 1795, married first Magdeline Scholastique Mius, married second Julie LeBlanc, daughter of Honoré LeBlanc and Anne Judith Mius.

[2] Rosalie, born 10 March 1798, married Benjamin Bertrand dit Maffre.

[3] Oliver Martin, born 8 November 1799, married Scholastique LeBlanc.

[4] Marie Thérèse, born 11 October 1801, married Guillaume Deveau dit Bill Couchique.

[5] Anne Elisabeth, born 7 December 1803, married Florent Mius.

[6] Louis Cyprien, born 1 February 1808, married Marie Julie Doucet.

[7] Anne Françoise, born 22 July 1808, married Basile Mius.

[8] Jeanne, born 26 January 1811. [1136]

Apparently, the name Dulin was gradually changed to Dulong in both Nova Scotia and Massachusetts, although I am unsure of when the Dulin-Dulong family started to migrate to Massachusetts; after 1900, however, descendants of the Montréal DuLongs as well as the Yarmouth Dulin-Dulongs were both living in the state, making it confusing to untangle family origins. [1137]

However, as soon as you find Yarmouth, or Nova Scotia, mentioned in the records of your family, then it is safe to assume that you are really a Dulin and not a Dulong. [1138]

[1136] The Dulin Family website belonging to John P. Dulong located at habitant.org/dulong/dulin.htm
[1137] Ibid.
[1138] Ibid.

To my knowledge, all the Dulongs in Nova Scotia are really Dulins; ultimately, you must trace back each generation to verify that you are indeed a Dulin.[1139]

The records in Nova Scotia for the nineteenth century are fairly thorough; having looked at the records, I have found that many of the Yarmouth Dulin-Dulongs were fisherman.[1140]

I find it very interesting that Louis Dulin would have arrived in Nova Scotia around 1790, a time period that was very unusual; I have often wondered if he was a fisherman, fleeing the French Revolution.[1141]

You will have noted that the Dulins often married into the Muis family; this family is really the noble Mius d'Entremont family and thus related to Rev. d'Entremont.[1142] To learn more about this noble family, I suggest you start with reading the article about Philippe Mius d'Entremont in the Dictionary of Canadian Biography (1966, vol. 1, p. 510).[1143] [1144]

Lastly, the Dulins have also intermarried with many other local Acadian families.

I, too, share Acadian ancestry that I am confident will be found to overlap with any found among the Dulins; therefore, ironically, we are cousins, not through the Dulong family, but through maternal Acadian lines.[1145]

[1139] The Dulin Family website belonging to John P. Dulong located at habitant.org/dulong/dulin.htm
[1140] Ibid.
[1141] Ibid.
[1142] Ibid.
[1143] Ibid.
[1144] http://www.biographi.ca/en/bio.php?id_nbr=472
[1145] The Dulin Family website belonging to John P. Dulong located at habitant.org/dulong/dulin.htm

[1] Louis Dulain was married to Jeanne Gauthier.[1146]

[2] Louis Dulain, born in the Minidray parish, diocese of Coutances, in Normandie, France, married Marie Apolline (dite Pauline) Frontain c. 1794.[1147][1148] The marriage was blessed, by Father Sigogne, in SAR on September 30, 1799.[1149][1150] Marie Apolline was born c. 1770.[1151]

[3] Louis Cyprien Dulain, born February 1, 1806,[1152][1153] married Anne Vitaline Mius (d/o Jean Cyrille dit Coco Mius and Scholastique Doucet).[1154] Anne Vitaline was born October 12, 1833.[1155] Louis died in August 1888.[1156]

[4] Adèle Dulain, born June 4, 1876, married **Jean Théophile (dit Câlin) Doucet** (s/o Michel Patrice (dit L'Anglais) Doucet and Anne Anastasie (dite Nanette) Mius) on January 10, 1893.[1157] Adèle died on March 5, 1903, after the birth of her last child, at the age of 27 in Quinan, Yarmouth County, Nova Scotia.[1158] She was buried on March 10,

---

[1146] https://novascotia.ca/archives/acadian/reborn/archives.asp?ID=48
[1147] d'Entremont, Father Clarence Joseph. (1984) <u>Histoire de Quinan, Nouvelle-Écosse</u>, pages 19 and 20.
[1148] https://novascotia.ca/archives/acadian/reborn/archives.asp?ID=48
[1149] d'Entremont, Father Clarence Joseph. (1984) <u>Histoire de Quinan, Nouvelle-Écosse</u>, pages 19 and 20.
[1150] https://novascotia.ca/archives/acadian/reborn/archives.asp?ID=48
[1151] d'Entremont, Father Clarence Joseph. (1984) <u>Histoire de Quinan, Nouvelle-Écosse</u>, page 102.
[1152] Ibid, page 127.
[1153] https://novascotia.ca/archives/acadian/reborn/archives.asp?ID=632
[1154] d'Entremont, Father Clarence Joseph. (1984) <u>Histoire de Quinan, Nouvelle-Écosse</u>, page 127.
[1155] https://novascotia.ca/archives/acadian/reborn/archives.asp?ID=2382
[1156] d'Entremont, Father Clarence Joseph. (1984) <u>Histoire de Quinan, Nouvelle-Écosse</u>, page 126.
[1157] Ibid, page 115.
[1158] Ste. Agnès RC Church records in Quinan, NS. Information obtained by Linda Joyce Campbell (first cousin once removed to my father) of Yarmouth, NS.

1903 in Quinan, Yarmouth County, Nova Scotia. [1159] Jean Théophile was baptized in April 1867. [1160]

Certificat de Baptême

Je Certifie que Marie Adèle Dulong
Enfant de Sylvain Dulong et Vitaline Mius
est né le 4e jour de juin 1876 à
baptisé le 5e jour de juin 1876 à Sainte-Anne-du-Ruisseau
confirmé le _____ jour de _____ 19__ à

SUIVANT LE RITE DE L'EGLISE CATHOLIQUE ROMAINE

par REV. William Mihan
Parrain et _____
Marraine _____

extrait conforme au registre des baptêmes de cette Eglise.

Père Crépin Khonde Curé

le 11 avril 2002   par _____

[1159] Ste. Agnès RC Church records in Quinan, NS. Information obtained by Linda Joyce Campbell (first cousin once removed to my father) of Yarmouth, NS.
[1160] Information obtained from Pauline d'Entremont in an email dated July 6, 2001.

Certificat de Mariage

Les présentes certifient que Jean Théophile Doucet

fils de Michel Doucet et de Rosalie Doucet

et

Adèle Dulin

fille de Louis Dulin et de Vitaline Doucet

ont contracté mariage le 10 janvier 1893

Témoins Ignace Mius et Anne Krentin

Prêtre officiant Jules Crouzier

Extrait des registres de la paroisse de Sainte-Anne-du-Ruisseau

Donné à Ste-Anne-du-Ruisseau le 11 avril 2002

Sr Yvette Duguay
Agente de Pastorale de Quinan

Paroisse Ste-Agnès

Death and Burial Certificate

This is to certify that Adèle Doucet who died on March 5th, 1904 was buried in our parish cemetery on March 10th, 1904. (27 years old)

Husband (Wife) of Théophile Doucet .

Rev. J. Crouzier officiating.

This is a true copy of the records of Ste-Agnès Parish.

Given at Quinan, N.S., on July 16th, 2004 .

Sr Yvette Duguay
~~Curé~~
Pastoral Agent

Duon

[1] Mathieu Duon, a merchant from Lyon, was married to Catherine Peyrieu about 1650. [1161]

[2] Jean Louis Duon married Jeanne Clémenson (d/o Mathieu Clémenson and Antoinette Soland) on June 22, 1683 at the St-Nizier de Lyon parish, in Lyonnais, France. [1162]

[3] Jean Baptiste (dit Lyonnais) Duon, born about 1684 at the St-Nizier de Lyon parish, in Lyonnais, France, [1163] married Agnès Hébert (d/o Antoine Hébert and Jeanne Corporon) on January 27, 1713 at PR. [1164] [1165] [1166] Agnès was born c. 1696. [1167] Jean Baptiste died at PR on May 5, 1746 and was buried on May 6, 1746. [1168] [1169]

[4] Jeanne Duon, born March 29, 1718 at PR, [1170] [1171] married **François Mius** (s/o Joseph Mius dit d'Azy and Marie Amirault) on February 14, 1735 at PR. [1172] [1173] [1174] François was

---

[1161] White, Stephen A. (1999) Dictionnaire Généalogique des Familles Acadiennes, Volume A to G, page 581.
[1162] Ibid.
[1163] Ibid.
[1164] Ibid.
[1165] White, Stephen A. (1999) Dictionnaire Généalogique des Familles Acadiennes, Volume H to Z, page 810.
[1166] https://novascotia.ca/archives/acadian/archives.asp?ID=1272
[1167] White, Stephen A. (1999) Dictionnaire Généalogique des Familles Acadiennes, Volume H to Z, page 810.
[1168] White, Stephen A. (1999) Dictionnaire Généalogique des Familles Acadiennes, Volume A to G, page 581.
[1169] https://novascotia.ca/archives/acadian/archives.asp?ID=2822
[1170] White, Stephen A. (1999) Dictionnaire Généalogique des Familles Acadiennes, Volume A to G, page 582.
[1171] https://novascotia.ca/archives/acadian/archives.asp?ID=680
[1172] White, Stephen A. (1999) Dictionnaire Généalogique des Familles Acadiennes, Volume A to G, page 582.

born March 19, 1703 at CS. [1175] [1176] According to Father Clarence Joseph d'Entremont, François died between 1766 and 1775. [1177]

[1173] White, Stephen A. (1999) <u>Dictionnaire Généalogique des Familles Acadiennes</u>, Volume H to Z, page 1207.
[1174] https://novascotia.ca/archives/acadian/archives.asp?ID=2037
[1175] White, Stephen A. (1999) <u>Dictionnaire Généalogique des Familles Acadiennes</u>, Volume H to Z, page 1207.
[1176] https://novascotia.ca/archives/acadian/archives.asp?ID=104
[1177] White, Stephen A. (1999) <u>Dictionnaire Généalogique des Familles Acadiennes</u>, Volume H to Z, page 1207.

de Forest

UPDATED JUNE 6, 2016

For several years, there had been a general theory expressed concerning the origins of the Acadian Michel Forest, one that stated him as having been part of the de Forest family of Huguenots who lived in the Netherlands before coming to North America.

This prestigious bourgeois family reaches back to Gaspard de Forest who was living in Avesnes, French Flanders, in 1450. As French-speaking Protestant Walloons from French Flanders, they sought refuge from religious persecution in the Netherlands; several of them became involved in various New World colonization efforts, including the New Netherlands (New York) and French Guiana. [1178]

There were two specific theories that full under the Walloon Forest origin theory for Michel de Forest.

[1] The Jessé theory claimed that Michel de Forest was the son of Henri de Forest (husband of Gertrude Bornstra) and the grandson of Jessé de Forest (husband of Marie du Cloux), the son of Jean or Jehan de Forest and Anne Maillard or Maillart. Father Vincent de Lérins, in his first edition of <u>Histoire de la famille Forest</u> (published in 1955), expressed that Michel came to New Amsterdam (New York) after the death of his mother, only to find that Jean de la Montagne, the husband of Rachel de Forest, his aunt, had possession of his father's property. When he became of age, he joined the Thomas Temple expedition to Nova Scotia. Michel was supposedly among the settlers who arrived in 1657. He settled down, married a

---

[1178] http://forum.famillesforest.org/articles.php?lng=en&pg=232&mnuid=283&tconfig=0

local woman and decided to remain when the French reclaimed the colony from the British in 1670.

[2] The Gérard theory claimed that Michel de Forest was really Gereyt de Forest, the son of Crispin de Forest (husband of Marguerite Bornstra) and the grandson of Gérard de Forest (husband of Esther de La Grange), another son of Jean or Jehan de Forest and Anne Maillard or Maillart (making him brother to Jessé de Forest, husband of Marie du Cloux), as expressed by Father Vincent de Lérins, in his second edition of Histoire de la famille Forest (published in 1965). Marguerite Bornstra was the sister of Gertrude Bornstra; she married Henri de Forest, Crispin's cousin, in a double wedding. These facts were verified by surviving primary documents, including the Walloon Register.

Whilst the Gérard theory is certainly stronger than the Jessé theory, the key to proving its authenticity lies in locating the list of colonists brought to Nova Scotia by Sir Thomas Temple.

Finding the 1658 list of settlers would be an important contribution to the origins of several Acadian families in the late 1650s; namely, the Melanson brothers (from England), Jean Pitre, Lawrence Granger (from Plymouth, England) and Roger Caissie (from Ireland).

We know that Michel de Forest married Marie Hébert about 1666. This time frame certainly lends credence to the idea that he may have arrived during the period of British control (1654 to 1670). However, Placide Gaudet was the first historian to suggest that Michel de Forest came to Acadie with Governor Charles de Menou d'Aulnay in 1650, before the English takeover. According to Nicole Bujold and Maurice Caillebeau in Les Origines françaises des premières familles acadiennes (1979, page 38), Governor d'Aulnay was recruiting young men to come to Acadie between 1645 and 1650.

Apparently, there is yet another theory, the Parthenay theory, one that is not tied to the Walloon de Forest family.

The papers of Gérald Forest, located at the Centre d'études acadiennes, show that he was pursuing the possibility that Michel de Forest might have been related to Pierre de Forest (from the parish of Ste-Croix, village of Parthenay, diocese of Poitiers, in Poitou, France). Pierre was the son of Michel de Forest and Renéee Bernardeau. He came to Montréal, Québec, marrying Elizabeth Langevin (daughter of Louis Langevin and Jeanne Gateau) on 10 April 1741, at the age of 28 years. Might there be a distant relation?

DNA EVIDENCE

Several descendants of Michel de Forest as well as a few descendants of Jessé de Forest have had their Y-DNA tested; they simply do not match. It is now clearly established that there is no genetic relationship between these two men.

It has become increasingly apparent that the more recent origins of the de Forest from Acadia is likely more centered toward the north region of France. Michel de Forest was not Gereyt de Forest.

UNPROVEN TO DATE

[1] Melchior de Forest, a merchant living in Avesnes, French Flanders, was married to Jacqueline Bronchin about 1510.[1179] Melchoir died c. 1549.[1180]

[2] Melchior de Forest, a cloth merchant, married Catherine DuFosset (d/o Antoine DuFosset and Isabeau Resteau from Mons) after the 4th Sunday of April 1533.[1181] Melchoir died before January 28, 1572.[1182] Catherine died in 1579, after the second Sunday following the festival of the Trinity, when there was a mass celebrated in her name.[1183]

[3] Jean de Forest, born c. 1548, married Anne Maillard (d/o Michel Maillard and Marguerite Raux) c. 1575.[1184] A cloth merchant located in Sedan, Champagne, Ardenne, France, he converted to Calvinism.[1185]

It was Father Vincent de Lérins, in his second edition of <u>Histoire de la famille Forest</u> (1965), who wrote … *Our unfortunate Jean, having been infected with Calvin's errors, ended up deciding that it was necessary to leave Avesnes, because of the threat of religious persecution. Little by little he sold his property and about 1600 his family, then composed of four children, split up: Melchior to Lille, Gérard to Leyden, in Holland, Anne with her mother to Amsterdam. Only Jesse remained with his father, who went to settle at Sedan, as*

[1179] White, Stephen A. (1999) <u>Dictionnaire Généalogique des Familles Acadiennes</u>, Volume A to G, pages 622 and 623.
[1180] Ibid.
[1181] Ibid, pages 623 and 624.
[1182] Ibid.
[1183] Ibid, page 624.
[1184] Ibid, pages 624 and 625.
[1185] Ibid, page 625.

a merchant-draper. At last, around 1615, Jean de Forest and his family were reunited at Leyden. [1186]

[4] Gérard de Forest, born c. 1583 in Avesnes, French Flanders, married Esther de La Grange (d/o Crispin de La Grange and unknown) on August 12, 1611 (Leyde, Wallon's church, Amsterdam, the Netherlands). [1187] Gérard, a Black Dyer at Leyde, was also associated with Kiliaen van Rensselaer, a Dutch diamond and pearl merchant from Amsterdam who was instrumental in the founding of Fort Orange, New Netherland (today known as Albany, New York). [1188] [1189] [1190] [1191] Gérard died in August 1654, according to the parish records at Leyde, Wallon's church, Amsterdam, the Netherlands. [1192]

[5] Crispin de Forest, baptized on December 9, 1612 in Leyde, Wallon's church, Amsterdam, the Netherlands, married Marguerite Bornstra (d/o Wybrant-Andriesz Bornstra and unknown) on July 1, 1636 (Leyde, Wallon's church, Amsterdam, the Netherlands). [1193]

[1186] White, Stephen A. (2000) <u>English Supplement to the Dictionnaire Généalogique des Familles Acadiennes</u> (page 131). Montréal, Québec: AGMV Marquis Imprimeur Inc.
[1187] White, Stephen A. (1999) <u>Dictionnaire Généalogique des Familles Acadiennes</u>, Volume A to G, pages 625 and 627.
[1188] Ibid, page 627
[1189] https://archive.org/details/vanrensselaerfam21spoo
[1190] https://en.wikipedia.org/wiki/Kiliaen_van_Rensselaer_(merchant)
[1191] https://en.wikipedia.org/wiki/Fort_Orange_(New_Netherland)
[1192] White, Stephen A. (1999) <u>Dictionnaire Généalogique des Familles Acadiennes</u>, Volume A to G, pages 625 and 627.
[1193] Ibid, pages 627 and 628.

THAT WHICH IS KNOWN TO US

[1] Michel (de) Forest, baptized on June 18, 1637 in Leyde, Wallon's church, Amsterdam, the Netherlands, [1194] married Marie Hébert (d/o Étienne Hébert and Marie Gaudet) c. 1666. [1195] [1196] [1197] Marie was born c. 1651. [1198] [1199] Michel died before 1691. [1200] Marie died in PR, in either 1677 or 1678. [1201] [1202]

It was Father Vincent de Lérins who suggested, in his second edition of Histoire de la famille Forest (1965), that the Acadian ancestor Michel was the same as Gereyt de Forest, son of Crispin de Forest and Marguerite Bornstra. In the persuing of this research, he found *that a persistent tradition, among the Forest families in the Gaspé peninsula, maintained that the Acadian ancestor came from a family originally from the French Flanders and that he converted to Catholicism in Acadie.* [1203]

[1194] White, Stephen A. (1999) Dictionnaire Généalogique des Familles Acadiennes, Volume A to G, pages 628 and 630.
[1195] Ibid.
[1196] White, Stephen A. (1999) Dictionnaire Généalogique des Familles Acadiennes, Volume H to Z, page 800.
[1197] www.francogene.com/genealogie-quebec-genealogy/115/115539.php
[1198] White, Stephen A. (1999) Dictionnaire Généalogique des Familles Acadiennes, Volume H to Z, page 800.
[1199] White, Stephen A. (1999) Dictionnaire Généalogique des Familles Acadiennes, Volume A to G, page 630.
[1200] White, Stephen A. (1999) Dictionnaire Généalogique des Familles Acadiennes, Volume A to G, pages 628 and 630.
[1201] White, Stephen A. (1999) Dictionnaire Généalogique des Familles Acadiennes, Volume H to Z, page 800.
[1202] White, Stephen A. (1999) Dictionnaire Généalogique des Familles Acadiennes, Volume A to G, page 630.
[1203] White, Stephen A. (2000) English Supplement to the Dictionnaire Généalogique des Familles Acadiennes (page 133). Montréal, Québec: AGMV Marquis Imprimeur Inc.

It must also be denoted that the Acadian ancestor called himself de Forest rather than Forest, Forêt, or La Forêt; according to Father Vincent de Lérins, the de Forest family *was widespread in the north of France.* [1204]

The archives of Amsterdam and Leyden contain no mention of Gereyt Forest after his birth, neither a record of his marriage, nor of his burial, nor any other documents in which he might have appeared; and that, furthermore, the archivists of these cities are inclined to believe that he left the country for America, as other members of his family did. [1205]

Considering further that this Gereyt de Forest is never mentioned in the censuses of PR, or of other places, in Acadie, it seems very clear that on the occasion of his conversion to Catholicism (for he was a Huguenot), Gereyt took a saint's name, that of Michel, as his patron and also in memory of his great grandfather, Michel Maillard, who had not passed over to Calvinism. [1206]

While this may, admittedly, be possible, additional proof is still needed.

[7] Gabrielle Forest dit Michel, born c. 1673, [1207] married **Pierre Brassaud** c. 1691. [1208] Pierre was born c. 1663. [1209] Gabrielle died at GP on November 9, 1710 and was buried on November 10, 1710. [1210] Pierre died before October 18, 1729. [1211]

[1204] White, Stephen A. (2000) English Supplement to the Dictionnaire Généalogique des Familles Acadiennes (page 133). Montréal, Québec: AGMV Marquis Imprimeur Inc.
[1205] Ibid.
[1206] Ibid.
[1207] White, Stephen A. (1999) Dictionnaire Généalogique des Familles Acadiennes, Volume A to G, pages 267 and 631.
[1208] Ibid, pages 267 and 631.
[1209] Ibid, page 267.
[1210] Ibid, pages 267 and 631.
[1211] Ibid, page 267.

Frontain

[1] Julien Alexandre Frontain married Anne Mius (d/o François Mius and Jeanne Duon) c. 1759 in MA (exile). [1212] Anne was born on November 4, 1736. [1213] [1214] Anne died on March 23, 1807 in Quinan, Yarmouth County, Nova Scotia. [1215]

[2] Marie Apolline (dite Pauline) Frontain, born c. 1770, [1216] married **Louis Dulain** (s/o Louis Dulain and Jeanne Gauthier) c. 1794. [1217] [1218] Louis was born in the parish of Minidray, diocese of Coutances, in Normandie, France.

[1212] d'Entremont, Father Clarence Joseph. (1984) <u>Histoire de Quinan, Nouvelle-Écosse</u>, page 17.
[1213] Ibid.
[1214] https://novascotia.ca/archives/acadian/archives.asp?ID=2169
[1215] d'Entremont, Father Clarence Joseph. (1984) <u>Histoire de Quinan, Nouvelle-Écosse</u>, page 17.
[1216] Ibid, page 102.
[1217] Ibid, pages 19 and 20.
[1218] https://novascotia.ca/archives/acadian/reborn/archives.asp?ID=48

Gaudet 1A

The oldest inhabitant of PR [in 1671] was the venerable *doyen* (senior member) of the colony; Jean Gaudet, aged ninety-six years. [1219]

[1] Jean Gaudet, born c. 1575, was married to a woman whose name is not known to us c. 1622. [1220]

[2] Françoise Gaudet, born c. 1623, [1221] [1222] married **Daniel LeBlanc** c. 1650. [1223] [1224] Daniel was her second husband. Daniel was born c. 1626. [1225] François died at PR, between the censuses of 1678 and 1700. [1226] [1227] Daniel died at PR, between the Oath of 1695 and the census of 1698. [1228]

[1219] White, Stephen A. (2000) English Supplement to the Dictionnaire Généalogique des Familles Acadiennes (page 139). Montréal, Québec: AGMV Marquis Imprimeur Inc.
[1220] White, Stephen A. (1999) Dictionnaire Généalogique des Familles Acadiennes, Volume A to G, page 666.
[1221] Ibid.
[1222] White, Stephen A. (1999) Dictionnaire Généalogique des Familles Acadiennes, Volume H to Z, page 983.
[1223] Ibid.
[1224] White, Stephen A. (1999) Dictionnaire Généalogique des Familles Acadiennes, Volume A to G, page 666.
[1225] White, Stephen A. (1999) Dictionnaire Généalogique des Familles Acadiennes, Volume H to Z, page 983.
[1226] White, Stephen A. (1999) Dictionnaire Généalogique des Familles Acadiennes, Volume A to G, page 666.
[1227] White, Stephen A. (1999) Dictionnaire Généalogique des Familles Acadiennes, Volume H to Z, page 983.
[1228] Ibid.

October 5, 1687: Account of the work accomplished in Acadia by Sr d'Aulnay; among those who made their marks: Daniel LeBlanc. Daniel thus arrived in Acadia before d'Aulnay's death in 1650. [1229]

Daniel LeBlanc *settled on the north bank of the Port Royal River (today the Annapolis River), to the northeast of the marsh at Bélisle, about nine miles above the fort at Port Royal, and a half mile below the chapel of Saint-Laurent, here he died between the years 1693 and 1698.* [1230]

May 24, 1690: Daniel LeBlanc was one of the six members of the council demanded by Phips charged with keeping the peace and meting out justice. [1231]

Although many residents took the oath unreservedly in 1695, by 1727 the Acadians were using it as a bargaining tool; they maintained they were neutral in any conflict the English had with the French and Mik'maq. [1232]

August 1695 (old style): Daniel LeBlanc took the oath of allegiance to the King of England at Port Royal; he made his mark on the document. [1233]

[1229] White, Stephen A. (2000) English Supplement to the Dictionnaire Généalogique des Familles Acadiennes (page 210). Montréal, Québec: AGMV Marquis Imprimeur Inc.
[1230] Ibid, page 209.
[1231] Ibid, page 210.
[1232] www.accesswave.ca/~cfraser/MarieBourg.html
[1233] White, Stephen A. (2000) English Supplement to the Dictionnaire Généalogique des Familles Acadiennes (page 210). Montréal, Québec: AGMV Marquis Imprimeur Inc.

Gaudet 1B

The oldest inhabitant of PR [in 1671] was the venerable doyen (senior member) of the colony; Jean Gaudet, aged ninety-six years. [1234]

[1] Jean Gaudet, born c. 1575, was married to a woman whose name is not known to us c. 1622. [1235]

[2] Marie Gaudet, born c. 1633, [1236] [1237] married **Étienne Hébert** c. 1650. [1238] [1239] Marie was buried at PR on July 30, 1710. [1240] [1241] [1242] Étienne died between 1669 and 1671. [1243]

[1234] White, Stephen A. (2000) English Supplement to the Dictionnaire Généalogique des Familles Acadiennes (page 139). Montréal, Québec: AGMV Marquis Imprimeur Inc.
[1235] White, Stephen A. (1999) Dictionnaire Généalogique des Familles Acadiennes, Volume A to G, page 666.
[1236] Ibid, page 667.
[1237] White, Stephen A. (1999) Dictionnaire Généalogique des Familles Acadiennes, Volume H to Z, page 800.
[1238] Ibid.
[1239] White, Stephen A. (1999) Dictionnaire Généalogique des Familles Acadiennes, Volume A to G, page 667.
[1240] Ibid.
[1241] White, Stephen A. (1999) Dictionnaire Généalogique des Familles Acadiennes, Volume H to Z, page 800.
[1242] https://novascotia.ca/archives/acadian/archives.asp?ID=1463
[1243] White, Stephen A. (1999) Dictionnaire Généalogique des Familles Acadiennes, Volume H to Z, page 800.

Gaudet 2

The oldest inhabitant of PR [in 1671] was the venerable *doyen* (senior member) of the colony; Jean Gaudet, aged ninety-six years. [1244]

[1] Jean Gaudet, born c. 1575, was married a second time to Nicole Colleson c. 1652. [1245] It is thought that she was probably a widow when she married Jean. Nicole was born c. 1607. [1246]

[2] Jean Gaudet, born c. 1653, married Jeanne Henry dit Robert c. 1680. [1247] [1248] Jeanne was born c. 1656. [1249] [1250] Jeanne was his second wife. Jeanne died before the census of 1693. [1251] [1252]

[3] Marie Gaudet, born c. 1681, [1253] [1254] married **Martin LeJeune dit Briard** (s/o Pierre Lejeune dit Briard and ---------- Doucet), widower of Jeanne Marie Kagigconiac (Mi'kmaq), c. 1699. [1255] [1256] Martin was born c. 1661. [1257] Marie died before October 16, 1729. [1258]

[1244] White, Stephen A. (2000) English Supplement to the Dictionnaire Généalogique des Familles Acadiennes (page 139). Montréal, Québec: AGMV Marquis Imprimeur Inc.
[1245] White, Stephen A. (1999) Dictionnaire Généalogique des Familles Acadiennes, Volume A to G, pages 369 and 667.
[1246] Ibid.
[1247] Ibid, pages 667 and 669.
[1248] White, Stephen A. (1999) Dictionnaire Généalogique des Familles Acadiennes, Volume H to Z, page 840.
[1249] Ibid.
[1250] White, Stephen A. (1999) Dictionnaire Généalogique des Familles Acadiennes, Volume A to G, page 669.
[1251] White, Stephen A. (1999) Dictionnaire Généalogique des Familles Acadiennes, Volume H to Z, page 840.
[1252] White, Stephen A. (1999) Dictionnaire Généalogique des Familles Acadiennes, Volume A to G, page 669.

[1253] White, Stephen A. (1999) <u>Dictionnaire Généalogique des Familles Acadiennes</u>, Volume A to G, page 669.
[1254] White, Stephen A. (1999) <u>Dictionnaire Généalogique des Familles Acadiennes</u>, Volume H to Z, page 1054.
[1255] White, Stephen A. (1999) <u>Dictionnaire Généalogique des Familles Acadiennes</u>, Volume A to G, page 669.
[1256] White, Stephen A. (1999) <u>Dictionnaire Généalogique des Familles Acadiennes</u>, Volume H to Z, page 1054.
[1257] Ibid, pages 1049 and 1054.
[1258] White, Stephen A. (1999) <u>Dictionnaire Généalogique des Familles Acadiennes</u>, Volume A to G, page 669.

Hébert 1

Antoine Hébert was a *tonnelier*. [1259] [1260] The French term *tonnelier* means barrel maker or cooper.

Antoine was also a brother to Étienne Hébert (as married to Marie Gaudet).

[1] Antoine Hébert, born c. 1621, married Geneviève Lefranc c. 1648. [1261] Geneviève was born c. 1613. [1262]

[2] Catherine Hébert, born c. 1656, married **Jacques LeBlanc** (s/o Daniel LeBlanc and Françoise Gaudet) c. 1673. [1263] Jacques was born c. 1651. [1264] Catherine died at St-Charles-des-Mines, the parish at GP. [1265] Jacques died at St-Charles-des-Mines, the parish at GP, after May 26, 1731. [1266]

[1259] Bujold, Nicole T. and Caillebeau, Maurice. (1979) <u>Les origins françaises des premières familles acadiennes</u> (page 16). Poitiers, France: Imprimerie l'Union.
[1260] https://en.wikipedia.org/wiki/Cooper_(profession)
[1261] White, Stephen A. (1999) <u>Dictionnaire Généalogique des Familles Acadiennes</u>, Volume H to Z, pages 798 and 1039.
[1262] Ibid.
[1263] Ibid, pages 799, 983 and 985.
[1264] Ibid, pages 983 and 985.
[1265] Ibid, pages 799 and 985.
[1266] Ibid, pages 983 and 985.

Hébert 2A

Étienne was a brother to Antoine Hébert (as married to Geneviève Lefranc).

[1] Étienne Hébert married Marie Gaudet c. 1650. [1267] [1268] Marie was born c. 1633. [1269] [1270] Étienne died between 1669 and 1671. [1271] Marie was buried at PR on July 30, 1710. [1272] [1273] [1274]

[2] Marie Hébert (born about 1651) [1275] [1276] married **Michel (Gereyt) (de) Forest** (s/o Crispin de Forest and Marguerite Bornstra) c. 1666. [1277] [1278] Michel (Gereyt) was

---

[1267] White, Stephen A. (1999) Dictionnaire Généalogique des Familles Acadiennes, Volume H to Z, page 800.
[1268] White, Stephen A. (1999) Dictionnaire Généalogique des Familles Acadiennes, Volume A to G, page 666.
[1269] Ibid.
[1270] White, Stephen A. (1999) Dictionnaire Généalogique des Familles Acadiennes, Volume H to Z, page 800.
[1271] Ibid.
[1272] White, Stephen A. (1999) Dictionnaire Généalogique des Familles Acadiennes, Volume A to G, page 666.
[1273] White, Stephen A. (1999) Dictionnaire Généalogique des Familles Acadiennes, Volume H to Z, page 800.
[1274] https://novascotia.ca/archives/acadian/archives.asp?ID=1463
[1275] White, Stephen A. (1999) Dictionnaire Généalogique des Familles Acadiennes, Volume H to Z, page 800.
[1276] White, Stephen A. (1999) Dictionnaire Généalogique des Familles Acadiennes, Volume A to G, pages 628 and 630.
[1277] White, Stephen A. (1999) Dictionnaire Généalogique des Familles Acadiennes, Volume H to Z, page 800.
[1278] White, Stephen A. (1999) Dictionnaire Généalogique des Familles Acadiennes, Volume A to G, pages 628 and 630.

baptized on June 18, 1637 in Leyde, Wallon's church, Amsterdam, the Netherlands.[1279] Marie died at PR, in either 1677 or 1678.[1280][1281] Michel died before 1691.[1282]

It was Father Vincent de Lérins who suggested, in his second edition of <u>Histoire de la famille Forest</u> (1965), that the Acadian ancestor Michel was the same as Gereyt de Forest, son of Crispin de Forest and Marguerite Bornstra. In the persuing of his research, he found *that a persistent tradition, among the Forest families in the Gaspé peninsula, maintained that the Acadian ancestor came from a family originally from the French Flanders and that he converted to Catholicism in Acadie.*[1283] It must also be denoted that the Acadian ancestor called himself de Forest rather than Forest, Forêt, or La Forêt. According to Father Vincent de Lérins, the de Forest family *was widespread in the north of France.*[1284]

The archives of Amsterdam and Leyden contain no mention of Gereyt Forest after his birth, neither a record of his marriage, nor of his burial, nor any other documents in which he might have appeared; and that, furthermore, the archivists of these cities are inclined to believe that he left the country for America, as other members of his family did.[1285]

[1279] White, Stephen A. (1999) <u>Dictionnaire Généalogique des Familles Acadiennes</u>, Volume A to G, pages 628 and 630.
[1280] White, Stephen A. (1999) <u>Dictionnaire Généalogique des Familles Acadiennes</u>, Volume H to Z, page 800.
[1281] White, Stephen A. (1999) <u>Dictionnaire Généalogique des Familles Acadiennes</u>, Volume A to G, page 630.
[1282] Ibid, pages 628 and 630.
[1283] White, Stephen A. (2000) <u>English Supplement to the Dictionnaire Généalogique des Familles Acadiennes</u> (page 133). Montréal, Québec: AGMV Marquis Imprimeur Inc.
[1284] Ibid.
[1285] Ibid.

Considering further that this Gereyt de Forest is never mentioned in the censuses of PR, or of other places, in Acadie, it seems very clear that on the occasion of his conversion to Catholicism (for he was a Huguenot), Gereyt took a saint's name, that of Michel, as his patron and also in memory of his great grandfather, Michel Maillard, who had not passed over to Calvinism. [1286]

While this may, admittedly, be possible, additional proof is still needed.

[1286] White, Stephen A. (2000) <u>English Supplement to the Dictionnaire Généalogique des Familles Acadiennes</u> (page 133). Montréal, Québec: AGMV Marquis Imprimeur Inc.

Hébert 2B

Étienne was a brother to Antoine Hébert (as married to Geneviève Lefranc).

[1] Étienne Hébert married Marie Gaudet c. 1650. [1287] [1288] Marie was born c. 1633. [1289] [1290] Étienne died between 1669 and 1671. [1291] Marie was buried at PR on July30, 1710. [1292] [1293] [1294]

[2] Catherine Hébert, born c. 1662, [1295] married **Philippe Pinet** (s/o ---------- Pinet and Anne Marie ----------) before the 1678 census of PR. [1296] Pierre was born c. 1654. [1297] Catherine died at Lbg on August 3, 1727 and was buried on August 4, 1727. [1298] Philippe died before October 1, 1710. [1299]

[1287] White, Stephen A. (1999) <u>Dictionnaire Généalogique des Familles Acadiennes</u>, Volume H to Z, page 800.
[1288] White, Stephen A. (1999) <u>Dictionnaire Généalogique des Familles Acadiennes</u>, Volume A to G, page 666.
[1289] Ibid.
[1290] White, Stephen A. (1999) <u>Dictionnaire Généalogique des Familles Acadiennes</u>, Volume H to Z, page 800.
[1291] Ibid.
[1292] White, Stephen A. (1999) <u>Dictionnaire Généalogique des Familles Acadiennes</u>, Volume A to G, page 666.
[1293] White, Stephen A. (1999) <u>Dictionnaire Généalogique des Familles Acadiennes</u>, Volume H to Z, page 800.
[1294] https://novascotia.ca/archives/acadian/archives.asp?ID=1463
[1295] White, Stephen A. (1999) <u>Dictionnaire Généalogique des Familles Acadiennes</u>, Volume H to Z, pages 800 and 1310.
[1296] Ibid, pages 800 and 1310.
[1297] Ibid, page 1310.
[1298] Ibid, pages 800 and 1310.
[1299] Ibid, page 1310.

Hébert 2C

Étienne was a brother to Antoine Hébert (as married to Geneviève Lefranc).

[1] Étienne Hébert married Marie Gaudet c. 1650. [1300] [1301] Marie was born c. 1633. [1302] [1303] Étienne died between 1669 and 1671. [1304] Marie was buried at PR on July30, 1710. [1305] [1306] [1307]

[2] Antoine Hébert, born c. 1670, married Jeanne Corporon (d/o Jean Corporon and Françoise Savoie) c. 1691. [1308] [1309] Jeanne was born c. 1673. [1310] [1311] Antoine died before

---

[1300] White, Stephen A. (1999) Dictionnaire Généalogique des Familles Acadiennes, Volume H to Z, page 800.
[1301] White, Stephen A. (1999) Dictionnaire Généalogique des Familles Acadiennes, Volume A to G, page 666.
[1302] Ibid.
[1303] White, Stephen A. (1999) Dictionnaire Généalogique des Familles Acadiennes, Volume H to Z, page 800.
[1304] Ibid.
[1305] White, Stephen A. (1999) Dictionnaire Généalogique des Familles Acadiennes, Volume A to G, page 666.
[1306] White, Stephen A. (1999) Dictionnaire Généalogique des Familles Acadiennes, Volume H to Z, page 800.
[1307] https://novascotia.ca/archives/acadian/archives.asp?ID=1463
[1308] White, Stephen A. (1999) Dictionnaire Généalogique des Familles Acadiennes, Volume H to Z, pages 801 and 810.
[1309] White, Stephen A. (1999) Dictionnaire Généalogique des Familles Acadiennes, Volume A to G, page 411.
[1310] Ibid.
[1311] White, Stephen A. (1999) Dictionnaire Généalogique des Familles Acadiennes, Volume H to Z, page 810.

July 31, 1753. [1312] Jeanne died at PR on August 11, 1735 and was buried on August 12, 1735. [1313] [1314] [1315]

[3] Agnès Hébert, born c. 1696, married **Jean Baptiste (dit Lyonnais) Duon** (s/o Jean Louis Duon and Jeanne Clémenson of Lyon) on February 27, 1713 in PR. [1316] [1317] [1318] Jean was baptized c. 1684 in the St-Nizier de Lyon parish, in Lyonnais, France. [1319] Jean Baptiste died at PR on May 5, 1746 and was buried on May 6, 1746. [1320] [1321]

[1312] White, Stephen A. (1999) Dictionnaire Généalogique des Familles Acadiennes, Volume H to Z, pages 801 and 810.
[1313] White, Stephen A. (1999) Dictionnaire Généalogique des Familles Acadiennes, Volume A to G, page 411.
[1314] White, Stephen A. (1999) Dictionnaire Généalogique des Familles Acadiennes, Volume H to Z, page 810.
[1315] https://novascotia.ca/archives/acadian/archives.asp?ID=2069
[1316] White, Stephen A. (1999) Dictionnaire Généalogique des Familles Acadiennes, Volume H to Z, page 810.
[1317] White, Stephen A. (1999) Dictionnaire Généalogique des Familles Acadiennes, Volume A to G, page 582.
[1318] https://novascotia.ca/archives/acadian/archives.asp?ID=1272
[1319] White, Stephen A. (1999) Dictionnaire Généalogique des Familles Acadiennes, Volume A to G, page 582.
[1320] Ibid.
[1321] https://novascotia.ca/archives/acadian/archives.asp?ID=2822

Étienne was a brother to Antoine Hébert (as married to Geneviève Lefranc).

[1] Étienne Hébert married Marie Gaudet c. 1650. [1322] [1323] Marie was born c. 1633. [1324] [1325] Étienne died between 1669 and 1671. [1326] Marie was buried at PR on July30, 1710. [1327] [1328] [1329]

[2] Antoine Hébert, born c. 1670, married Jeanne Corporon (d/o Jean Corporon and Françoise Savoie) c. 1691. [1330] [1331] Jeanne was born c. 1673. [1332] [1333] Antoine died before July 31, 1753. [1334] Jeanne died at PR on August 11, 1735 and was buried on August 12, 1735. [1335] [1336] [1337]

[1322] White, Stephen A. (1999) Dictionnaire Généalogique des Familles Acadiennes, Volume H to Z, page 800.
[1323] White, Stephen A. (1999) Dictionnaire Généalogique des Familles Acadiennes, Volume A to G, page 666.
[1324] Ibid.
[1325] White, Stephen A. (1999) Dictionnaire Généalogique des Familles Acadiennes, Volume H to Z, page 800.
[1326] Ibid.
[1327] White, Stephen A. (1999) Dictionnaire Généalogique des Familles Acadiennes, Volume A to G, page 666.
[1328] White, Stephen A. (1999) Dictionnaire Généalogique des Familles Acadiennes, Volume H to Z, page 800.
[1329] https://novascotia.ca/archives/acadian/archives.asp?ID=1463
[1330] White, Stephen A. (1999) Dictionnaire Généalogique des Familles Acadiennes, Volume H to Z, pages 801 and 810.
[1331] White, Stephen A. (1999) Dictionnaire Généalogique des Familles Acadiennes, Volume A to G, page 411.
[1332] Ibid.
[1333] White, Stephen A. (1999) Dictionnaire Généalogique des Familles Acadiennes, Volume H to Z, page 810.
[1334] White, Stephen A. (1999) Dictionnaire Généalogique des Familles Acadiennes, Volume H to Z, pages 801 and 810.
[1335] White, Stephen A. (1999) Dictionnaire Généalogique des Familles Acadiennes, Volume A to G, page 411.

[3] Marie Marthe Hébert, born July 12, 1710 in Port Royal, Acadie, [1338] [1339] married **Charles-Amand I Mius** (s/o Joseph Mius dit d'Azy and Marie Amirault) on January 21, 1731 in Port Royal. [1340] [1341] [1342] Charles was born December 17, 1702 at CS. [1343] [1344]

[1336] White, Stephen A. (1999) <u>Dictionnaire Généalogique des Familles Acadiennes</u>, Volume H to Z, page 810.
[1337] https://novascotia.ca/archives/acadian/archives.asp?ID=2069
[1338] White, Stephen A. (1999) <u>Dictionnaire Généalogique des Familles Acadiennes</u>, Volume H to Z, page 811.
[1339] https://novascotia.ca/archives/acadian/archives.asp?ID=337
[1340] White, Stephen A. (1999) <u>Dictionnaire Généalogique des Familles Acadiennes</u>, Volume H to Z, page 811.
[1341] Ibid, 1207.
[1342] https://novascotia.ca/archives/acadian/archives.asp?ID=1811
[1343] White, Stephen A. (1999) <u>Dictionnaire Généalogique des Familles Acadiennes</u>, Volume H to Z, page 1207.
[1344] https://novascotia.ca/archives/acadian/archives.asp?ID=102

Housseau

[1] Nicolas Housseau was married to Marguerite Bolduc.[1345] They were from the Saint-Jean diocese, in Troyes, Champagne, France.[1346]

[2] Marguerite Housseau married **Jean Meunier** (s/o Mathurin Meunier and Françoise Fafard) on October 5, 1670 at Sainte-Anne de Beaupré, Québec.[1347] [1348] Jean was baptized at Trois Rivières, Québec, on January 8, 1651.[1349] [1350]

[1345] White, Stephen A. (1999) Dictionnaire Généalogique des Familles Acadiennes, Volume H to Z, page 1179.
[1346] Ibid.
[1347] Tanguay, Mgr Cyprien. (1975) Dictionnaire Généalogique des Familles Canadiennes, Volume 1, page 428.
bibnum2.banq.qc.ca/bna/dicoGenealogie/src/0002/0022/0047/0048/3957-1-468.pdf
[1348] White, Stephen A. (1999) Dictionnaire Généalogique des Familles Acadiennes, Volume H to Z, page 1179.
[1349] Tanguay, Mgr Cyprien. (1975) Dictionnaire Généalogique des Familles Canadiennes, Volume 1, page 428.
bibnum2.banq.qc.ca/bna/dicoGenealogie/src/0002/0022/0047/0048/3957-1-468.pdf
[1350] White, Stephen A. (1999) Dictionnaire Généalogique des Familles Acadiennes, Volume H to Z, page 1179.

Lafleur

[1] Charles Lafleur was married to Jeanne Gachet. [1351] [1352] [1353] They were from Chataigneraye, the diocese of Poitiers, in Poitou, France. [1354]

[2] Joachine Lafleur, born c. 1642, [1355] married **Pierre Martin** (s/o Louis Martin and Sébastienne Coutande) on February 11, 1664 in Québec. [1356] [1357] [1358] [1359] [1360] [1361] Pierre was born c. 1643. [1362]

[1351] Tanguay, Mgr Cyprien. (1975) Dictionnaire Généalogique des Familles Canadiennes, Volume 5, page 536. bibnum2.banq.qc.ca/bna/dicoGenealogie/src/0174/0178/0202/0207/3957-5-543.pdf

[1352] Colonel John B. Devoe. (2000) Devoe-deVaux Family History 1691 to 1991 (a self published work shared with the author in email correspondence).

[1353] http://genealogie.quebec/testphp/info.php?no=63209

[1354] Tanguay, Mgr Cyprien. (1975) Dictionnaire Généalogique des Familles Canadiennes, Volume 5, page 536. bibnum2.banq.qc.ca/bna/dicoGenealogie/src/0174/0178/0202/0207/3957-5-543.pdf

[1355] Colonel John B. Devoe. (2000) Devoe-deVaux Family History 1691 to 1991 (a self published work shared with the author in email correspondence).

[1356] Tanguay, Mgr Cyprien. (1975) Dictionnaire Généalogique des Familles Canadiennes, Volume 1, page 89. bibnum2.banq.qc.ca/bna/dicoGenealogie/src/0002/0022/0047/0048/3957-1-456.pdf

[1357] Tanguay, Mgr Cyprien. (1975) Dictionnaire Généalogique des Familles Canadiennes, Volume 5, page 536. bibnum2.banq.qc.ca/bna/dicoGenealogie/src/0174/0178/0202/0207/3957-5-543.pdf

[1358] www.francogene.com/genealogie-quebec-genealogy/003/003812.php

[1359] Colonel John B. Devoe. (2000) Devoe-deVaux Family History 1691 to 1991 (a self published work shared with the author in email correspondence).

[1360] http://genealogie.quebec/testphp/info.php?no=63209

[1361] http://yamachiche.ca/toponymie/genealogie/section6.html

[1362] Colonel John B. Devoe. (2000) Devoe-deVaux Family History 1691 to 1991 (a self published work shared with the author in email correspondence).

Joachine Lafleur was a *Fille du Roi*, a term that meant meaning daughters (wards) of the King.

These ladies, in large part, started the French Canadian population explosion that has, over 350 years, spread across North America. France was colonizing in North America. With fur traders, storekeepers, indentured servants, dockhands, clerics, farmers, settlers, and soldiers in New France, the population was mostly men.

The King quickly came to realize that for this new colony to thrive there must be marriageable women. The King offered 50 livres dowry in addition to whatever the lady brought with her. He also sponsored her transportation.

There is a very specific timeframe that identifies the *Filles du Roi*.

They came between 1663 and 1673. Of the nearly 1000 women who undertook the journey, about 800 made it to Canada. These were not ladies of ill repute. Some were from wealthy families.

With all that is written about them, the details of *why* they chose to come to New France are, for the most part, lost to history. One can only hope that at least one made the journey merely to experience the unknown and satisfy a pioneer spirit.

de La Grange

[1] Crispin de La Grange, a member of the Corporation of Dyers (meaning the Dyers of textiles and wools), was married to a woman whose name is not known to us. [1363]

[2] Esther de La Grange married to **Gérard de Forest** (s/o Jean de Forest and Anne Maillard) on August 12, 1611 (Leyde, Wallon's church, Amsterdam, the Netherlands). [1364] Géerard was born c. 1583 in Avesnes, French Flanders. [1365] Gérard died in August 1654, according to the parish records at Leyde, Wallon's church, Amsterdam, the Netherlands. [1366]

[1363] White, Stephen A. (1999) <u>Dictionnaire Généalogique des Familles Acadiennes</u>, Volume A to G, pages 625 and 627.
[1364] Ibid.
[1365] Ibid.
[1366] Ibid.

Landry 1

René Landry, the elder, is the brother of Antoinette Landry, wife of Antoine Bourg. There exists no relationship between René Landry, the elder, and René Landry, the younger, husband of Marie Bernard (meaning that he was neither brother, nor nephew).

[1] René Landry dit l'aîné, meaning *the elder*, born c. 1618, married Perrine Bourg, widow of Simon Pelletret, c. 1645. [1367] [1368] Perrine Bourg was born c. 1626. [1369] [1370]

[2] Marie Landry, born c. 1646, married **Germain Doucet** (s/o Germain Doucet, Sieur de LaVerdure, and unknown) c. 1664. [1371] [1372] Germain was born c. 1641. [1373] Marie died at PR. [1374] [1375] Germain died at PR, before the census of 1698. [1376]

[1367] White, Stephen A. (1999) Dictionnaire Généalogique des Familles Acadiennes, Volume H to Z, pages 915 and 1283.
[1368] White, Stephen A. (1999) Dictionnaire Généalogique des Familles Acadiennes, Volume A to G, page 221.
[1369] Ibid.
[1370] White, Stephen A. (1999) Dictionnaire Généalogique des Familles Acadiennes, Volume H to Z, pages 915 and 1283.
[1371] Ibid, page 915.
[1372] White, Stephen A. (1999) Dictionnaire Généalogique des Familles Acadiennes, Volume A to G, pages 526 and 530.
[1373] Ibid.
[1374] White, Stephen A. (1999) Dictionnaire Généalogique des Familles Acadiennes, Volume H to Z, page 915.
[1375] White, Stephen A. (1999) Dictionnaire Généalogique des Familles Acadiennes, Volume A to G, page 530.
[1376] Ibid, pages 526 and 530.

Landry 2

There exists no relationship between René Landry, the younger, and René Landry, the elder, husband of Perrine Bourg.

[1] René Landry dit lejeune, meaning *the younger*, born c. 1634, married Marie Bernard (d/o ---------- Bernard and Andrée Guyon) c. 1659. [1377] [1378] Marie Bernard was born c. 1645. [1379] [1380] René died at PR, before the census of 1693. [1381] Marie was buried at PR on January 11, 1719. [1382] [1383] [1384]

[2] Claude Landry, born c. 1663, married Marie Catherine Thibodeau (d/o Pierre Thibodeau and Jeanne Thériot) c. 1684. [1385] Marie Catherine was born c. 1667. [1386] Claude was buried at GP on September 4, 1747. [1387] Marie Catherine died before November 11, 1721. [1388]

[1377] White, Stephen A. (1999) Dictionnaire Généalogique des Familles Acadiennes, Volume H to Z, page 916.
[1378] White, Stephen A. (1999) Dictionnaire Généalogique des Familles Acadiennes, Volume A to G, page 125.
[1379] Ibid.
[1380] White, Stephen A. (1999) Dictionnaire Généalogique des Familles Acadiennes, Volume H to Z, page 916.
[1381] Ibid.
[1382] White, Stephen A. (1999) Dictionnaire Généalogique des Familles Acadiennes, Volume A to G, page 125.
[1383] White, Stephen A. (1999) Dictionnaire Généalogique des Familles Acadiennes, Volume H to Z, page 916.
[1384] https://novascotia.ca/archives/acadian/archives.asp?ID=1533
[1385] White, Stephen A. (1999) Dictionnaire Généalogique des Familles Acadiennes, Volume H to Z, pages 917, 924 and 1508.
[1386] Ibid, pages 924 and 1508.
[1387] Ibid, page 924.

[3] Jeanne Landry, born c. 1685, married **René LeBlanc** (s/o Jacques LeBlanc and Catherine Hébert) c. 1708. [1389] René was born c. December 1685. [1390]

[1388] White, Stephen A. (1999) <u>Dictionnaire Généalogique des Familles Acadiennes</u>, Volume H to Z, pages 924 and 1508.
[1389] Ibid.
[1390] Ibid, pages 986 and 1006.

LeBlanc

The place of origin and the ancestors of Daniel LeBlanc are unknown.

Some have alleged that Daniel descended from a noble family from Dauphiné, basing themselves on the research of H. Léandre d'Entremont, but the line he suggested (à René à Alphonse à Pierre) is of a family named Blanc or de Blanc, rather than LeBlanc. [1391]

[1] Daniel LeBlanc, born c. 1626, married Françoise Gaudet (d/o Jean Gaudet and unknown) c. 1650. [1392] [1393] Françoise was born c. 1623. [1394] [1395] Daniel died at PR, between the Oath of 1695 and the census of 1698. [1396] François died at PR, between the censuses of 1678 and 1700. [1397] [1398]

[1391] White, Stephen A. (2000) English Supplement to the Dictionnaire Généalogique des Familles Acadiennes (page 209). Montréal, Québec: AGMV Marquis Imprimeur Inc.

[1392] White, Stephen A. (1999) Dictionnaire Généalogique des Familles Acadiennes, Volume H to Z, page 983.

[1393] White, Stephen A. (1999) Dictionnaire Généalogique des Familles Acadiennes, Volume A to G, page 666.

[1394] Ibid.

[1395] White, Stephen A. (1999) Dictionnaire Généalogique des Familles Acadiennes, Volume H to Z, page 983.

[1396] Ibid.

[1397] White, Stephen A. (1999) Dictionnaire Généalogique des Familles Acadiennes, Volume A to G, page 666.

[1398] White, Stephen A. (1999) Dictionnaire Généalogique des Familles Acadiennes, Volume H to Z, page 983.

October 5, 1687: Account of the work accomplished in Acadia by Sr d'Aulnay; among those who made their marks: Daniel LeBlanc. Daniel thus arrived in Acadia before d'Aulnay's death in 1650. [1399]

Daniel LeBlanc settled on the north bank of the Port Royal River (today the Annapolis River), to the northeast of the marsh at Bélisle, about nine miles above the fort at Port Royal, and a half mile below the chapel of Saint-Laurent, here he died between the years 1693 and 1698. [1400]

May 24, 1690: Daniel LeBlanc was one of the six members of the council demanded by Phips charged with keeping the peace and meting out justice. [1401]

Although many residents took the oath unreservedly in 1695, by 1727 the Acadians were using it as a bargaining tool; they maintained they were neutral in any conflict the English had with the French and Mik'maq. [1402]

August 1695 (old style): Daniel LeBlanc took the oath of allegiance to the King of England at Port Royal; he made his mark on the document. [1403]

[2] Jacques LeBlanc, born c. 1651, married Catherine Hébert (d/o Antoine Hébert and Geneviève Lefranc) c. 1673. [1404] Catherine was born c. 1656. [1405] Jacques died at

---

[1399] White, Stephen A. (2000) English Supplement to the Dictionnaire Généalogique des Familles Acadiennes (page 210). Montréal, Québec: AGMV Marquis Imprimeur Inc.
[1400] Ibid, page 209.
[1401] Ibid, page 210.
[1402] www.accesswave.ca/~cfraser/MarieBourg.html
[1403] White, Stephen A. (2000) English Supplement to the Dictionnaire Généalogique des Familles Acadiennes (page 210). Montréal, Québec: AGMV Marquis Imprimeur Inc.
[1404] White, Stephen A. (1999) Dictionnaire Généalogique des Familles Acadiennes, Volume H to Z, pages 799, 983 and 985.
[1405] Ibid, pages 799 and 985.

St-Charles-des-Mines, the parish at GP, after May 26, 1731. [1406] Catherine died at St-Charles-des-Mines, the parish at GP. [1407]

[3] René LeBlanc, born c. December 1685, married Jeanne Landry (d/o Claude Landry and Catherine Thibodeau) c. 1708. [1408] Jeanne was born c. 1685. [1409]

[4] Pierre LeBlanc, born August 21, 1718 in GP, married Claire Boudrot (d/o Claude Boudrot and Catherine Meunier) on October 24, 1740 in GP. [1410] [1411] Claire was born on December 27, 1719 at GP. [1412] Claire died on November 1, 1741 at GP at the age of 22 years [1413] and was buried on November 2, 1741. [1414]

[5] Pierre LeBlanc, born about 1741 in GP, [1415] married Marguerite Amirault (d/o Charles Amirault and Claire Dugas) in MA (exile). [1416] On August 16, 1769, Father Bailly blessed the marriage that had taken place in MA (exile), as no priests were allowed to go near the Acadians while in exile. If they did, imprisonment or death awaited them. [1417] This couple is amongst one of the first group of settlers to resettle at SAR.

[1406] White, Stephen A. (1999) <u>Dictionnaire Généalogique des Familles Acadiennes</u>, Volume H to Z, pages 983 and 985.
[1407] Ibid, pages 799 and 985.
[1408] Ibid, pages 924, 986 and 1006.
[1409] Ibid, pages 924 and 1006.
[1410] Ibid, page 1007.
[1411] White, Stephen A. (1999) <u>Dictionnaire Généalogique des Familles Acadiennes</u>, Volume A to G, page 192.
[1412] Ibid.
[1413] Ibid.
[1414] Ibid.
[1415] www.acadian-home.org/ste-anne-du-ruisseau.html
[1416] d'Entremont, Father Clarence Joseph. (1984) <u>Histoire de Quinan, Nouvelle-Écosse</u>, page 89.
[1417] www.acadian-home.org/ste-anne-du-ruisseau.html

[6] Marie LeBlanc, born February 24, 1767, [1418] married **Paul Mius** (s/o Jean Baptiste I Mius and Marie Josèphe Surette). [1419] Paul was born at CS, either towards the end of 1755 or the beginning of 1756. [1420] Marie died on April 7, 1835 in Quinan, Yarmouth County, Nova Scotia. [1421] [1422]

[1418] www.acadian-home.org/ste-anne-du-ruisseau.html
[1419] d'Entremont, Father Clarence Joseph. (1984) <u>Histoire de Quinan, Nouvelle-Écosse</u>, page 89.
[1420] Ibid.
[1421] Ibid.
[1422] https://novascotia.ca/archives/acadian/reborn/archives.asp?ID=2540

Lefebvre

[1] Jean Lefebvre, the Master Goldsmith at Reims, was married to Jeanne Doubleau. [1423]

[2] Martin Lefebvre, baptized at St-Symphorien de Reims parish, Marne, France, [1424] was married to Barbe Bajolet (born May 22, 1608 in Piney, Champagne, France) [1425] [1426] on January 10, 1647 at the St-Barthélemy de LaRochelle parish, in Aunis, France. [1427] [1428] In addition to being Sieur de Montespy, Martin (her second husband) was also the Ordinary Secretary to the Money Chamber of King Louis XIV. [1429] Martin died on November 15, 1651 at St. Jean du Perrot, La Rochelle, France. [1430]

The marriage contract made by Martin and Barbe indicates that he had *but shortly returned from the country of Canada*, when he became engaged to Barbe Bajolet, widow of Isaac Pesseley, adjutant of the garrison at Port Royal, *whence she had also but shortly returned.* [1431]

[1423] White, Stephen A. (1999) Dictionnaire Généalogique des Familles Acadiennes, Volume H to Z, page 1034.
[1424] Ibid.
[1425] Ibid.
[1426] White, Stephen A. (1999) Dictionnaire Généalogique des Familles Acadiennes, Volume A to G, page 70.
[1427] Ibid.
[1428] White, Stephen A. (1999) Dictionnaire Généalogique des Familles Acadiennes, Volume H to Z, page 1034.
[1429] Ibid.
[1430] Ibid.
[1431] White, Stephen A. (2000) English Supplement to the Dictionnaire Généalogique des Familles Acadiennes (page 220). Montréal, Québec: AGMV Marquis Imprimeur Inc.

[3] Marie Anne Lefebvre was born on October 10, 1649 according to the St-Jean de La Rochelle parish register, province of Aunis, France. [1432] [1433] Marie Anne was baptized on April 18, 1650. [1434] [1435] She married **Étienne Comeau** (s/o Pierre Comeau and Rose Bayon) c. 1670. [1436] [1437] Étienne was born c. 1650. [1438] Marie Anne died before the census of 1693. [1439] [1440] Étienne was buried at PR on January 22, 1723. [1441] [1442]

[1432] White, Stephen A. (1999) Dictionnaire Généalogique des Familles Acadiennes, Volume H to Z, page 1034.
[1433] White, Stephen A. (1999) Dictionnaire Généalogique des Familles Acadiennes, Volume A to G, page 371.
[1434] White, Stephen A. (1999) Dictionnaire Généalogique des Familles Acadiennes, Volume H to Z, page 1034.
[1435] White, Stephen A. (1999) Dictionnaire Généalogique des Familles Acadiennes, Volume A to G, page 371.
[1436] White, Stephen A. (1999) Dictionnaire Généalogique des Familles Acadiennes, Volume H to Z, page 1034.
[1437] White, Stephen A. (1999) Dictionnaire Généalogique des Familles Acadiennes, Volume A to G, page 371.
[1438] Ibid, pages 369 and 371.
[1439] White, Stephen A. (1999) Dictionnaire Généalogique des Familles Acadiennes, Volume H to Z, page 1034.
[1440] White, Stephen A. (1999) Dictionnaire Généalogique des Familles Acadiennes, Volume A to G, page 371.
[1441] Ibid, pages 369 and 371.
[1442] https://novascotia.ca/archives/acadian/archives.asp?ID=1555

Lejeune

[1] Pierre Lejeune dit Briard was married to ---------- Doucet (d/o Germain Doucet, Sieur de LaVerdure, and unknown) c. 1650 in PR. [1443] [1444] According to researcher Denis Savard, the nickname Briard means *native of Brie*, a large region located east of Paris. [1445]

[2] Martin Lejeune dit Briard, born c. 1661, married Marie Gaudet (d/o Jean Gaudet and Jeanne Henry dit Robert) c. 1699. [1446] [1447] This was a second marriage for Martin. Marie Gaudet was born c. 1681. [1448] [1449]

[3] Claire Lejeune, born c. 1706, married **François Viger** (s/o François Viger and Marie Mius) c. 1722. [1450] François was born August 16, 1699 at PR. [1451] Claire died before November 23, 1768. [1452] François was buried at Très-Ste-Trinité de Cherbourg (Normandie, France) on March 13, 1760. [1453]

[1443] White, Stephen A. (1999) <u>Dictionnaire Généalogique des Familles Acadiennes</u>, Volume H to Z, page 1048.
[1444] White, Stephen A. (1999) <u>Dictionnaire Généalogique des Familles Acadiennes</u>, Volume A to G, page 526.
[1445] http://www.acadienouvelle.com/chroniques/2016/03/20/la-famille-lejeune/
[1446] White, Stephen A. (1999) <u>Dictionnaire Généalogique des Familles Acadiennes</u>, Volume H to Z, pages 1049 and 1054.
[1447] White, Stephen A. (1999) <u>Dictionnaire Généalogique des Familles Acadiennes</u>, Volume A to G, page 669.
[1448] Ibid.
[1449] White, Stephen A. (1999) <u>Dictionnaire Généalogique des Familles Acadiennes</u>, Volume H to Z, page 1054.
[1450] Ibid, pages 1055 and 1566.
[1451] Ibid, page 1566.
[1452] Ibid, page 1055.
[1453] Ibid, page 1566.

Maillard

[1] Michel Maillard, mayor of Felleries, Avesnes, French Flanders, was married to Marguerite Raux. [1454]

[2] Anne Maillard married **Jean de Forest** (s/o Melchior de Forest and Catherine Du Fosset) c. 1575. [1455] Jean, born c. 1548, was a cloth merchant living in Sedan, Champagne, Ardenne, France, who converted to Calvinism. [1456]

It was Father Vincent de Lérins who wrote, in his second edition of Histoire de la famille Forest (1965) ... *Our unfortunate Jean, having been infected with Calvin's errors, ended up deciding that it was necessary to leave Avesnes, because of the threat of religious persecution. Little by little he sold his property and about 1600 his family, then composed of four children, split up: Melchior to Lille, Gérard to Leyden, in Holland, Anne with her mother to Amsterdam. Only Jesse remained with his father, who went to settle at Sedan, as a merchant-draper. At last, around 1615, Jean de Forest and his family were reunited at Leyden.* [1457]

[1454] White, Stephen A. (1999) Dictionnaire Généalogique des Familles Acadiennes, Volume A to G, page 625.
[1455] Ibid.
[1456] Ibid.
[1457] White, Stephen A. (2000) English Supplement to the Dictionnaire Généalogique des Familles Acadiennes (page 131). Montréal, Québec: AGMV Marquis Imprimeur Inc.

Martin 1

[1] Louis Martin was married to Sébastienne Coutande. [1458] [1459] [1460] They were from Ste-Vierge, the diocese of Poitiers, in Poitou, France. [1461]

[2] Pierre Martin, born c. 1643, [1462] married Joachine Lafleur (d/o Charles Lafleur and Jeanne Gachet) on February 11, 1664 in Québec. [1463] [1464] [1465] [1466] [1467] [1468] Joachine LaFleur was born c. 1642. [1469]

[1458] Tanguay, Mgr Cyprien. (1975) Dictionnaire Généalogique des Familles Canadiennes, Volume 1, page 89.
bibnum2.banq.qc.ca/bna/dicoGenealogie/src/0002/0022/0047/0048/3957-1-456.pdf
[1459] Tanguay, Mgr Cyprien. (1975) Dictionnaire Généalogique des Familles Canadiennes, Volume 5, page 536.
bibnum2.banq.qc.ca/bna/dicoGenealogie/src/0174/0178/0202/0207/3957-5-543.pdf
[1460] Colonel John B. Devoe. (2000) Devoe-deVaux Family History 1691 to 1991 (a self published work shared with the author in email correspondence).
[1461] Tanguay, Mgr Cyprien. (1975) Dictionnaire Généalogique des Familles Canadiennes, Volume 5, page 536.
bibnum2.banq.qc.ca/bna/dicoGenealogie/src/0174/0178/0202/0207/3957-5-543.pdf
[1462] Colonel John B. Devoe. (2000) Devoe-deVaux Family History 1691 to 1991 (a self published work shared with the author in email correspondence).
[1463] Tanguay, Mgr Cyprien. (1975) Dictionnaire Généalogique des Familles Canadiennes, Volume 1, page 89.
bibnum2.banq.qc.ca/bna/dicoGenealogie/src/0002/0022/0047/0048/3957-1-456.pdf
[1464] Tanguay, Mgr Cyprien. (1975) Dictionnaire Généalogique des Familles Canadiennes, Volume 5, page 536.
bibnum2.banq.qc.ca/bna/dicoGenealogie/src/0174/0178/0202/0207/3957-5-543.pdf
[1465] www.francogene.com/genealogie-quebec-genealogy/000/000640.php
[1466] Colonel John B. Devoe. (2000) Devoe-deVaux Family History 1691 to 1991 (a self published work shared with the author in email correspondence).
[1467] http://genealogie.quebec/testphp/info.php?no=63209
[1468] http://yamachiche.ca/toponymie/genealogie/section6.html

Joachine Lafleur was a *Fille du Roi*, a term that meant meaning daughters (wards) of the King.

These ladies, in large part, started the French Canadian population explosion that has, over 350 years, spread across North America. France was colonizing in North America. With fur traders, storekeepers, indentured servants, dockhands, clerics, farmers, settlers, and soldiers in New France, the population was mostly men.

The King quickly came to realize that for this new colony to thrive there must be marriageable women. The King offered 50 livres dowry in addition to whatever the lady brought with her. He also sponsored her transportation.

There is a very specific timeframe that identifies the *Filles du Roi*.

They came between 1663 and 1673. Of the nearly 1000 women who undertook the journey, about 800 made it to Canada. These were not ladies of ill repute. Some were from wealthy families.

With all that is written about them, the details of *why* they chose to come to New France are, for the most part, lost to history. One can only hope that at least one made the journey merely to experience the unknown and satisfy a pioneer spirit.

[3] Marie Madeleine Martin, baptized on June 29, 1666 in Sillery, Québec, [1470] [1471] married **Michel Deveau (dit Dauphiné)** c. 1693. [1472] [1473] [1474] [1475] Michel was born c. 1663. [1476] [1477]

[1469] Colonel John B. Devoe. (2000) Devoe-deVaux Family History 1691 to 1991 (a self published work shared with the author in email correspondence).
[1470] White, Stephen A. (1999) Dictionnaire Généalogique des Familles Acadiennes, Volume A to G, page 508.
[1471] Tanguay, Mgr Cyprien. (1975) Dictionnaire Généalogique des Familles Canadiennes, Volume 1, page 89.

bibnum2.banq.qc.ca/bna/dicoGenealogie/src/0002/0022/0047/0048/3957-1-456.pdf
[1472] White, Stephen A. (1999) Dictionnaire Généalogique des Familles Acadiennes, Volume A to G, page 508.
[1473] www.francogene.com/genealogie-quebec-genealogy/084/084606.php
[1474] Colonel John B. Devoe. (2000) Devoe-deVaux Family History 1691 to 1991 (a self published work shared with the author in email correspondence).
[1475] csapstaff.ednet.ns.ca/jldeveau/deveau1.html
[1476] White, Stephen A. (1999) Dictionnaire Généalogique des Familles Acadiennes, Volume A to G, page 508.
[1477] csapstaff.ednet.ns.ca/jldeveau/deveau1.html

Martin 2

In keeping with the Roster of the *Saint-Jehan*, dated April 1, 1636, *Pierre Martin, ploughman, with his wife and a child residing at Bourgueil* was among the passengers. [1478]

There was a grant (dated August 6, 1679) of a parcel of land near PR, bounded to the east by the great meadow, to the west by the Domanchin Brook, to the south by the Dauphin River (today known as the Annapolis River), and to the north by the mountain, by Alexandre Le Borgne de Bélisle, in the name of Emmanuel Le Borgne Du Coudray, seigneur for part of Acadie, to Pierre Martin and Mathieu Martin, his son. [1479]

[1] René Martin was married to Étiennette Poirier. [1480]

[1] Pierre Martin, born c. 1601, married Catherine Vigneau (d/o Olivier Vigneau and Renée Courtin) on June 30, 1630 at the St-Germain de Bourgeuil parish, in Touraine, France. [1481] Pierre died before the census of 1678. [1482] Catherine died before the census of 1678. [1483]

[2] Marguerite Martin, born about 1644, married **Jean Bourg** (s/o Antoine Bourg and Antoinette Landry) c. 1667. [1484] [1485] Jean was born c. 1646. [1486] Marguerite died at PR on

---

[1478] White, Stephen A. (2000) <u>English Supplement to the Dictionnaire Généalogique des Familles Acadiennes</u> (page 243). Montréal, Québec: AGMV Marquis Imprimeur Inc.
[1479] Ibid.
[1480] White, Stephen A. (1999) <u>Dictionnaire Généalogique des Familles Acadiennes</u>, Volume H to Z, page 1125.
[1481] Ibid.
[1482] Ibid.
[1483] Ibid.
[1484] Ibid.
[1485] White, Stephen A. (1999) <u>Dictionnaire Généalogique des Familles Acadiennes</u>, Volume A to G, pages 221 and 224.

April 24, 1707 and was buried on April 25, 1707. [1487] [1488] [1489] Jean died between the censuses of 1693 and 1698. [1490]

[1486] White, Stephen A. (1999) Dictionnaire Généalogique des Familles Acadiennes, Volume A to G, pages 221 and 224.
[1487] White, Stephen A. (1999) Dictionnaire Généalogique des Familles Acadiennes, Volume H to Z, page 1125.
[1488] White, Stephen A. (1999) Dictionnaire Généalogique des Familles Acadiennes, Volume A to G, page 224.
[1489] https://novascotia.ca/archives/acadian/archives.asp?ID=1405
[1490] White, Stephen A. (1999) Dictionnaire Généalogique des Familles Acadiennes, Volume A to G, page 224.

Meunier

[1] René Meunier (Le Mounier) was married to Marie Leroux.[1491] They were from Clermont, in the Auvergne region (province) of France.[1492,1493]

[1] Mathurin Meunier married Françoise Fafard (d/o Jean Fafard and Elisabeth Tibou from Argence, near the village of Caen in Normandie, France) on November 3, 1647 in Montréal, Québec.[1494,1495] Mathurin was baptized in 1619.[1496] Françoise was baptized in 1624.[1497] Françoise was buried on January 13, 1702 at Sainte-Anne de Beaupré, Québec.[1498]

[2] Jean Meunier married Marguerite Housseau (d/o Nicolas Housseau and Marguerite Bolduc) on October 5, 1670 at Sainte-Anne de Beaupré, Québec.[1499,1500] Jean was baptized at Trois Rivières, Québec, on January 8, 1651.[1501,1502]

[1491] Tanguay, Mgr Cyprien. (1975) <u>Dictionnaire Généalogique des Familles Canadiennes</u>, Volume 1, page 428. bibnum2.banq.qc.ca/bna/dicoGenealogie/src/0002/0022/0047/0048/3957-1-468.pdf
[1492] Ibid.
[1493] https://en.wikipedia.org/wiki/Auvergne_(province)
[1494] Tanguay, Mgr Cyprien. (1975) <u>Dictionnaire Généalogique des Familles Canadiennes</u>, Volume 1, page 428. bibnum2.banq.qc.ca/bna/dicoGenealogie/src/0002/0022/0047/0048/3957-1-468.pdf
[1495] White, Stephen A. (1999) <u>Dictionnaire Généalogique des Familles Acadiennes</u>, Volume H to Z, page 1179.
[1496] Tanguay, Mgr Cyprien. (1975) <u>Dictionnaire Généalogique des Familles Canadiennes</u>, Volume 1, page 428. bibnum2.banq.qc.ca/bna/dicoGenealogie/src/0002/0022/0047/0048/3957-1-468.pdf
[1497] Ibid.
[1498] Ibid.
[1499] Ibid.
[1500] White, Stephen A. (1999) <u>Dictionnaire Généalogique des Familles Acadiennes</u>, Volume H to Z, page 1179.

[3] Catherine Meunier married **Claude Boudrot** (s/o Michel Boudrot and Michelle Aucoin) c. 1700. [1503] [1504] Catherine was his second wife. Claude was born c. 1663. [1505] Claude was buried at GP on March 7, 1740. [1506]

[1501] Tanguay, Mgr Cyprien. (1975) <u>Dictionnaire Généalogique des Familles Canadiennes</u>, Volume 1, page 428.
bibnum2.banq.qc.ca/bna/dicoGenealogie/src/0002/0022/0047/0048/3957-1-468.pdf
[1502] White, Stephen A. (1999) <u>Dictionnaire Généalogique des Familles Acadiennes</u>, Volume H to Z, page 1179.
[1503] Ibid.
[1504] White, Stephen A. (1999) <u>Dictionnaire Généalogique des Familles Acadiennes</u>, Volume A to G, pages 185 and 191.
[1505] Ibid, pages 185 and 190.
[1506] Ibid.

Mius

In 1557, the name Nicolaus Mius of Grÿnn appears on the register of the University of Orléans, one of five German students. [1507]

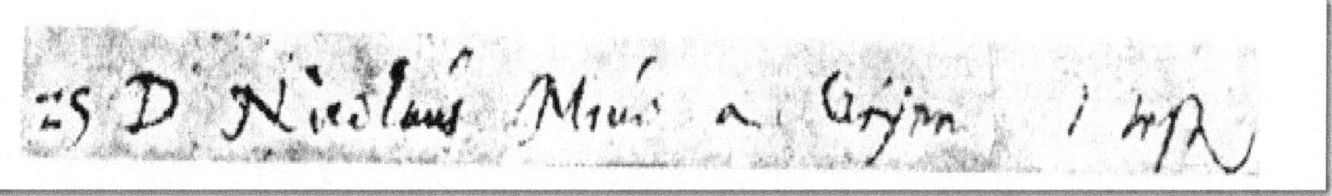

http://mius-dentremont-dna-project.tripod.com/miusdentremontdnaproject

It reads *D Nicolaus Mius a Grÿnn*.

The D stands for *Dominus* which is Latin for Mister, and Grÿnn, which follows, indicates where he came from.

By 1569, Nicolaus was married to Jeanne, surname unknown; they had several children. It is this same Nicolaus (Nicolas) Mius who was the chamber valet of Admiral Gaspard de Coligny II, the French Huguenot leader. In Admiral Gaspard de Coligny's will, Nicolaus is mentioned.

To Nicolas Mouche (Mius), my chamber valet and his wife, Jeanne, for their good services, to me and my wife, I give them five hundred francs in money one time and six septiers of bled metal (mixture of wheat and rye) the rest of their lives solely so they can have more children. [1508]

[1507] doris_muise.tripod.com/muise2.htm
[1508] Ibid.

Nicolaus also served as interpreter for Admiral Gaspard de Coligny, the military and political leader of the Huguenots. Both of these men were killed on August 24, 1572 during the St. Bartholomew's Day Massacre in Paris.

The slaughter of French Huguenots quickly spread to the provinces and about 20,000 Huguenots were ultimately killed by Roman Catholic mobs. The prime responsibility for the massacre was borne by Catherine de Medici, who opposed the influence of the Protestant leader, Admiral Gaspard II de Colignay, over her weak son, King Charles IX. [1509]

Father Clarence d'Entremont, author of <u>Histoire du Cap-Sable</u>, read Grÿnn simply as Grynn. In searching for Grynn (minus the two dots above the y), the closest he could find was the village of Gryon located in the Canton of Vaud (Switzerland).

In a question posed to the Cantonales Vaudroises, in Lausanne, Switzerland, touching on the origin of Nicolas Mius, a response, dated September 13, 1978, shared that this family name did not appear in the region of Vaud, and specifically, not in Gryon; so, too, did it become known, in 2008, and validated, once again, in 2013, that Gryon was never called, or spelled, as either Grynn or Grÿnn. [1510]

The dotted y, as found in Grÿnn, was apparently used often in place of a simple y. It is also used as a Dutch or Flemish ij, as in Grijnn, which looks like Grÿnn in cursive writing.

Neither Grijnn nor Grÿnn has been located on maps, both modern and 16th century, of Holland or Belgium.

[1509] https://en.wikisource.org/wiki/Lectures_on_Modern_History/The_Huguenots_and_the_League

[1510] https://www.familytreedna.com/public/Mius-dEntremont

While Grÿnn has not been found on modern maps of Germany, historical maps have yet to be investigated.

There was also another German student in attendance (at the University of Orléans) by the name of Conrad Maius; he could have been from the same family. [1511]

The name, originally Majus, was often written as Maius. [1512] In German, the letters ai are pronounced as i, thereby resulting in the present pronunciation Mius (my-us). [1513]

Given that these times were significantly dangerous for Calvinist Protestants, could it be that Nicolaus Mius may have written a fictitious place name (Grÿnn) in the register of the University of Orléans in order to further protect his family?

Admiral Gaspard II de Coligny, Seigneur de Châtillon, had been married twice. [1514] His first wife, Charlotte de Laval, died on March 3, 1568. [1515] He was then married, a second time, to Countess Jacqueline d'Entremont of the House of Montbel d'Entremont of Savoie, in 1571. [1516] Following the death of her husband, Countess Jacqueline (the only daughter and heiress of the Montbel d'Entremont family of Savoy), [1517] a widow for the second time, felt indebted to the orphaned children of Nicolaus, taking a son (unfortunately there is no record of his first name) under her protection. [1518]

[1511] doris_muise.tripod.com/muise2.htm
[1512] Ibid.
[1513] Ibid.
[1514] https://en.wikipedia.org/wiki/Gaspard_II_de_Coligny
[1515] https://en.wikipedia.org/wiki/Charlotte_de_Laval
[1516] https://fr.wikipedia.org/wiki/Jacqueline_de_Montbel_d'Entremont
[1517] Ibid.
[1518] doris_muise.tripod.com/muise2.htm

In the marriage contract between the Admiral and Jacqueline, there is a clause that reads as follows: *The first originating from the marriage and his descendants, whether male or female, would carry the name and coat of arms of Count d'Entremont* (denoted by Jacqueline's father). [1519]

Béatrice de Coligny, Countess d'Entremont, was born on December 21, 1572. [1520]

On November 30, 1600, she married Claude Antoine Bon, Baron of Meuillon and Montauban, Governor of Marseilles; and their first born, a son, was named François Virgine. [1521] It has been further speculated that Claude Antoine Bon de Meuillon was the biological son of Nicolaus Mius (killed while defending the wounded Coligny), adopted by the Bon de Meuillon family of Marseilles. [1522] [1523]

Nicolas Mius also left two daughters, Charlotte Mousche and Louyse Mousche, both of whom were put in the care of Louise de Coligny, Princess of Orange, daughter of the Admiral and his first wife, widow of William of Nassau, Prince of Orange (dit *le Taciturne*). [1524]

It is plausible that Philippe Mius d'Entremont, aka François Virgine, Count d'Entremont, could have deliberately hid his true identity, in Acadie, to avoid complications from past Huguenot related activities in France.

[1519] doris_muise.tripod.com/muise2.htm
[1520] https://fr.wikipedia.org/wiki/Jacqueline_de_Montbel_d'Entremont
[1521] michaelmarcotte.com/dentremontOrigin.htm
[1522] Ibid.
[1523] Ibid.
[1524] doris_muise.tripod.com/muise2.htm

In 1651, it is known that Philippe Mius d'Entremont, his wife Madeleine Hélie, and their 4 year old daughter, Marguerite, sailed from La Rochelle, France, with Charles de Latour, and a number of his men, arriving in Acadie during the month of August. [1525]

As denoted on the Mius d'Entremont Family Tree DNA project website, [1526] *we are actively endeavoring to determine if, indeed, François Virgine d'Entremont and Philippe Mius d'Entremont were one and the same person; likewise, for the two wives of these two fellows, namely, Madeleine Élie du Tillet and Madeleine Hélie.*

An artist's rendition of what Philippe Mius may have looked like.

Mius d'Entremont: A Baron in Acadia (article is in French) [1527]

[1525] http://doris_muise.tripod.com/muise2.htm
[1526] https://www.familytreedna.com/public/mius-dentremont/default.aspx
[1527] https://www.acadienouvelle.com/etc/gensdici/2017/01/22/mius-dentremont-baron-acadie/

Mius d'Entremont 1A

Philippe Mius came to Acadie, about 1651, with his wife Madeleine Hélie, as adjutant to Governor Charles de Saint-Étienne de La Tour; he served as commandant in the colony when La Tour was absent. [1528]

On July 17, 1653, he received, jointly with Pierre Ferrand, by letters patent from Charles de Saint-Étienne de La Tour, the fief of Pobomcoup (today known as Pubnico), at Cape Sable. [1529]

In 1670, he became the King's attorney. [1530]

On October 5, 1687, Philippe Mius d'Entremont signed an attestation in favour of the accomplishments of Governor d'Aulnay. [1531]

The connections that follow herein are those re François, son of Joseph Mius dit d'Azy and Marie Amirault.

[1528] White, Stephen A. (2000) English Supplement to the Dictionnaire Généalogique des Familles Acadiennes (page 256). Montréal, Québec: AGMV Marquis Imprimeur Inc.
[1529] Ibid.
[1530] Ibid.
[1531] Ibid.

[1] Philippe Mius, born c. 1609 in Normandie, France, was married to Madeleine Hélie c. 1649. [1532] Madeleine was born c. 1626. [1533] According to Father Clarence Joseph d'Entremont, Philippe died at GP at the end of 1700. [1534] Madeleine died before the PR census of 1678. [1535]

[2] Philippe Mius (dit d'Azy), born c. 1660, married a Mi'kmaq woman (whose name is not known to us) c. 1678. [1536]

[3] Joseph Mius (dit d'Azy), born c. 1679, married Marie Amirault (d/o François Amirault dit Tourangeau and Marie Pitre) c. 1699. [1537] [1538] Marie was born c. 1684 at CS. [1539]

NOTE: This couple has been genetically traced to the fatal Niemann-Pick (variant C) disease as per the French Acadian population of Yarmouth County, Nova Scotia.

[4] François Mius, born March 19, 1703 at CS, [1540] [1541] married Jeanne Duon (d/o Jean Baptiste Duon dit Lyonnais and Agnès Hébert) on February 14, 1735 in PR. [1542] [1543] [1544] Jeanne was born March 29, 1718 in PR. [1545] [1546] François died between 1766 and 1775. [1547]

[1532] White, Stephen A. (1999) Dictionnaire Généalogique des Familles Acadiennes, Volume H to Z, pages 840 and 1201.
[1533] Ibid.
[1534] Ibid.
[1535] Ibid.
[1536] Ibid, pages 1201 and 1206.
[1537] Ibid, pages 1206 and 1207.
[1538] White, Stephen A. (1999) Dictionnaire Généalogique des Familles Acadiennes, Volume A to G, page 17.
[1539] Ibid.
[1540] White, Stephen A. (1999) Dictionnaire Généalogique des Familles Acadiennes, Volume H to Z, page 1207.
[1541] https://novascotia.ca/archives/acadian/archives.asp?ID=104
[1542] White, Stephen A. (1999) Dictionnaire Généalogique des Familles Acadiennes, Volume A to G, page 582.

[5] Marie Suzanne Mius, born c. 1758 in MA (exile), [1548] married **Michel Doucet** (s/o Joseph Doucet and Anne Surette) c. 1778. [1549] [1550] Michel was born October 17, 1754 in PR. [1551] [1552] [1553] Michel died on April 19, 1830 [1554] [1555] at the age of 75 in Quinan, Yarmouth County, Nova Scotia. He was buried on April 30, 1830. [1556] According to parish records, Marie Suzanne died after her husband at a date that is not registered.

NOTE: This couple has been genetically traced to Alström Syndrome as per the French Acadian population of Yarmouth County, Nova Scotia.

[1543] White, Stephen A. (1999) <u>Dictionnaire Généalogique des Familles Acadiennes</u>, Volume H to Z, page 1207.
[1544] https://novascotia.ca/archives/acadian/archives.asp?ID=2037
[1545] White, Stephen A. (1999) <u>Dictionnaire Généalogique des Familles Acadiennes</u>, Volume A to G, page 582.
[1546] https://novascotia.ca/archives/acadian/archives.asp?ID=680
[1547] White, Stephen A. (1999) <u>Dictionnaire Généalogique des Familles Acadiennes</u>, Volume H to Z, page 1207.
[1548] d'Entremont, Father Clarence Joseph. (1984) <u>Histoire de Quinan, Nouvelle-Écosse</u>, page 18.
[1549] Ibid.
[1550] Information received from Kenneth Breau, cousin and archivist at the Université de Moncton.
[1551] d'Entremont, Father Clarence Joseph. (1984) <u>Histoire de Quinan, Nouvelle-Écosse</u>, page 18.
[1552] Information received from Kenneth Breau, cousin and archivist at the Université de Moncton.
[1553] https://novascotia.ca/archives/acadian/archives.asp?ID=3522
[1554] Information received from Kenneth Breau, cousin and archivist at the Université de Moncton.
[1555] https://novascotia.ca/archives/acadian/reborn/archives.asp?ID=2031
[1556] Ibid.

[1] Philippe Mius, born c. 1609 in Normandie, France, was married to Madeleine Hélie c. 1649. [1557] Madeleine was born c. 1626. [1558] According to Father Clarence Joseph d'Entremont, Philippe died at GP at the end of 1700. [1559] Madeleine died before the PR census of 1678. [1560]

[2] Philippe Mius (dit d'Azy), born c. 1660, married a Mi' kmaq woman (whose name is not known to us) c. 1678. [1561]

[3] Joseph Mius (dit d'Azy), born c. 1679, married Marie Amirault (d/o François Amirault dit Tourangeau and Marie Pitre) c. 1699. [1562] [1563] Marie was born c. 1684 at CS. [1564]

NOTE: This couple has been genetically traced to the fatal Niemann-Pick (variant C) disease as per the French Acadian population of Yarmouth County, Nova Scotia.

[4] François Mius, born March 19, 1703 at CS, [1565] [1566] married Jeanne Duon (d/o Jean Baptiste Duon dit Lyonnais and Agnès Hébert) on February 14, 1735 in PR. [1567] [1568] [1569] Jeanne was born March 29, 1718 in PR. [1570] [1571] François died between 1766 and 1775. [1572]

[1557] White, Stephen A. (1999) Dictionnaire Généalogique des Familles Acadiennes, Volume H to Z, pages 840 and 1201.
[1558] Ibid.
[1559] Ibid.
[1560] Ibid.
[1561] Ibid, pages 1201 and 1206.
[1562] Ibid, pages 1206 and 1207.
[1563] White, Stephen A. (1999) Dictionnaire Généalogique des Familles Acadiennes, Volume A to G, page 17.
[1564] Ibid.
[1565] White, Stephen A. (1999) Dictionnaire Généalogique des Familles Acadiennes, Volume H to Z, page 1207.
[1566] https://novascotia.ca/archives/acadian/archives.asp?ID=104
[1567] White, Stephen A. (1999) Dictionnaire Généalogique des Familles Acadiennes, Volume A to G, page 582.

[5] Anne Mius, born November 4, 1736, [1573] [1574] was married to **Julien Alexandre Frontain** c. 1759 in MA (exile). [1575] Anne died on March 23, 1807 in Quinan, Yarmouth County, Nova Scotia. [1576] [1577]

[1568] White, Stephen A. (1999) <u>Dictionnaire Généalogique des Familles Acadiennes</u>, Volume H to Z, page 1207.
[1569] https://novascotia.ca/archives/acadian/archives.asp?ID=2037
[1570] White, Stephen A. (1999) <u>Dictionnaire Généalogique des Familles Acadiennes</u>, Volume A to G, page 582.
[1571] https://novascotia.ca/archives/acadian/archives.asp?ID=680
[1572] White, Stephen A. (1999) <u>Dictionnaire Généalogique des Familles Acadiennes</u>, Volume H to Z, page 1207.
[1573] d'Entremont, Father Clarence Joseph. (1984) <u>Histoire de Quinan, Nouvelle-Écosse</u>, page 17.
[1574] https://novascotia.ca/archives/acadian/archives.asp?ID=2169
[1575] d'Entremont, Father Clarence Joseph. (1984) <u>Histoire de Quinan, Nouvelle-Écosse</u>, page 17.
[1576] Ibid.
[1577] https://novascotia.ca/archives/acadian/reborn/archives.asp?ID=697

[1] Philippe Mius, born c. 1609 in Normandie, France, was married to Madeleine Hélie c. 1649. [1578] Madeleine was born c. 1626. [1579] According to Father Clarence Joseph d'Entremont, Philippe died at GP at the end of 1700. [1580] Madeleine died before the PR census of 1678. [1581]

[2] Philippe Mius (dit d'Azy), born c. 1660, married a Mi'kmaq woman (whose name is not known to us) c. 1678. [1582]

[3] Joseph Mius (dit d'Azy), born c. 1679, married Marie Amirault (d/o François Amirault dit Tourangeau and Marie Pitre) c. 1699. [1583] [1584] Marie was born c. 1684 at CS. [1585]

NOTE: This couple has been genetically traced to the fatal Niemann-Pick (variant C) disease as per the French Acadian population of Yarmouth County, Nova Scotia.

[4] François Mius, born March 19, 1703 at CS, [1586] [1587] married Jeanne Duon (d/o Jean Baptiste Duon dit Lyonnais and Agnès Hébert) on February 14, 1735 in PR. [1588] [1589] [1590] Jeanne was born March 29, 1718 in PR. [1591] [1592] François died between 1766 and 1775. [1593]

[1578] White, Stephen A. (1999) Dictionnaire Généalogique des Familles Acadiennes, Volume H to Z, pages 840 and 1201.
[1579] Ibid.
[1580] Ibid.
[1581] Ibid.
[1582] Ibid, pages 1201 and 1206.
[1583] Ibid, pages 1206 and 1207.
[1584] White, Stephen A. (1999) Dictionnaire Généalogique des Familles Acadiennes, Volume A to G, page 17.
[1585] Ibid.
[1586] White, Stephen A. (1999) Dictionnaire Généalogique des Familles Acadiennes, Volume H to Z, page 1207.
[1587] https://novascotia.ca/archives/acadian/archives.asp?ID=104
[1588] White, Stephen A. (1999) Dictionnaire Généalogique des Familles Acadiennes, Volume A to G, page 582.

[5] Jean Pierre Mius, born February 3, 1743, [1594] married Anne Doucet (d/o Joseph Doucet and Anne Surette) c. 1768 in MA (exile). [1595] [1596] Anne was born April 1, 1747 in PR. [1597] [1598] Jean Pierre died on February 7, 1825 in SAR and was buried on February 8, 1825. [1599] [1600] [1601] Anne was buried on January 4, 1838 in SAR. [1602] [1603]

[6] François Mius, born c. 1770 in MA (exile) [1604] married Marie Osithe O'Bird (Hubbard) (d/o John O' Bird and Madeleine Modeste Mius) on February 19, 1798 in SAR. [1605] [1606] Marie Osithe was born c. 1775. [1607]

[1589] White, Stephen A. (1999) Dictionnaire Généalogique des Familles Acadiennes, Volume H to Z, page 1207.
[1590] https://novascotia.ca/archives/acadian/archives.asp?ID=2037
[1591] White, Stephen A. (1999) Dictionnaire Généalogique des Familles Acadiennes, Volume A to G, page 582.
[1592] https://novascotia.ca/archives/acadian/archives.asp?ID=680
[1593] White, Stephen A. (1999) Dictionnaire Généalogique des Familles Acadiennes, Volume H to Z, page 1207.
[1594] Information received from Kenneth Breau, cousin and archivist at the Université de Moncton.
[1595] d'Entremont, Father Clarence Joseph. (1984) Histoire de Quinan, Nouvelle-Écosse, page 15.
[1596] Information received from Kenneth Breau, cousin and archivist at the Université de Moncton.
[1597] d'Entremont, Father Clarence Joseph. (1984) Histoire de Quinan, Nouvelle-Écosse, page 15.
[1598] https://novascotia.ca/archives/acadian/archives.asp?ID=2893
[1599] d'Entremont, Father Clarence Joseph. (1984) Histoire de Quinan, Nouvelle-Écosse, page 15.
[1600] Information received from Kenneth Breau, cousin and archivist at the Université de Moncton.
[1601] https://novascotia.ca/archives/acadian/reborn/archives.asp?ID=1512
[1602] Information received from Kenneth Breau, cousin and archivist at the Université de Moncton.
[1603] https://novascotia.ca/archives/acadian/reborn/archives.asp?ID=4262
[1604] d'Entremont, Father Clarence Joseph. (1984) Histoire de Quinan, Nouvelle-Écosse, page 73.

Paroisse Ste-Agnès

Death and Burial certificate

This is to certify that _Osithe Muis_ who _16th, 1865_ was buried in our parish cemetry on _September_ Husband (wife) of _____ Rev. _Cosmas J. Quinan_ officiating.

This is a true copy of the records of Ste_Agnès Parish.

Given at Quinan, N.S. on _July 16th, 2004_.

Sr Yvette
Curé

[1605] d'Entremont, Father Clarence Joseph. (1984) <u>Histoire de Quinan, Nouvelle-Écosse</u>, page 73.
[1606] https://novascotia.ca/archives/acadian/reborn/archives.asp?ID=18
[1607] Macauley, Sheila Hubbard. (1996) <u>The Hubbard Family of Nova Scotia</u>, page 6. Baltimore, MD: Gateway Press, Inc.

[7] Anne Anastasie (dite Nanette) Mius, born December 25, 1817 in Quinan, Nova Scotia, [1608] [1609] married **Michel Patrice (dit L'Anglais) Doucet** (s/o Joseph Mathurin Doucet and Angélique Mathilde Mius) c. 1839. Michel Patrice, born March 16, 1817 in Quinan, Nova Scotia, [1610] was baptized on March 16, 1817 in SAR. [1611] Anne died on November 17, 1885 at the age of 62. [1612]

[1608] d'Entremont, Father Clarence Joseph. (1984) Histoire de Quinan, Nouvelle-Écosse, page 75.
[1609] https://novascotia.ca/archives/acadian/reborn/archives.asp?ID=1362
[1610] d'Entremont, Father Clarence Joseph. (1984) Histoire de Quinan, Nouvelle-Écosse, page 75.
[1611] https://novascotia.ca/archives/acadian/reborn/archives.asp?ID=1335
[1612] d'Entremont, Father Clarence Joseph. (1984) Histoire de Quinan, Nouvelle-Écosse, page 75.

[1] Philippe Mius, born c. 1609 in Normandie, France, was married to Madeleine Hélie c. 1649. [1613] Madeleine was born c. 1626. [1614] According to Father Clarence Joseph d'Entremont, Philippe died at GP at the end of 1700. [1615] Madeleine died before the PR census of 1678. [1616]

[2] Philippe Mius (dit d'Azy), born c. 1660, married a Mi'kmaq woman (whose name is not known to us) c. 1678. [1617]

[3] Joseph Mius (dit d'Azy), born c. 1679, married Marie Amirault (d/o François Amirault dit Tourangeau and Marie Pitre) c. 1699. [1618] [1619] Marie was born c. 1684 at CS. [1620]

NOTE: This couple has been genetically traced to the fatal Niemann-Pick (variant C) disease as per the French Acadian population of Yarmouth County, Nova Scotia.

[4] François Mius, born March 19, 1703 at CS, [1621] [1622] married Jeanne Duon (d/o Jean Baptiste Duon dit Lyonnais and Agnès Hébert) on February 14, 1735 in PR. [1623] [1624] [1625] Jeanne was born March 29, 1718 in PR. [1626] [1627] François died between 1766 and 1775. [1628]

[1613] White, Stephen A. (1999) <u>Dictionnaire Généalogique des Familles Acadiennes</u>, Volume H to Z, pages 840 and 1201.
[1614] Ibid.
[1615] Ibid.
[1616] Ibid.
[1617] Ibid, pages 1201 and 1206.
[1618] Ibid, pages 1206 and 1207.
[1619] White, Stephen A. (1999) <u>Dictionnaire Généalogique des Familles Acadiennes</u>, Volume A to G, page 17.
[1620] Ibid.
[1621] White, Stephen A. (1999) <u>Dictionnaire Généalogique des Familles Acadiennes</u>, Volume H to Z, page 1207.
[1622] https://novascotia.ca/archives/acadian/archives.asp?ID=104
[1623] White, Stephen A. (1999) <u>Dictionnaire Généalogique des Familles Acadiennes</u>, Volume A to G, page 582.

[5] Jean Pierre Mius, born February 3, 1743, [1629] married Anne Doucet (d/o Joseph Doucet and Anne Surette) c. 1768 in MA (exile). [1630] [1631] Anne was born April 1, 1747 in PR. [1632] [1633] Jean Pierre died on February 7, 1825 in SAR and was buried on February 8, 1825. [1634] [1635] [1636] Anne was buried on January 4, 1838 in SAR. [1637] [1638]

[6] François Mius, born c. 1770 in MA (exile) [1639] married Marie Osithe O'Bird (Hubbard) (d/o John O' Bird and Madeleine Modeste Mius) on February 19, 1798 in SAR. [1640] [1641] Marie Osithe was born c. 1775. [1642]

[1624] White, Stephen A. (1999) Dictionnaire Généalogique des Familles Acadiennes, Volume H to Z, page 1207.
[1625] http://novascotia.ca/archives/acadian/archives.asp?ID=2037
[1626] White, Stephen A. (1999) Dictionnaire Généalogique des Familles Acadiennes, Volume A to G, page 582.
[1627] https://novascotia.ca/archives/acadian/archives.asp?ID=680
[1628] White, Stephen A. (1999) Dictionnaire Généalogique des Familles Acadiennes, Volume H to Z, page 1207.
[1629] Information received from Kenneth Breau, cousin and archivist at the Université de Moncton.
[1630] d'Entremont, Father Clarence Joseph. (1984) Histoire de Quinan, Nouvelle-Écosse, page 15.
[1631] Information received from Kenneth Breau, cousin and archivist at the Université de Moncton.
[1632] d'Entremont, Father Clarence Joseph. (1984) Histoire de Quinan, Nouvelle-Écosse, page 15.
[1633] https://novascotia.ca/archives/acadian/archives.asp?ID=2893
[1634] d'Entremont, Father Clarence Joseph. (1984) Histoire de Quinan, Nouvelle-Écosse, page 15.
[1635] Information received from Kenneth Breau, cousin and archivist at the Université de Moncton.
[1636] https://novascotia.ca/archives/acadian/reborn/archives.asp?ID=1512
[1637] Information received from Kenneth Breau, cousin and archivist at the Université de Moncton.
[1638] https://novascotia.ca/archives/acadian/reborn/archives.asp?ID=4262
[1639] d'Entremont, Father Clarence Joseph. (1984) Histoire de Quinan, Nouvelle-Écosse, page 73.

Paroisse Ste-Agnès

Death and Burial certificate

This is to certify that _Osithe Mius_ who _16th 1865_ was buried in our parish cemetry on _September_

Husband (wife) of _____

Rev. _James J. Quinan_ officiating.

This is a true copy of the records of Ste_Agnès Parish.

Given at Quinan, N.S. on _July 16th, 2004_.

Sr. Yvette
Curé

---

[7] Charles Séraphin Mius, born May 1, 1803,[1643][1644][1645] married Marguerite Mius (d/o Paul Mius and Marie LeBlanc) on April 18, 1825.[1646][1647] Marguerite was born on December 7, 1801.[1648][1649]

[1640] d'Entremont, Father Clarence Joseph. (1984) Histoire de Quinan, Nouvelle-Écosse, page 73.

[1641] https://novascotia.ca/archives/acadian/reborn/archives.asp?ID=18

[1642] Macauley, Sheila Hubbard. (1996) The Hubbard Family of Nova Scotia, page 6. Baltimore, MD: Gateway Press, Inc.

[1643] d'Entremont, Father Clarence Joseph. (1984) Histoire de Quinan, Nouvelle-Écosse, page 73.

[1644] Macauley, Sheila Hubbard. (1996) The Hubbard Family of Nova Scotia, page 6. Baltimore, MD: Gateway Press, Inc.

[1645] https://novascotia.ca/archives/acadian/reborn/archives.asp?ID=532

[1646] d'Entremont, Father Clarence Joseph. (1984) Histoire de Quinan, Nouvelle-Écosse, pages 73 and 94.

Certificat de Baptême

Les présentes certifient que **Charles Séraphin Mius (Miuce)**
Fils ou fille de **François Mius** et de **Osithe O'Bird (O'Burd)**
Est né(e) à _____ le **1 mai 1803**
et a été baptisé(e) **25 juin 1803** par **Rév. Sigogne**
Parrain **Jean Baptiste Miuce** Marraine _____
a été confirmé(e) le _____ à _____
a été marié(e) le _____ à _____
Extrait des registres de la paroisse de **Ste-Anne-du-Ruisseau**
Donné à **Ste -Anne-du-Ruisseau** le **10 oct. 2003**

P. Crépin Kbondé
Curé

[1647] https://novascotia.ca/archives/acadian/reborn/archives.asp?ID=1524
[1648] d'Entremont, Father Clarence Joseph. (1984) <u>Histoire de Quinan, Nouvelle-Écosse,</u> page 94.
[1649] https://novascotia.ca/archives/acadian/reborn/archives.asp?ID=271

[8] Rosalie Angèle (dite Angélique) Mius, born September 17, 1834 in Quinan, Nova Scotia, [1650] was married to **Vital Mius** (s/o Pierre Eusèbe (dit Petit John) Mius and Scholastique Boutier) on November 8, 1853 at SAR. [1651] [1652] Vital was born November 17, 1828 in Quinan, Nova Scotia. [1653] Rosalie Angèle died in Yarmouth on January 21, 1916. [1654]

[1650] htts://novascotia.ca/archives/acadian/reborn/archives.asp?ID=2624
[1651] d'Entremont, Father Clarence Joseph. (1984) <u>Histoire de Quinan, Nouvelle-Écosse</u>, page 74.
[1652] Sainte-Anne-du-Ruisseau Parish Records, Book 3(1841-1867) Marriages, Page 115.
[1653] https://novascotia.ca/archives/acadian/reborn/archives.asp?ID=1929
[1654] d'Entremont, Father Clarence Joseph. (1984) <u>Histoire de Quinan, Nouvelle-Écosse</u>, page 74.

Certificat de Mariage

Les présentes certifient que **Vital Mius**

fils de **Eusebe Mius** et de **Scholastique Bouquet (Boutier)**

et

Rosalie Angélique Mius

fille de **Séraphin Mius** et de **Marguerite Mius**

ont contracté mariage le **8 nov. 1853**

Témoins **Mande Mius et Urbain Miraux**

Prêtre officiant **Rév. Joseph Goudot**

Extrait des registres de la paroisse de **Ste-Anne-du-Ruisseau**

Donné à **Ste-Anne-du-Ruisseau** le **10 oct. 2003**

Rév. Crépin Khonde
Curé

[1] Philippe Mius, born c. 1609 in Normandie, France, was married to Madeleine Hélie c. 1649. [1655] Madeleine was born c. 1626. [1656] According to Father Clarence Joseph d'Entremont, Philippe died at GP at the end of 1700. [1657] Madeleine died before the PR census of 1678. [1658]

[2] Philippe Mius (dit d'Azy), born c. 1660, married a Mi'kmaq woman (whose name is not known to us) c. 1678. [1659]

[3] Joseph Mius (dit d'Azy), born c. 1679, married Marie Amirault (d/o François Amirault dit Tourangeau and Marie Pitre) c. 1699. [1660] [1661] Marie was born c. 1684 at CS. [1662]

NOTE: This couple has been genetically traced to the fatal Niemann-Pick (variant C) disease as per the French Acadian population of Yarmouth County, Nova Scotia.

[4] François Mius, born March 19, 1703 at CS, [1663] [1664] married Jeanne Duon (d/o Jean Baptiste Duon dit Lyonnais and Agnès Hébert) on February 14, 1735 in PR. [1665] [1666] [1667] Jeanne was born March 29, 1718 in PR. [1668] [1669] François died between 1766 and 1775. [1670]

[1655] White, Stephen A. (1999) <u>Dictionnaire Généalogique des Familles Acadiennes</u>, Volume H to Z, pages 840 and 1201.
[1656] Ibid.
[1657] Ibid.
[1658] Ibid.
[1659] Ibid, pages 1201 and 1206.
[1660] Ibid, pages 1206 and 1207.
[1661] White, Stephen A. (1999) <u>Dictionnaire Généalogique des Familles Acadiennes</u>, Volume A to G, page 17.
[1662] Ibid.
[1663] White, Stephen A. (1999) <u>Dictionnaire Généalogique des Familles Acadiennes</u>, Volume H to Z, page 1207.
[1664] https://novascotia.ca/archives/acadian/archives.asp?ID=104
[1665] White, Stephen A. (1999) <u>Dictionnaire Généalogique des Familles Acadiennes</u>, Volume A to G, page 582.

[5] Jean Pierre Mius, born February 3, 1743, [1671] married Anne Doucet (d/o Joseph Doucet and Anne Surette) c. 1768 in MA (exile). [1672] [1673] Anne was born April 1, 1747 in PR. [1674] [1675] Jean Pierre died on February 7, 1825 in SAR and was buried on February 8, 1825. [1676] [1677] [1678] Anne was buried on January 4, 1838 in SAR. [1679] [1680]

[6] Cécile Mius was married to **François Chrysostôme (dit Couchique) Deveau** (s/o Jacques Deveau and Marie Madeleine Robichaud dit Cadet) c. 1791. [1681] [1682] [1683]

[1666] White, Stephen A. (1999) <u>Dictionnaire Généalogique des Familles Acadiennes</u>, Volume H to Z, page 1207.
[1667] https://novascotia.ca/archives/acadian/archives.asp?ID=2037
[1668] White, Stephen A. (1999) <u>Dictionnaire Généalogique des Familles Acadiennes</u>, Volume A to G, page 582.
[1669] https://novascotia.ca/archives/acadian/archives.asp?ID=680
[1670] White, Stephen A. (1999) <u>Dictionnaire Généalogique des Familles Acadiennes</u>, Volume H to Z, page 1207.
[1671] Information received from Kenneth Breau, cousin and archivist at the Université de Moncton.
[1672] d'Entremont, Father Clarence Joseph. (1984) <u>Histoire de Quinan, Nouvelle-Écosse</u>, page 15.
[1673] Information received from Kenneth Breau, cousin and archivist at the Université de Moncton.
[1674] d'Entremont, Father Clarence Joseph. (1984) <u>Histoire de Quinan, Nouvelle-Écosse</u>, page 15.
[1675] https://novascotia.ca/archives/acadian/archives.asp?ID=2893
[1676] d'Entremont, Father Clarence Joseph. (1984) <u>Histoire de Quinan, Nouvelle-Écosse</u>, page 15.
[1677] Information received from Kenneth Breau, cousin and archivist at the Université de Moncton.
[1678] https://novascotia.ca/archives/acadian/reborn/archives.asp?ID=1512
[1679] Information received from Kenneth Breau, cousin and archivist at the Université de Moncton.
[1680] https://novascotia.ca/archives/acadian/reborn/archives.asp?ID=4262
[1681] d'Entremont, Father Clarence Joseph. (1984) <u>Histoire de Quinan, Nouvelle-Écosse</u>, page 75.
[1682] Information received from Kenneth Breau, cousin and archivist at the Université de Moncton.

François Chrysostôme (dit Couchique) was born May 1764 in Pointe du Diable, near Halifax, Nova Scotia.[1684][1685] François Chrysostôme (dit Couchique) died on November 25, 1842 in Salmon River, Digby County, Nova Scotia.[1686][1687]

[1683] Information received in an email from Fred Chandler Union III, dated July 2, 2001 (based on the research of Nova Scotia Acadian historian, J. Alphonse Deveau).
[1684] Ibid.
[1685] Information received in an email from Fred Chandler Union III, dated July 2, 2001 (based on the research of Nova Scotia Acadian historian, J. Alphonse Deveau).
[1686] Information received from Kenneth Breau, cousin and archivist at the Université de Moncton.
[1687] csapstaff.ednet.ns.ca/jldeveau/deveau3.html

[1] Philippe Mius, born c. 1609 in Normandie, France, was married to Madeleine Hélie c. 1649. [1688] Madeleine was born c. 1626. [1689] According to Father Clarence Joseph d'Entremont, Philippe died at GP at the end of 1700. [1690] Madeleine died before the PR census of 1678. [1691]

[2] Philippe Mius (dit d'Azy), born c. 1660, married a Mi'kmaq woman (whose name is not known to us) c. 1678. [1692]

[3] Joseph Mius (dit d'Azy), born c. 1679, married Marie Amirault (d/o François Amirault dit Tourangeau and Marie Pitre) c. 1699. [1693] [1694] Marie was born c. 1684 at CS. [1695]

NOTE: This couple has been genetically traced to the fatal Niemann-Pick (variant C) disease as per the French Acadian population of Yarmouth County, Nova Scotia.

[4] François Mius, born March 19, 1703 at CS, [1696] [1697] married Jeanne Duon (d/o Jean Baptiste Duon dit Lyonnais and Agnès Hébert) on February 14, 1735 in PR. [1698] [1699] [1700] Jeanne was born March 29, 1718 in PR. [1701] [1702] François died between 1766 and 1775. [1703]

[1688] White, Stephen A. (1999) Dictionnaire Généalogique des Familles Acadiennes, Volume H to Z, pages 840 and 1201.
[1689] Ibid.
[1690] Ibid.
[1691] Ibid.
[1692] Ibid, pages 1201 and 1206.
[1693] Ibid, pages 1206 and 1207.
[1694] White, Stephen A. (1999) Dictionnaire Généalogique des Familles Acadiennes, Volume A to G, page 17.
[1695] Ibid.
[1696] White, Stephen A. (1999) Dictionnaire Généalogique des Familles Acadiennes, Volume H to Z, page 1207.
[1697] https://novascotia.ca/archives/acadian/archives.asp?ID=104
[1698] White, Stephen A. (1999) Dictionnaire Généalogique des Familles Acadiennes, Volume A to G, page 582.

[5] Jean Pierre Mius, born February 3, 1743,[1704] married Anne Doucet (d/o Joseph Doucet and Anne Surette) c. 1768 in MA (exile).[1705][1706] Anne was born April 1, 1747 in PR.[1707][1708] Jean Pierre died on February 7, 1825 in SAR and was buried on February 8, 1825.[1709][1710][1711] Anne was buried on January 4, 1838 in SAR.[1712][1713]

[6] Jean Baptiste (dit Petit John) Mius was married to Marguerite Robichaud (d/o Pierre Robichaud dit Cadet and Marie Rose Corporon) on November 29, 1797.[1714][1715][1716] They

---

[1699] White, Stephen A. (1999) Dictionnaire Généalogique des Familles Acadiennes, Volume H to Z, page 1207.
[1700] https://novascotia.ca/archives/acadian/archives.asp?ID=2037
[1701] White, Stephen A. (1999) Dictionnaire Généalogique des Familles Acadiennes, Volume A to G, page 582.
[1702] https://novascotia.ca/archives/acadian/archives.asp?ID=680
[1703] White, Stephen A. (1999) Dictionnaire Généalogique des Familles Acadiennes, Volume H to Z, page 1207.
[1704] Information received from Kenneth Breau, cousin and archivist at the Université de Moncton.
[1705] d'Entremont, Father Clarence Joseph. (1984) Histoire de Quinan, Nouvelle-Écosse, page 15.
[1706] Information received from Kenneth Breau, cousin and archivist at the Université de Moncton.
[1707] d'Entremont, Father Clarence Joseph. (1984) Histoire de Quinan, Nouvelle-Écosse, page 15.
[1708] https://novascotia.ca/archives/acadian/archives.asp?ID=2893
[1709] d'Entremont, Father Clarence Joseph. (1984) Histoire de Quinan, Nouvelle-Écosse, page 15.
[1710] Information received from Kenneth Breau, cousin and archivist at the Université de Moncton.
[1711] https://novascotia.ca/archives/acadian/reborn/archives.asp?ID=1512
[1712] Information received from Kenneth Breau, cousin and archivist at the Université de Moncton.
[1713] https://novascotia.ca/archives/acadian/reborn/archives.asp?ID=4262
[1714] d'Entremont, Father Clarence Joseph. (1984) Histoire de Quinan, Nouvelle-Écosse, page 75.
[1715] Information received from Kenneth Breau, cousin and archivist at the Université de Moncton.
[1716] https://novascotia.ca/archives/acadian/reborn/archives.asp?ID=101

were married in front of witnesses due to the absence of a priest. The marriage was blessed by Father Sigogne on November 9, 1799. [1717] Marguerite was born on October 1, 1770. [1718]

[7] Pierre Eusèbe (dit Petit John) Mius, born June 28, 1801, [1719] married Scholastique Boutier (d/o Jean Boutier and Anne Marguerite Doucet) on October 25, 1825. [1720] Scholastique was born on November 22, 1806. [1721]

Certificat de Baptême

Les présentes certifient que **Pierre Eusebe Mius**
Fils ou fille de **Jean Baptiste Mius** et de **Marguerite Robichaud**
Est né(e) à _____ le **28 juin 1801**
et a été baptisé(e) **2 août 1801** par **Frederic Suret**
Parrain **Pierre Robichaud** Marraine **Marguerite Mius**
a été confirmé(e) le _____ à _____
a été marié(e) le _____ à _____
Extrait des registres de la paroisse de **Ste-Anne-du-Ruisseau**
Donné à **Ste Anne-du-Ruisseau** le **10 oct. 2003**

[1717] https://novascotia.ca/archives/acadian/reborn/archives.asp?ID=101
[1718] Information received from Kenneth Breau, cousin and archivist at the Université de Moncton.
[1719] https://novascotia.ca/archives/acadian/reborn/archives.asp?ID=261
[1720] https://novascotia.ca/archives/acadian/reborn/archives.asp?ID=1605
[1721] https://novascotia.ca/archives/acadian/reborn/archives.asp?ID=701

[8] Vital Mius, born November 17, 1828 in Quinan, Nova Scotia, [1722] married Rosalie Angèle (dite Angélique) Mius (d/o Charles Séraphin Mius and Marguerite Mius) on November 8, 1853 at SAR. [1723] [1724] Rosalie Angèle was born on September 17, 1834 in Quinan, Nova Scotia. [1725] Rosalie Angèle died in Yarmouth on January 21, 1916. [1726]

[1722] https://novascotia.ca/archives/acadian/reborn/archives.asp?ID=1929
[1723] d'Entremont, Father Clarence Joseph. (1984) Histoire de Quinan, Nouvelle-Écosse, page 74.
[1724] Sainte-Anne-du-Ruisseau Parish Records, Book 3(1841-1867) Marriages, Page 115.
[1725] https://novascotia.ca/archives/acadian/reborn/archives.asp?ID=2624
[1726] d'Entremont, Father Clarence Joseph. (1984) Histoire de Quinan, Nouvelle-Écosse, page 74.

[9] Peter Muise, born c. 1854, married Martha Roach (d/o John William Henry Roach and Marie Elizabeth Deveau) on December 8, 1877. [1727] Martha was born on March 29, 1862 in Wedgeport, Yarmouth County, Nova Scotia. [1728] However, the Certificate of Death (which follows) states March 12, 1860 as having been the date of her birth. Peter died on February 20, 1916 in Yarmouth, Yarmouth County, Nova Scotia. [1729] He was buried on February 23, 1916. [1730] Martha died on February 3, 1940 in Yarmouth, Yarmouth County, Nova Scotia. [1731] She was buried on February 7, 1940. [1732]

[1727] Parish of the Holy Trinity (Reel 2. Page 85, Number 257) located at the Argyle Courthouse in Tusket, NS.
[1728] E-mail from Susan Surette dated Tuesday, June 5, 2001.
[1729] Ibid.
[1730] Ibid.
[1731] E-mails from Susan Surette dated Wednesday, May 30, 2001 and Tuesday, June 5, 2001.
[1732] E-mail from Susan Surette dated Tuesday, June 5, 2001.

Peter Muire Bachelor of this Parish and Martha Roach Spinster of this Parish were married in this Parish by License with Consent of Friends this 8th Day of December in the Year One thousand eight hundred and 1877

Dec 8, 1877

By me J.T.T. Moody

This Marriage was solemnized between us { Peter + Muire Rector
Martha + Roach

In the Presence of { Sam Churchill
Mary Muire

NO. 251

Certificate of Death

№ 005238

Name of Deceased Person:	PETER MEUSE
Sex:	MALE
Date of Death:	Feb 20, 1916
Place of Death:	YARMOUTH
Date of Birth:	NOT STATED
Age:	64 YRS
Place of Birth:	YARMOUTH, NOVA SCOTIA
Residence:	YARMOUTH, NOVA SCOTIA
Occupation:	NOT STATED
Marital Status:	MARRIED
Name of Spouse:	NOT STATED
Name of Father:	NOT STATED
Name of Mother:	NOT STATED
Name of Attending Physician:	G. W. T. FARISH
Name of Funeral Director:	V. S. SWEENY
Disposition:	NOT STATED
Place of Disposition:	ST. AMBROSE
At:	YARMOUTH, NOVA SCOTIA
Name of Informant:	FRED MUISE
Address:	NOT STATED
Relationship:	NOT STATED
Date of Registration:	Feb 22, 1916
Registration No:	1916-02-050712

This is to certify that the record herein contained is from a Record of Death on file in the office of the REGISTRAR GENERAL of NOVA SCOTIA.

Given under my hand and the SEAL of the DEPUTY REGISTRAR GENERAL at Halifax, THIS 7th DAY OF September 2001

Deputy Registrar General

Certificate of Death

Nº 005769

Name of Deceased Person:	MARTHA MUISE
Sex:	FEMALE
Date of Death:	Feb 03, 1940
Place of Death:	YARMOUTH
Date of Birth:	Mar 12, 1860
Age:	79 YRS
Place of Birth:	YARMOUTH, NOVA SCOTIA
Residence:	YARMOUTH, NOVA SCOTIA
Occupation:	HOUSEWIFE
Marital Status:	WIDOWED
Name of Spouse:	PETER MUISE
Name of Father:	JAMES ROACH
Name of Mother:	ELIZABETH DEVEAU
Name of Attending Physician:	S. N. WILLIAMSON
Name of Funeral Director:	J. S. SWEENY
Disposition:	NOT STATED
Place of Disposition:	ST. AMBBROSE
At:	NOT STATED
Name of Informant:	FRED MUISE
Address:	YARMOUTH, NS
Relationship:	SON
Date of Registration:	Feb 28, 1940
Registration No:	1940-02-184602

This is to certify that the record herein contained is from a Record of Death on file in the office of the REGISTRAR GENERAL of NOVA SCOTIA.

Given under my hand and the SEAL of the DEPUTY REGISTRAR GENERAL at Halifax, THIS 13th DAY OF June 2002

Deputy Registrar General

According to my father, Peter and Martha lived at 16 Regent Street in Yarmouth.

Peter's death notice was located in the Yarmouth Times (dated February 26, 1916): Peter Meuse, of Regent Street, died on Sunday after a five week illness of pneumonia. He was 64 years old and leaves three sons and a daughter. [1733]

There is a shared headstone of Peter and Martha at the Our Lady of Calvary Cemetery (Section A - 136) in Yarmouth. The stone reads: Peter Muise died February 20, 1916, aged 64 years (as well as) Martha Muise born March 29, 1862 and Died February 3, 1940. [1734]

It was in locating a copy of their marriage certificate during the July 1999 visit that I also located the parents of Peter Muise; namely, Vital (Laborer) and Angelica. Parents of Martha were also denoted thusly, as W (Ship Carpenter) and Elizabeth.

[10] Beatrice Muise, born October 14, 1898, married **Jean Avite (Harvey) Doucet** (s/o Jean Théophile Doucet dit Câlin and Adèle Dulain) on November 15, 1915 in Yarmouth, Yarmouth County, Nova Scotia. [1735] They were married at St. Ambrose Catholic Church in Yarmouth by Reverend W. E. Young. Jean Avite (Harvey) was born on August 7, 1896 in East Quinan, Yarmouth County, Nova Scotia. [1736]

[1733] E-mail from Susan Surette dated Tuesday, June 5, 2001.
[1734] Ibid.
[1735] https://www.novascotiagenealogy.com/ItemView.aspx?ImageFile=16-992&Event=marriage&ID=147091
[1736] Ste. Agnès RC Church records in Quinan, NS. Information obtained by Linda Joyce Campbell (first cousin once removed to my father) of Yarmouth, NS.

St. Ambrose Cathedral

65 Green Street
Yarmouth, Nova Scotia
B5A 1Z6
(902) 742-7151
Fax: (902) 742-7152
E-mail: ycc@ns.aliantzinc.ca

Certificate of Baptism

++

Name:	Beatrice Muise
Father:	Peter Muise
Mother:	Martha Roach
Date of Birth:	14 Oct 1898
Place of Birth:	
Date of Baptism:	Oct 18, 1898
Sponsors:	George Roach
	Mary Muise
Presider:	Rev. W.B. Hamilton
Confirmation:	
Marriage:	
Issued by:	Mary Sweeney
Date:	25 August 2011

Province of Nova Scotia
MARRIAGE REGISTER

Date of Marriage	November 15th 1915
Place of Marriage	Yarmouth NS
County	Yarmouth
How Married; by License or Banns	Banns
Dates of Publication, if by Banns	3 preceding Sundays
Full name of Groom	Harvé Doucette
Age	19
Condition (Bachelor or Widower)	Bachelor
Religious Denomination	Catholic
Occupation	Laborer
Residence	Yarmouth NS
Where Born	Quinan NS
Names of Parents	Theophile & Adele Doucette
Occupation of Parent	Laborer
Full name of Bride	Beatrice Meuse
Age	17
Condition (Spinster or Widow)	Spinster
Religious Denomination	Catholic
Her Place of Residence	Yarmouth NS
Where Born	
Names of Parents	Peter & Martha Meuse
Occupation of Parent	Laborer
Names of Witnesses	William H. Doucette / Lillian Titus
Signature of Parties Married	Harvé Doucette / Beatrice Muise
Officiating Clergyman	W. E. Young
Denomination of Clergyman	Catholic Priest

I Certify, That the marriage of the persons above named was duly celebrated by me at the time and place and in the manner stated in this Register.

W. E. Young
Officiating Clergyman.

[1] Philippe Mius, born c. 1609 in Normandie, France, was married to Madeleine Hélie c. 1649. [1737] Madeleine was born c. 1626. [1738] According to Father Clarence Joseph d'Entremont, Philippe died at GP at the end of 1700. [1739] Madeleine died before the PR census of 1678. [1740]

[2] Philippe Mius (dit d'Azy), born c. 1660, married a Mi'kmaq woman (whose name is not known to us) c. 1678. [1741]

[3] Joseph Mius (dit d'Azy), born c. 1679, married Marie Amirault (d/o François Amirault dit Tourangeau and Marie Pitre) c. 1699. [1742] [1743] Marie was born c. 1684 at CS. [1744]

NOTE: This couple has been genetically traced to the fatal Niemann-Pick (variant C) disease as per the French Acadian population of Yarmouth County, Nova Scotia.

[4] François Mius, born March 19, 1703 at CS, [1745] [1746] married Jeanne Duon (d/o Jean Baptiste Duon dit Lyonnais and Agnès Hébert) on February 14, 1735 in PR. [1747] [1748] [1749] Jeanne was born March 29, 1718 in PR. [1750] [1751] François died between 1766 and 1775. [1752]

[1737] White, Stephen A. (1999) Dictionnaire Généalogique des Familles Acadiennes, Volume H to Z, pages 840 and 1201.
[1738] Ibid.
[1739] Ibid.
[1740] Ibid.
[1741] Ibid, pages 1201 and 1206.
[1742] Ibid, pages 1206 and 1207.
[1743] White, Stephen A. (1999) Dictionnaire Généalogique des Familles Acadiennes, Volume A to G, page 17.
[1744] Ibid.
[1745] White, Stephen A. (1999) Dictionnaire Généalogique des Familles Acadiennes, Volume H to Z, page 1207.
[1746] https://novascotia.ca/archives/acadian/archives.asp?ID=104
[1747] White, Stephen A. (1999) Dictionnaire Généalogique des Familles Acadiennes, Volume A to G, page 582.

[5] Jean Pierre Mius, born February 3, 1743, [1753] married Anne Doucet (d/o Joseph Doucet and Anne Surette) c. 1768 in MA (exile). [1754] [1755] Anne was born April 1, 1747 in PR. [1756] [1757] Jean Pierre died on February 7, 1825 in SAR and was buried on February 8, 1825. [1758] [1759] [1760] Anne was buried on January 4, 1838 in SAR. [1761] [1762]

[6] Marguerite Mius was married to **Anselme Mius**, s/o Paul Mius and Marie LeBlanc, on September 29, 1807. [1763] [1764]

[1748] White, Stephen A. (1999) <u>Dictionnaire Généalogique des Familles Acadiennes</u>, Volume H to Z, page 1207.
[1749] https://novascotia.ca/archives/acadian/archives.asp?ID=2037
[1750] White, Stephen A. (1999) <u>Dictionnaire Généalogique des Familles Acadiennes</u>, Volume A to G, page 582.
[1751] https://novascotia.ca/archives/acadian/archives.asp?ID=680
[1752] White, Stephen A. (1999) <u>Dictionnaire Généalogique des Familles Acadiennes</u>, Volume H to Z, page 1207.
[1753] Information received from Kenneth Breau, cousin and archivist at the Université de Moncton.
[1754] d'Entremont, Father Clarence Joseph. (1984) <u>Histoire de Quinan, Nouvelle-Écosse</u>, page 15.
[1755] Information received from Kenneth Breau, cousin and archivist at the Université de Moncton.
[1756] d'Entremont, Father Clarence Joseph. (1984) <u>Histoire de Quinan, Nouvelle-Écosse</u>, page 15.
[1757] https://novascotia.ca/archives/acadian/archives.asp?ID=2893
[1758] d'Entremont, Father Clarence Joseph. (1984) <u>Histoire de Quinan, Nouvelle-Écosse</u>, page 15.
[1759] Information received from Kenneth Breau, cousin and archivist at the Université de Moncton.
[1760] https://novascotia.ca/archives/acadian/reborn/archives.asp?ID=1512
[1761] Information received from Kenneth Breau, cousin and archivist at the Université de Moncton.
[1762] https://novascotia.ca/archives/acadian/reborn/archives.asp?ID=4262
[1763] d'Entremont, Father Clarence Joseph. (1984) <u>Histoire de Quinan, Nouvelle-Écosse</u>, pages 75 and 89.
[1764] https://novascotia.ca/archives/acadian/reborn/archives.asp?ID=748

Mius d'Entremont 1B

Philippe Mius came to Acadie, about 1651, with his wife Madeleine Hélie, as adjutant to Governor Charles de Saint-Étienne de La Tour; he served as commandant in the colony when La Tour was absent. [1765]

On July 17, 1653, he received, jointly with Pierre Ferrand, by letters patent from Charles de Saint-Étienne de La Tour, the fief of Pobomcoup (today known as Pubnico), at Cape Sable. [1766]

In 1670, he became the King's attorney. [1767]

On October 5, 1687, Philippe Mius d'Entremont signed an attestation in favour of the accomplishments of Governor d'Aulnay. [1768]

The connections that follow herein are those re Jean Baptiste I, son of Joseph Mius dit d'Azy and Marie Amirault.

[1765] White, Stephen A. (2000) English Supplement to the Dictionnaire Généalogique des Familles Acadiennes (page 256). Montréal, Québec: AGMV Marquis Imprimeur Inc.
[1766] Ibid.
[1767] Ibid.
[1768] Ibid.

[1] Philippe Mius, born c. 1609 in Normandie, France, was married to Madeleine Hélie c. 1649. [1769] Madeleine was born c. 1626. [1770] According to Father Clarence Joseph d'Entremont, Philippe died at GP at the end of 1700. [1771] Madeleine died before the PR census of 1678. [1772]

[2] Philippe Mius (dit d'Azy), born c. 1660, married a Mi' kmaq woman (whose name is not known to us) c. 1678. [1773]

[3] Joseph Mius (dit d'Azy), born c. 1679, married Marie Amirault (d/o François Amirault dit Tourangeau and Marie Pitre) c. 1699. [1774] [1775] Marie was born c. 1684 at CS. [1776]

NOTE: This couple has been genetically traced to the fatal Niemann-Pick (variant C) disease as per the French Acadian population of Yarmouth County, Nova Scotia.

[4] Jean Baptiste I Mius, born 1713, [1777] was married to Marie Josèphe Surette (d/o Pierre Surette and Jeanne Pellerin) on October 3, 1735 in Port Royal, Acadie. [1778] [1779] Marie Josèphe was born on October 13, 1718 in Port Royal, Acadie. [1780] [1781] Jean Baptiste died at

---

[1769] White, Stephen A. (1999) Dictionnaire Généalogique des Familles Acadiennes, Volume H to Z, pages 840 and 1201.
[1770] Ibid.
[1771] Ibid.
[1772] Ibid.
[1773] Ibid, pages 1201 and 1206.
[1774] Ibid, pages 1206 and 1207.
[1775] White, Stephen A. (1999) Dictionnaire Généalogique des Familles Acadiennes, Volume A to G, page 17.
[1776] Ibid.
[1777] White, Stephen A. (1999) Dictionnaire Généalogique des Familles Acadiennes, Volume H to Z, page 1208.
[1778] Ibid, pages 1208 and 1476.
[1779] https://novascotia.ca/archives/acadian/archives.asp?ID=2084
[1780] White, Stephen A. (1999) Dictionnaire Généalogique des Familles Acadiennes, Volume H to Z, page 1476.

SAR on June 29, 1806 and was buried on June 30, 1806. [1782] [1783] Marie died before the census of August 14, 1763. [1784]

[5] Paul Mius, born either towards the end of 1755 or the beginning of 1756 at CS, [1785] married Marie LeBlanc (d/o Pierre LeBlanc and Marguerite Amirault). [1786] Marie was born c. 1767. [1787] Marie died on April 7, 1835 in Quinan, Yarmouth County, Nova Scotia. [1788] [1789]

[6] Angélique Mathilde Mius, born June 28, 1795 in Quinan, Nova Scotia, [1790] [1791] [1792] married **Joseph Mathurin Doucet** (s/o Michel Doucet and Marie Suzanne Mius) on October

---

[1781] htttps://novascotia.ca/archives/acadian/archives.asp?ID=725
[1782] White, Stephen A. (1999) <u>Dictionnaire Généalogique des Familles Acadiennes</u>, Volume H to Z, page 1208.
[1783] https://novascotia.ca/archives/acadian/reborn/archives.asp?ID=652
[1784] White, Stephen A. (1999) <u>Dictionnaire Généalogique des Familles Acadiennes</u>, Volume H to Z, page 1476.
[1785] d'Entremont, Father Clarence Joseph. (1984) <u>Histoire de Quinan, Nouvelle-Écosse</u>, page 89.
[1786] Ibid.
[1787] Ibid.
[1788] Ibid.
[1789] https://novascotia.ca/archives/acadian/reborn/archives.asp?ID=2540
[1790] Information received from Kenneth Breau, cousin and archivist at the Université de Moncton.
[1791] d'Entremont, Father Clarence Joseph. (1984) <u>Histoire de Quinan, Nouvelle-Écosse</u>, page 94.
[1792] https://novascotia.ca/archives/acadian/reborn/archives.asp?ID=90

28, 1816 in SAR. [1793] [1794] [1795]   Joseph Mathurin was born on May 7, 1795 probably at Pointe-des Ben, part of Sluice Point. [1796] [1797]

[1793] Information received from Kenneth Breau, cousin and archivist at the Université de Moncton.
[1794] d'Entremont, Father Clarence Joseph. (1984) <u>Histoire de Quinan, Nouvelle-Écosse</u>, pages 94 and 113.
[1795] https://novascotia.ca/archives/acadian/reborn/archives.asp?ID=1292
[1796] d'Entremont, Father Clarence Joseph. (1984) <u>Histoire de Quinan, Nouvelle-Écosse</u>, page 94.
[1797] https://novascotia.ca/archives/acadian/reborn/archives.asp?ID=109

[1] Philippe Mius, born c. 1609 in Normandie, France, was married to Madeleine Hélie c. 1649.[1798] Madeleine was born c. 1626.[1799] According to Father Clarence Joseph d'Entremont, Philippe died at GP at the end of 1700.[1800] Madeleine died before the PR census of 1678.[1801]

[2] Philippe Mius (dit d'Azy), born c. 1660, married a Mi'kmaq woman (whose name is not known to us) c. 1678.[1802]

[3] Joseph Mius (dit d'Azy), born c. 1679, married Marie Amirault (d/o François Amirault dit Tourangeau and Marie Pitre) c. 1699.[1803] [1804] Marie was born c. 1684 at CS.[1805]

NOTE: This couple has been genetically traced to the fatal Niemann-Pick (variant C) disease as per the French Acadian population of Yarmouth County, Nova Scotia.

[4]] Jean Baptiste I Mius, born 1713,[1806] was married to Marie Josèphe Surette (d/o Pierre Surette and Jeanne Pellerin) on October 3, 1735 in Port Royal, Acadie.[1807] [1808] Marie Josèphe was born on October 13, 1718 in Port Royal, Acadie.[1809] [1810] Jean Baptiste died at

---

[1798] White, Stephen A. (1999) <u>Dictionnaire Généalogique des Familles Acadiennes</u>, Volume H to Z, pages 840 and 1201.
[1799] Ibid.
[1800] Ibid.
[1801] Ibid.
[1802] Ibid, pages 1201 and 1206.
[1803] Ibid, pages 1206 and 1207.
[1804] White, Stephen A. (1999) <u>Dictionnaire Généalogique des Familles Acadiennes</u>, Volume A to G, page 17.
[1805] Ibid.
[1806] White, Stephen A. (1999) <u>Dictionnaire Généalogique des Familles Acadiennes</u>, Volume H to Z, page 1208.
[1807] Ibid, pages 1208 and 1476.
[1808] https://novascotia.ca/archives/acadian/archives.asp?ID=2084
[1809] White, Stephen A. (1999) <u>Dictionnaire Généalogique des Familles Acadiennes</u>, Volume H to Z, page 1476.

SAR on June 29, 1806 and was buried on June 30, 1806. [1811] [1812] Marie died before the census of August 14, 1763. [1813]

[5] Paul Mius, born either towards the end of 1755 or the beginning of 1756 at CS, [1814] married Marie LeBlanc (d/o Pierre LeBlanc and Marguerite Amirault). [1815] Marie was born c. 1767. [1816] Marie died on April 7, 1835 in Quinan, Yarmouth County, Nova Scotia. [1817] [1818]

[6] Anselme Mius married Marguerite Mius (d/o Jean Pierre Mius and Anne Doucet) on September 29, 1807. [1819] [1820]

[7] Jean Cyrille (dit Coco) Mius, born August 17, 1812, [1821] [1822] married Scholastique Doucet (d/o Charles (dit Tania) Doucet and Anne Mius) on October 29, 1832. [1823] [1824]

[1810] https://novascotia.ca/archives/acadian/archives.asp?ID=725
[1811] White, Stephen A. (1999) Dictionnaire Généalogique des Familles Acadiennes, Volume H to Z, page 1208.
[1812] httsp://novascotia.ca/archives/acadian/reborn/archives.asp?ID=652
[1813] White, Stephen A. (1999) Dictionnaire Généalogique des Familles Acadiennes, Volume H to Z, page 1476.
[1814] d'Entremont, Father Clarence Joseph. (1984) Histoire de Quinan, Nouvelle-Écosse, page 89.
[1815] Ibid.
[1816] Ibid.
[1817] Ibid.
[1818] https://novascotia.ca/archives/acadian/reborn/archives.asp?ID=2540
[1819] d'Entremont, Father Clarence Joseph. (1984) Histoire de Quinan, Nouvelle-Écosse, pages 75 and 89.
[1820] https://novascotia.ca/archives/acadian/reborn/archives.asp?ID=748
[1821] d'Entremont, Father Clarence Joseph. (1984) Histoire de Quinan, Nouvelle-Écosse, page 89.
[1822] https://novascotia.ca/archives/acadian/reborn/archives.asp?ID=995
[1823] d'Entremont, Father Clarence Joseph. (1984) Histoire de Quinan, Nouvelle-Écosse, page 89.
[1824] https://novascotia.ca/archives/acadian/reborn/archives.asp?ID=2290

Scholastique was born on April 23, 1812. [1825] [1826] Scholastique died on March 14, 1896 in Quinan, Yarmouth County, Nova Scotia. [1827]

Paroisse Ste-Agnès

Death and Burial certificate

This is to certify that *Scholastique Mius* who died on *Mar 14th /1896* was buried in our parish cemetry on *March 17, 1896*. Husband (wife) of *Daughter of Charles Doucet and widower of (?)* Rev. *J. Creagier* officiating. *She was 85 years old.*

This is a true copy of the records of Ste_Agnès Parish.

Given at Quinan, N.S. on *July 16th, 2004*.

Sr. Yvette Duguay
Curé

[8] **Anne Vitaline Mius**, born October 12, 1833, [1828] [1829] married **Louis Cyprien Dulain** (s/o Louis Dulain and Marie Apolline Frontain). [1830] Louis Cyprien was born on February 1, 1806. [1831] [1832] Louis Cyprien died in August 1888. [1833]

[1825] d'Entremont, Father Clarence Joseph. (1984) Histoire de Quinan, Nouvelle-Écosse page 89.
[1826] https://novascotia.ca/archives/acadian/reborn/archives.asp?ID=971
[1827] d'Entremont, Father Clarence Joseph. (1984) Histoire de Quinan, Nouvelle-Écosse, page 89.
[1828] Ibid.
[1829] https://novascotia.ca/archives/acadian/reborn/archives.asp?ID=2382
[1830] d'Entremont, Father Clarence Joseph. (1984) Histoire de Quinan, Nouvelle-Écosse, pages 89 and 127.
[1831] Ibid, page 126.
[1832] https://novascotia.ca/archives/acadian/reborn/archives.asp?ID=632

[1] Philippe Mius, born c. 1609 in Normandie, France, was married to Madeleine Hélie c. 1649. [1834] Madeleine was born c. 1626. [1835] According to Father Clarence Joseph d'Entremont, Philippe died at GP at the end of 1700. [1836] Madeleine died before the PR census of 1678. [1837]

[2] Philippe Mius (dit d'Azy), born c. 1660, married a Mi'kmaq woman (whose name is not known to us) c. 1678. [1838]

[3] Joseph Mius (dit d'Azy), born c. 1679, married Marie Amirault (d/o François Amirault dit Tourangeau and Marie Pitre) c. 1699. [1839] [1840] Marie was born c. 1684 at CS. [1841]

NOTE: This couple has been genetically traced to the fatal Niemann-Pick (variant C) disease as per the French Acadian population of Yarmouth County, Nova Scotia.

[4]] Jean Baptiste I Mius, born 1713, [1842] was married to Marie Josèphe Surette (d/o Pierre Surette and Jeanne Pellerin) on October 3, 1735 in Port Royal, Acadie. [1843] [1844] Marie

---

[1833] d'Entremont, Father Clarence Joseph. (1984) Histoire de Quinan, Nouvelle-Écosse, page 126.
[1834] White, Stephen A. (1999) Dictionnaire Généalogique des Familles Acadiennes, Volume H to Z, pages 840 and 1201.
[1835] Ibid.
[1836] Ibid.
[1837] Ibid.
[1838] Ibid, pages 1201 and 1206.
[1839] Ibid, pages 1206 and 1207.
[1840] White, Stephen A. (1999) Dictionnaire Généalogique des Familles Acadiennes, Volume A to G, page 17.
[1841] Ibid.
[1842] White, Stephen A. (1999) Dictionnaire Généalogique des Familles Acadiennes, Volume H to Z, page 1208.
[1843] Ibid, pages 1208 and 1476.
[1844] https://novascotia.ca/archives/acadian/archives.asp?ID=2084

Josèphe was born on October 13, 1718 in Port Royal, Acadie. [1845] [1846] Jean Baptiste died at SAR on June 29, 1806 and was buried on June 30, 1806. [1847] [1848] Marie died before the census of August 14, 1763. [1849]

[5] Paul Mius, born either towards the end of 1755 or the beginning of 1756 at CS, [1850] married Marie LeBlanc (d/o Pierre LeBlanc and Marguerite Amirault). [1851] Marie was born c. 1767. [1852] Marie died on April 7, 1835 in Quinan, Yarmouth County, Nova Scotia. [1853] [1854]

[6] Marguerite Mius, born December 7, 1801, [1855] married **Charles Séraphin Mius** (s/o François Mius and Marie Osithe O'Bird) on April 18, 1825. [1856] [1857] Charles Séraphin was born on May 1, 1803. [1858] [1859]

[1845] White, Stephen A. (1999) Dictionnaire Généalogique des Familles Acadiennes, Volume H to Z, page 1476.
[1846] https://novascotia.ca/archives/acadian/archives.asp?ID=725
[1847] White, Stephen A. (1999) Dictionnaire Généalogique des Familles Acadiennes, Volume H to Z, page 1208.
[1848] https://novascotia.ca/archives/acadian/reborn/archives.asp?ID=652
[1849] White, Stephen A. (1999) Dictionnaire Généalogique des Familles Acadiennes, Volume H to Z, page 1476.
[1850] d'Entremont, Father Clarence Joseph. (1984) Histoire de Quinan, Nouvelle-Écosse, page 89.
[1851] Ibid.
[1852] Ibid.
[1853] Ibid.
[1854] https://novascotia.ca/archives/acadian/reborn/archives.asp?ID=2540
[1855] d'Entremont, Father Clarence Joseph. (1984) Histoire de Quinan, Nouvelle-Écosse, page 94.
[1856] Ibid, pages 73 and 94.
[1857] https://novascotia.ca/archives/acadian/reborn/archives.asp?ID=1524
[1858] d'Entremont, Father Clarence Joseph. (1984) Histoire de Quinan, Nouvelle-Écosse, page 73.
[1859] Macauley, Sheila Hubbard. (1996) The Hubbard Family of Nova Scotia, page 6. Baltimore, MD: Gateway Press, Inc.

Certificat de Baptême

Les présentes certifient que **Marguerite Mius (Miuce)**
Fils ou fille de **Paul Mius** et de **Marie LeBlanc**
Est né(e) à _____ le **7 déc. 1801**
et a été baptisé(e) **8 déc. 1801** par **Rév. Sigogne**
Parrain **Joseph Babin** Marraine **Marguerite Bourque**
a été confirmé(e) le _____ à _____
a été marié(e) le _____ à _____
Extrait des registres de la paroisse de **Ste-Anne-du-Ruisseau**
Donné à **Ste-Anne-du-Ruisseau** le **10 oct. 2003**

P. Crépin Khonde
Curé

Certificat de Mariage

Les présentes certifient que **Charles Séraphin Mius**
fils de **François Mius** et de **Osithe O'Bird (O'Burd)**
et
Marguerite Mius
fille de **Paul Mius** et de **Marie LeBlanc**
ont contracté mariage le **18 avril 1825**
Témoins **Louis Dulain et Benjamin Mius**
Prêtre officiant **Rév. Sigogne**
Extrait des registres de la paroisse de **Ste-Anne-du-Ruisseau**
Donné à **Ste-Anne-du-Ruisseau** le **10 oct. 2003**

Rév. Crépin Khonde
Curé

Mius d'Entremont 1C

Philippe Mius came to Acadie, about 1651, with his wife Madeleine Hélie, as adjutant to Governor Charles de Saint-Étienne de La Tour; he served as commandant in the colony when La Tour was absent. [1860]

On July 17, 1653, he received, jointly with Pierre Ferrand, by letters patent from Charles de Saint-Étienne de La Tour, the fief of Pobomcoup (today known as Pubnico), at Cape Sable. [1861]

In 1670, he became the King's attorney. [1862]

On October 5, 1687, Philippe Mius d'Entremont signed an attestation in favour of the accomplishments of Governor d'Aulnay. [1863]

The connections that follow herein are those re Charles-Amand I, son of Joseph Mius dit d'Azy and Marie Amirault.

[1860] White, Stephen A. (2000) <u>English Supplement to the Dictionnaire Généalogique des Familles Acadiennes</u> (page 256). Montréal, Québec: AGMV Marquis Imprimeur Inc.
[1861] Ibid.
[1862] Ibid.
[1863] Ibid.

[1] Philippe Mius, born c. 1609 in Normandie, France, was married to Madeleine Hélie c. 1649. [1864] Madeleine was born c. 1626. [1865] According to Father Clarence Joseph d'Entremont, Philippe died at GP at the end of 1700. [1866] Madeleine died before the PR census of 1678. [1867]

[2] Philippe Mius (dit d'Azy), born c. 1660, married a Mi' kmaq woman (whose name is not known to us) c. 1678. [1868]

[3] Joseph Mius (dit d'Azy), born c. 1679, married Marie Amirault (d/o François Amirault dit Tourangeau and Marie Pitre) c. 1699. [1869] [1870] Marie was born c. 1684 at CS. [1871]

NOTE: This couple has been genetically traced to the fatal Niemann-Pick (variant C) disease as per the French Acadian population of Yarmouth County, Nova Scotia.

[4] Charles Amand I Mius, born December 17, 1702 at CS, [1872] [1873] married Marie Marthe Hébert (d/o Antoine Hébert and Jeanne Corporon) on January 21, 1731 in PR. [1874] [1875] [1876]

[1864] White, Stephen A. (1999) <u>Dictionnaire Généalogique des Familles Acadiennes</u>, Volume H to Z, pages 840 and 1201.
[1865] Ibid.
[1866] Ibid.
[1867] Ibid.
[1868] Ibid, pages 1201 and 1206.
[1869] Ibid, pages 1206 and 1207.
[1870] White, Stephen A. (1999) <u>Dictionnaire Généalogique des Familles Acadiennes</u>, Volume A to G, page 17.
[1871] Ibid.
[1872] White, Stephen A. (1999) <u>Dictionnaire Généalogique des Familles Acadiennes</u>, Volume H to Z, page 1207.
[1873] https://novascotia.ca/archives/acadian/archives.asp?ID=102
[1874] White, Stephen A. (1999) <u>Dictionnaire Généalogique des Familles Acadiennes</u>, Volume H to Z, page 811.
[1875] Ibid, page 1207.
[1876] https://novascotia.ca/archives/acadian/archives.asp?ID=1811

Marie Marthe was born on July 12, 1710 in PR. [1877] [1878] Marie Marthe died at SAR on February 22, 1803 and was buried on February 23, 1803. [1879] [1880]

[5] Félicité Mius, born c. 1745, [1881] married **Charles Doucet** (s/o Joseph Doucet and Anne Surette) c. 1775. [1882] Charles was born on December 21, 1735 in PR. [1883] [1884] Félicité died at SAR on February 8, 1828 and was buried on February 10, 1828. [1885] [1886] [1887] Charles died on March 1, 1817 in Quinan, Yarmouth County, Nova Scotia and was buried on March 3, 1817. [1888] [1889]

[1877] White, Stephen A. (1999) <u>Dictionnaire Généalogique des Familles Acadiennes</u>, Volume H to Z, page 811.
[1878] https://novascotia.ca/archives/acadian/archives.asp?ID=337
[1879] White, Stephen A. (1999) <u>Dictionnaire Généalogique des Familles Acadiennes</u>, Volume H to Z, page 811.
[1880] https://novascotia.ca/archives/acadian/reborn/archives.asp?ID=300
[1881] Information received from Kenneth Breau, cousin and archivist at the Université de Moncton.
[1882] Ibid.
[1883] Ibid.
[1884] https://novascotia.ca/archives/acadian/archives.asp?ID=2115
[1885] Information received from Kenneth Breau, cousin and archivist at the Université de Moncton.
[1886] Email received from Lloyd d'Entremont, dated June 30, 1999.
[1887] http://novascotia.ca/archives/acadian/reborn/archives.asp?ID=1881
[1888] Information received from Kenneth Breau, cousin and archivist at the Université de Moncton.
[1889] https://novascotia.ca/archives/acadian/reborn/archives.asp?ID=1333

[1] Philippe Mius, born c. 1609 in Normandie, France, was married to Madeleine Hélie c. 1649. [1890] Madeleine was born c. 1626. [1891] According to Father Clarence Joseph d'Entremont, Philippe died at GP at the end of 1700. [1892] Madeleine died before the PR census of 1678. [1893]

[2] Philippe Mius (dit d'Azy), born c. 1660, married a Mi' kmaq woman (whose name is not known to us) c. 1678. [1894]

[3] Joseph Mius (dit d'Azy), born c. 1679, married Marie Amirault (d/o François Amirault dit Tourangeau and Marie Pitre) c. 1699. [1895] [1896] Marie was born c. 1684 at CS. [1897]

NOTE: This couple has been genetically traced to the fatal Niemann-Pick (variant C) disease as per the French Acadian population of Yarmouth County, Nova Scotia.

[4] Charles-Amand I Mius, born December 17, 1702 at CS, [1898] [1899] married Marie Marthe Hébert (d/o Antoine Hébert and Jeanne Corporon) on January 21, 1731 in PR. [1900] [1901] [1902]

[1890] White, Stephen A. (1999) Dictionnaire Généalogique des Familles Acadiennes, Volume H to Z, pages 840 and 1201.
[1891] Ibid.
[1892] Ibid.
[1893] Ibid.
[1894] Ibid, pages 1201 and 1206.
[1895] Ibid, pages 1206 and 1207.
[1896] White, Stephen A. (1999) Dictionnaire Généalogique des Familles Acadiennes, Volume A to G, page 17.
[1897] Ibid.
[1898] White, Stephen A. (1999) Dictionnaire Généalogique des Familles Acadiennes, Volume H to Z, page 1207.
[1899] https://novascotia.ca/archives/acadian/archives.asp?ID=102
[1900] White, Stephen A. (1999) Dictionnaire Généalogique des Familles Acadiennes, Volume H to Z, page 811.
[1901] Ibid, page 1207.
[1902] https://novascotia.ca/archives/acadian/archives.asp?ID=1811

Marie Marthe was born on July 12, 1710 in PR. [1903] [1904] Marie Marthe died at SAR on February 22, 1803 and was buried on February 23, 1803. [1905] [1906]

[5] Madeleine Modeste Mius, born c. 1742, [1907] married **John O'Bird (Hubbard)** on January 16, 1772 in Salem, Essex County, Massachusetts (while in exile). [1908] [1909] John died in 1824. [1910] Madeleine Modeste died on February 10, 1826 at Hubbard's Point, Yarmouth County, Nova Scotia. [1911]

[1903] White, Stephen A. (1999) <u>Dictionnaire Généalogique des Familles Acadiennes</u>, Volume H to Z, page 811.
[1904] https://novascotia.ca/archives/acadian/archives.asp?ID=337
[1905] White, Stephen A. (1999) <u>Dictionnaire Généalogique des Familles Acadiennes</u>, Volume H to Z, page 811.
[1906] https://novascotia.ca/archives/acadian/reborn/archives.asp?ID=300
[1907] Macauley, Sheila Hubbard. (1996) <u>The Hubbard Family of Nova Scotia</u>, page 1. Baltimore, MD: Gateway Press, Inc.
[1908] Ibid.
[1909] d'Entremont, Father Clarence Joseph. (1984) <u>Histoire de Quinan, Nouvelle-Écosse</u>, page 19.
[1910] Macauley, Sheila Hubbard. (1996) <u>The Hubbard Family of Nova Scotia</u>, page 2. Baltimore, MD: Gateway Press, Inc.
[1911] Ibid, page 1.

Mius d'Entremont 1D

Philippe Mius came to Acadie, about 1651, with his wife Madeleine Hélie, as adjutant to Governor Charles de Saint-Étienne de La Tour; he served as commandant in the colony when La Tour was absent. [1912]

On July 17, 1653, he received, jointly with Pierre Ferrand, by letters patent from Charles de Saint-Étienne de La Tour, the fief of Pobomcoup (today known as Pubnico), at Cape Sable. [1913]

In 1670, he became the King's attorney. [1914]

On October 5, 1687, Philippe Mius d'Entremont signed an attestation in favour of the accomplishments of Governor d'Aulnay. [1915]

The connections that follow herein are those re Joseph, son of Joseph Mius dit d'Azy and Marie Amirault.

[1912] White, Stephen A. (2000) <u>English Supplement to the Dictionnaire Généalogique des Familles Acadiennes</u> (page 256). Montréal, Québec: AGMV Marquis Imprimeur Inc.
[1913] Ibid.
[1914] Ibid.
[1915] Ibid.

[1] Philippe Mius, born c. 1609 in Normandie, France, was married to Madeleine Hélie c. 1649. [1916] Madeleine was born c. 1626. [1917] According to Father Clarence Joseph d'Entremont, Philippe died at GP at the end of 1700. [1918] Madeleine died before the PR census of 1678. [1919]

[2] Philippe Mius (dit d'Azy), born c. 1660, married a Mi' kmaq woman (whose name is not known to us) c. 1678. [1920]

[3] Joseph Mius (dit d'Azy), born c. 1679, married Marie Amirault (d/o François Amirault dit Tourangeau and Marie Pitre) c. 1699. [1921] [1922] Marie was born c. 1684 at CS. [1923]

NOTE: This couple has been genetically traced to the fatal Niemann-Pick (variant C) disease as per the French Acadian population of Yarmouth County, Nova Scotia.

[4] Joseph Mius, born June 27, 1700 at CS, [1924] [1925] married Marie Josèphe Préjean (d/o Jean Préjean and Andrée Savoie) on September 9, 1726 at PR. [1926] [1927] Marie Josèphe was born on April 22, 1702 in PR. [1928] [1929]

[1916] White, Stephen A. (1999) Dictionnaire Généalogique des Familles Acadiennes, Volume H to Z, pages 840 and 1201.
[1917] Ibid.
[1918] Ibid.
[1919] Ibid.
[1920] Ibid, pages 1201 and 1206.
[1921] Ibid, pages 1206 and 1207.
[1922] White, Stephen A. (1999) Dictionnaire Généalogique des Familles Acadiennes, Volume A to G, page 17.
[1923] Ibid.
[1924] Ibid, page 1207.
[1925] https://novascotia.ca/archives/acadian/archives.asp?ID=103
[1926] White, Stephen A. (1999) Dictionnaire Généalogique des Familles Acadiennes, Volume H to Z, pages 1207 and 1351.
[1927] https://novascotia.ca/archives/acadian/archives.asp?ID=1122

[5] Louis Mius, born c. 1746, married Anne Josèphe Corporon (d/o Eustache Corporon and Angélique Viger dit Brigeau) c. 1768. [1930]

[6] Anne Mius, born c. 1792, married **Charles (dit Tania) Doucet** (s/o Charles Doucet and Félicité Mius) on April 29, 1811. [1931] [1932] [1933] Charles was born c. 1788. [1934]

[1928] White, Stephen A. (1999) <u>Dictionnaire Généalogique des Familles Acadiennes</u>, Volume H to Z, page 1351.
[1929] https://novascotia.ca/archives/acadian/archives.asp?ID=1
[1930] Information received from Kenneth Breau, cousin and archivist at the Université de Moncton
[1931] Ibid.
[1932] d'Entremont, Father Clarence Joseph. <u>Histoire de Sainte-Anne-du-Ruisseau, Belleville et Rivière Abram</u>, page 21.
[1933] Email received from Pauline d'Entremont, dated July 6, 2001.
[1934] Information received from Kenneth Breau, cousin and archivist at the Université de Moncton

Mius d'Entremont 2

Philippe Mius came to Acadie, about 1651, with his wife Madeleine Hélie, as adjutant to Governor Charles de Saint-Étienne de La Tour; he served as commandant in the colony when La Tour was absent. [1935]

On July 17, 1653, he received, jointly with Pierre Ferrand, by letters patent from Charles de Saint-Étienne de La Tour, the fief of Pobomcoup (today known as Pubnico), at Cape Sable. [1936]

In 1670, he became the King's attorney. [1937]

On October 5, 1687, Philippe Mius d'Entremont signed an attestation in favour of the accomplishments of Governor d'Aulnay. [1938]

[1] Philippe Mius, born c. 1609 in Normandie, France, was married to Madeleine Hélie c. 1649. [1939] Madeleine was born c. 1626. [1940] According to Father Clarence Joseph d'Entremont, Philippe died at GP at the end of 1700. [1941] Madeleine died before the PR census of 1678. [1942]

[1935] White, Stephen A. (2000) English Supplement to the Dictionnaire Généalogique des Familles Acadiennes (page 256). Montréal, Québec: AGMV Marquis Imprimeur Inc.
[1936] Ibid.
[1937] Ibid.
[1938] Ibid.
[1939] White, Stephen A. (1999) Dictionnaire Généalogique des Familles Acadiennes, Volume H to Z, pages 840 and 1201.
[1940] Ibid.
[1941] Ibid.
[1942] Ibid.

[2] Philippe Mius (dit d'Azy), born c. 1660, married a Mi' kmaq woman (whose name is not known to us) c. 1678. [1943]

[3] Marie Mius, born c. 1680, [1944] was married to **François Viger** (s/o François Viger and ----------) c. 1697. [1945] François was born c. 1662. [1946]

[1943] White, Stephen A. (1999) <u>Dictionnaire Généalogique des Familles Acadiennes</u>, Volume H to Z, pages 1201 and 1206.
[1944] Ibid, pages 1206 and 1566.
[1945] Ibid.
[1946] Ibid, page 1566.

A Little Controversy

There has been talk, with *unproven allegations*, that François Virgine de Montbel, Count d'Entremont, the son of Beatrice de Coligny d'Entremont and Claude Antoine de Meouillon de Montauban, might actually be Philippe Mius d'Entremont (as married to Madeleine Hélie). Feel free to explore on your own.

Actes du Colloque l'Amiral de Coligny et son Temps [1947]

A Little Controversy [1948]

Famille du Tillet [1949]

François Virgine Bon, Comte d'Entremont et de Montbel [1950]

Marcotte Genealogy [1951]

Marcotte Genealogy via Melançon [1952]

[1947] michaelmarcotte.com/MiusdEntremont.htm
[1948] http://www.museeacadien.ca/argyle/html/egenealogy5.htm
[1949] racineshistoire.free.fr/LGN/PDF/du_Tillet.pdf (page 5)
[1950] http://genealogie.quebec/testphp/info.php?no=193963
[1951] michaelmarcotte.com/francoisebon.htm
[1952] michaelmarcotte.com/melancon.htm

O'Bird 1A

According to the Sainte-Anne-du-Rousseau church records, John Hubbard was born in Ireland.

Father Jean Mandé Sigogne, serving as priest, beginning in 1799, referred to John Hubbard as *Jean O'Bird or O'Burd of the Irish nation* in the marriage record of John's daughter Marie Vénérante in 1799. [1953] [1954] He referred to him as *Jean O'Bird, Irish* in the marriage record of John's daughter Marie Osithe, also in 1799. [1955]

These are the only historical documents that record the nationality of John Hubbard. [1956]

[1] John O'Bird (Hubbard) married Madeleine Modeste Mius (on January 16, 1772 in Salem, Essex County, Massachusetts (while in exile). [1957] Madeleine Modeste was born c. 1742. [1958] John died sometime between May and September of 1824, as this was when he wrote his will and it was probated. [1959]

[1953] Sheila Hubbard Macauley. (1996) The Hubbard Family of Nova Scotia, page xiii. Baltimore, Maryland: Gateway Press Incorporated.
[1954] https://novascotia.ca/archives/acadian/reborn/archives.asp?ID=26
[1955] https://novascotia.ca/archives/acadian/reborn/archives.asp?ID=18
[1956] Sheila Hubbard Macauley. (1996) The Hubbard Family of Nova Scotia, page xiii. Baltimore, Maryland: Gateway Press Incorporated.
[1957] Ibid.
[1958] Ibid, page 1.
[1959] Ibid, page xiii.

Louis Robichaud, another French Acadian [refugee from Nova Scotia], had been given instructions by the Abbé Maillard, vicar general of Halifax, Nova Scotia, to receive the promises of marriage from all Acadians in the region of Boston who wished to marry. [1960]

John Hubbard's name was written as *Jean Hobord* in their marriage record, and witnessed by Louis Robichaud who was acting in place of a priest, as no priest was available at this time in Massachusetts to perform marriages. [1961]

[2] Jean O'Bird (Hubbard) JR, born c. 1774, [1962] married Marie Anne Doucet (d/o Michel Doucet and Marie Suzanne Mius) on January 10, 1794 in SAR. [1963] [1964] Jean died on August 12, 1817 in Argyle, Yarmouth County, Nova Scotia and was buried on August 13, 1817. [1965] [1966]

[3] Marie Madeleine O'Bird (Hubbard), born October 31, 1802, [1967] [1968] married **Jean Séraphin Deveau** (s/o François Chrysostôme (dit Couchique) Deveau and Cécile Mius) c. 1821. [1969] [1970] Marie Madeleine was born March 27, 1799 in Salmon River, Nova Scotia.

[1960] Sheila Hubbard Macauley. (1996) The Hubbard Family of Nova Scotia, page xiii. Baltimore, Maryland: Gateway Press Incorporated.
[1961] Ibid.
[1962] Ibid, page 5.
[1963] Ibid.
[1964] Information received from Kenneth Breau, cousin and archivist at the Université de Moncton.
[1965] Sheila Hubbard Macauley. (1996) The Hubbard Family of Nova Scotia, page 5. Baltimore, Maryland: Gateway Press Incorporated.
[1966] https://novascotia.ca/archives/acadian/reborn/archives.asp?ID=1355
[1967] Sheila Hubbard Macauley. (1996) The Hubbard Family of Nova Scotia, page 10. Baltimore, Maryland: Gateway Press Incorporated.
[1968] Sigogne, Father Jean Mandé. Cape Sable Vital Statistics Catalogue of Families (1799 to 1841). Information received in an email from Fred Chandler Union III, dated July 2, 2001.
[1969] Macauley, Sheila Hubbard. (1996) The Hubbard Family of Nova Scotia, page 10. Baltimore, MD: Gateway Press, Inc.

[1971] [1972] Jean died at Lake Doucet, Digby County, Nova Scotia. [1973] Marie Anne died at Lake Doucet, Digby County, Nova Scotia, sometime after 1843. [1974]

[1970] Sigogne, Father Jean Mandé. St. Mary's Bay Catalogue of Familles (1818 to 1829). Information received in an email from Fred Chandler Union III, dated July 2, 2001.
[1971] Ibid.
[1972] Information received in an email from Sheila Hubbard Macauley, dated July 2, 2001.
[1973] Information obtained from David A. Mallet.
[1974] Macauley, Sheila Hubbard. (1996) The Hubbard Family of Nova Scotia, page 10. Baltimore, MD: Gateway Press, Inc.

O'Bird 1B

According to the Sainte-Anne-du-Rousseau church records, John Hubbard was born in Ireland.

Father Jean Mandé Sigogne, serving as priest, beginning in 1799, referred to John Hubbard as *Jean O'Bird or O'Burd of the Irish nation* in the marriage record of John's daughter Marie Vénérante in 1799. [1975] [1976] He referred to him as *Jean O'Bird, Irish* in the marriage record of John's daughter Marie Osithe, also in 1799. [1977]

These are the only historical documents that record the nationality of John Hubbard. [1978]

[1] John O'Bird (Hubbard) married Madeleine Modeste Mius (on January 16, 1772 in Salem, Essex County, Massachusetts (while in exile). [1979] Madeleine Modeste was born c. 1742. [1980] John died sometime between May and September of 1824, as this was when he wrote his will and it was probated. [1981]

[1975] Sheila Hubbard Macauley. (1996) The Hubbard Family of Nova Scotia, page xiii. Baltimore, Maryland: Gateway Press Incorporated.
[1976] https://novascotia.ca/archives/acadian/reborn/archives.asp?ID=26
[1977] https://novascotia.ca/archives/acadian/reborn/archives.asp?ID=18
[1978] Sheila Hubbard Macauley. (1996) The Hubbard Family of Nova Scotia, page xiii. Baltimore, Maryland: Gateway Press Incorporated.
[1979] Ibid.
[1980] Ibid, page 1.
[1981] Ibid, page xiii.

Louis Robichaud, another French Acadian [refugee from Nova Scotia], had been given instructions by the Abbé Maillard, vicar general of Halifax, Nova Scotia, to receive the promises of marriage from all Acadians in the region of Boston who wished to marry. [1982]

John Hubbard's name was written as *Jean Hobord* in their marriage record, and witnessed by Louis Robichaud who was acting in place of a priest, as no priest was available at this time in Massachusetts to perform marriages. [1983]

[2] Marie Osithe O' Bird (Hubbard), born c. 1775, [1984] married **François Mius** (s/o Jean Pierre Mius and Anne Doucet) on February 19, 1798 in SAR. [1985] [1986] They were married in front of witnesses due to the absence of a priest. The marriage was blessed by Father Sigogne on August 12, 1799. [1987] François was born c. 1770 in MA (exile). [1988] Marie Osithe died on September 16, 1865 in Quinan, Yarmouth County, Nova Scotia and was buried on September 18, 1865. [1989]

[1982] Sheila Hubbard Macauley. (1996) The Hubbard Family of Nova Scotia, page xiii. Baltimore, Maryland: Gateway Press Incorporated.
[1983] Ibid.
[1984] Ibid, page 6.
[1985] Ibid.
[1986] https://novascotia.ca/archives/acadian/reborn/archives.asp?ID=18
[1987] Ibid.
[1988] d'Entremont, Father Clarence Joseph. (1984) Histoire de Quinan, Nouvelle-Écosse, page 73.
[1989] Ibid.

Paroisse Ste-Agnès

Death and Burial certificate

This is to certify that _Osithe Muis_ who _16th, 1865_ was buried in our parish cemetry on _September_
Husband (wife) of _____
Rev. _Joannes J. Quinan_ officiating.

This is a true copy of the records of Ste_Agnès Parish.

Given at Quinan, N.S. on _July 16th, 2004_.

Sr Yvette
Curé

Pellerin

[1] Étienne Pellerin, born c. 1647, [1990] married Jeanne Savoie (d/o François Savoie and Catherine Lejeune) c. 1675. [1991] Jeanne was born c. 1658. [1992] Étienne died at PR on November 17, 1722 and was buried on November 18, 1722. [1993] [1994] Jeanne died at PR on November 3, 1735 and was buried on November 4, 1735. [1995] [1996]

[2] Jeanne Pellerin, born c. 1688, married **Pierre Surette** (s/o Noël Surette and Françoise Colarde from the parish of Mauset, in La Rochelle, Aunis, France) on February 4, 1709 in PR. [1997] [1998] Pierre was born in the parish of Marais, in La Rochelle, Aunis, France c. 1679. [1999] Jeanne died on January 27, 1758 and was buried on January 28, 1758, according to the Notre-Dame parish register in Québec. [2000] Pierre died at PR on October 30, 1749 and was buried on October 31, 1749. [2001] [2002]

[1990] White, Stephen A. (1999) <u>Dictionnaire Généalogique des Familles Acadiennes</u>, Volume H to Z, page 1278.
[1991] Ibid, pages 1278 and 1457.
[1992] Ibid.
[1993] White, Stephen A. (1999) <u>Dictionnaire Généalogique des Familles Acadiennes</u>, Volume H to Z, page 1278.
[1994] https://novascotia.ca/archives/acadian/archives.asp?ID=1554
[1995] White, Stephen A. (1999) <u>Dictionnaire Généalogique des Familles Acadiennes</u>, Volume H to Z, pages 1278 and 1457.
[1996] https://novascotia.ca/archives/acadian/archives.asp?ID=2095
[1997] White, Stephen A. (1999) <u>Dictionnaire Généalogique des Familles Acadiennes</u>, Volume H to Z, pages 1279 and 1476.
[1998] https://novascotia.ca/archives/acadian/archives.asp?ID=1231
[1999] White, Stephen A. (1999) <u>Dictionnaire Généalogique des Familles Acadiennes</u>, Volume H to Z, page 1476.
[2000] Ibid, pages 1279 and 1476.
[2001] Ibid, page 1476.
[2002] https://novascotia.ca/archives/acadian/archives.asp?ID=3095

Pesseley

On July 14, 1640 there was an inquiry presided over by Mathieu Cappon, clerk and registrar, against Charles de Saint-Étienne de La Tour, at which appeared Germain Doucet dit LaVerdure, Isaac Pesseley, and Guillaume Trahan. [2003]

[1] Isaac Pesseley, a merchant from Piney, three miles from Troyes, in the department of Champagne, was married to Barbe Bajolet (d/o Antoine Bajolet and Jeanne Baudinet) c. 1629 in France. [2004] [2005] Barbe was born on May 22, 1608, according to the Parish Register of Piney in the department of Champagne. [2006] [2007] Isaac arrived in Acadia on the *Saint-Jehan* in 1636. [2008] [2009] Isaac's death was probably due to the assault on Fort Saint Jean (located in present-day St. John, NewBrunswick) where d'Aulnay lost many men on April 16, 1645. [2010] [2011]

[2003] White, Stephen A. (2000) English Supplement to the Dictionnaire Généalogique des Familles Acadiennes (page 274). Montréal, Québec: AGMV Marquis Imprimeur Inc.
[2004] White, Stephen A. (1999) Dictionnaire Généalogique des Familles Acadiennes, Volume H to Z, page 1288.
[2005] White, Stephen A. (1999) Dictionnaire Généalogique des Familles Acadiennes, Volume A to G, page 70.
[2006] Ibid.
[2007] White, Stephen A. (1999) Dictionnaire Généalogique des Familles Acadiennes, Volume H to Z, page 1288.
[2008] http://www.pitretrail.com/
[2009] http://acadian-cajun.com/stjehan.htm
[2010] White, Stephen A. (1999) Dictionnaire Généalogique des Familles Acadiennes, Volume H to Z, page 1288.
[2011] http://www.pitretrail.com/

[2] Marie Pesseley, born about 1645, [2012] married **Jean Pitre** c. 1665. [2013]

[2012] White, Stephen A. (1999) <u>Dictionnaire Généalogique des Familles Acadiennes</u>, Volume H to Z, pages 1289 and 1318.
[2013] Ibid.

Pinet

[1] ---------- Pinet was married to Anne-Marie ---------- about 1653. [2014]

[2] Philippe Pinet, born c. 1654, married Catherine Hébert (d/o Étienne Hébert and Marie Gaudet) before the 1678 Census of Port Royal, Acadie. [2015] Catherine was born c. 1662. [2016] Philippe died before October 1, 1710. [2017] Catherine died at Louisbourg on August 3, 1727 and was buried on August 4, 1727. [2018]

[3] Marie Pinet, born October 8, 1685 in LM, [2019] [2020] married **Jean Baptiste Corporon dit l'aîné** (s/o Jean Corporon and Françoise Savoie) c. 1702. [2021] [2022] Jean Baptiste was born c. 1677. [2023] Marie died at Lbg on December 15, 1732 and was buried on December 16, 1732. [2024] [2025] Jean Baptiste died at Lbg on March 16, 1741 and was buried on March 17, 1741. [2026]

[2014] White, Stephen A. (1999) <u>Dictionnaire Généalogique des Familles Acadiennes</u>, Volume H to Z, page 1310.
[2015] Ibid, pages 800 and 1310.
[2016] Ibid.
[2017] Ibid, page 1310.
[2018] Ibid, pages 800 and 1310.
[2019] Ibid, page 1311.
[2020] White, Stephen A. (1999) <u>Dictionnaire Généalogique des Familles Acadiennes</u>, Volume A to G, pages 411 and 413.
[2021] White, Stephen A. (1999) <u>Dictionnaire Généalogique des Familles Acadiennes</u>, Volume H to Z, page 1311.
[2022] White, Stephen A. (1999) <u>Dictionnaire Généalogique des Familles Acadiennes</u>, Volume A to G, pages 411 and 413.
[2023] Ibid.
[2024] White, Stephen A. (1999) <u>Dictionnaire Généalogique des Familles Acadiennes</u>, Volume H to Z, page 1311.

DNA tests have revealed that the mutations in Anne Marie's mtDNA link her to haplogroup A, one that is traceable to the Siberian Arctic and Aleutian Indians.

The Inuit peoples are known to have migrated east from the Arctic regions, crossing Canada, and later dropping down into Newfoundland and Nova Scotia.

Since haplogroup A is consistent with a mother that has North American ancestry and not European ancestry, the initial test indicates that Anne Marie was of Aboriginal ancestry and not of European French descent.

Marie Rundquist, author of Revisiting Anne Marie: How an American Woman of Seventeenth Century Nova Scotia and a DNA Match Redefine American Heritage, is the mtDNA descendant of Anne Marie.

You can read more about Marie's story at

https://www.cbu.ca/indigenous-affairs/unamaki-college/mikmaq-resource-centre/essays/finding-anne-marie-the-hidden-history-of-our-acadian-ancestors/

You can locate Marie's book at https://www.amazon.com/dp/1439205000/

[2025] White, Stephen A. (1999) Dictionnaire Généalogique des Familles Acadiennes, Volume A to G, page 413.
[2026] Ibid.

Pitre

According to the declaration at Belle-Île-en-Mer, by his grandson Claude Pitre, the pioneer of the Acadian Pitre family is of Flemish origin. However, Father Clarence d'Entremont was of the opinion that it was "more likely that he was English," given *An Account of the Customs and Manners of the Micmakis and Maricheets* (as published in London in 1758; page 105), "where it is said that *Peters*, a blacksmith from England ... was of English origin." [2027]

Between this mention of a blacksmith named John Peters in Acadie, who came from England, and the 1671 census showing a Jean Pitre who specialized as some sort of metalworker, such presents the hypothesis that this was the same man. [2028]

Stephen White, author of Dictionnaire Généalogique des Familles Acadiennes, says ... *While there is no proof that the blacksmith and the edge-tool maker were one and the same, there is no real contradiction in supposing that they might have been, inasmuch as there were many Flemish artisans in England during the middle part of the seventeenth century, and one of them might have chosen to emigrate to Acadia sometime after the English capture of the colony in 1654.* [2029]

The publication, as referenced (above) by Father Clarence d'Entremont, was fully entitled, *An Account of the Customs and Manners of the Micmakis and Maricheets Savage Nations, Now Dependent On The Government Of Cape-Breton*, was from an original French

---

[2027] White, Stephen A. (2000) English Supplement to the Dictionnaire Généalogique des Familles Acadiennes (page 280). Montréal, Québec: AGMV Marquis Imprimeur Inc.
[2028] http://www.pitretrail.com/
[2029] Ibid.

manuscript letter, written by a French Abbot who had lived as a missionary, for many years, in Nova Scotia. [2030]

In this letter he writes … *Except a few families from Boston or New England I could never learn there were above three of purely British subjects, who also, ultimately conforming both in the religious and civil institutions to the French, became incorporated with them. These families were the Peterses, the Grangers, the Cartys. These last indeed descended from one Roger John Baptist Carty, an Irish Roman Catholic. He had been an indented servant in New England, and had obtained at length his discharge from his master, with permission to remain with the French Acadians for the freer exercise of his religion. Peters was an iron-smith in England, and together with Granger, married in Acadia, and was there naturalized a Frenchman. Granger made his abjuration before M. Petit, secular-priest of the seminary of Paris, then missionary at Port-Royal (Annapolis). These and other European families then soon became united with the French Acadians, and were no longer distinguished from them.* [2031]

Is it possible, still, that Jean Pitre was really Jan Pietr from Holland?

Leopold Lanctot theorizes that in about 1656 Jean immigrated to the American colonies founded by the Dutch, either to Fort Orange (Albany, NY) or New Amsterdam (New York, NY). [2032]

England had seized Acadie in 1654, renamed it New Scotland, and sent an expedition, led by Sir Thomas Temple, which arrived there on May 1, 1657; when war broke out between England and Holland in 1664, Bostonians seized Fort Orange and New Amsterdam. [2033]

[2030] http://www.pitretrail.com/
[2031] Ibid.
[2032] Ibid.
[2033] Ibid.

Temple recruited the Dutch colonists for his new seignory, supposedly including Jan Pietr; while there is no list of settlers from this expedition, the timing allows for the possibility. [2034]

Another theory of origins appeared in The History of St. Anthony's Parish 1803-1980 (which includes the descendants of Jean Pitre in Prince Edward Island, most of whom have taken the name Peters); this account would have him in Permambuco, Brazil, escaping the Dutch wars in South America by hopping a schooner to Acadie. [2035]

Excerpted from a letter (dated 1984) from Stephen White, author of Dictionnaire Généalogique des Familles Acadiennes, to Leo F. Peters ... *The best direct evidence of Jean Pitre's parentage and origin would have been the record of his marriage to Marie Pesseley. Without that one will have to be very lucky indeed to trace him in Europe, even with the area of research narrowed to Flanders. Even if you found a Jean Pitre born in Flanders in 1636, it would be impossible to be sure he was the same Jean Pitre who settled in Acadia without some positive evidence making the connection, such as a record showing his departure for Acadia. Such a record might be almost anywhere, if it exists at all.* [2036]

He could have arrived in Acadie, in 1666, on *Le Saint Jean Baptiste* from France to New France (Québec), listed as Jean Pitran; his name may have been different from that which exists in the 1671 census. [2037]

Whatever his origins, there are, today, thousands of descendants across Canada, the United States and France, who all of whom can trace their way back to Jean Pitre of Acadie.

[2034] http://www.pitretrail.com/
[2035] Ibid.
[2036] Ibid.
[2037] Ibid.

[1] Jean Pitre, born c. 1636, married Marie Pesseley (d/o Isaac Pesseley and Barbe Bajolet) c. 1665. [2038] Marie was born c. 1645. [2039]

[2] Marie Pitre, born c. 1666, [2040] [2041] married **François Amirault dit Tourangeau** c. 1683. [2042] [2043] François was born c. 1644. [2044]

[2038] White, Stephen A. (1999) <u>Dictionnaire Généalogique des Familles Acadiennes</u>, Volume H to Z, page 1318.
[2039] Ibid, pages 1289 and 1318.
[2040] Ibid, page 1318.
[2041] White, Stephen A. (1999) <u>Dictionnaire Généalogique des Familles Acadiennes</u>, Volume A to G, page 17.
[2042] White, Stephen A. (1999) <u>Dictionnaire Généalogique des Familles Acadiennes</u>, Volume H to Z, page 1318.
[2043] White, Stephen A. (1999) <u>Dictionnaire Généalogique des Familles Acadiennes</u>, Volume A to G, page 17.
[2044] Ibid.

Poirier

[1] Jean Poirier married Jeanne Chebrat (d/o Antoine Chebrat and Françoise Chaumoret) c. 1647. [2045] [2046] Jeanne was baptized on February 5, 1627 in the La Chaussée parish, located in Poitou, France. [2047] [2048]

[2] Michel Poirier, born about 1650, married Marie Boudrot (d/o Michel Boudrot and Michelle Aucoin) c. 1673. [2049] [2050] Marie was born c. 1650. [2051] [2052] Michel died at Bbn. [2053]

[3] Anne Poirier, born c. 1678, married **Jean Pothier** c. 1699. [2054] Jean was born c. 1672. [2055] Anne died before 1710. [2056] Jean died in either 1724 or 1725. [2057]

[2045] White, Stephen A. (1999) <u>Dictionnaire Généalogique des Familles Acadiennes</u>, Volume H to Z, page 1327.
[2046] White, Stephen A. (1999) <u>Dictionnaire Généalogique des Familles Acadiennes</u>, Volume A to G, page 338.
[2047] Ibid.
[2048] White, Stephen A. (1999) <u>Dictionnaire Généalogique des Familles Acadiennes</u>, Volume H to Z, page 1327.
[2049] Ibid, pages 1327 and 1328.
[2050] White, Stephen A. (1999) <u>Dictionnaire Généalogique des Familles Acadiennes</u>, Volume A to G, page 185.
[2051] Ibid.
[2052] White, Stephen A. (1999) <u>Dictionnaire Généalogique des Familles Acadiennes</u>, Volume H to Z, page 1328.
[2053] Ibid.
[2054] Ibid, pages 1328 and 1346.
[2055] Ibid, page 1346.
[2056] Ibid, page 1328.
[2057] Ibid, page 1346.

Pothier

[1] Jean Pothier, born c. 1672, married Anne Poirier (d/o Michel Poirier and Marie Boudrot) c. 1699. [2058] Anne was born c. 1678. [2059] Jean died in either 1724 or 1725. [2060] Anne died before 1710. [2061]

[2] Marie Pothier, born c. 1701, [2062] married **Jacques Deveau dit Dauphiné** (s/o Michel Deveau dit Dauphiné and Marie Madeleine Martin) on October 17, 1719 in Bbn. [2063] [2064] [2065] Jacques was born c. 1699. [2066] [2067] Both died before August 12, 1760. [2068] [2069]

[2058] White, Stephen A. (1999) <u>Dictionnaire Généalogique des Familles Acadiennes</u>, Volume H to Z, pages 1328 and 1346.
[2059] Ibid.
[2060] Ibid, page 1346.
[2061] Ibid, page 1328.
[2062] Ibid, page 1346.
[2063] Ibid.
[2064] White, Stephen A. (1999) <u>Dictionnaire Généalogique des Familles Acadiennes</u>, Volume A to G, page 508.
[2065] csapstaff.ednet.ns.ca/jldeveau/deveau2.html
[2066] White, Stephen A. (1999) <u>Dictionnaire Généalogique des Familles Acadiennes</u>, Volume A to G, page 508.
[2067] csapstaff.ednet.ns.ca/jldeveau/deveau2.html
[2068] White, Stephen A. (1999) <u>Dictionnaire Généalogique des Familles Acadiennes</u>, Volume H to Z, page 1346.
[2069] White, Stephen A. (1999) <u>Dictionnaire Généalogique des Familles Acadiennes</u>, Volume A to G, page 508.

Préjean

[1] Jean Préjean dit LeBreton, born c. 1651, [2070] married Andrée Savoie (d/o François Savoie and Catherine Lejeune) c. 1683. [2071] Andrée was born c. 1667. [2072] Jean died at PR on either June 4 or June 5, 1733 and was buried on June 6, 1733. [2073] [2074]

[2] Marie Josèphe Préjean, born April 22, 1702 in PR, [2075] [2076] married **Joseph Mius** (s/o Joseph Mius dit d'Azy and Marie Amirault) on September 9, 1726 in PR. [2077] [2078] Joseph was born on June 27, 1700 in CS. [2079] [2080]

[2070] White, Stephen A. (1999) Dictionnaire Généalogique des Familles Acadiennes, Volume H to Z, page 1351.
[2071] Ibid, pages 1351 and 1457.
[2072] Ibid, pages 1351 and 1457.
[2073] Ibid, page 1351.
[2074] https://novascotia.ca/archives/acadian/archives.asp?ID=1916
[2075] White, Stephen A. (1999) Dictionnaire Généalogique des Familles Acadiennes, Volume H to Z, page 1351.
[2076] https://novascotia.ca/archives/acadian/archives.asp?ID=1
[2077] White, Stephen A. (1999) Dictionnaire Généalogique des Familles Acadiennes, Volume H to Z, pages 1207 and 1351.
[2078] https://novascotia.ca/archives/acadian/archives.asp?ID=1122
[2079] White, Stephen A. (1999) Dictionnaire Généalogique des Familles Acadiennes, Volume H to Z, pages 1207.
[2080] https://novascotia.ca/archives/acadian/archives.asp?ID=103

Roach

While I have reason to believe that John William Henry Roach *may* have been born on May 10, 1821 in Granville, Annapolis County, Nova Scotia, s/o Frederic Roach and Elizabeth Ricketson,[2081] I have yet to secure documentation that validates this information. To further complicate matters, there was another Roach (Roche) family also living in the Granville area.

In keeping with the marriage certificate copy, dated September 5, 1853, the groom is stated as having been from Granville, the bride from Beaver River (a rural community in Digby County, situated near the town of Yarmouth). The marriage record states the Holy Trinity Anglican Church of Yarmouth County, Nova Scotia.

Knowing that John William Henry Roach died, in Yarmouth, Yarmouth County, Nova Scotia, between the censuses of 1871 and 1881 also provides me with a further window of opportunity, at present, to try and locate a death and/or burial certificate.

[1] John William Henry Roach married Marie Elizabeth Deveau (d/o Jean Séraphin Deveau and Marie Madeleine O'Bird (Hubbard)) on September 5, 1853.[2082] Marie Elizabeth was born on March 30, 1830 in Digby County, Nova Scotia.[2083] [2084]

[2081] Information received from Lorraine Newman, researcher at ATCHA (Argyle Township Court House and Archives.
[2082] Parish of the Holy Trinity (Reel 2, Page 1, Number 2) located at the Argyle Courthouse in Tusket, NS.
[2083] Information received from Lorraine Newman, researcher at ATCHA (Argyle Township Court House and Archives.
[2084] Sigogne, Father Jean Mandé. St. Mary's Bay Catalogue of Familles (1840 to 1844). Information received in an email from Fred Chandler Union III, dated July 2, 2001.

[2] Martha Roach, born March 29, 1862 in Wedgeport, Yarmouth County, Nova Scotia,[2085] married **Peter Muise** (s/o Vital Mius and Rosalie Angèle (dite Angélique) Mius) on December 8, 1877.[2086] However, the Certificate of Death (which follows) states March 12, 1860 as having been her date of birth. Peter was born about 1854. Martha died on February 3, 1940 in Yarmouth, Yarmouth County, Nova Scotia.[2087] She was buried on February 7, 1940.[2088] Peter died on February 20, 1916 in Yarmouth, Yarmouth County, Nova Scotia.[2089] He was buried on February 23, 1916.[2090]

[2085] Information received in an email from Susan Surette, dated June 5, 2001.
[2086] Parish of the Holy Trinity (Reel 2, Page 85, Number 257) located at the Argyle Courthouse in Tusket, NS.
[2087] E-mails from Susan Surette dated Wednesday, May 30, 2001 and Tuesday, June 5, 2001.
[2088] E-mail from Susan Surette dated Tuesday, June 5, 2001.
[2089] Ibid.

> Peter Muise Bachelor _____ of this ___ Parish
> _____ and
> Martha Roach Spinster _____ of this ___ Parish
> _____ were married in this
> Parish _____ by Licence
> with Consent of Friends ____ this 8th Day of December
> in the Year One thousand eight hundred and 1877
>
> Dec 8, 1877   By me J.T.T. Moody
> This Marriage was solemnized between us { Peter x Muise Rector
>   Martha x Roach
> In the Presence of { Sam Churchill
>   Mary Muise
>
> NO. 251

[2090] E-mail from Susan Surette dated Tuesday, June 5, 2001.

№ 005238

Certificate of Death

Name of Deceased Person:	PETER MEUSE
Sex:	MALE
Date of Death:	Feb 20, 1916
Place of Death:	YARMOUTH
Date of Birth:	NOT STATED
Age:	64 YRS
Place of Birth:	YARMOUTH, NOVA SCOTIA
Residence:	YARMOUTH, NOVA SCOTIA
Occupation:	NOT STATED
Marital Status:	MARRIED
Name of Spouse:	NOT STATED
Name of Father:	NOT STATED
Name of Mother:	NOT STATED
Name of Attending Physician:	G. W. T. FARISH
Name of Funeral Director:	V. S. SWEENY
Disposition:	NOT STATED
Place of Disposition:	ST. AMBROSE
At:	YARMOUTH, NOVA SCOTIA
Name of Informant:	FRED MUISE
Address:	NOT STATED
Relationship:	NOT STATED
Date of Registration:	Feb 22, 1916
Registration No:	1916-02-050712

This is to certify that the record herein contained is from a Record of Death on file in the office of the REGISTRAR GENERAL of NOVA SCOTIA.

Given under my hand and the SEAL of the DEPUTY REGISTRAR GENERAL at Halifax, THIS 7th DAY OF September 2001

Deputy Registrar General

Nº 005769

Certificate of Death

Name of Deceased Person:	MARTHA MUISE
Sex:	FEMALE
Date of Death:	Feb 03, 1940
Place of Death:	YARMOUTH
Date of Birth:	Mar 12, 1860
Age:	79 YRS
Place of Birth:	YARMOUTH, NOVA SCOTIA
Residence:	YARMOUTH, NOVA SCOTIA
Occupation:	HOUSEWIFE
Marital Status:	WIDOWED
Name of Spouse:	PETER MUISE
Name of Father:	JAMES ROACH
Name of Mother:	ELIZABETH DEVEAU
Name of Attending Physician:	S. N. WILLIAMSON
Name of Funeral Director:	J. S. SWEENY
Disposition:	NOT STATED
Place of Disposition:	ST. AMBBROSE
At:	NOT STATED
Name of Informant:	FRED MUISE
Address:	YARMOUTH, NS
Relationship:	SON
Date of Registration:	Feb 28, 1940
Registration No:	1940-02-184602

This is to certify that the record herein contained is from a Record of Death on file in the office of the REGISTRAR GENERAL of NOVA SCOTIA.

Given under my hand and the SEAL of the DEPUTY REGISTRAR GENERAL at Halifax, THIS 13th DAY OF June 2002

Deputy Registrar General

According to my father, Peter and Martha lived at 16 Regent Street in Yarmouth.

Peter's death notice was located in the Yarmouth Times (dated February 26, 1916) ... Peter Meuse, of Regent Street, died on Sunday after a five week illness of pneumonia. He was 64 years old and leaves three sons and a daughter. [2091]

There is a shared headstone of Peter and Martha at the Our Lady of Calvary Cemetery (Section A - 136) in Yarmouth. The stone reads: Peter Muise died February 20, 1916, aged 64 years (as well as) Martha Muise born March 29, 1862 and Died February 3, 1940. [2092]

It was in locating a copy of their marriage certificate during the July 1999 visit that I also located the parents of Peter Muise; namely, Vital (Laborer) and Angelica. Parents of Martha were also denoted thusly, as W (Ship Carpenter) and Elizabeth.

[2091] E-mail from Susan Surette dated Tuesday, June 5, 2001.
[2092] Ibid.

Robichaud 1A

[1] Étienne Robichaud, born c. 1640, [2093] married Françoise Boudrot (d/o Michel Boudrot and Michelle Aucoin) c. 1663. [2094] [2095] Françoise was born c. 1642. [2096] [2097] Étienne died in PR, before the census of 1686. [2098] Françoise died after the census of 1714. [2099]

[2] Charles Robichaud dit Cadet, born c. 1667, [2100] married Marie Bourg (d/o Jean Bourg and Marguerite Martin) on June 18, 1703 in PR. [2101] [2102] [2103] Marie was born c. 1673. [2104] [2105] Charles died at PR before May 18, 1737. [2106]

[2093] White, Stephen A. (1999) <u>Dictionnaire Généalogique des Familles Acadiennes</u>, Volume H to Z, page 1403.
[2094] Ibid.
[2095] White, Stephen A. (1999) <u>Dictionnaire Généalogique des Familles Acadiennes</u>, Volume A to G, page 184.
[2096] Ibid.
[2097] White, Stephen A. (1999) <u>Dictionnaire Généalogique des Familles Acadiennes</u>, Volume H to Z, page 1403.
[2098] Ibid.
[2099] White, Stephen A. (1999) <u>Dictionnaire Généalogique des Familles Acadiennes</u>, Volume A to G, page 184.
[2100] White, Stephen A. (1999) <u>Dictionnaire Généalogique des Familles Acadiennes</u>, Volume H to Z, page 1403.
[2101] Ibid, pages 1403 and 1405.
[2102] White, Stephen A. (1999) <u>Dictionnaire Généalogique des Familles Acadiennes</u>, Volume A to G, page 224.
[2103] https://novascotia.ca/archives/acadian/archives.asp?ID=1170
[2104] White, Stephen A. (1999) <u>Dictionnaire Généalogique des Familles Acadiennes</u>, Volume A to G, page 224.
[2105] White, Stephen A. (1999) <u>Dictionnaire Généalogique des Familles Acadiennes</u>, Volume H to Z, page 1405.
[2106] Ibid, pages 1403 and 1405.

[3] Pierre Robichaud dit Cadet, born April 25, 1707 in PR,[2107] [2108] married Suzanne Brassaud (d/o Pierre Brassaud and Gabrielle Forest) c. 1730.[2109] [2110] Suzanne was born c. 1707.[2111]

By 1750, Pierre and Suzanne had eight children and were settled at Rivière des Blonds (Tryon River, Prince Edward Island).[2112]

[4] Marie Madeleine Robichaud dit Cadet, born c. 1731 in Cbd, married **Jacques Deveau** (s/o Jacques Deveau dit Dauphiné and Marie Pothier) on November 22, 1751 in PLJ.[2113] [2114] Jacques was born c. 1726 on ISJ.[2115] Jacques died, April 1770, in Salmon River, Digby County, Nova Scotia.[2116]

[2107] White, Stephen A. (1999) <u>Dictionnaire Généalogique des Familles Acadiennes</u>, Volume H to Z, page 1405.
[2108] https://novascotia.ca/archives/acadian/archives.asp?ID=184
[2109] White, Stephen A. (1999) <u>Dictionnaire Généalogique des Familles Acadiennes</u>, Volume H to Z, page 1405.
[2110] White, Stephen A. (1999) <u>Dictionnaire Généalogique des Familles Acadiennes</u>, Volume A to G, page 267.
[2111] Ibid.
[2112] www.acadian-home.org/wedgeport.html
[2113] Information received in an email from Fred Chandler Union III, dated July 2, 2001 (based on the research of Nova Scotia Acadian historian, J. Alphonse Deveau).
[2114] csapstaff.ednet.ns.ca/jldeveau/deveau3.html
[2115] Ibid.
[2116] Information obtained from David A. Mallet.

Robichaud 1B

[1] Étienne Robichaud, born c. 1640, [2117] married Françoise Boudrot (d/o Michel Boudrot and Michelle Aucoin) c. 1663. [2118] [2119] Françoise was born c. 1642. [2120] [2121] Étienne died in PR, before the census of 1686. [2122] Françoise died after the census of 1714. [2123]

[2] Charles Robichaud dit Cadet, born c. 1667, [2124] married Marie Bourg (d/o Jean Bourg and Marguerite Martin) on June 18, 1703 in PR. [2125] [2126] [2127] Marie was born c. 1673. [2128] [2129] Charles died at PR before May 18, 1737. [2130]

[2117] White, Stephen A. (1999) Dictionnaire Généalogique des Familles Acadiennes, Volume H to Z, page 1403.
[2118] Ibid.
[2119] White, Stephen A. (1999) Dictionnaire Généalogique des Familles Acadiennes, Volume A to G, page 184.
[2120] Ibid.
[2121] White, Stephen A. (1999) Dictionnaire Généalogique des Familles Acadiennes, Volume H to Z, page 1403.
[2122] Ibid.
[2123] White, Stephen A. (1999) Dictionnaire Généalogique des Familles Acadiennes, Volume A to G, page 184.
[2124] White, Stephen A. (1999) Dictionnaire Généalogique des Familles Acadiennes, Volume H to Z, page 1403.
[2125] Ibid, pages 1403 and 1405.
[2126] White, Stephen A. (1999) Dictionnaire Généalogique des Familles Acadiennes, Volume A to G, page 224.
[2127] https://novascotia.ca/archives/acadian/archives.asp?ID=1170
[2128] White, Stephen A. (1999) Dictionnaire Généalogique des Familles Acadiennes, Volume A to G, page 224.
[2129] White, Stephen A. (1999) Dictionnaire Généalogique des Familles Acadiennes, Volume H to Z, page 1405.
[2130] Ibid, pages 1403 and 1405.

[3] Pierre Robichaud dit Cadet, born April 25, 1707 in PR, [2131] [2132] married Suzanne Brassaud (d/o Pierre Brassaud and Gabrielle Forest) c. 1730. [2133] [2134] Suzanne was born c. 1707. [2135]

By 1750, Pierre and Suzanne had eight children and were settled at Rivière des Blonds (Tryon River, Prince Edward Island). [2136]

[4] Pierre Robichaud dit Cadet, born c. 1737, married Marie Rose Corporon (d/o Eustache Corporon and Angélique Viger dit Brigeau) c. 1763. [2137] Marie Rose was born c. 1752. Their marriage was ratified by Father Bailly on October 1, 1770 at Pointe-de-l'Est (Eastern Passage, Nova Scotia). [2138] This family settled in Wedgeport sometime after the baptism of their daughter Agnès on December 1, 1771. [2139]

This Pierre Robichaud would be known, at Bas-de-Tousquet (Wedgeport) as Pierre Cadet. He settled on land left by Joseph and Benjamin Robichaud, sons of Maximin Robichaud (à Pierre à Pierre). [2140]

[2131] White, Stephen A. (1999) Dictionnaire Généalogique des Familles Acadiennes, Volume H to Z, page 1405.
[2132] htttps://novascotia.ca/archives/acadian/archives.asp?ID=184
[2133] White, Stephen A. (1999) Dictionnaire Généalogique des Familles Acadiennes, Volume H to Z, page 1405.
[2134] White, Stephen A. (1999) Dictionnaire Généalogique des Familles Acadiennes, Volume A to G, page 267.
[2135] Ibid.
[2136] www.acadian-home.org/wedgeport.html
[2137] Ibid.
[2138] Ibid.
[2139] Ibid.
[2140] Ibid.

Pierre was among the 200 young Acadians and Natives of Villejouin recruited on Île-Saint-Jean to defend the French fort at Louisbourg. He was taken prisoner there in 1758. Nothing is known as to the lot of this family during the Deportation. [2141]

[5] Marguerite Robichaud, born October 1, 1770, [2142] married **Jean Baptiste (dit Petit John) Mius** (s/o Jean Pierre Mius and Anne Doucet) on November 29, 1797. [2143] [2144] [2145] They were married in front of witnesses due to the absence of a priest. The marriage was blessed by Father Sigogne on November 9, 1799. [2146]

[2141] www.acadian-home.org/wedgeport.html
[2142] Information received from Kenneth Breau, cousin and archivist at the Université de Moncton.
[2143] d'Entremont, Father Clarence Joseph. (1984) <u>Histoire de Quinan, Nouvelle-Écosse</u>, page 75.
[2144] Information received from Kenneth Breau, cousin and archivist at the Université de Moncton.
[2145] https://novascotia.ca/archives/acadian/reborn/archives.asp?ID=101
[2146] Ibid.

Savoie 1A

[1] François Savoie, born c. 1621, married Catherine Lejeune c. 1651. [2147] Catherine was born c. 1633. [2148]

[2] Françoise Savoie, born c. 1652, married **Jean Corporon** c. 1670. [2149] [2150] Jean was born c. 1647. [2151] Françoise was buried at PR on December 27, 1711. [2152] [2153] [2154] Jean died at PR on February 12, 1713 and was buried on the same day. [2155] [2156] He died during the English rule.

[2147] White, Stephen A. (1999) <u>Dictionnaire Généalogique des Familles Acadiennes</u>, Volume H to Z, pages 1048 and 1456.
[2148] Ibid, pages 1048 and 1456.
[2149] Ibid, page 1456.
[2150] White, Stephen A. (1999) <u>Dictionnaire Généalogique des Familles Acadiennes</u>, Volume A to G, page 411.
[2151] Ibid.
[2152] White, Stephen A. (1999) <u>Dictionnaire Généalogique des Familles Acadiennes</u>, Volume H to Z, page 1456.
[2153] White, Stephen A. (1999) <u>Dictionnaire Généalogique des Familles Acadiennes</u>, Volume A to G, page 411.
[2154] https://novascotia.ca/archives/acadian/archives.asp?ID=1470
[2155] White, Stephen A. (1999) <u>Dictionnaire Généalogique des Familles Acadiennes</u>, Volume A to G, page 411.
[2156] https://novascotia.ca/archives/acadian/archives.asp?ID=1480

Savoie 1B

[1] François Savoie, born c. 1621, married Catherine Lejeune c. 1651. [2157] Catherine was born c. 1633. [2158]

[2] Jeanne Savoie, born c. 1658, married **Étienne Pellerin** c. 1675. [2159] Étienne was born c. 1647. [2160] Jeanne died at PR on November 3, 1735 and was buried on November 4, 1735. [2161] [2162] Étienne died at PR on November 17, 1722 and was buried on November 18, 1722. [2163] [2164]

[2157] White, Stephen A. (1999) <u>Dictionnaire Généalogique des Familles Acadiennes</u>, Volume H to Z, pages 1048 and 1456.
[2158] Ibid, pages 1048 and 1456.
[2159] Ibid, pages 1278 and 1457
[2160] Ibid, page 1278.
[2161] Ibid, pages 1278 and 1457.
[2162] https://novascotia.ca/archives/acadian/archives.asp?ID=2095
[2163] White, Stephen A. (1999) <u>Dictionnaire Généalogique des Familles Acadiennes</u>, Volume H to Z, page 1278.
[2164] https://novascotia.ca/archives/acadian/archives.asp?ID=1554

Savoie 1C

[1] François Savoie, born c. 1621, married Catherine Lejeune c. 1651. [2165] Catherine was born c. 1633. [2166]

[2] Andrée Savoie, born c. 1667, married **Jean Préjean dit LeBreton** c. 1683. [2167] Jean was born c. 1651. [2168] Jean died at PR on either June 4 or June 5, 1733 and was buried on June 6, 1733. [2169] [2170]

[2165] White, Stephen A. (1999) Dictionnaire Généalogique des Familles Acadiennes, Volume H to Z, pages 1048 and 1456.
[2166] Ibid, pages 1048 and 1456.
[2167] Ibid, pages 1351 and 1457.
[2168] Ibid, page 1351.
[2169] Ibid.
[2170] https://novascotia.ca/archives/acadian/archives.asp?ID=1916

A Little More Controversy

There has been talk, with *unproven allegations*, that François Savoie (as married to Catherine Lejeune) might actually be the illegitimate son of Thomas François Savoie, Prince of Carignan. Feel free to explore on your own.

Carignan Regiment [2171]

Lineage from Adam (Michael Marcotte) [2172]

Maison de Savoie (House of Savoy) [2173]

Marcotte Genealogy via Frechette [2174]

Michael Marcotte's Genealogy re Savoy [2175]

Savoie Genealogy [2176]

Spanish Royal Lineage (Michael Marcotte) [2177]

[2171] www.acadian-home.org/carignan-regiment.html
[2172] michaelmarcotte.com/Adam.htm
[2173] https://fr.wikipedia.org/wiki/Maison_de_Savoie
[2174] michaelmarcotte.com/frechette.html
[2175] michaelmarcotte.com/savoy.htm
[2176] savoiegenealogy.blogspot.ca/
[2177] michaelmarcotte.com/spkings.htm

Thomas Francis, 1st Prince of Carignan [2178] [2179]

https://commons.wikimedia.org/wiki/Category:Thomas_Francis,_Prince_of_Carignan#/media/File:Tomasso_Francisco_savoycarignano.jpg

---

[2178] http://www.princeton.edu/~achaney/tmve/wiki100k/docs/Thomas_Francis,_1st_Prince_of_Carignano.html

[2179] https://en.wikipedia.org/wiki/Thomas_Francis,_Prince_of_Carignano

Surette 1A

[1] Noël Surette was married to François Colarde. [2180]

[2] Pierre Surette, born c. 1679 in the Marais parish of La Rochelle, Aunis, France, married Jeanne Pellerin (d/o Étienne Pellerin and Jeanne Savoie) on February 4, 1709 in PR. [2181] [2182] Jeanne was born c. 1688. [2183] Pierre died at PR on October 30, 1749 and was buried on October 31, 1749. [2184] [2185] Jeanne died on January 27, 1758 and was buried on January 28, 1758, according to the Notre-Dame parish register in Québec. [2186]

[3] Anne Surette, born September 28, 1715 in PR, [2187] [2188] married **Joseph Doucet** (s/o Claude dit Maître Jean Doucet and Marie Comeau) on January 8, 1731 in PR. [2189] [2190] [2191] Joseph was born on March 12, 1706 in PR. [2192] [2193]

[2180] White, Stephen A. (1999) Dictionnaire Généalogique des Familles Acadiennes, Volume H to Z, page 1476.
[2181] Ibid, pages 1279 and 1476.
[2182] https://novascotia.ca/archives/acadian/archives.asp?ID=1231
[2183] White, Stephen A. (1999) Dictionnaire Généalogique des Familles Acadiennes, Volume H to Z, pages 1279 and 1476.
[2184] Ibid, page 1476.
[2185] https://novascotia.ca/archives/acadian/archives.asp?ID=3095
[2186] White, Stephen A. (1999) Dictionnaire Généalogique des Familles Acadiennes, Volume H to Z, pages 1279 and 1476.
[2187] Ibid, page 1476.
[2188] https://novascotia.ca/archives/acadian/archives.asp?ID=562
[2189] White, Stephen A. (1999) Dictionnaire Généalogique des Familles Acadiennes, Volume H to Z, page 1476.
[2190] White, Stephen A. (1999) Dictionnaire Généalogique des Familles Acadiennes, Volume A to G, page 541.
[2191] https://novascotia.ca/archives/acadian/archives.asp?ID=1807

[2192] White, Stephen A. (1999) Dictionnaire Généalogique des Familles Acadiennes, Volume A to G, page 541.
[2193] https://novascotia.ca/archives/acadian/archives.asp?ID=127

Surette 1B

[1] Noël Surette was married to François Colarde. [2194]

[2] Pierre Surette, born c. 1679 in the Marais parish of La Rochelle, Aunis, France, married Jeanne Pellerin (d/o Étienne Pellerin and Jeanne Savoie) on February 4, 1709 in PR. [2195] [2196] Jeanne was born c. 1688. [2197] Pierre died at PR on October 30, 1749 and was buried on October 31, 1749. [2198] [2199] Jeanne died on January 27, 1758 and was buried on January 28, 1758, according to the Notre-Dame parish register in Québec. [2200]

[3] Marie Josèphe Surette, born October 13, 1718 in PR, [2201] [2202] married **Jean Baptiste I Mius** (s/o Joseph Mius dit d'Azy and Marie Amirault) on October 3, 1735 in PR. [2203] [2204] Jean Baptiste was born c. 1713. [2205] Marie Josèphe died before the census of August 14,

---

[2194] White, Stephen A. (1999) <u>Dictionnaire Généalogique des Familles Acadiennes</u>, Volume H to Z, page 1476.
[2195] Ibid, pages 1279 and 1476.
[2196] https://novascotia.ca/archives/acadian/archives.asp?ID=1231
[2197] White, Stephen A. (1999) <u>Dictionnaire Généalogique des Familles Acadiennes</u>, Volume H to Z, pages 1279 and 1476.
[2198] Ibid, page 1476.
[2199] https://novascotia.ca/archives/acadian/archives.asp?ID=3095
[2200] White, Stephen A. (1999) <u>Dictionnaire Généalogique des Familles Acadiennes</u>, Volume H to Z, pages 1279 and 1476.
[2201] Ibid, page 1476.
[2202] https://novascotia.ca/archives/acadian/archives.asp?ID=725
[2203] White, Stephen A. (1999) <u>Dictionnaire Généalogique des Familles Acadiennes</u>, Volume H to Z, pages 1208 and 1476.
[2204] https://novascotia.ca/archives/acadian/archives.asp?ID=2084
[2205] White, Stephen A. (1999) <u>Dictionnaire Généalogique des Familles Acadiennes</u>, Volume H to Z, page 1208.

1763. [2206] Jean Baptiste died at SAR on June 29, 1806 and was buried on June 30, 1806. [2207] [2208]

[2206] White, Stephen A. (1999) <u>Dictionnaire Généalogique des Familles Acadiennes</u>, Volume H to Z, page 1476.
[2207] Ibid, page 1208.
[2208] https://novascotia.ca/archives/acadian/reborn/archives.asp?ID=652

Thériot

[1] Jean Thériot, born c. 1601, married Perrine Rau c. 1636. [2209] Perrine was born c. 1611. [2210]

[2] Jeanne Thériot, born c. 1643, married **Pierre Thibodeau** c. 1660 in PR. [2211] Pierre was born c. 1631. [2212] Jeanne died at PR on December 7, 1726 and was buried on December 8, 1726. [2213] [2214] Pierre died at PR on December 26, 1704 and was buried on December 27, 1704. [2215] [2216]

[2209] White, Stephen A. (1999) <u>Dictionnaire Généalogique des Familles Acadiennes</u>, Volume H to Z, pages 1365 and 1483.
[2210] Ibid.
[2211] Ibid, pages 1484 and 1508
[2212] Ibid, page 1508.
[2213] Ibid, pages 1484 and 1508.
[2214] https://novascotia.ca/archives/acadian/archives.asp?ID=1565
[2215] White, Stephen A. (1999) <u>Dictionnaire Généalogique des Familles Acadiennes</u>, Volume H to Z, page 1508.
[2216] https://novascotia.ca/archives/acadian/archives.asp?ID=1377

Thibodeau

There was a grant (dated 26 June 1695) of a parcel of land by Frotenac and Bochart de Champigny to Pierre Thibodeau, a resident of PR, of the K8askag8she River, between Mount Desert and Machias, *with a league on either side of the said river by two leagues of depth, to be measured from its mouth, with the islands and islets if any be found there.* [2217]

This grant was confirmed by the King's warrant of May 9, 1696. [2218]

[1] Pierre Thibodeau, born c. 1631, married Jeanne Thériot (d/o Jean Thériot and Perrine Rau) c. 1660 in PR. [2219] Jeanne was born c. 1643. [2220] Pierre died at PR on December 26, 1704 and was buried on December 27, 1704. [2221] [2222] Jeanne died at PR on December 7, 1726 and was buried on December 8, 1726. [2223] [2224]

[2] Marie Catherine Thibodeau, born c. 1667, married **Claude Landry** (s/o René Landry and Marie Bernard) c. 1684. [2225] Claude was born c. 1663. [2226] Marie Catherine died before November 11, 1721. [2227] Claude was buried at GP on September 4, 1747. [2228]

[2217] White, Stephen A. (2000) <u>English Supplement to the Dictionnaire Généalogique des Familles Acadiennes</u> (page 319). Montréal, Québec: AGMV Marquis Imprimeur Inc.
[2218] Ibid.
[2219] White, Stephen A. (1999) <u>Dictionnaire Généalogique des Familles Acadiennes</u>, Volume H to Z, pages 1484 and 1508.
[2220] Ibid.
[2221] Ibid, page 1508.
[2222] https://novascotia.ca/archives/acadian/archives.asp?ID=1377
[2223] White, Stephen A. (1999) <u>Dictionnaire Généalogique des Familles Acadiennes</u>, Volume H to Z, page 1484.
[2224] https://novascotia.ca/archives/acadian/archives.asp?ID=1565
[2225] White, Stephen A. (1999) <u>Dictionnaire Généalogique des Familles Acadiennes</u>, Volume H to Z, pages 917, 924 and 1508.

[2226] White, Stephen A. (1999) Dictionnaire Généalogique des Familles Acadiennes, Volume H to Z, pages 917 and 924.
[2227] Ibid, pages 924 and 1508.
[2228] Ibid, page 924.

Trahan

[1] Nicolas Trahan was married to Renée Desloges c. 1600 in the St-Pierre de Montreuil-Bellay parish, province of Anjou, France. [2229]

[2] Guillaume Trahan, born c. 1601, married Françoise Corbineau on July 13, 1627 in the St-Étienne de Chinon parish, province of Touraine, France. [2230]

Guillaume Trahan was a *maréchal*, [2231] the French equivalent to an English Marshal.

[3] Jeanne Trahan, born c. 1629, [2232] [2233] married **Jacques (dit Jacob) Bourgeois** c. 1643. [2234] [2235] Jacques (dit Jacob) was baptized on January 8, 1621 in the church of Saint-Romain in La Ferté-Gaucher, France; a town located some fifty kilometers to the east of Paris. [2236]

While Jacques (dit Jacob) Bourgeois does not figure into my ancestry per sé, he does figure into the history of the Doucet family; hence, his placement herein.

[2229] White, Stephen A. (1999) <u>Dictionnaire Généalogique des Familles Acadiennes</u>, Volume H to Z, page 1535.
[2230] Ibid, pages 1535 and 1536.
[2231] Bujold, Nicole T. and Caillebeau, Maurice. (1979) <u>Les origins françaises des premières familles acadiennes</u> (page 16). Poitiers, France: Imprimerie l'Union.
[2232] White, Stephen A. (1999) <u>Dictionnaire Généalogique des Familles Acadiennes</u>, Volume H to Z, page 1536.
[2233] White, Stephen A. (1999) <u>Dictionnaire Généalogique des Familles Acadiennes</u>, Volume A to G, page 251.
[2234] Ibid.
[2235] White, Stephen A. (1999) <u>Dictionnaire Généalogique des Familles Acadiennes</u>, Volume H to Z, page 1536.
[2236] Bourgeois, Paul-Pierre. (1994) <u>À la recherche des Bourgeois d'Acadie (1641 à 1800)</u> (pages 13 and 14). Sackville, NB: Tribune Press Ltée.

Given the August 16, 1654 capitulation of Port Royal, we know that Germain left his brother-in-law, Jacques Bourgeois, surgeon, as both Lieutenant of Port Royal and a witness to see that the conditions of the treaty were carried out.

It is quite possible that Germain Doucet married a second time before 1654. Even though the wife has never been identified, Stephen A. White states that she may possibly have been either the daughter of Guillaume Trahan or the sister of Jacques Bourgeois. No children have been traced to this marriage.

It is important to make mention of further notations per Stephen A. White as noted in the Dictionnaire Généalogique des Familles Acadiennes, Volume A to G, page 527.

[i]. It is not possible that the mother of the children of Germain Doucet is a sister of Jacques Bourgeois' wife, as certain authors have proposed, given that the in-laws of Jacques Bourgeois did not get married until 1627. There exists the possibility that Germain Doucet nevertheless married, in second nuptials, to a daughter of Guillaume Trahan who gave him no surviving children; but it is as possible that such a second wife is the sister of Jacques Bourgeois and not the sister of his wife. (Refer to *La Société Généalogique Canadienne Française*, Volume VI, 1955, page 372).

According to Father Archange Godbout, the second child who came to Acadia with Guillaume Trahan might well have been a daughter who was to marry, sometime before 1654, Germain Doucet, Sieur de LaVerdure. [2237]

[2237] White, Stephen A. (2000) English Supplement to the Dictionnaire Généalogique des Familles Acadiennes (page 139). Montréal, Québec: AGMV Marquis Imprimeur Inc.

Viger

[1] François Viger was married to unknown c. 1661. [2238]

[2] François Viger, born c. 1662, married Marie Mius (d/o Philippe Mius dit d'Azy and his first Amérindienne wife) c. 1697. [2239] Marie was born c. 1680. [2240] François was an inhabitant of Ouimakagan in 1705. [2241]

[3] François Viger, born August 16, 1699 in PR, [2242] [2243] married Claire Lejeune (d/o Martin Lejeune dit Briard and Marie Gaudet) c. 1722. [2244] Claire was born c. 1706. [2245]

[4] Angélique Viger dit Brigeau married **Eustache Corporon** (s/o Jean Baptiste Corporon dit l'aîné and Marie Pinet) c. 1749. [2246]

[2238] White, Stephen A. (1999) <u>Dictionnaire Généalogique des Familles Acadiennes</u>, Volume H to Z, page 1565.
[2239] Ibid, pages 1565 and 1566.
[2240] Ibid, pages 1206 and 1566.
[2241] Ibid, page 1566.
[2242] Ibid, page 1566.
[2243] https://novascotia.ca/archives/acadian/archives.asp?ID=113
[2244] White, Stephen A. (1999) <u>Dictionnaire Généalogique des Familles Acadiennes</u>, Volume H to Z, pages 1055 and 1566.
[2245] Ibid, page 1055.
[2246] White, Stephen A. (1999) <u>Dictionnaire Généalogique des Familles Acadiennes</u>, Volume A to G, page 413.

Vigneau

[1] Olivier Vigneau was married to Renée Courtin.[2247]

[2] Catherine Vigneau, born c. 1603, married **Pierre Martin** (s/o René Martin and Étiennette Poirier) on June 30, 1630 in the parish of St-Germain de Bourgeuil parish, province of Touraine, France.[2248] Pierre was born c. 1601.[2249] Catherine died before the census of 1678.[2250] Pierre died before the census of 1678.[2251]

[2247] White, Stephen A. (1999) <u>Dictionnaire Généalogique des Familles Acadiennes</u>, Volume H to Z, page 1125.
[2248] Ibid, pages 1125 and 1567.
[2249] Ibid, page 1125.
[2250] Ibid, pages 1125 and 1567.
[2251] Ibid, page 1125.

Kinship List

Relative	Relationship
----------, Anne-Marie (NATIVE)	Ninth great grandmother
----------, Mi'kmaq (NATIVE)	Seventh great grandmother
----------, Rachel	Spouse of fourth great granduncle
(de) Forest, Michel (Gereyt)	Eighth great grandfather
Amirault, Charles	Sixth great grandfather
Amirault, François (dit Tourangeau)	Seventh great grandfather
Amirault, Hélène (Padène)	Spouse of fourth great granduncle
Amirault, Marguerite	Fifth great grandmother
Amirault, Marie	Sixth great grandmother
AuCoin, Michelle	Eighth great grandmother
Babin, Jeanne	Spouse of sixth great granduncle
Bajolet, Antoine	Ninth great grandfather
Bajolet, Barbe (dit Bayol)	Eighth great grandmother
Baudinet, Jeanne	Ninth great grandmother
Bayon, Rose	Eighth great grandmother

Relative	Relationship
Bernard, ----------	Tenth great grandfather
Bernard, Marie	Ninth great grandmother
Bolduc, Marguerite	Ninth great grandmother
Bornstra, Marguerite	Ninth great grandmother
Bornstra, Wybrant-Andriesz	Tenth great grandfather
Boudreau, Alice Anne	Spouse of granduncle
Boudrot, Claire	Sixth great grandmother
Boudrot, Claude	Seventh great grandfather
Boudrot, Françoise	Eighth great grandmother
Boudrot, Marie	Eighth great grandmother
Boudrot, Michel	Eighth great grandfather
Bourg, Antoine	Ninth great grandfather
Bourg, Bernard	Eighth great grandfather
Bourg, Jean	Eighth great grandfather
Bourg, Marguerite	Seventh great grandmother
Bourg, Marie	Seventh great grandmother
Bourg, Perrine	Eighth great grandmother

Relative	Relationship
Boutier, Jean	Fourth great grandfather
Boutier, Jean	Fifth great grandfather
Boutier, Scholastique	Third great grandmother
Brassaud, Pierre	Seventh great grandfather
Brassaud, Suzanne	Sixth great grandmother
Breau, Marie Catherine (Kay)	Grandmother
Breau, Renée	Ninth great grandmother
Bronchin, Jacqueline	Thirteenth great grandmother
Brun, Françoise	Eighth great grandmother
Brun, Vincent	Ninth great grandfather
Charest, Charles	Spouse of second great grandaunt
Chaumoret, Françoise	Tenth great grandmother
Chebrat, Antoine	Tenth great grandfather
Chebrat, Jeanne	Ninth great grandmother
Chiasson, François	Spouse of fifth great grandaunt
Clémenson, Jeanne	Seventh great grandmother
Clémenson, Mathieu	Eighth great grandfather

Relative	Relationship
Colarde, Françoise	Seventh great grandmother
Colleson, Nicole	Tenth great grandmother
Comeau, Étienne	Seventh great grandfather
Comeau, Marie	Sixth great grandmother
Comeau, Pierre	Eighth great grandfather
Corporon, Anne Josèphe	Fifth great grandmother
Corporon, Eustache	Sixth great grandfather
Corporon, Jean	Seventh great grandfather
Corporon, Jean (Baptiste) (dit l'aîné)	Seventh great grandfather
Corporon, Jeanne	Sixth great grandmother
Corporon, Madeleine	Spouse of sixth great granduncle
Corporon, Marie Rose	Fifth great grandmother
Courtin, Renée	Tenth great grandmother
Coutande, Sebastienne	Ninth great grandmother
de Forest, Crispin	Ninth great grandfather
de Forest, Gérard	Tenth great grandfather
de Forest, Jean	Eleventh great grandfather

Relative	Relationship
de Forest, Melchior	Thirteenth great grandfather
de Forest, Melchior	Twelfth great grandfather
de Forest, Michel (Gereyt)	Eighth great grandfather
de La Grange, Crispin	Eleventh great grandfather
de La Grange, Esther	Tenth great grandmother
Deveau, François Chrysostôme (Couchique)	Fourth great grandfather
Deveau, Jacques (dit Dauphiné)	Sixth great grandfather
Deveau, Jacques	Fifth great grandfather
Deveau, Jean Séraphin	Third great grandfather
Deveau, Marie Elizabeth	Second great grandmother
Deveau, Michel (dit Dauphiné)	Seventh great grandfather
Doubleau, Jeanne	Ninth great grandmother
Doucet, ----------	Ninth great grandmother
Doucet, Alexis	Sixth great granduncle
Doucet, Anne	Fifth great grandaunt
Doucet, Anne	Fourth great grandaunt
Doucet, Anne	Fourth great grandmother

Relative	Relationship
Doucet, Anne Élisabeth	Second great grandaunt
Doucet, Anne Julienne	Second great grandaunt
Doucet, Anne Marguerite	Fourth great grandmother
Doucet, Anne Rosalie	Second great grandaunt
Doucet, Anne Scholastique	Second great grandaunt
Doucet, Anne Vitaline	Grandaunt
Doucet, Avite	Great granduncle
Doucet, Bernard (dit LaVerdure)	Sixth great granduncle
Doucet, Cécile	Fifth great grandaunt
Doucet, Charles	Sixth great granduncle
Doucet, Charles	Fifth great granduncle
Doucet, Charles	Fifth great grandfather
Doucet, Charles (dit Tania)	Fourth great grandfather
Doucet, Claude	Fifth great granduncle
Doucet, Claude (dit Maître Jean)	Sixth great grandfather
Doucet, Dominique	Fourth great granduncle
Doucet, Édouard	Third great granduncle

Relative	Relationship
Doucet, Élizabeth (Isabelle)	Third great grandaunt
Doucet, François	Fourth great granduncle
Doucet, François David	Third great granduncle
Doucet, François David (dit Catoon)	Second great granduncle
Doucet, François David (dit Quançois)	Great granduncle
Doucet, Françoise	Second great grandaunt
Doucet, Geneviève	Third great grandaunt
Doucet, Germain (Sieur de La Verdure)	Eighth great grandfather
Doucet, Germain	Seventh great grandfather
Doucet, Henri Adolphe	Great granduncle
Doucet, Henriette Concorde	Third great grandaunt
Doucet, Isidore	Fourth great granduncle
Doucet, Jacques (dit Maillard)	Sixth great granduncle
Doucet, Jacques	Third great granduncle
Doucet, Jean Avite (Harvey)	Grandfather
Doucet, Jean Baptiste Toussaint	Second great granduncle
Doucet, Jean Émilien	Great granduncle

Relative	Relationship
Doucet, Jean Magloire	Fourth great granduncle
Doucet, Jean Robert	Second great granduncle
Doucet, Jean Théophile (dit Câlin)	Great grandfather
Doucet, Jeanne	Third great grandaunt
Doucet, Jeanne	Sixth great grandaunt
Doucet, Joseph	Fifth great grandfather
Doucet, Joseph	Fourth great granduncle
Doucet, Joseph Harris	Granduncle
Doucet, Joseph Mathurin	Third great grandfather
Doucet, Joseph Mathurin	Second great granduncle
Doucet, Julienne	Spouse of great granduncle
Doucet, Laurent	Sixth great granduncle
Doucet, Laurent	Fourth great granduncle
Doucet, Louis	Fifth great granduncle
Doucet, Louis Théophile	Granduncle
Doucet, Lucie Ursule	Third great grandaunt
Doucet, Madeleine	Fifth great grandaunt

Relative	Relationship
Doucet, Madeleine Honorine (Honorme)	Spouse of second great granduncle
Doucet, Mandé	Spouse of second great grandaunt
Doucet, Marguerite	Eighth great grandmother
Doucet, Marguerite	Fifth great grandaunt
Doucet, Marguerite	Third great grandaunt
Doucet, Marie	Sixth great grandaunt
Doucet, Marie	Fifth great grandaunt
Doucet, Marie Anne	Fourth great grandmother
Doucet, Marie Anne	Second great grandaunt
Doucet, Marie Modeste	Spouse of fourth great granduncle
Doucet, Marie Osite	Fourth great grandaunt
Doucet, Marie Rose	Grandaunt
Doucet, Michel	Third great granduncle
Doucet, Michel	Fourth great grandfather
Doucet, Michel Patrice	Great granduncle
Doucet, Michel Patrice (L'Anglais)	Second great grandfather
Doucet, Monique	Spouse of third great granduncle

Relative	Relationship
Doucet, Paul	Fourth great granduncle
Doucet, Pierre	Seventh great granduncle
Doucet, Pierre	Sixth great granduncle
Doucet, Pierre	Fifth great granduncle
Doucet, Pierre	Fourth great granduncle
Doucet, Pierre Ambroise	Spouse of second great grandaunt
Doucet, Rosalie	Third great grandaunt
Doucet, Rosalie Angélique	Great grandaunt
Doucet, Rosalie Ursule	Second great grandaunt
Doucet, Scholastique	Third great grandmother
Doucet, Sophie	Second great grandaunt
Doucet, Ursule	Fifth great grandaunt
Doucette, Albert (Al)	Father
Doucette, Andrea Jean	Sister
Doucette, Beatrice Martha	Aunt
Doucette, Catherine Beatrice	Sister
Doucette, David Percy (Popeye)	Uncle

Relative	Relationship
Doucette, Denise Helen	Sister
Doucette, George Harvey (Harvey)	Uncle
Doucette, Helen	Aunt
Doucette, Jean E.	Aunt
Doucette, John	Uncle
Doucette, John	Uncle
Doucette, Lynette Marie	Sister
Doucette, Martha	Aunt
Doucette, Mary May	Aunt
Doucette, Michele Anne	Self
Doucette, Peter Patrick	Uncle
Doucette, Raymond L	Uncle
Doucette, Thomas Anthony	Uncle
Doucette, William	Uncle
Doucette, William Henry	Uncle
Du Fosset, Antoine	Thirteenth great grandfather
Du Fosset, Catherine	Twelfth great grandmother

Relative	Relationship
Dugas, Abraham	Eighth great grandfather
Dugas, Claire	Sixth great grandmother
Dugas, Claude	Seventh great grandfather
Dulain, Jeanne Cyprienne	Spouse of great granduncle
Dulain, Louis	Third great grandfather
Dulain, Louis	Fourth great grandfather
Dulain, Louis Cyprien	Second great grandfather
Dulain, Marie Adèle	Great grandmother
Dulain, Simon	Spouse of second great grandaunt
Duon, Jean Baptiste (dit Lyonnais)	Sixth great grandfather
Duon, Jean Louis	Seventh great grandfather
Duon, Jeanne	Fifth great grandmother
Duon, Mathieu	Eighth great grandfather
Fafard, Françoise	Ninth great grandmother
Feeley, Anne Elizabeth	Mother
Feeley, James Henry (Harry)	Grandfather
Forest, Gabrielle (dit Michel)	Seventh great grandmother

Relative	Relationship
Frontain, Augustin (Justin)	Spouse of third great grandaunt
Frontain, Julien Alexandre	Fourth great grandfather
Frontain, Marguerite	Spouse of third great granduncle
Frontain, Marie Apolline (Pauline)	Third great grandmother
Frontain, Marie Élisabeth	Spouse of great granduncle
Frontain, Rosalie	Spouse of second great granduncle
Gachet, Jeanne	Ninth great grandmother
Gaudet, Bernard (Blèche)	Spouse of fifth great grandaunt
Gaudet, Françoise	Ninth great grandmother
Gaudet, Jean	Eighth great grandfather
Gaudet, Jean	Ninth great grandfather
Gaudet, Marie	Seventh great grandmother
Gaudet, Marie	Eighth great grandmother
Gauthier, Jeanne	Fourth great grandmother
Godreau, Marie	Fifth great grandmother
Grosvalet, François	Spouse of fifth great grandaunt
Guérin, Huguette	Spouse of sixth great granduncle

Relative	Relationship
Guyon, Andrée	Tenth great grandmother
Hébert, Agnès	Sixth great grandmother
Hébert, Antoine	Ninth great grandfather
Hébert, Antoine	Sixth great grandfather
Hébert, Catherine	Eighth great grandmother
Hébert, Catherine	Eighth great grandmother
Hébert, Étienne	Seventh great grandfather
Hébert, Marie	Eighth great grandmother
Hébert, Marie Marthe	Fifth great grandmother
Hélie, Madeleine	Eighth great grandmother
Henry (Henri), Jeanne (dit Robert)	Ninth great grandmother
Housseau, Marguerite	Eighth great grandmother
Housseau, Nicolas	Ninth great grandfather
Jacquard, Marie	Spouse of great granduncle
Lafleur, Charles	Ninth great grandfather
Lafleur, Joachine (FILLE DU ROI)	Eighth great grandmother
Landry, Antoinette	Ninth great grandmother

Relative	Relationship
Landry, Claude	Eighth great grandfather
Landry, Jeanne	Seventh great grandmother
Landry, Marie	Seventh great grandmother
Landry, René (dit l'aîné)	Eighth great grandfather
Landry, René (dit le jeune)	Ninth great grandfather
Le Borgne, Jacques (dit Cotte)	Spouse of fifth great grandaunt
LeBlanc, Anne	Spouse of third great granduncle
LeBlanc, Bernard	Spouse of third great grandaunt
LeBlanc, Daniel	Ninth great grandfather
LeBlanc, Honoré	Fourth great granduncle
LeBlanc, Jacques	Eighth great grandfather
LeBlanc, Jean Baptiste	Spouse of third great grandaunt
LeBlanc, Marguerite	Spouse of third great granduncle
LeBlanc, Marie	Fourth great grandmother
LeBlanc, Pierre	Sixth great grandfather
LeBlanc, Pierre	Fifth great grandfather
LeBlanc, René	Seventh great grandfather

Relative	Relationship
LeBlanc, Rosalie	Spouse of great granduncle
Lefebvre, Jean	Ninth great grandfather
Lefebvre, Marie-Anne	Seventh great grandmother
Lefebvre, Martin	Eighth great grandfather
Lefranc, Geneviève	Ninth great grandmother
LeJeune, Catherine	Eighth great grandmother
LeJeune, Claire	Seventh great grandmother
LeJeune, Martin (dit Briard)	Eighth great grandfather
LeJeune, Pierre (dit Briard)	Ninth great grandfather
Loppinot, Jean Chrysostôme	Spouse of sixth great grandaunt
Maillard, Anne	Eleventh great grandmother
Maillard, Michel	Twelfth great grandfather
Martin, Louis	Ninth great grandfather
Martin, Marguerite	Eighth great grandmother
Martin, Marie-Madeleine	Seventh great grandmother
Martin, René	Tenth great grandfather
Martin, Pierre	Ninth great grandfather

Relative	Relationship
Martin, Pierre	Eighth great grandfather
Meunier, Catherine	Seventh great grandmother
Meunier, Jean	Eighth great grandfather
Meunier, Mathurin	Ninth great grandfather
Mius, Angélique Mathilde	Third great grandmother
Mius, Anne	Spouse of great granduncle
Mius, Anne	Fourth great grandmother
Mius, Anne	Fourth great grandmother
Mius, Anne Anastasie (Nanette)	Second great grandmother
Mius, Anne Élisabeth (Zabeth)	Spouse of second great granduncle
Mius, Anne Judith	Spouse of fourth great granduncle
Mius, Anne Julienne	Spouse of second great granduncle
Mius, Anne Mathilde	Spouse of great granduncle
Mius, Anne Théotiste	Spouse of third great granduncle
Mius, Anne Vitaline	Second great grandmother
Mius, Anselme	Fourth great grandfather
Mius, Cécile	Fourth great grandmother

Relative	Relationship
Mius, Charles-Amand I	Fifth great grandfather
Mius, Charles Séraphin	Third great grandfather
Mius, Cyrille Baptiste	Spouse of second great grandaunt
Mius, Félicité	Fifth great grandmother
Mius, Firmin	Spouse of third great grandaunt
Mius, Firmin	Spouse of third great grandaunt
Mius, François	Fifth great grandfather
Mius, François	Third great grandfather
Mius, Isabelle	Spouse of third great granduncle
Mius, Jean Baptiste (dit Petit John)	Fourth great grandfather
Mius, Jean Baptiste I	Fifth great grandfather
Mius, Jean Baptiste II	Fourth great granduncle
Mius, Jean Cyrille (dit Coco)	Third great grandfather
Mius, Jean Pierre	Fourth great grandfather
Mius, Joseph (dit d'Azy)	Sixth great grandfather
Mius, Joseph	Sixth great grandfather
Mius, Louis	Fifth great grandfather

Relative	Relationship
Mius, Ludivine	Spouse of fourth great granduncle
Mius, Madeleine Modeste	Fourth great grandmother
Mius, Marguerite	Fourth great grandmother
Mius, Marguerite	Third great grandmother
Mius, Marie	Eighth great grandmother
Mius, Marie Suzanne	Fourth great grandmother
Mius, Paul	Fourth great grandfather
Mius, Philippe (dit d'Azy)	Seventh great grandfather
Mius, Pierre Eusèbe (dit Petit John)	Third great grandfather
Mius, Rosalie-Angèle (Angélique)	Second great grandmother
Mius, Sylvain (Senteur)	Spouse of second great grandaunt
Mius, Vital	Second great grandfather
Mius, Zacharie	Spouse of second great grandaunt
Mius d'Entremont, Philippe	Eighth great grandfather
Moulaison, Anne Juliette (Julie)	Spouse of second great granduncle
Moulaison, Joseph	Spouse of fourth great grandaunt
Muise, Beatrice	Grandmother

Relative	Relationship
Muise, Charles	Granduncle
Muise, Frederick	Granduncle
Muise, George	Granduncle
Muise, Martha	Grandaunt
Muise, Mary	Grandaunt
Muise, Peter	Granduncle
Muise, Peter	Great grandfather
Muise, William Henry	Granduncle
O'Bird (Hubbard), Jean Jr.	Fourth great grandfather
O'Bird (Hubbard), John	Fourth great grandfather
O'Bird (Hubbard), Marie Madeleine	Third great grandmother
O'Bird (Hubbard), Marie Osithe	Third great grandmother
Pellerin, Étienne	Seventh great grandfather
Pellerin, Jeanne	Sixth great grandmother
Pellerin, Marguerite	Spouse of fifth great granduncle
Pellerin, Marie	Spouse of sixth great granduncle
Pelletret, Henriette	Spouse of seventh great granduncle

Relative	Relationship
Pesseley, Isaac	Ninth great grandfather
Pesseley, Marie	Eighth great grandmother
Peyrieu, Catherine	Eighth great grandmother
Pinet, ----------	Ninth great grandfather
Pinet, Marie	Seventh great grandmother
Pinet, Philippe	Eighth great grandfather
Pitre, Jean	Eighth great grandfather
Pitre, Marie	Seventh great grandmother
Poirier, Anne	Seventh great grandmother
Poirier, Étiennette	Tenth great grandmother
Poirier, Jean	Ninth great grandfather
Poirier, Michel	Eighth great grandfather
Pothier, Jean	Seventh great grandfather
Pothier, Marie	Sixth great grandmother
Préjean, Jean dit LeBreton	Seventh great grandfather
Préjean, Madeleine	Spouse of fifth great granduncle
Préjean, Marie Josèphe	Sixth great grandmother

Relative	Relationship
Préjean (dit l'aîné), Pierre	Spouse of fifth great grandaunt
Rau (Reau), Perrine	Tenth great grandmother
Raux, Marguerite	Twelfth great grandmother
Resteau, Isabeau	Thirteenth great grandmother
Roach, Edmond	Great granduncle
Roach, John William Henry	Second great grandfather
Roach, Martha	Great grandmother
Roach, Mary Elizabeth	Great grandaunt
Robichaud, Charles (dit Cadet)	Seventh great grandfather
Robichaud, Étienne	Eighth great grandfather
Robichaud, Marguerite	Fourth great grandmother
Robichaud, Marie-Madeleine (dit Cadet)	Fifth great grandmother
Robichaud, Marie Josèphe	Spouse of fifth great granduncle
Robichaud, Pierre (dit Cadet)	Sixth great grandfather
Robichaud, Pierre (dit Cadet)	Fifth great grandfather
Savoie, Andrée	Seventh great grandmother
Savoie, François	Eighth great grandfather

Relative	Relationship
Savoie, Françoise	Seventh great grandmother
Savoie, Jeanne	Seventh great grandmother
Soland, Antoinette	Eighth great grandmother
Stewart, Albert Joseph	Spouse
Stewart, Alyssa Kathleen	Daughter
Stewart, Niall Alexander	Son
Surette, Anne	Fifth great grandmother
Surette, Marie Josèphe	Fifth great grandmother
Surette, Marie Sarah	Spouse of granduncle
Surette, Noël	Seventh great grandfather
Surette, Pierre	Sixth great grandfather
Thériot, Jean	Tenth great grandfather
Thériot, Jeanne	Ninth great grandmother
Thibeau, Jean Baptiste	Spouse of third great grandaunt
Thibodeau, Marie Catherine	Eighth great grandmother
Thibodeau, Pierre	Ninth great grandfather
UNKNOWN	Tenth great grandmother

Relative	Relationship
UNKNOWN	Eleventh great grandmother
UNKNOWN	Fourteenth great grandmother
UNKNOWN	Fifteenth great grandmother
UNKNOWN	Eighth great grandmother
UNKNOWN	Ninth great grandmother
UNKNOWN	Eighth great grandmother
UNKNOWN	Sixteenth great grandmother
Viger, Angélique (dit Brigeau)	Sixth great grandmother
Viger, François	Ninth great grandfather
Viger, François	Eighth great grandfather
Viger, François	Seventh great grandfather
Vigneau, Catherine	Ninth great grandmother
Vigneau, Olivier	Tenth great grandfather

Marriage List

Husband	Wife	Year	Place
(de) Forest, Michel (Gereyt)	Hébert, Marie	1666	PR
Amirault, Charles	Dugas, Claire	1726	PR
Amirault, François	Pitre, Marie	1683	
Bajolet, Antoine	Baudinet, Jeanne		
Bernard, ----------	Guyon, Andrée	1644	
Bornstra, Wybrant-Andriesz	UNKNOWN		
Boudrot, Claude	Meunier, Catherine	1700	
Boudrot, Michel	AuCoin, Michelle	1641	
Bourg, Antoine	Landry, Antoinette	1642	PR
Bourg, Bernard	Brun, Françoise	1670	PR
Bourg, Jean	Martin, Marguerite	1667	
Bourgeois, Jacques (Jacob)	Trahan, Jeanne	1643	
Boutier, Jean	Doucet, Anne Marguerite	1802	SAR
Boutier, Jean	Godreau, Marie		
Brassaud, Pierre	Forest, Gabrielle	1691	PR

Husband	Wife	Year	Place
Brun, Vincent	Breau, Renée	1644	France
Charest, Charles	Doucet, Anne Scholastique	1856	
Chebrat, Antoine	Chaumoret, Françoise		
Chiasson, François	Doucet, Anne	1722	PR
Clémenson, Mathieu	Soland, Antoinette		
Comeau, Pierre	Bayon, Rose	1649	
Comeau, Étienne	Lefebvre, Marie-Anne	1670	PR
Corporon, Eustache	Viger, Angélique	1749	
Corporon, Jean	Savoie, Françoise	1670	PR
Corporon, Jean	Savoie, Françoise		
Corporon, Jean (Baptiste)	Pinet, Marie	1702	
Deveau, François Christophe	Mius, Cécile	1791	
Deveau, Jacques	Pothier, Marie	1719	Bbn
Deveau, Jacques	Robichaud, Marie-Madeleine	1751	PLJ
Deveau, Jean Séraphin	O'Bird, Marie Madeleine	1821	
Deveau, Michel	Martin, Marie-Madeleine	1693	
Doucet, Avite	Doucet, Julienne		

Husband	Wife	Year	Place
Doucet, Avite	Jacquard, Marie		
Doucet, Bernard	Corporon, Madeleine	1690	
Doucet, Charles	Guérin, Huguette	1684	
Doucet, Charles	Mius, Félicité	1775	
Doucet, Charles	Préjean, Madeleine	1725	PR
Doucet, Charles (Tania)	Mius, Anne	1811	
Doucet, Claude	Pellerin, Marguerite	1739	PR
Doucet, Claude (Maître Jean)	Comeau, Marie	1696	PR
Doucet, Dominique	Mius, Madeleine Modeste	1761	MA (exile)
Doucet, François David	Mius, Isabelle	1808	SAR
Doucet, François David	Doucet, Madeleine Honorine		
Doucet, François David	Dulain, Jeanne Cyprienne		
Doucet, Germain	Landry, Marie	1664	PR
Doucet, Germain	UNKNOWN	1620	
Doucet, Isidore	----------, Rachel	1760	
Doucet, Jacques	LeBlanc, Anne	1812	SAR
Doucet, Jacques	Mius, Anne Théotiste	1842	SAR

Husband	Wife	Year	Place
Doucet, Jacques	Pellerin, Marie	1695	
Doucet, Jean Avite (Harvey)	Muise, Beatrice	1915	Yarmouth, NS
Doucet, Jean Baptiste T.	Mius, Anne Julienne		
Doucet, Jean Magloire	Amirault, Hélène (Padène)	1770	
Doucet, Jean Robert	Frontain, Rosalie		
Doucet, Jean Robert	Mius, Anne Élisabeth	1868	
Doucet, Jean Théophile	Dulain, Marie Adèle	1893	Quinan, NS
Doucet, Jean Émilien	Mius, Anne Mathilde	1887	
Doucet, Joseph	Mius, Ludivine	1770	
Doucet, Joseph	Surette, Anne	1731	PR
Doucet, Joseph Harris	Surette, Marie Sarah	1928	Surette's Island
Doucet, Joseph Mathurin	Mius, Angélique Mathilde	1816	SAR
Doucet, Joseph Mathurin	Moulaison, Anne Juliette	1840	
Doucet, Laurent	Babin, Jeanne	1689	
Doucet, Louis Théophile	Boudreau, Alice Anne	1922	Wakefield, MA
Doucet, Mandé	Doucet, Sophie	1851	
Doucet, Michel	Frontain, Marguerite	1807	SAR

Husband	Wife	Year	Place
Doucet, Michel	Mius, Marie Suzanne	1778	
Doucet, Michel Patrice	Frontain, Marie Élisabeth	1861	
Doucet, Michel Patrice	LeBlanc, Rosalie	1893	Yarmouth, NS
Doucet, Michel Patrice	Mius, Anne		
Doucet, Michel Patrice	Mius, Anne Anastasie	1838	Quinan, NS
Doucet, Pierre	Pelletret, Henriette	1660	
Doucet, Pierre	Robichaud, Marie Josèphe	1732	PR
Doucet, Pierre Ambroise	Doucet, Rosalie Ursule	1844	
Doucet, Édouard	Doucet, Monique	1818	
Doucet, Édouard	LeBlanc, Marguerite	1818	SAR
Doucette, Albert (Al)	Feeley, Anne Elizabeth	1961	Truro, NS
Du Fosset, Antoine	Resteau, Isabeau		
Dugas, Abraham	Doucet, Marguerite	1647	PR
Dugas, Claude	Bourg, Marguerite	1697	PR
Dulain, Louis	Frontain, Marie Apolline	1794	
Dulain, Louis	Gauthier, Jeanne		
Dulain, Louis Cyprien	Mius, Anne Vitaline		

Husband	Wife	Year	Place
Dulain, Simon	Doucet, Anne Julienne	1859	
Duon, Jean Baptiste	Hébert, Agnès	1713	PR
Duon, Jean Louis	Clémenson, Jeanne	1683	France
Duon, Mathieu	Peyrieu, Catherine	1650	France
Feeley, James Henry	Breau, Marie Catherine	1930	Amherst, NS
Frontain, Augustin (Justin)	Doucet, Élizabeth (Isabelle)	1806	SAR
Frontain, Joseph	Robichaud, Geneviève		
Frontain, Julien Alexandre	Mius, Anne	1759	
Gaudet, Bernard (Blèche)	Doucet, Marie	1724	
Gaudet, Jean	Colleson, Nicole	1652	
Gaudet, Jean	Henry (Henri), Jeanne	1680	
Gaudet, Jean	UNKNOWN	1622	
Grosvalet, François	Doucet, Madeleine	1743	PR
Housseau, Nicolas	Bolduc, Marguerite		
Hébert, Antoine	Corporon, Jeanne	1691	
Hébert, Antoine	Lefranc, Geneviève	1648	
Hébert, Étienne	Gaudet, Marie	1650	

Husband	Wife	Year	Place
Lafleur, Charles	Gachet, Jeanne		
Landry, Claude	Thibodeau, Marie Catherine	1684	
Landry, René	Bernard, Marie	1659	
Landry, René	Bourg, Perrine	1645	PR
Le Borgne, Jacques	Doucet, Cécile	1752	PR
LeBlanc, Bernard	Doucet, Marguerite		
LeBlanc, Daniel	Gaudet, Françoise	1650	PR
LeBlanc, Honoré	Mius, Anne Judith	1790	
LeBlanc, Jacques	Hébert, Catherine	1673	
LeBlanc, Jean Baptiste	Doucet, Lucie Ursule	1810	SAR
LeBlanc, Pierre	Amirault, Marguerit		MA (exile)
LeBlanc, Pierre	Boudrot, Claire	1740	GP
LeBlanc, René	Landry, Jeanne	1708	GP
LeJeune, Martin	Gaudet, Marie	1699	
LeJeune, Pierre	Doucet, ----------	1650	PR
Lefebvre, Jean	Doubleau, Jeanne		
Lefebvre, Martin	Bajolet, Barbe	1647	France

Husband	Wife	Year	Place
Loppinot, Jean Chrysostôme	Doucet, Jeanne	1702	
Maillard, Michel	Raux, Marguerite		
Martin, Louis	Coutande, Sebastienne		
Martin, Pierre	Lafleur, Joachine	1664	Québec
Martin, Pierre	Vigneau, Catherine	1630	France
Meunier, Jean	Housseau, Marguerite	1670	Québec
Meunier, Mathurin	Fafard, Françoise		
Mius d'Entremont, Philippe	Hélie, Madeleine	1649	
Mius, Anselme	Mius, Marguerite	1807	
Mius, Charles Séraphin	Mius, Marguerite	1825	
Mius, Charles-Amand I	Hébert, Marie Marthe	1731	PR
Mius, Cyrille Baptiste	Doucet, Anne Rosalie	1842	
Mius, Firmin	Doucet, Geneviève		
Mius, Firmin	Doucet, Jeanne	1807	SAR
Mius, François	Duon, Jeanne	1735	PR
Mius, François	O'Bird, Marie Osithe	1798	SAR
Mius, Jean Baptiste	Robichaud, Marguerite	1797	

Husband	Wife	Year	Place
Mius, Jean Baptiste I	Surette, Marie Josèphe	1735	PR
Mius, Jean Baptiste II	Doucet, Marie Modeste	1770	
Mius, Jean Cyrille (Coco)	Doucet, Scholastique	1832	
Mius, Jean Pierre	Doucet, Anne	1768	MA (exile)
Mius, Joseph	Amirault, Marie	1699	
Mius, Joseph	Préjean, Marie Josèphe	1726	PR
Mius, Louis	Corporon, Anne Josèphe	1768	
Mius, Paul	LeBlanc, Marie		
Mius, Philippe	----------, Mi'kmaq	1678	
Mius, Pierre	UNKNOWN		
Mius, Pierre Eusèbe	Boutier, Scholastique	1825	
Mius, Sylvain (Senteur)	Doucet, Anne Élisabeth	1847	
Mius, Vital	Mius, Rosalie-Angèle	1853	SAR
Mius, Zacharie	Doucet, Marie Anne	1857	
Moulaison, Joseph	Doucet, Marie Osite	1780	
Muise, Peter	Roach, Martha	1877	Yarmouth, NS
O'Bird, Jean	Doucet, Marie Anne	1794	

Husband	Wife	Year	Place
O'Bird, John	Mius, Madeleine Modeste	1772	MA (exile)
Pellerin, Étienne	Savoie, Jeanne	1675	
Pesseley, Isaac	Bajolet, Barbe	1629	France
Pinet, ----------	----------, Anne-Marie	1653	
Pinet, Philippe	Hébert, Catherine		PR
Pitre, Jean	Pesseley, Marie	1665	
Poirier, Jean	Chebrat, Jeanne	1647	
Poirier, Michel	Boudrot, Marie	1673	
Pothier, Jean	Poirier, Anne	1699	
Préjean Pierre	Doucet, Marguerite	1722	Bbn
Préjean, Jean	Savoie, Andrée	1683	
Roach, John William Henry	Deveau, Marie Elizabeth	1853	
Robichaud, Charles	Bourg, Marie	1703	PR
Robichaud, Pierre	Brassaud, Suzanne	1730	
Robichaud, Pierre	Corporon, Marie Rose	1763	
Robichaud, Étienne	Boudrot, Françoise	1663	
Savoie, François	LeJeune, Catherine	1651	

Husband	Wife	Year	Place
Stewart, Albert Joseph	Doucette, Michele Anne	1985	Truro, NS
Surette (Frontain), Cyprien	Boutier, Léonisse		
Surette (Frontain), Jean	Muise, Anne Adèle (Delphine)		
Surette, Noël	Colarde, Françoise		
Surette, Pierre	Pellerin, Jeanne	1709	PR
Thibeau, Jean Baptiste	Doucet, Rosalie	1807	SAR
Thibodeau, Pierre	Thériot, Jeanne	1660	PR
Thériot, Jean	Rau (Reau), Perrine	1636	
Trahan, Guillaume	Corbineau, Françoise	1627	France
Trahan, Nicolas	Desloges, Renée	1600	France
UNKNOWN	Bourgeois, Marguerite		
Viger, François	LeJeune, Claire	1722	
Viger, François	Mius, Marie	1697	
Viger, François	UNKNOWN	1661	
de Forest, ----------	UNKNOWN	1485	
de Forest, ----------	UNKNOWN	1440	
de Forest, Crispin	Bornstra, Marguerite	1636	Netherlands

Husband	Wife	Year	Place
de Forest, Gérard	de La Grange, Esther	1611	Netherlands
de Forest, Jean	Maillard, Anne	1575	
de Forest, Melchior	Bronchin, Jacqueline	1510	
de Forest, Melchior	Du Fosset, Catherine	1533	
de Forest, Melchior	UNKNOWN	1470	
de La Grange, Crispin	UNKNOWN		

Genealogy Forms

This segment directs the reader to a variety of online (and free) Pedigree Chart sources.

The information you acquire and collect needs to be recorded and organized so that it is easily understood. Researching the origins of your family takes considerable time as well as a good deal of organization. It becomes pertinent, then, that you avail of the many free forms available to you for this very purpose.

To download some of these free forms, and print them off, you need to ensure that <u>Adobe Acrobat Reader</u> [2252] is installed on your computer.

BASIC CHARTS AND WORKSHEETS

<u>Adoptive Family Tree</u> [2253] has spaces for recording both a person's biological and adoptive parents.

<u>Biographical Outline</u> [2254] notes information on events in an ancestor's life, such as education, military service, marriage and children.

<u>Family Group Sheet</u> [2255] is designed for recording information about a nuclear family.

<u>Family Group Record Form</u> [2256]

[2252] https://get.adobe.com/reader/
[2253] https://www.familytreemagazine.com/upload/images/PDF/adoptiontree.pdf
[2254] https://www.familytreemagazine.com/freebie/biographicaloutline/
[2255] https://www.familytreemagazine.com/freebie/familygroupsheet/
[2256] https://familysearch.org/sites/all/themes/frankie/documents/Step-2-Family-Group-Record.pdf

Interactive Family Group Record Sheet [2257] must be completed before printing.

Relationship Chart [2258] [2259] used to figure out how family members are related.

Record Marriage Records [2260]

Stepfamily Tree [2261]

CEMETERY

Cemetery Record 1 [2262]

Cemetery Record 2 [2263]

Cemetery Transcription Form [2264]

GENEALOGY RECORDS

Genealogy Records Worksheets [2265] includes Deed Index: Grantees, Deed Index: Grantors, Statewide Marriage Index, Military Records Checklist, Cemetery Transcription Form, Vital Records Chart, Military Biography Form. Some are solely US based; others can be utilized, regardless of country wherein research is based.

[2257] misbach.org/download/FamilyGroupRecord.pdf
[2258] https://www.familytreemagazine.com/upload/images/PDF/relationship.pdf
[2259] www.wakefieldfhs.org.uk/RELATE.pdf
[2260] https://www.familytreemagazine.com/freebie/free-form-record-marriage-records/
[2261] https://www.familytreemagazine.com/upload/images/PDF/stepfamily.pdf
[2262] dept.cs.williams.edu/~bailey/genealogy/index_files/Cemetery1.pdf
[2263] dept.cs.williams.edu/~bailey/genealogy/index_files/Cemetery2.pdf
[2264] https://www.familytreemagazine.com/upload/images/pdf/cemetery.pdf
[2265] https://www.familytreemagazine.com/freeforms/recordworksheets/

IMMIGRATION

Immigration Forms (US) [2266] are designed for transcribing names of, and information about, early immigrants you find on customs lists (the name for early passenger lists) and ship manifests (more-modern passenger lists). Due to changing immigration laws, shipping companies had to record different information about passengers through the years. Record your ancestor's passenger information on the form corresponding to the year he or she immigrated to America.

ORAL HISTORY

Family history isn't just about records and vital statistics; It's also about the stories, memories and traditions you want to pass on to future generations.

How Do I Conduct an Oral History Interview? [2267]

Oral Histories Kit [2268]

Oral History Forms [2269] includes: Artifacts and Heirlooms Form, Tradition Recording Form, Time Capsule Form, Oral History Interview Record Form, Heirloom Inventory Form, Photo Inventory Form and Home Movie Cataloging Record Form.

Oral History Techniques [2270]

Sample Questions to Conduct an Oral History Interview [2271]

[2266] https://www.familytreemagazine.com/freeforms/immigrationforms/
[2267] https://www.le.ac.uk/emoha/training/no2.pdf
[2268] www.aa.org/assets/en_US/en_oralhistorieskit.pdf
[2269] https://www.familytreemagazine.com/freeforms/oralhistoryforms/
[2270] www.indiana.edu/~cshm/oral_history_techniques.pdf
[2271] www.gphistorical.org/pdf-files/oralhistory.pdf

Talking History: Oral History Guidelines [2272]

The Smithsonian Folklife and Oral History Interviewing Guide [2273]

Writing Good Questions [2274]

RESEARCH TRACKERS AND ORGANIZERS

Article Reading List [2275] for cataloguing articles you want to read or refer to later.

Book Wish List [2276] assists you in making a checklist of genealogy books you'd like to buy or borrow.

Correspondence Log [2277] allows you to keep track of general research requests you send to libraries and archives.

Correspondence Record Sheet [2278]

Family Correspondence Log [2279] for organizing research requests sent to (and received from) family members.

Note Taking Form 1 [2280] for filing your notes by surname and record type.

[2272] https://www.environment.nsw.gov.au/resources/cultureheritage/TalkingHistoryOralHistoryGuidelines.pdf
[2273] https://folklife.si.edu/resources/pdf/InterviewingGuide.pdf
[2274] home.earthlink.net/~ahickling/interviewsuggestions.html
[2275] https://www.familytreemagazine.com/upload/images/PDF/reading.pdf
[2276] https://www.familytreemagazine.com/freebie/bookwishlist/
[2277] https://www.familytreemagazine.com/upload/images/PDF/correspondence.pdf
[2278] dept.cs.williams.edu/~bailey/genealogy/index_files/CorrespondenceRecordSheet.pdf
[2279] https://www.familytreemagazine.com/upload/images/PDF/familycorrespond.pdf
[2280] https://www.familytreemagazine.com/upload/images/PDF/note1.pdf

Note Taking Form 2 [2281] for filing your notes by couple or family group.

Online Database Search Tracker [2282]

Personal Records Inventory [2283] is a formatted template to record a detailed inventory of your personal records.

Repository Checklist [2284] enables you to plan a research trip by recording details about the archive or library you intend to visit.

Research Calendar [2285] allows you to keep track of materials you've searched.

Research Checklist of Books [2286] is to be used for listing books that you want to check regarding your ancestors.

Research Journal [2287] for listing sources you have already checked or are planning to check.

Research Log [2288] is a form that helps researchers plan their research, while also recording and documenting their findings.

Research Record Sheet [2289]

Research Worksheet [2290] is ideal for tracking research on long-lost relatives or 20th-century ancestors.

[2281] https://www.familytreemagazine.com/upload/images/PDF/note2.pdf
[2282] https://www.familytreemagazine.com/upload/images/PDF/online-search-tracker.pdf
[2283] https://www.familytreemagazine.com/freebie/personalrecordsinventory/
[2284] https://www.familytreemagazine.com/freebie/repositorychecklist/
[2285] https://www.familytreemagazine.com/freebie/researchcalendar/
[2286] https://www.familytreemagazine.com/upload/images/PDF/books.pdf
[2287] https://www.familytreemagazine.com/upload/images/PDF/researchjournal.pdf
[2288] https://familysearch.org/learn/wiki/en/images/0/0f/Research_Log.doc
[2289] dept.cs.williams.edu/~bailey/genealogy/index_files/ResearchRecordSheet.pdf

Surname Variant Chart [2291] keeps track of surnames you're researching, as well as their variant forms and spellings.

Table of Contents (for files) [2292] form for listing the documents in a file folder so you can find them quickly.

You can also purchase, online, the following traditional pedigree charts.

15 Generation Pedigree Chart (10 pack) [2293] [2294]

[2290] https://www.familytreemagazine.com/freebie/researchworksheet/
[2291] https://www.familytreemagazine.com/freebie/surnamevariantchart/
[2292] https://www.familytreemagazine.com/freebie/tableofcontents/
[2293] https://www.amazon.com/15-Generation-Pedigree-Chart-pack/dp/B006ZZQNMI/
[2294] https://www.amazon.ca/15-Generation-Pedigree-Chart-pack/dp/B006ZZQNMI/

Associations

La Société Historique Acadienne (unable to determine if still operable)

Case Postale 632, Moncton, New Brunswick, Canada, E1C 8M7

$ 25 membership fee (Canada)

$ 30 membership fee (outside Canada)

Members will receive quarterly copies of <u>Les Cahiers</u>.

La Société Généalogique Canadienne Française [2295]

3440, rue Davidson, Montréal, Québec, Canada, H1W 2Z5

$ 45 membership fee (Canada) one year

$ 45 membership fee US funds (outside Canada) one year

Email: info@sgcf.com

Due to the proliferation of viruses, only emails with the word **Genealogy** in the subject line will be considered.

Members will receive quarterly copies of <u>Mémoires</u> (published since 1944).

[2295] www.sgcf.com/

La Société Historique du Madawaska

165, Boul. Hébert, Edmundston, New Brunswick, Canada, E3V 2S8

Telephone: (506) 737-5280

Fax: (506) 737-5281

Members receive copies of La Revue de La Société Historique du Madawaska.

American-Canadian Genealogical Society [2296]

P.O. Box 6478, Manchester, NH, USA, 03108-6478

$ 35 membership fee (US)

$ 40 membership fee for Canadians (US funds)

Email: ACGS@acgs.org

Members will receive quarterly copies of American-Canadian Genealogist.

[2296] https://acgs.org/

Acadian Genealogy Exchange (AGE) (unable to determine if still operable) [2297]

3265 Wayman Branch Road, Covington, KY, USA, 41015-4601

Phone, Fax and Modem: 859-356-9825

Email: janjehn@hotmail.com

$ 17 membership fee (US)

Members will receive copies of the AGE publication twice yearly. Contents include genealogical and historical information of interest to Acadians, French-Canadian Acadians and Cajuns. Queries are free to anyone as long as they pertain to the ethnic groups as cited above.

American-French Genealogical Society [2298]

P.O. Box 830, Woonsocket, RI, USA, 02895-0870

$ 35 membership fee (US)

$ 45 membership fee for Canadians (US funds)

Members receive Je Me Souviens, a semi-annual, 100+ page journal filled with resources for genealogists, members' research stories, new member listings, and facts and tips. A bi-monthly newsletter, AFGnewS, keeps members informed of Society activities.

[2297] www.acadiangenexch.com/
[2298] https://afgs.org/site/

Argyle Municipality Historical and Genealogical Society [2299]

P.O. Box 101, Tusket, Nova Scotia, Canada, B0W 3M0

$ 30 membership fee (individual)

$ 35 membership fee (family)

Those living in the US should pay in US finds to help cover additional mailing charges. Members receive a quarterly newsletter called The Argus.

La Société Historique Acadienne de Pubnico-Ouest [2300]

Case Postale 92, Pubnico-Ouest, Nova Scotia, Canada, B0W 3S0

$ 10 membership fee

Email: musee.acadien@ns.sympatico.ca

Members receive a quarterly Bulletin that keeps them up-to-date with respect to this Acadian Centre that houses the renowned works of the deceased Père Clarence d'Entremont.

[2299] www.argylecourthouse.com/content/
[2300] www.museeacadien.ca/english/society/index.htm

L'Association Histoire de Chez Nous (unable to determine if still operable) [2301]

339, route La Vallée, Memramcook, New Brunswick, Canada, E4K 3C5

Telephone: (506) 776-8600

Email: ahcn@ahcn.ca

$ 20 membership fee for Canadians

$ 30 membership fee for those living outside Canada

Membership entails you to a genealogical and folklore magazine entitled La Voix du Passé. This organization deals with the communities of Allainville, Bas-Néguac, Canton-des-Robichaud, Chemin des Breau, Chemin des Caissie, Chemin des Drisdelle, Chemin des Grattan, Chemin des Stymiest, Comeau Settlement, Covedell, Fair-Isle, Lagacéville, Lavillette, Néguac, Rivière-des-Caches, St-Wilfred, Village Saint-Laurent.

[2301] ahcn.ca/

Bibliography 1

This particular bibliography of material represents the sources that were used to derive information with regards to my personal pedigree.

An Acadian Parish Remembered [2302]

An Acadian Parish Reborn [2303]

ATCHA: Argyle Township Courthouse and Archives [2304]

Les Doucet du Monde [2305] [2306]

Murdoch, Beamish. (1865) A History of Nova Scotia or Acadie: Volume 1

Murdoch, Beamish. (1866) A History of Nova Scotia or Acadie: Volume 2

Murdoch, Beamish. (1867) A History of Nova Scotia or Acadie: Volume 3

Occupations and Trades in New France [2307]

Arsenault, Bona. (1978). Histoire et Généalogie des Acadiens.

Bergeron, Père Adrien. (1981). Le Grand Arrangement des Acadiens au Québec.

Bourgeois, Paul Pierre. (1994). À la recherche des Bourgeois d'Acadie (1641 à 1800).

[2302] https://novascotia.ca/archives/acadian/
[2303] https://novascotia.ca/archives/acadian/reborn/
[2304] www.argylecourthouse.com/content/
[2305] http://doucetfamily.org/home.htm
[2306] https://www.facebook.com/groups/LDoucetDM/
[2307] www.acadian-home.org/occupations.html

Bujold, Nicole T. and Caillebeau, Maurice. (1979) Les origins françaises des premières familles acadiennes.

C'entre d'études acadiennes, Université de Moncton. (1995). Acadia of The Maritimes.

Clark, Andrew Hill. (1968). Acadia: The Geography of Early Nova Scotia to 1760.

Doucet, Mme L. J. (1955). "*Généalogie des familles Doucet*" as published by La Société Généalogique Canadienne Française, Memoires (Volume VI, 1955, pages 371-388)

Doucette, Wilfred. One of the Directors of the Acadian Heritage and Culture Foundation Incorporated in Erath, Louisiana. Research material received courtesy of his nephew, Robert (Bob) Doucet.

d'Entremont, Père Clarence. (1984). Histoire de Quinan, Nouvelle-Écosse.

Devoe, Colonel John B. (2000). Devoe-DeVaux Family History 1691 - 1991.

Herbin, John Frederi. (1991). The History of Grand-Pré.

Jehn, Janet. *Acadian Genealogy Exchange* material.

Macauley Hubbard, Sheila. (1996). The Hubbard Family of Nova Scotia.

Perron, F. René. (1991). "*De Germain Doucet à Jacob Bourgeois*" as published by La Société Historique Acadienne, Les Cahiers, Octobre - Décembre 1991 (Volume 22, Number 4, pages 86-114)

Perron, F. René. (1992). "*Bourgeois & Doucet: à Bassevelle des suites surprenantes*" as published by La Société Historique Acadienne, Les Cahiers, Janvier - Mars 1992 (Volume 23, Number 1, pages 27-46)

Perron, F. René. "*Mystère de la famille Doucet*" (an article as sent to me by Paul Pierre Bourgeois)

Perron, F. René. "*De La Verdure aux Ant-Isles et Vice-Versa*" (an article as sent to me by Carol Doucet)

Ross, Sally and Deveau, J. Alphonse. (1992). The Acadians of Nova Scotia: Past and Present.

White, Stephen A. (1999). Dictionnaire Généalogique des Familles Acadiannes.

White, Stephen A. (2000). English Supplement to Dictionnaire Généalogique des Familles Acadiannes.

Bibliography 2

This particular bibliography of material represents a multitude of Acadian resources. They are listed here in the hope that they will serve to generate further interest with respect to the "Acadie" that we all share.

BOOKS

Arceneaux, Leon M. (2002) <u>Beyond the Storm: An Acadian Odyssey</u>.

Arsenault, Bona. (1994). <u>History of The Acadians</u>.

Arsenault, Georges. (2002) <u>Acadian Legends, Folktales and Songs from Prince Edward Island</u>.

Aucoin, Réjean and Tremblay, Jean-Claude. (1999) <u>The Magic Rug of Grand Pré</u>.

Barrett, Wayne. (1990). <u>Acadian Pictorial Cookbook</u>.

Bleakney, J. Sherman. (2004) <u>Sods, Soil, and Spades: The Acadians at Grand Pré and Their Dykeland Legacy</u>.

Boudreau, Amy. (2002) <u>The Story of the Acadians</u>.

Boudreau, Hélène. (2008) <u>Acadian Star</u>.

Boudreau Vaughn, Betty. (1997). <u>I'll Buy You An Ox: An Acadian Daughter's Bittersweet Passage into Womanhood</u>.

Comeau Poirier, Léonie. (1985). <u>My Acadian Heritage</u>.

Cormier-Boudreau, Marielle and Gallant, Melvin. (1991). A Taste of Acadie.

Brasseaux, Carl A. (1991). Scattered To The Wind: Dispersal and Wanderings of The Acadians 1755-1809.

Chevrier, Cécile. (1994). Acadie - Sketches of A Journey.

Chiasson, Anselme. (1998). Chéticamp - History and Acadian Traditions.

Davison, Marion and Marsh, Audrey. (1983). Smoke Over Grand-Pré.

Deveau, J. Alphonse. Two Beginnings - A Brief Acadian History.

Donovan, Lois. (2007) Winds of L'Acadie.

Doucet, Clive. (2000) Notes from Exile: On Being Acadian.

Doucet, Clive. (2004) Lost and Found in Acadie.

Doucet, Clive. (2005) Acadian Homecoming.

Doucette, Michele. (2010) A Travel in Time to Grand Pré (revised edition).

Doucette, Michele. (2011) Back Home With Evangeline.

Doucette, Sister Therese and Doucette, Dr. Francis. The History of Madawaska - An English Translation.

Doughty, Arthur G. (2008) The Acadian Exiles: A Chronicle of the Land of Evangeline.

Faragher, John Mack. (2005) A Great and Noble Scheme: The Tragic Story of the Expulsion of the French Acadians from Their American Homeland.

Gerrior, William. (2003) Acadian Awakenings: Roots & Routes, International Links, an Acadian Family in Exile.

Griffiths, Naomi E. S. (1992). The Contexts of Acadian History 1686-1784.

Griffiths, Naomi. (2004) From Migrant to Acadian: A North American Border People, 1604-1735.

Hope-Simpson, Lila. (2005) Fiddles and Spoons.

Jobb, Dean W. (2005) The Acadians: A People's Story of Exile and Triumph.

Johnston, John and Kerr, Wayne. (2004) Grand-Pré: Heart of Acadie.

Laxer, James. (2007) The Acadians: In Search of a Homeland.

LeBlanc, Dudley J. (1966). The Acadian Miracle.

Léger, Yvon. (1992). Beloved Acadia of My Ancestors (translated by Antoine Bugeaud)

Longfellow, Henry Wadsworth. (1951). Evangeline.

Mahaffie Jr., Charles D. (1995). A Land of Discord Always - Acadia From Its Beginnings to The Expulsion of Its People 1604-1755.

Maillet, Antoine. (2004) Pélagie: The Return to Acadie.

Paratte, Henri-Domonique. (1998). Peoples of the Maritimes - Acadians.

Roberts, Charles G. D. (1898) A Sister to Evangeline: Being the Story of Yvonne de Lamourie, and How She Went Into Exile with the Villagers of Grand Pré.

Roberts, Charles G. D. (2003) The Forge in the Forest: An Acadian Romance (first published in 1896).

Silver, Alfred. (2002) Three Hills Home.

Stewart, Sharon. (2004) Dear Canada: Banished from Our Home: The Acadian Diary of Angélique Richard, Grand Pré, Acadie, 1755.

Tallant, Robert and Boyd Dillon, Corinne. (2001) Evangeline and The Acadians.

Yesterday In Acadia - Scenes From The Acadian Historical Village (Caraquet, New Brunswick)

WEBSITES: ACADIAN RELATED

300 Year Old Village Unearthed [2308]

1755: The History and the Stories [2309]

Aboriginal Education [2310]

Acadian and French Canadian Ancestral Home [2311]

Acadian and French Canadian Genealogy [2312]

Acadian Archives: UMFK [2313]

Acadian Cajun Genealogy, History and Culture [2314]

[2308] https://www.cbc.ca/news/canada/300-year-old-acadian-village-unearthed-1.198771
[2309] 139.103.17.56/1755-html/entree6cfe.html
[2310] https://novascotia.ca/abor/education/other-resources/
[2311] www.acadian-home.org/frames.html
[2312] habitant.org/
[2313] https://www.umfk.edu/archives/
[2314] www.acadian-cajun.com/index.htm

Acadian Census Records: The True Acadian Period 1604-1755 [2315]

Acadian Church Records: The True Acadian Period 1604-1755 [2316]

Acadian Compiled Works: The True Acadian Period 1604-1755 [2317]

Acadian Culture in Nova Scotia [2318]

Acadian Culture in Maine [2319]

Acadian Heartland: Records of the Deportation and Le Grand Dérangement [2320]

Acadian Historic Atlas [2321]

Acadian House Museum (Chezzetcook, Nova Scotia) [2322]

Acadian Museum (Miscouche, Prince Edward Island) [2323]

Acadian Notarial Records: The True Acadian Period 1604-1755 [2324]

Acadian Place Names: Yesterday and Today [2325]

[2315] www.acadian-cajun.com/genac1.htm
[2316] www.acadian-cajun.com/genac2.htm
[2317] www.acadian-cajun.com/genac4.htm
[2318] https://www.novascotia.com/explore/culture/acadian-culture
[2319] acim.umfk.maine.edu/
[2320] https://novascotia.ca/archives/deportation/
[2321] epe.lac-bac.gc.ca/100/205/301/ic/cdc/neo-ecossaise/en/index.htm
[2322] https://www.novascotia.com/see-do/attractions/acadian-house-museum-lacadie-de-chezzetcook/1539
[2323] museeacadien.org/an/
[2324] www.acadian-cajun.com/genac3.htm
[2325] www.acadian-home.org/places-yesterday-today.html

Acadian Surnames: The True Acadian Period 1604-1755 [2326]

Archaeological Field School at Grand Pré, Nova Scotia [2327]

Archaeologist Digs Up Artifacts Along Border from 1700s [2328]

Archaeologists Searching for Grand Pré Church Site [2329]

Archaeology in Nova Scotia [2330]

Argyle District Acadians [2331]

Beaubassin Village: Our Living History [2332]

CyberAcadie (French website of Daniel Robichaud) [2333]

Doucet House (Hunter River, Prince Edward Island) [2334]

Erosion threatens historic Acadian site [2335]

Former Acadian Border settlement (Beaubassin) being recognized by Parks Canada [2336]

[2326] www.acadian-cajun.com/genac5.htm
[2327] https://www.smu.ca/academics/departments/grand-pre-archaeology.html
[2328] https://www.cbc.ca/news/canada/new-brunswick/fort-lawrence-beausejour-charles-burke-1.3421687
[2329] https://www.cbc.ca/news/canada/nova-scotia/acadian-church-1.3290859
[2330] https://museum.novascotia.ca/collections/archaeology
[2331] epe.lac-bac.gc.ca/100/205/301/ic/cdc/argyle/html/home.htm
[2332] https://bcasey.liberal.ca/news-nouvelles/beaubassin-village-our-living-history/
[2333] cyberacadie.com/cyberacadie.com/index.html
[2334] www.farmersbank.ca/en/doucet-house
[2335] https://www.pressreader.com/canada/journal-pioneer/20110624/281917359706248
[2336] thechronicleherald.ca/novascotia/1415760-former-acadian-border-settlement-being-recognized-by-parks-canada-project

Fowler Strives to Uncover Grand Pré [2337]

Grand Pré National Historic Site [2338] [2339] [2340]

Grand Pré: UNESCO World Heritage Site [2341] [2342] [2343] [2344]

H. Léander d'Entremont Notebooks 1 to 27 (in English) [2345]

H. Léander d'Entremont Notebooks 28 to 58 (in English) [2346]

Histoire du Canada et de l'Acadie [2347]

Historic Acadian Village of Nova Scotia (Lower West Pubnico) [2348]

History of Nova Scotia (website belonging to Peter Landry) [2349]

History of the County of Annapolis (including Old Port Royal and Acadia) [2350]

Île Saint-Croix [2351]

[2337] thechronicleherald.ca/opinion/1291762-demont-fowler-strives-to-uncover-grand-pre
[2338] https://www.pc.gc.ca/en/lhn-nhs/ns/grandpre/index
[2339] https://www.novascotia.com/see-do/attractions/grand-pr-national-historic-site/1335
[2340] www.experiencegrandpre.ca/
[2341] https://www.pc.gc.ca/en/culture/spm-whs/sites-canada/sec02p
[2342] https://www.worldheritagesite.org/list/Grand+Pr%C3%A9
[2343] https://whc.unesco.org/en/list/1404
[2344] https://cch.novascotia.ca/stories/grand-pre-unesco-world-heritage-site
[2345] www.museeacadien.ca/french/archives/fonds/microfilms/1-27.htm
[2346] www.museeacadien.ca/french/archives/fonds/microfilms/28-53.htm
[2347] web.archive.org/web/20021216212432/http://pages.infinit.net/lej/index.htm
[2348] https://levillage.novascotia.ca/
[2349] www.blupete.com/History.htm
[2350] https://archive.org/stream/cihm_00386#page/n5/mode/2up
[2351] epe.lac-bac.gc.ca/100/205/301/ic/cdc/ile-ste-croix/english/before.html

L'Acadie CD-Rom (produced by Portage Technologies, unsure if still available) [2352]

L'Acadie Toujours (blog belonging to William Cork) [2353]

Le Grand Dérangement: The Acadian Exile in Massachusetts [2354]

Les Ami(e)s de Grand Pré [2355]

Les Archives Père Clarence d'Entremont [2356]

Maps of Acadia [2357]

Melanson Settlement National Historic Site [2358] [2359]

Mi'kmaw Spirit [2360]

Mi'kmaw Spirit: The History of Kejimkujik [2361]

Mi'kmaw Timeline: pre-Contact [2362]

Mi'kmaw Timeline: post-Contact [2363]

[2352] web.archive.org/web/19991022004216/http://www.portageinc.com/emain.html
[2353] acadietoujours.blogspot.com/2005/
[2354] https://www.sec.state.ma.us/mus/muspdf/Lobby-Exhibits/Acadien-Exhibit.pdf
[2355] amis-de-grand-pre.ca/
[2356] www.museeacadien.ca/english/archives/index.htm
[2357] www.acadian-home.org/map-of-acadia.html
[2358] https://www.pc.gc.ca/en/lhn-nhs/ns/melanson/index
[2359] https://www.novascotia.com/see-do/attractions/melanson-settlement-national-historic-site/1651
[2360] www.muiniskw.org/index.htm
[2361] www.muiniskw.org/pgHistory3.htm
[2362] www.muiniskw.org/pgHistory1.htm
[2363] www.muiniskw.org/pgHistory2.htm

Minas Basin Archaeological Project [2364]

Nova Scotia Archives: Acadians [2365]

Nova Scotia Archives: Mi'kmaq Holding Resources Guide [2366]

Nova Scotia Museum: The Mi'kmaq [2367]

Port Royal History [2368]

Port Royal National Historic Site [2369] [2370]

Records of Life on the Tantramar [2371]

Saint-Pierre-et-Miquelon [2372]

In reference to the surnames links, prior to deportation, that follow, there may be times when they appear not to work; simply go to Nova Scotia Genealogy Records Online, [2373] as these sites are also listed therein.

Surnames of People in the Beaubassin region (Amherst, Nova Scotia) [2374]

[2364] https://www.mun.ca/archaeology/people/faculty/mdeal/minas_project.php
[2365] https://novascotia.ca/archives/virtual/?Search=THaca&List=all
[2366] https://novascotia.ca/archives/mikmaq/
[2367] https://museum.novascotia.ca/resources/mikmaq
[2368] web.archive.org/web/20020207062215/http://users.andara.com/~grose/portroy.html
[2369] https://www.pc.gc.ca/en/lhn-nhs/ns/portroyal
[2370] https://www.novascotia.com/see-do/attractions/port-royal-national-historic-site/1462
[2371] https://www.mta.ca/marshland/topic4_acadians/acadian.htm
[2372] https://en.wikipedia.org/wiki/Saint_Pierre_and_Miquelon
[2373] http://www.genealogysearch.org/canada/novascotia.html
[2374] web.archive.org/web/20070209200757/http://www.cdene.ns.ca/neo-ecossaise/en/region/beauNoms.cfm?alpha=a

Surnames of People in the Cobequid region (Truro, Nova Scotia) [2375]

Surnames of People in the Grand Pré region (Grand Pré, Nova Scotia) [2376]

Surnames of People in the Louisbourg region (Louisbourg, Cape Breton, Nova Scotia) [2377]

Surnames of People in the Pisiquit region (Windsor, Nova Scotia) [2378]

Surnames of People in the Port Royal region (Annapolis Royal, Nova Scotia) [2379]

Surnames of People in the Pubnico region (Pubnico, Nova Scotia) [2380]

The Acadian Odyssey [2381]

The Acadians of Cape Breton [2382]

The Fortress of Louisbourg [2383]

The Fortress of Louisbourg Digital Collection [2384]

[2375] web.archive.org/web/20070209201018/http://www.cdene.ns.ca/neo-ecossaise/en/region/cobequidNoms.cfm?alpha=a
[2376] web.archive.org/web/20070209200821/http://www.cdene.ns.ca/neo-ecossaise/en/region/grandNoms.cfm?alpha=a
[2377] web.archive.org/web/20070209200859/http://www.cdene.ns.ca/neo-ecossaise/en/region/louisbourgNoms.cfm?alpha=a
[2378] web.archive.org/web/20040307085941/http://www.cdene.ns.ca/neo-ecossaise/en/region/pisiquitNoms.cfm?alpha=a
[2379] web.archive.org/web/20070209200954/http://www.cdene.ns.ca/neo-ecossaise/en/region/portNoms.cfm?alpha=a
[2380] web.archive.org/web/20040307085624/http://www.cdene.ns.ca/neo-ecossaise/en/region/pubnicoNoms.cfm?alpha=a
[2381] epe.lac-bac.gc.ca/100/205/301/ic/cdc/acadian/english/toce/toce.htm
[2382] web.archive.org/web/20070321170218/fortress.uccb.ns.ca/search/AcadiaPaperE.html
[2383] epe.lac-bac.gc.ca/100/205/301/ic/cdc/louisbourg/enghome.html
[2384] epe.lac-bac.gc.ca/100/205/301/ic/cdc/fortress/default.htm

The Island Acadians (Prince Edward Island) [2385]

The Origins of the Acadian Michel Forest [2386]

Village Historique Acadien (Bertrand, New Brunswick) [2387]

WEBSITES: FRANCE RELATED

Bassevelle [2388]

Commanderie de Coutran (Saint-Martin-des-Champs) [2389] [2390] [2391] [2392]

Commanderie de Coutran Map [2393] [2394]

Église Saint-Croix, Bassevelle [2395] [2396] [2397]

France GenWeb [2398]

[2385] epe.lac-bac.gc.ca/100/205/301/ic/cdc/acadiedelile/index.htm
[2386] habitant.org/forest/index.htm
[2387] www.villagehistoriqueacadien.com/en
[2388] www.bassevelle.fr/
[2389] https://www.facebook.com/pages/Commanderie-de-Saint-Martin-des-Champs/152266578141732
[2390] www.petitrandonneur.fr/randonnee-a-st-martin-des-champs-77-a117888340
[2391] https://fr.wikipedia.org/wiki/Commanderie_de_Saint-Martin-des-Champs
[2392] https://www.cybevasion.fr/cirkwi-la-commanderie-de-coutran-48678.html
[2393] tinypic.com/view.php?pic=fmnpqv&s=4#.W3Xf79VKjX4
[2394] www.t4t35.fr/Megalithes/AfficheSite.aspx?NumSite=6351
[2395] www.patrimoine-religieux.fr/eglises_edifices/77-Seine-et-Marne/77024-Bassevelle/165695-EglisedelInvention-de-la-Sainte-Croix
[2396] https://www.sauvegardeartfrancais.fr/projets/bassevelle-eglise-de-la-sainte-croix/
[2397] www.fratcatho-lfsj.fr/Historique%20Communes/SITE%20Bassevelle%20Historique.pdf
[2398] www.francegenweb.org/

French Origins of Acadian Familes (website of deceased François Roux of France) [2399]

Les Commanderies des Templiers (Département de la Seine-et-Marne) [2400]

→ Click Seine-et-Marne (77) department. Scroll down to Ferté-Gaucher (La); you can also scroll to view Saint-Martin-des-Champs.

Poitou, Acadie, Brétagne (website of deceased François Roux of France) [2401]

Seine-et-Marne Archives [2402]

WEBSITES: NEW FRANCE RELATED

FrancoGene (website belonging to Denis Beauregard) [2403]

Genealogy of the French in North America (website belonging to Denis Beauregard) [2404]

The Drouin Collection: QuébecVital Records and Church Records (cost involved) [2405]

Virtual Museum of New France [2406]

[2399] froux.pagesperso-orange.fr/familles/frame1.htm
[2400] www.templiers.net/departements/index.php?page=77
[2401] froux.pagesperso-orange.fr/index.htm
[2402] archives.seine-et-marne.fr/archives-en-ligne
[2403] www.francogene.com/genealogy/
[2404] www.francogene.com/gfna/gfna/998/
[2405] www.ancestry.com/drouin/
[2406] https://www.historymuseum.ca/virtual-museum-of-new-france/

About the Author

Michele Doucette holds a Master's Degree in Literacy Education from Mount Saint Vincent University (Halifax, NS). A native of Truro, NS, she has been living on the west coast of Newfoundland since 1985 where she is employed as a Special Education teacher.

She is the author of many spiritual (metaphysical) works; namely, [1] *The Ultimate Enlightenment For 2012: All We Need Is Ourselves*, a book that was nominated for the Allbooks Review Best Inspirational Book for 2011, [2] *Turn Off The TV: Turn On Your Mind*, [3] *Veracity At Its Best*, [4] *The Collective: Essays on Reality* (a composition of essays in relation to the Matrix), [5] *Sleepers Awaken: The Time Is Now To Consciously Create Your Own Reality*, [6] *Healing the Planet and Ourselves: How To Raise Your Vibration*, [7] *You Are Everything: Everything Is You*, [8] *The Awakening of Humanity: A Foremost Necessity*, [9] *The Cosmos of the Soul: A Spiritual Biography*, [10] *Getting Out Of Our Own Way: Love Is The Only Answer*, [11] *Living The Jedi Way* and [12] *Vicarius Christi: The Vicar of Christ*, all of which have been published through St. Clair Publications. In addition, she has written a volume that deals with crystals, aptly entitled *The Wisdom of Crystals*.

She is also the author of *A Travel in Time to Grand Pré*, a visionary metaphysical novel that historically ties the descendants of Yeshua (Jesus) to modern day Nova Scotia. As shared by a reviewer, *Veracity At Its Best* "constructs the context for the spiritual message" parted in *A Travel in Time to Grand Pré*.

Against the backdrop of 1754 Acadie, it was the blending of French Acadian history with current DNA testing that contributed to the weaving of this alchemical tale of time travel, romance and intrigue.

From Henry I Sinclair to the Merovingians, from the Cathari treasure at Montségur to the Knights Templar, this novel, together with the words of Yeshua as spoken at the height of his ministry, has the potential to inspire others; for it is herein that we learn how individuals can find their way, their truth(s), in order to live their lives to the fullest.

Several years in the making, she was also driven to write *Back Home With Evangeline*, the sequel to *A Travel in Time to Grand Pré*. It is here that Madeleine and Michel find themselves back in the twentieth century with a message that must be shared with the world. So, too, and even more importantly, must the message be lived, and experienced, by one and all.

So, too, is she the author of *Time Will Tell*, a uniquely moving tale that begins in the present day before weaving its way backward through time to connect a glowing thread of historic discoveries. Courtesy of past-life regression, Michaela (Dr. Mike) Callaghan, a brilliant metaphysical scientist, in the twenty-first century, discovers that she lived as a young, noble, Cathari herbalist healer, in the Languedoc area of France, during a time when political change was in the air.

When not working as a Special Education teacher, she continues to read, research and write, exploring her personal genealogies, all of which constitute her passion. She is currently working on the finishing touches of *Men and Women of Renown: My Maternal Ancestry*.

In the words of the Dalai Lama … *In order to be happy, one must first possess inner contentment; and inner contentment cannot come from having all we want; rather it comes from having and appreciating all we have.*

www.ingramcontent.com/pod-product-compliance
Lightning Source LLC
Chambersburg PA
CBHW082018300426
44117CB00015B/2272